Software Reuse in the Emerging Cloud Computing Era

Hongji Yang
DeMontfort University, UK

Xiaodong Liu
Edinburg Napier University, UK

Managing Director:	Lindsay Johnston
Senior Editorial Director:	Heather A. Probst
Book Production Manager:	Sean Woznicki
Development Manager:	Joel Gamon
Development Editor:	Michael Killian
Acquisitions Editor:	Erika Gallagher
Typesetter:	Milan Vracarich, Jr.
Cover Design:	Nick Newcomer, Lisandro Gonzalez

Published in the United States of America by
Information Science Reference (an imprint of IGI Global)
701 E. Chocolate Avenue
Hershey PA 17033
Tel: 717-533-8845
Fax: 717-533-8661
E-mail: cust@igi-global.com
Web site: http://www.igi-global.com

Library of Congress Cataloging-in-Publication Data

Software reuse in the emerging cloud computing era / Hongji Yang and Xiaodong Liu, editors.
    p. cm.
  Includes bibliographical references and index.
  ISBN 978-1-4666-0897-9 (hardcover) -- ISBN 978-1-4666-0898-6 (ebook) -- ISBN 978-1-4666-0899-3 (print & perpetual access) 1. Computer software--Reusability. 2. Cloud computing. 3. Service-oriented architecture (Computer science) I. Yang, Hongji. II. Liu, Xiaodong, 1966-
  QA76.76.R47S64586 2012
  004.6782--dc23
                              2011048474

British Cataloguing in Publication Data
A Cataloguing in Publication record for this book is available from the British Library.

All work contributed to this book is new, previously-unpublished material. The views expressed in this book are those of the authors, but not necessarily of the publisher.

Editorial Advisory Board & List of Reviewers

Table of Contents

Section 1
Reuse Assets

Section 2
Reuse of Architecture, Infrastructure, Platforms, and Services

Detailed Table of Contents

Section 1
Reuse Assets

Chapter 1

Richard Millham, University of Bahamas, Bahamas & Durban University of Technology, South Africa

This chapter examines the migration process of a legacy system, as a software-as-a-service model, to the Web and looks at some of the reasons that drive this legacy system migration. As migration is often a multi-step process, depending on the legacy system being migrated, the author outlines several techniques and transformations for each step of the migration process in order to enable legacy systems, of different types, to be migrated to the cloud.

Chapter 2

Tsung Lee, National Sun Yat-Sen University, Taiwan
Jhih-Syan Hou, National Sun Yat-Sen University, Taiwan

This chapter introduces a model expansion method that is used in a new methodology of model composition and evolution for broad design domains. In the methodology, hierarchical model compositional relationships are captured in a model composition graph (MCG) as a schema of designs. An MCG schema can be used as a blueprint for systematic and flexible evolution of designs with three hierarchical model refinement operations: expansion, synthesis, and configuration.

This chapter describes some of the most popular and innovative software reuse in the Cloud. By categorizing software in these dual categories, the authors glimpse the practices of source code, binary code, components, and frameworks that prime them for massive reuse and establish them as building blocks of software innovation.

This chapter lists the most important challenges that might prevent adopters from successfully implementing SOA in their organizations, with the help of some recommended solutions. Furthermore, it presents a step-by-step implementation case study in order to teach beginners the best ways to apply SOA to their organizations.

Section 2
Reuse of Architecture, Infrastructure, Platforms, and Services

This chapter describes the development of software systems having different architectures reusing most of the implementations of the required functionalities as-is. It presents a systematic process for crafting multi-architecture reusable components and for using those components in formulating software systems. Furthermore, the chapter highlights the significance of the strategic reuse across systems in three contemporary research spheres.

This chapter follows the contours of evolution from object orientation to Cloud Computing and Service-oriented Architecture (SOA) to understand reusability in the context of service syndication based on the API handshake approach between diverse systems.

To produce several ESB variations successfully, a systematic reuse across ESB systems is crucial. Therefore, the commonality in ESB products, which is comprised mainly of ESB services, should be strategically exploited, and this chapter discusses an approach to realize it. The authors present a platform that can derive architecturally heterogeneous ESB products from reusable ESB services. Their approach for building the platform leverages aspect oriented programming.

Chapter 8

Although it is transparent to the user through virtualization, that is also a strength of cloud computing, the runtime scalability of resources to cater for a variety of services is to be addressed to meet the critical factor of the agreed quality of service. In this work, an architecture based on information feed-back is presented to address this issue. The findings have been supported by the simulation results.

Section 3
Reuse in Cloud Applications

This chapter tries to demystify cloud computing by means of introducing and simplifying its terms to readers with different IT interests.

This chapter provides an overview of social customer relationship management (CRM) and explores the Web-based platforms that provide social CRM solution in software as a service (SaaS) model as well as the applications and tools that complement traditional CRM systems. Based on a review of current practices, the chapter also outlines the potential benefits social CRM provides to organizations in their sales, service, and marketing efforts.

In the literature, several transaction models exist. Choosing (reusing entirely) or introducing (reusing partially) transaction models for cloud computing is not an easy task. The difficulty of this task is due to the fact that it requires a deep understanding of the properties that characterize transaction models to be able to discriminate reusable from non reusable properties with respect to cloud computing characteristics.

This chapter formulates the service-oriented requirements analysis as an automated feedback control process, in which the classical once for all philosophy is replaced with a continuous learning, negotiation, and adaptation process. Based on the existing requirements model and new service requests, the proposed service requirements elicitation framework ASREGL aims to achieve an optimal service supply and demand relationship. The current control variable is the similarity of the service requirements and capabilities.

Preface

Welcome to this new research book from IGI Global.

With the rapid development of computing hardware, high-speed network, web programming, distributed and parallel computing, and other technologies, cloud computing has recently emerged as a commercial reality.

Cloud Computing is rapidly emerging as the new computing paradigm of the coming decade. The idea of virtualizing, not just hardware, but software resources as well, has attracted the attention of academicians, as well as the industry. Cloud computing not only offers a viable solution to the problem of addressing scalability and availability concerns for large-scale applications but also displays the promise of sharing resources to reduce cost of ownership. The concept has evolved over the years starting from data centers to present day infrastructure virtualization. Technically, Cloud computing is still to mature, and there are still many challenges, including fundamental models, infrastructures and architectures, provision of services, and development of applications.

Software reuse is the use of existing software, or software knowledge, to build new software. At the early days, programmers have always reused sections of code, templates, functions, and procedures. Software reuse as a recognized area of study in software engineering, however, dates only from 1968 when Douglas McIlroy of Bell Laboratories proposed basing the software industry on reusable components.

Service-Oriented Computing is a computing paradigm that exploits both web services and Service-Oriented Architecture (SOA) as fundamental elements for developing software systems. This paradigm changes the way software systems are designed, architected, delivered, and consumed. The service-oriented paradigm is emerging as a new way to engineer systems that are composed of and exposed as services for use through standardized protocols.

Software reuse has been a major driver for the successful development of software systems for decades and has resulted in tremendous savings in costs and time. Over time, new reuse requirements keep initiating new techniques and approaches for the up to date implementation of the concept, from libraries of reusable assets to product lines, to generative methods. Reusable assets have always been the core of successful reuse, ranging from component to design pattern, and recently to software service.

With the advent of emerging software systems and advances in software reuse, the level of software reuse has recently been raised to services in SOA, large-scale components and agglomeration of components in the advanced context of service-oriented systems, pervasive computing, cloud computing, high confidence systems, embedded software, and globalized software development. Systematic and large-scale reuse of reusable assets at multiple development levels is improving the efficiency of software development activities significantly in terms of cost and time. New approaches and products keep emerging from research community and industry.

One of the important aspects for Cloud computing to develop rapidly is software asset reuse, i.e. to reuse assts that are available to computing systems presently. Asset reuse can be in the following groups: reuse of computing models, reuse of architecture and infrastructure, reuse of platforms and services, and reuse of platforms and services.

In answering the above challenges, the research and industry communities have been actively creating new approaches and tools on the development, specification, retrieval, reuse and evolution of reusable assets. It is worthy to systematically collect such new approaches and resultant tools to promote their acceptance, foster further developments, and speed up their commercialization. This book of research will be the first book that serves the above purposes. It will act as an effective means to summarize the current state of art and knowledge in this area, guide researchers, and foster new advances.

The book will help to clarify the present fast-advancing literature of the current state of art and knowledge in the areas of the development and reuse of reusable assets in emerging software systems and applications, as part of the information science and technology literature. It will no doubt expand the above literature, and promote the exchange and evolution of the above advances in software reuse and cloud computing among multiple disciplines, and a wide spectrum of research, industry, and user communities.

The book targets a spectrum of readers, including researcher, practitioners, educators, and students, and even part of the end users in software engineering, computing, networks and distributed systems, and information systems.

Here, we would heartily thank the invaluable contributions from the chapter authors, invited reviewers, and the IGI Global publisher. Without their support, the publication of the book would not be a reality.

We hope you all find the book informative and memorable.

The Editors,

Hongji Yang
De Montfort University, UK

Xiaodong Liu
Edinburgh Napier University, UK

Acknowledgment

We hereby would express our sincere thanks to the members of the Editorial Advisory Board and invited Reviewers, who have provided valuable reviews on the submitted chapter proposals and the follow-on selected full chapters. We appreciate their support very much, which was indispensible for the publication of this book.

Hongji Yang
De Montfort University, UK

Xiaodong Liu
Edinburgh Napier University, UK

Section 1
Reuse Assets

Chapter 1
Software Asset Re-Use:
Migration of Data-Intensive Legacy System to the Cloud Computing Paradigm

Richard Millham
University of Bahamas, Bahamas & Durban University of Technology, South Africa

ABSTRACT

In this chapter, the author examines the migration process of a legacy system, as a software-as-a-service model, to the Web, and he looks at some of the reasons that drive this legacy system migration. As migration is often a multi-step process, depending on the legacy system being migrated, the author outlines several techniques and transformations for each step of the migration process in order to enable legacy systems, of different types, to be migrated to the cloud. Of particular interest are the different methods to handle data-intensive legacy systems to enable them to function in a cloud computing environment with reduced bandwidth. Unlike the migration of an unstructured legacy system to a locally-distributed desktop system, system migration to a cloud computing environment poses some unique challenges such as restricted bandwidth, scalability, and security. Part of this migration process is adapting the transformed legacy system to be able to function in such an environment. At the end of the chapter, several small case studies of legacy systems, each of a different nature successfully migrated to the cloud, will be given.

DOI: 10.4018/978-1-4666-0897-9.ch001

INTRODUCTION

What is cloud computing? Cloud computing could be defined as an emerging paradigm of data and computation sharing over a scalable network of nodes (the "cloud"); these nodes include clients, data centers, and Web services (Mirzaei, 2009). Focusing on service provision, Betty defines cloud computing as Internet-based services and resources that are delivered to clients on-demand from a service provider (Beatty, 2009).

In order to access these services, these clients do not need expertise or control over the technology that they access; however, these clients are able to gain access to technology which both improves end-user productivity and is cost-effective (Mirzaei, 2009). For the service provider, these services consists of applications, such as payroll systems, with portals, which use standard interfaces and messages protocols, that can be accessed by clients (Schluting, 2010; Mirzaei, 2009). In addition to services, the providers supply resources to their clients such as servers, network, memory, CPU, and storage (Schluting, 2010).

This chapter describes the process of migrating a legacy system, often data-intensive, to a Web-based environment along with the challenges and possible solutions of such a migration. Unlike other users of cloud computing that utilise services supplied by other Web-based service providers in the "cloud", this chapter focuses on enterprises that migrate their own legacy systems to the Web and provide services to their own clients using these migrated systems. In the chapter, several short case studies of legacy systems that were successfully migrated to the Web are given with an analysis of each migration.

Reasons to Move to the Cloud

Cloud computing offers many advantages to businesses. The Internet is often the driving force behind legacy modernization today. The Web can save an organization time and money by delivering to customers and partners, business processes and information locked within a legacy system. The approach used in accessing back-office functionality will depend on how much of the system needs to be Internet-enabled (Zoufaly, 2002). For businesses, cloud hosted applications mean that they can access these applications with all of its functionality but without the hassle of hosting the application oneself. This advantage means that business have access to technology but at a lower cost, with less required staff and management time and with the use of outside expertise (Schluting, 2010; Duggan 2010). Cloud computing has even been recommended as a method to reduce the technological gap between developed and developing countries by enabling IT firms in developing countries to access the most current technology while not requiring expertise in the area (Duggan, 2010). Additional advantages include the ability to dynamic scale the application's capacity depending on clients' needs, usage based pricing, quick service provision, and standardized services that can be accessed by many different clients (Beatty, 2009). Possible disadvantages include lack of stability, lack of customization ability, and security concerns (Schluting, 2010).

Cloud computing is particularly advantageous to small-to-medium sized enterprises (SME's) because they have access to enterprise systems at a fraction of the cost without requiring the resources or expertise to host these systems in-house. For larger enterprises, which already have built-in enterprise systems and in-house expertise, using the cloud to host one's enterprise system rather than to act as a client to a service provider is more feasible. As companies expand and merge, many companies increasingly have disparate locations that need to communicate with each other via their enterprise system. Utilizing the internet and cloud computing offers a cheaper solution than trying to incorporate all of these locations within a company intra-net that accesses the company's enterprise system. In addition, hosting one's own system avoids the lack of customizability problem for clients with many cloud hosted applications (Zoufaly, 2002).

In addition, many corporations, such as insurance, are under mounting pressure to enable their systems to be accessed by sales representatives in the field and by customers outside. Migration of the system to the Internet is the most feasible option (Sneed, 2008). Businesses face changing consumer demand, which they must address, and their processes must change to reflect this demand. An example, banking systems traditionally were accessed by clerks, who interacted with customers, within a set time period of banking hours. Today, banks are under increasing pressure to enable their customers to access their banking systems on-line at all times. This change requires a change in the bank's business processes as well as addressing other issues, such as enabling customers of diverse skills and background rather than trained bank clerks, to easily access and to be able to interact with their banking systems (Aversano, 2001).

In conjunction with accessibility of their Web-enabled applications to a wider user base, corporations are under pressure to streamline their business processes. This streamlining of business processes is often in conjunction with allowing a wider user base access to current online transactions (Sneed, 2008). An example, insurance companies, through a Web-based application, can enable their customers to go online to receive quotes and sign up for insurance coverage; processes that were formerly reserved for insurance agents as they interacted with their customers (Sneed, 2008).

Moving an application to the web offers additional advantages such as uniform access, platform independency, modular design, and simplified client configuration. In workplaces where users must regularly access several distributed applications each with a different user interfaces, migrating the system to the web allows the system interfaces to be standardized into a consistent display format. This standardised interface has the benefits of lower user training costs and of enabling users to more easily transition between applications. Be-

cause Web applications are platform-independent unlike client-server applications, client interfaces for Web will work on heterogeneous platforms. The modular design of Web applications enables modifications and enhancements from user requirements can easily be added to the system. Because users already have access to the Internet via Web browsers, there is no need to install client software. (Tan, 1998)

In addition, legacy systems contain a wealth of business logic and rules of their organization as well as a considerable investment (Fergen, 1994). Despite their age, legacy systems support unique business processes and contain invaluable knowledge and historical data. For these reasons, these systems often provide a strong competitive advantage to business (Zoufaly, 2002). Legacy systems, particularly transaction-based systems, are heavily data-intensive and contain huge amounts of data gathered through years of use (Spruth, 2007).

Consequently, modernisation of legacy systems is crucial for organisations that spend too much on maintenance to retain the business value of their system. Another reason for modernisation is the industry's movement toward new Internet-based platforms that utilise a component-based, distributed computing model that is able to automate business processes internally or through Web services using partners. Through the adoption of newer computer paradigms, operating costs may be reduced and IS can more easily be adapted to fit in with market changes.(Zoufaly, 2002)

BACKGROUND

Although more modern technological and cost-effective platforms have been available for some time, it is estimated that approximately 80% of IT systems are running on legacy platforms. International Data Corporation estimates that 200 billion lines of legacy code still operate on more than 10 000 large mainframe platforms. The Hurwitz

Group discovered that only 10% of enterprises have fully integrated their most mission-critical business processes (Zoufaly, 2002). Because of high conversion and redevelopment costs, developing a replacement for the legacy system in a new paradigm, such as the cloud environment, often is infeasible (Bisbal, 1999).

Legacy systems vary tremendously by application domain, programming language, platform, and architecture (Weber, 2006). Because of the tremendous variation in legacy systems, migration strategies tend to be based on a particular legacy system rather than legacy systems in general (Moore, 2000).

In migrating legacy systems to a cloud computing environment, existing legacy system architectures pose challenges to this migration. Existing monolithic legacy architectures are anti-thetical to more modern distributed and layered architectures used by most cloud computing architectures (Zoufaly, 2002).

In order to better understand legacy systems and their migration to a cloud computing environment, it is necessary to distinguish the different user-interface architectures of a legacy system. These user-interface architectures range from dumb terminals to Web browsers; each architecture type may impose a different approach to its underlying system's migration.

As computers began to gain widespread use during the 1960s, the most common architecture was a large central processor, a mainframe, which was accessed by users using simple, directly connected terminals. Mainframe technology remained the dominant architecture through the mid-1980s and it remains the key part of data processing in many businesses. These systems are retained due to their low operating cost, the high expense and risk of replacement, and the high speed of the user interface. Because of their original physical isolation, little consideration was paid during their development to the issues of security. Similarly, due to their simple design, dumb terminals are unable to do any processing on their own such as input validation or handling encryption (Weber, 2006).

During the 1980's with the advent of personal computers, local area networks began to connect these computers together while allowing these computers access to central facilities such as data storage and printing. Developers began to design systems that took advantage of personal computer's desktop processing capabilities and the capabilities of the local area network. The user's personal computer acted as a client and performed most of the processing while accessing centralized data on database servers via the network (Weber, 2006).

With the arrival of the widespread use of the Internet from the mid-1990's, applications were able to use a new form of interface, Web browsers on connected workstations, which allowed them to access and update data of centralized business systems via Web pages. A browser sends a request, with or without data, to a centralized Web server. The Web server then processes the request and accompanying data and generates a Web page in response. The advantage of the Web-based architecture was that it allowed any Internet user access to the business system; thus, the accessibility of this system was greatly increased. Some disadvantages of this architecture include concerns regarding security, reliability, and high performance (Weber, 2006).

MIGRATION STRATEGIES

Introduction

There are numerous migration strategies. One factor that leads to such diversity in migration strategies is the fact that many of these migration strategies were developed using a specific legacy system as their test case. Unfortunately, because legacy system vary widely in their nature, composition, and paradigms, it is difficult to evaluate each strategy objectively (Colosimo,

2007). As an example, De Lucia's legacy system was a monolithic COBOL system whose ad-hoc analysis tool revealed to be composed of a number of closely-coupled modules, particularly in regards to the subsystem and system layers which communicated via global variables and files. This system had a high business value but a high degree of obsolescence (De Lucia, 2007). Consequently, it is very difficult to decompose this type of system into server and client components that is needed for the Web migration model. Strategies also differ as to whether the migrated system should simply mimic the old system with a new Web interface or whether the migrated system should incorporate new functionalities. Tan argues that in order for the Web-based application to be accepted by the users, changes to the legacy system must be minimized and most of the original system functionalities must be kept. In order to ensure universal Web accessibility, HTTP and HTML standards must be kept to ensure the system can be accessed from any browser and no specialized client software is required (Tan, 1998). Zoufaly argues that new functionalities may be added to the migrated system provided that the system is first migrated to the Web and its existing functionalities are tested after migration before adding new functionalities. In order to accomplish this, the migration might need to be divided up into two phases. The first phase involved code conversion, data migration, and associated testing. This first phase involves testing for functional equivalence of the target system with that of the original legacy system. The next phase, once this equivalency is established, is to add and test new system functionalities (Zoufaly, 2002).

Besides the question of adding new functionalities, an analysis must be performed on the system, particularly a monolithic system, in order to evaluate the degree of coupling among components which need to be separated during migration. This analysis also aids the determination of the cost:benefit of migrating these different components. Aversano identifies areas of a legacy system as consisting of the user interface, application logic, and database layer. In a monolithic legacy system, these areas must be identified and decoupled from each other into components in order to enable this system's migration to the Web. The user interface is replaced by a Web browser, the application logic is replaced by applications residing on the Web server, and the database layer is replaced by a database server connected to the Web server applications. Both the application and database server are enclosed by wrappers in order to aid the ease of migration to the Web. Each of these components need to be analysed as to their degree of coupling with one another. If there is too high a degree of coupling, the costs of migration for this legacy system may be too high and it may be more cost-effective to develop a new replacement system. If the degree of coupling is acceptable, these parts of the legacy system are decoupled and put into components. Each part of the legacy system must be evaluated as to it criticality, strategic value, and peculiarity along with the risks and costs of its migration; if these costs exceed their value, it is more cost-effective to develop new replacement components (Aversano, 2001).

Zoufaly follows this cost:benefit analysis along with identification of components with their associated business logic of the system. At the beginning of the migration, the core business logic embedded within the system along with the corresponding code sections that implement them, must be identified. Using program-affinity analysis, call maps and process flow diagrams can be created that show program-to-program call/link relationships and related business activities (Zoufaly, 2002).

After these code sections that implement the core business logic have been identified and related, the system can be divided up into standalone components that can be deployed on Internet-based environments. Collections of these components now perform specific business functions. Components that interact between the Web client and server are wrapped using Web-capable API wrappers. One advantage of this approach is that it provides more flexibility with the user interface and pre-built in functionality in regards to Web protocols and standards. Web wrappers enable vendors to focus on the communication and connectivity aspects of their wrappers without worrying about the complexity of the legacy system that they embrace. One drawback is that wrapping keeps the static functionality of the legacy system with no capability to add methods that provide new functionalities or services. Wrapping is suitable for situations where there is no need to add new business functionalities to the system. In addition to those components that perform business logic, these are special components that perform common system utility functions such as error reporting and transaction logging. In order to prevent redundant components and to ensure consistent system behaviour, these components should be standardised into a system-wide reusable utility library (Zoufaly, 2002). In terms of a user interface, screen scrapers are developed to provide client-server access to legacy system functionality. In most cases, these screen scrapers provide a graphical user interface that mimics the original dumb terminal client screens of the mainframe. These screen scrapers are then developed into HTML forms and migrated to Web browsers where they are able to provide Internet access to legacy applications without requiring changes to the underlying platform. Because little change has been made to the legacy application, these screen scrapers require very little migration time but suffer from scalability problems because most legacy systems cannot handle as many users as Web-based platforms (Zoufaly, 2002). One problem with this approach is that the fundamental nature of a traditional legacy user interface is different from that of a Web-based interface. Legacy user interfaces were often system dependent where they relied on the system prompting them for input and choices of actions. Web-based interfaces are event-driven where the users' actions are system

pre-emptive. These interfaces rely on the user invoking an event, such as clicking on a link, in order to activate a corresponding function of the legacy system (Moore, 2000).

Types of Legacy Systems to be Migrated

The migration of a legacy system to a cloud, Web-based environment is a multi-phase process that depends heavily on the type of legacy system being migrated. If the legacy system is a monolithic mainframe system, phases from call analysis to separation of the user interface must be performed; if the legacy system is a componentized system with a separate user interface, feature analysis in conjunction with migration of the user interface and system need only be performed.

Call Analysis of Legacy Systems

In order to restructure a legacy system to serve as potential Web components, the legacy system code must be analysed. Sneed analyses this code in regards to the number of lines of code, the number of data structures and elements, the number of file and database accesses, the number of decisions, and the number of subroutines and subroutine calls. The measurement of these attributes is necessary to determine the degree of modularity, reusability, and flexibility that is an important consideration for their reuse as Web server components. If the analysis reveals that certain individual program parts have few dependencies between them, the higher their modularity and the easier these parts are to extract and to serve as components. Similarly, if individual program parts have no I/O operations and no direct branches into other code blocks, they have a high degree of self-containment and reusability. If a code section does not contain any hard coded data that prevents it from being used in another context, it has a high degree of flexibility. The degree of flexibility, reusability, and modularity possessed by an individual program part has a direct correlation to its wrapping cost when migrating to the Web (Sneed, 2008).

Through the use of code analysis and slicing techniques, Bodhuin identifies the user interface and server sides as well as code sections that manage one persistent data store. These code sections are earmarked as potential persistent objects. Through analysis of data flow at the intra and inter-procedural level, the set of parameters that are used between legacy components are identified. After the components are wrapped, these parameters act as messages between the wrapped components (Bodhuin, 2002; Sneed, 2008). Analysis of data flow plays an additional role in identifying relevant and redundant data and in semantic understanding of the data (Bianchi, 2000; Hainaut, 1993b). Jarzabek proposes the use of design pattern analysis of code in order to determine what sections of code access a particular piece of data (Jarzabek, 1998).

Object Clustering

If the source legacy system is procedurally-structured, it is necessary to restructure it as an object-oriented system before it can be migrated to a Web-based environment. There are several methods to identify potential objects among procedural code. Some of these methods are dependent on the source system programming language. Newcomb and Kotik (Newcomb, 1995) utlise an object identification method that bases its objects on COBOL records – each top-level COBOL record declaration becomes a single object with procedures accessing these records becoming the methods of the new object. Other methods are programming language independent. Bodhuin's approach to object clustering is to identify, through program slicing, sections of code that access only one persistent data store. The data structure that is associated with this data store becomes the object attributes while the object methods are the code sections that have exclusive access to those attributes (Bodhuin, 2002). Still

other methods rely on analysis of the degree of interaction between procedures and variables. If certain variables and procedures have a high degree of interaction between them (high coupling), these variables and procedures form an object. Similarly, data dependencies among variables are used for object clustering; if two variables have a common data dependency, such as both of them belonging to the same record structure, these two variables should be clustered into the same object (Gall, 1998). Van Deursen distinguishes between regular procedures and those procedures with a high degree of fan-out (procedures that call many other procedures) or fan-in (procedures that are called by many other procedures). It is necessary to separate high fan-in and fan-out procedures from further object clustering analysis in order to avoid creating illogical objects whose only associativity is their functionality. High fan-out procedures are usually controller procedures that should be in their own controller object while high fan-in procedures often perform a common function for all classes, such as logging, and likewise should be put in their own class (van Deursen, 1999). Procedures called by a controller function may often be reused as objects in different contexts (Sneed, 2008) Millham combined the methods of Gall and van Deursen to cluster procedures and variables together as objects based on their high degree of coupling but avoiding clustering procedures that have only functional cohesiveness with other procedures (Millham, 2002)

A component may consist of one or more of these identified objects, depending on the granularity of functionality required by the system (Sneed, 1996; McRobb, 2005). Components, operating in a cloud computing environment, require consideration of different factors, such as security and performance, than those than operate in a desktop networked environment (Kumar, 2007).

Separation of User Interface and Server Functionalities

One of the most important steps in legacy system migration to the Web is the separation of the user interface from the server functionalities. After separation, the user interface becomes a Web browser and the server functionalities are migrated to a Web server. Different approaches, such as data-flow analysis (Merlo, 1995) and state transition diagrams (Bovenzi, 2003), have been proposed to aid in reengineering user interfaces.

Often, the legacy system user interface is simply translated into its HTML equivalent, through middleware, and represented in a Web page. Middleware is used to translate requests from the web page and redirect them to the appropriate server component functionality. Middleware then translates the response from the server into a format that can be displayed on the Web page (Bodhuin, 2002). De Lucia translates this request/ response action into XML files that are passed in between the server and web page (De Lucia, 2007).

One challenge in reengineering user interfaces is that the legacy user interfaces often invoked embedded procedures to validate its input or do some additional processing. Separating these embedded procedures from the user interface is difficult and often requires manual intervention (Cosimo, 2006). One approach is to transfer the embedded procedures of the user interface to the server components (Arsano, 2001). One disadvantage of this approach is that any data validation, formerly invoked on the client side, must now be passed on, as a round trip, to the server. This approach greatly increases server load, network traffic, and delays in processing. Bodhuin uses middleware to produce client-side scripted functions within the Web browser to emulate the user interface embedded functions, particularly for data validation. If a legacy screen used function keys, these keys are replaced by HTML links on the client Web page which invoke the appropriate client-scripted function. The function then con-

verts the request to an http request to be passed on to the server and the function then displays the server response in the appropriate form fields of the Web page (Bodhuin, 2002).

Another challenge in reengineering user interfaces to a Web-based front end is that the legacy screens were often designed to be procedural rather than event-driven. Web pages that are event-driven are better able to response to user actions (Moore, 2000). Event-driven systems are characterised by multiple, rather than single, entry points and a requirement to keep track of the state of the user interface in order to ensure that only allowable actions, from this state, are permitted. Static analysis of the program is performed in order to determine its entry points, along with their permissible future states from any given state. In order to hold the current state of the user interface, a place variable is used to hold the current state and from this current state, the set of allowable actions, which correspond to what set of event-handling functions can be invoked, can be determined. The original legacy function, with one entry point, is split into two. The first function consists of code that displays data and prompts the user for input. The second function, reconstructed with multiple entry points, consists of code that acts as an event handler in response to the user interface event that invoked it (Moore, 2002).

Other than migrating the user interface and the server with its functionalities to the Web as distinct entities, the server and client (user interface) have different resource characteristics which must be considered during migration. Servers have a more predictable resource requirements based on their transactional nature. On the other hand, clients tend to be single user based and have sudden bursts of user interaction, corresponding to computing and "think" time, that make resource requirements highly unpredictable. During server and client migration to the cloud, planning is required to determine resource requirements and how to allocate these requirements to their corresponding physical hardware. Clients, in addition, require further consideration during their migration in terms of what data is gathered from clients and how this data is optimally provisioned and processed within the cloud (Beaty, 2009)

Data Reengineering and Management of Data-Intensive Applications

Data Reengineering

Data of legacy systems often come with issues such as data model deprecation, missing data documentation, shared data between different legacy systems, and redundant data (Strobl, 2009). In addition to data structure, data value problems may exist such as duplicate and incorrect data, multi-valued lists, and different encoding schemes (Aebi, 1994; Aebi, 1997). In order to reengineer this legacy data to a more modern relational database for use in its migration to a new paradigm, two approaches may be used. The first approach, physical conversion, is the transfer of existing data structures within the legacy system to their relational database (Aiken, 1993; Joris, 1992; Sabanis, 1992; Pomerlani, 1993). Millham proposes the using working storage records as structures in the target database rather than file records, which often are structureless (Millham, 2009a). Hainaut proposes detecting legacy referential constraints through a careful analysis of the legacy procedural code, file contents, and secondary keys. Multi-valued lists of attribute B of record A are converted to a many-to-one relationship of B to A. Multi-record types within a sequential file may be portrayed as a many-to-one relationship. If foreign keys use multi-valued attributes they are converted to a many-to-many relationship with their parent table linked, via an intermediate table of values, to their linked table (Hainaut, 1993b). One drawback of this approach is that mistakes and database degradation from the legacy data system are carried over to the new system. In

addition, this legacy data was often designed for a particular environment and may be unsuitable for migration to another environment, such as the cloud. (Henrard, 2002).

The other database conversion approach is conceptual where the physical artefacts of the new legacy database are analysed and reengineered, often with user expertise, into a logical normalised relational database (Henrard, 2002). The first phase of this transfer is to perform a dynamic trace of calls to the legacy data system along with dataflow and dependency analysis (Bianchi, 2000; Millham, 2005; Cleve, 2006). This analysis is used to identify which data could be classified as conceptual (data specific to the application domain and that describe specific application concepts), control (data that is used for program decisions or to record an event), structural (data that is used to organise and support the data structures of the system), and calculated (data that is calculated by the application). After the dependencies among data are determined using both this analysis and identification of keys between records, the legacy data (records, foreign keys, indexes, constraints, and fields) is converted into a new target schema. (Bianchi, 2000; Pomerlani, 1993). Strobl also uses a dynamic analysis of legacy calls to the database in order to determine both which data is being used and relevant and to determine database performance requirements. Irrelevant business data is discarded. Because Strobl's analysis records the number of accesses to specific data tables, over a long period of time, transaction volumes can be measured for future performance goals (Strobl, 2009).

Often this conversion is not always straightforward; for example, constraints may be added, dropped, or changed and entity sets in the new system may have to be identified though new attributes (Aebi, 1994). In addition, although some database attributes' semantic meaning came be derived through domain analysis (Millham, 2009a), user expertise is usually required to obtain semantic meaning for all attributes.

Data-Intensive Applications

One of the reasons that enterprise systems tend to be data-intensive are that these systems tend to collect and analyse huge amounts of data for their business' competitive advantage.(Liu, 2008) An example, a telecommunications company might analyse the calling period of its customers for several years in order to develop a better marketing plan for them. Often this analysis involves collecting statistics, such as how often a specific event occurred, from a very large data set (Liu, 2008).

Often, when trying to analyse this large data set, it is found that this set is usually split into several sub-sets and analysis involves correlating data from these subsets. In database terms, this means analysis involves queries which entail table joins. Often these data sets and subsets and inoptimally distributed across the network. If data is not located on a node where table joins often occur but instead is located on a remote node, this remote data must be transmitted to the target node where the join is being performed. In addition, the queries that manipulate this data utilise a high-level SQL query language whose optimisations are hidden. Depending on the algorithm used, these queries may scan the same data set more than once with resulting performance degradation. Liu argues that an expert programmer could program an optimised query than scans the same dataset only once (Liu, 2008).

Often, different enterprise systems access the same core database (Strobl, 2009). When an enterprise system is moved to the Web, data dependency problems emerge (Liu, 2008). Teng, as a solution, proposes the use of a middleware that tracks data usage and their dependencies and conflict for later resolution. If a dependency is detected, any shared data is monitored. If this data is modified by one service, the developer is notified (Teng, 2006).

Enterprise systems typically were designed to operate within a high performance intra-net. When this system is migrated to the Web, the performance of the Internet is not comparable to the original intra-net. An example, an enterprise system was designed to operate within a high-bandwidth intra-net with centralised data storage with multiple fiber channel links and switches to provide both high bandwidth and fault tolerance. This design utilised the high bandwidth, often 10G, between servers and storage. When migrated to the Internet, this bandwidth is reduced to 250 Mbps. (Liu, 2008).

In order to address the problem of reduced bandwidth on the Web, Liu re-architectured the enterprise system to utilise local hard drive bandwidth rather than rely on network bandwidth. Rather than increasing the network bandwidth in the case of new demands being placed on the enterprise system, the local disk I/O bandwidth is increased instead (Liu, 2008). Logan uses object caching to improve data access times in parallel I/O operations. Objects are non-overlapping file regions which contain the minimum amount of shared data. Requests for data are directed to the object that manages this data. The speed-up in object caching is that data fetching occurs in parallel, load balancing among objects is performed, and that contention is reduced, because each object controls its own subset of data which is inaccessible to other objects (Logan, 2007). Logan's method focuses on reducing file contention but does not have a clear method to determine data distribution that increased I/O data bandwidth. To prevent long data transfer times in a cloud environment, Chang proposes data striping across multiple nodes before data access occur (pre-staging) (Chang, 2005; Chang, 2007). In order to increase data transfer speeds during this stages, multiple data streams copy duplicate parts of large files in parallel. One problem with this approach is that often an application does not require all of the data files but only requires parts of it resulting in a waste of network and data bandwidth. Fen proposes using on-demand data provision – providing data fragments to an application only when this application demands it. Besides eliminating wasted bandwidth, this approach allows data access and analysis to occur concurrently and, thus, it improves the application's performance. An example, while the application is analysing one data fragment, the next needed data fragment is being fetched (Fen, 2009). Although pre-staging of data access commonly is implemented in legacy systems, on-demand data fetching requires a specialised middleware for on-demand data transfer. This middleware keeps track of the mapping of a logical file name to the physical location of its many corresponding replicated data fragments. When a data fragment is needed, the corresponding fragment is obtained from the server with the lowest contention time. In order to decrease data access times further, prefetching of data fragments using data read-aheads is employed. Prefetching of data fragments assumes patterns of application data demand within the legacy application based on temporary locality (Chang, 2007). Although Change assumes application demand will be based on temporary locality, no algorithm is provided to manage on-demand access of these fragments.

Liu proposes allowing programmers to control the location and size of data to ensure data storage optimization and with this knowledge, custom program queries to optimally retrieve data. Explicit programming operators, such as map and Cartesian, are provided to programmers to manage data distributed across various nodes. Unlike traditional SQL queries, the responsibility is placed upon the programmer to ensure that the tables being joined are located on two distributed data partitions to facilitate a parallel read, thus speeding up the query's performance. Using these customised queries with optimised data deployments and parallel processing, significant performance improvements can be achieved – 1.7 Gbps throughput as compared to the customary 250 Mbps. One challenge with this approach is that because optimal data deployment often consists of huge amounts of data being located on one node, many performance issues emerge

such as memory-to-disk misses, swapping, etc. (Liu, 2008).

In the case of hardware unreliability, Liu rearchitectures migrated enterprise systems to tolerate hardware failures through data replication and transaction-recovery mechanisms (Liu, 2008).

Feature Identification

Feature Identification might be defined as a methodology to derive features from a given system (Jiang, 2004). A feature could be defined as a logical operation of the system while a service could be defined as a logical grouping of one or more features; this grouping often corresponds to a business process modeled by the system (Chen, 2005). An example, a feature might update certain details in a customer's contract while a service might manage the customer's contract with the business. Although components are utilised by both object oriented and cloud computing systems, cloud computing utilises them in a different way. Cloud computing models these components in terms of the services that a specific component provides, publishes, and uses (Ali Arsajani, 2001; Bieber, 2001). The service description and semantics of the agreement between server and client components determine these components' interaction (Papazoglou, 2007).

In order to identify features within components, different approaches have been used. Features have been identified through dynamic traces of program execution runs (Wilde, 1995); however, this method lacks the ability to identify both the interface and the different sections of the code that implement a feature. In order to identify which subprograms are associated with a particular feature, static and dynamic analysis of a program has been used (Eisenbarth, 2001). Analysis of the data and control flow of programs have been conducted as means of determining what subprograms are called when a feature is invoked, to determine workflow parallelism that can be exploited for increased performance, and to use these results for component/object cluster-ing (Glatard, 2006; Wilde, 1995; Millham, 2002; Millham, 2003; Zhang, 2004). Often, if the legacy systems are modeled through UML diagrams, certain UML diagrams, such as component dia-grams can be used to relate features with their associated subsystem (Millham, 2005). Using a data decomposition strategy, Glatard transforms and migrates a batch-oriented legacy system to an interactive one (Glatard, 2006). User expertise is used by Vemuri to identify features within a program (Vemuri, 2008); however, this method is highly dependent on this expertise being available. Lecue uses pattern matching to identify features; a dictionary is used in conjunction with this pat-tern matching in order to give semantic meaning to the patterns that have been extracted from the code (Lecue, 2008). Jiang uses a combination of a dynamic trace of a system and pattern matching for feature identification. The results of this pat-tern matching are refined through user expertise (Jiang, 2004). Lecue's and Jiang's methods assume an object-oriented web-based source architecture as their source architecture; if the source archi-tecture is different, such as procedurally-based non object-oriented system, these methods are ineffective. Once features are found, these features are categorised into different types through an analysis of their relationships (Li, 2005).

After features have been identified, it is neces-sary to group these features, and the objects that implement them, into services and component groups respectively that perform related func-tionalities. (Glatard, 2006).

The main goal of a service-oriented architecture is that the modeled business process, which uses the Web service, should determine the sequence and combination of business rules to be executed. In conjunction with this goal and in order to ensure that a component is reusable for a Web service, this component should perform one and only one business rule. This standard often conflicts with legacy system modules which were often designed, for efficiency reasons, to implement several business rules at once. In order to split these modules up into one business rule components, user expertise and tools are used to determine what sections of code manipulate a particular data structure in order to achieve a desired output that corresponds to a business rule. Once this section of code is determined, this code is split off into its own component that implements this one business rule. Using this method, multiple components, along with their corresponding Web services, can be extracted from a single legacy program (Sneed, 2008).

Web Wrapping

The purpose of wrapping is to allow new applica-tions, whether Web browser-based or otherwise, to interact with their legacy components. A wrapper could be defined as an interface that allows these applications to access legacy components through the exchange of messages. The wrappers convert these messages into invocations of methods within the legacy system components that perform the requested service (Bodhuin, 2002; Sneed 1996).

The level of wrapping that encapsulate a legacy system varies by their degree of granularity. At the highest degree of granularity, all the application logic and data management functions of the legacy system are encapsulated within a single wrapper on the server. This single wrapper minimises the changes to code that would be required during migration but it has the downside of preventing after future modifications of code after migration. The legacy system architecture remains largely intact. A lesser degree of wrapping granularity would be enclosing individual components each within their own wrapper. Although this wrap-ping level is more costly, this approach has the advantage of enabling components to be replaced individually as system functionality needs change (Aversano, 2001).

Individual wrapping tools are used to enclose components, and their calls, with wrappers. Legacy terminal input/output operations are replaced by these wrapping tools with a call to their corresponding wrapped component that implements these operations. Using the input parameter declaration of these calls as a guide, these tools create a WSDL schema to describe the web service request. These tools then create a wrapper module to translate the web service requests into input parameters for the corresponding method of the implementing component. The tools also create another WSDL schema to describe the web server response and create a wrapper module to translate the output parameters of the implementing component into a WSDL response (Sneed, 2008). One disadvantage with Sneed's methodology is that it did not consider control logic with the user interface such as input validation. De Lucia's methodology utilises another tool, with manual developer intervention, to represent this embedded user interface control logic as client-side scripted function code (De Lucia, 2007). Mei identifies a problem with WSDL schemas in that they hard-wire the location of a particular Web service to a particular node within this schema; cloud computing contains the notion of location transparency which moves Web services around its network of nodes to handle network faults and to maintain load balancing. These schemas must be able to adapt to a relocatable Web service (Mei, 2008)

Aversano separates the client interface, which is converted into Web pages with embedded client-scripted functions, from the server, which is encapsulated by a wrapper. The Web page invokes a function, through invoking its corresponding embedded client function. This function creates a message, with input parameters of the call encapsulated within the message, and passes it to the server wrapper. The server wrapper accepts the message and invokes the corresponding legacy module's function that implements the called operation. The wrapper then encapsulates the module function's response in a wrapper which is then passed back to the client's function which, in turn, extracts the

necessary data from the message and displays it on the Web form (Aversano, 2001).

In object-oriented based systems, a SOAP/CORBA IDL (Interface Definition Parser) translator tool can be used (Glatard, 2006). Class interfaces are parsed by this tool in order to determine their data types, references to external components, public properties descriptions, and return types and input/output parameters. Once the interface has been parsed, the tool uses this interface specification to create stub classes on the client side and skeleton classes on the server side. These wrappers handle any message passing between components. If a client invokes a method, the client-side class passes the invocation as a SOAP-enclosed message to the corresponding Web service on the server. The server-side class then accepts this message, unwraps it, and then redirects the invocation to the corresponding server component that implements the method being called. Once the method has been executed, the output parameters of this method are then encapsulated as a SOAP message by this server-side class and passed back to the client-side class to be passed on to the originating caller module (Zou, 2001).

Although different wrapping approaches have been used with legacy systems, some approaches include more than simply enabling the client, through wrappers, to invoke a method on the server in a similar way that it did so in the original legacy system. Some wrapping approaches entail the use of specialised proxy classes that redirect client requests to the server and then handle the corresponding response from the server (Zou, 2001; Guo, 2005). These classes have additional properties, which are set by developers, such as CacheDuration, EnableSession, TransactionOption, and BufferResponse that are specialised functionalities needed to function in a Web environment (Glatard, 2006). Through the use of specialised, pre-built wrapping classes, the developers can focus on migration issues of their legacy system while the vendors of these classes can concentrate on the communications and connectivity aspects of their environment (Zoufaly, 2002).

Migration Case Studies

This section highlights several case studies of different legacy systems that were migrated to the Web or cloud computing environment along with a description of the methods and tools used in their migration. The type of the legacy system to be migrated plays an enormous role in determining the type of migration strategy used (Weber, 2006; Moore, 2000).

The first case study is a monolithic, procedurally-driven COBOL system with a sequential file system that underwent a few modifications before its migration to the Web. During the 1980's, the original legacy screens were separated from the rest of the system and were replaced with screen scrapers that interacted, via files, with the legacy system server. In order to migrate this system to the Web, a tool, TAGDUR, was used to analyse the system and identify potential object clusters which were then reengineered into object components. Because the legacy file records were unstructured, the corresponding temporary records, in which the file records were transferred into and which had a more meaningful structure, were used, along with domain analysis, to identify the potential data structures of the legacy system (Millham 2009a; Millham 2009b). After the potential data structures of the legacy system were identified, the sequential file system was reengineered into a relational database. The next reengineering step was to separate sections of legacy code into relevant components. The original legacy system was grouped into separate source code files; often, a group of these files would perform a particular service and a particular file would produce a particular feature of the service. Source code files, grouped by a particular service they performed or business process they modeled, typically would communicate via shared sequential files rather than message passing. Consequently, because of this shared file usage with separate source code files, it was easier to separate the server part of the application program into distinct components providing a service. Through domain analysis of each source file and an analysis of communication patterns involving files among source files, features within the system were identified and grouped into web services along with the components that supported the implementation of these services. Using a SOAP/CORBA IDL parser, the reengineered object components were analysed and wrapped with the generated client and server wrapper classes. The screen scrapers were replaced by a Web browser client; this client, using the client server class, sent and received data after invoking the appropriate Web services, through the server wrapper class, on the legacy system. These services, in turn, manipulated the relevant data in the relational database (Millham, 2010).

Figure 1 shows the architecture of the legacy system migrated to a Web-based environment. De Lucia chose a ACUTCOBOL-GT supplier management legacy system for his case study. Unlike a Web-based architecture that requires separate presentation, business logic, and data layers, this system combined these layers into a monolithic system. The original VSAM legacy database was retained rather than being reengineered into a relational database. In an attempt to preserve as much of the original legacy system as possible, the legacy system, minus its screens, were wrapped, through automated migration tools, in a single wrapper and legacy screens were replaced by a Web interface screens. This strategy was dictated by the results of a previous analysis of the legacy system which found this system as consisting of closely-coupled modules interacting via global variables; consequently, due to this fact, it was very difficult to separate the server part into distinct components each providing a service. Instead, because of the close-coupling of modules, it was much easier to wrap the entire server part within a single wrapper. Because most of the legacy system was retained, only 8.2% of

Figure 1. Transformation from legacy to service-oriented architecture (Millham, 2010)

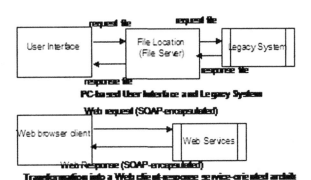

the legacy code had to be re-written manually. Analysis of the system before and after migration was conducted in order to evaluate performance. This analysis determined that the migrated system had significantly less visualization times for its Web interface compared to its legacy screens. However, the analysis determined that most of this visualization time, for either interface, was consumed by read/write operations of the screen fields to/from the original VSAM database (De Lucia, 2007). This case study demonstrates that through the use of tools and retaining most of the original legacy system, the legacy system could be migrated to a Web environment with a minimum of effort. However, because the original VSAM database was retained rather than being reengineered into an optimized relational database, data access times remained slow. Furthermore, because the original system was encapsulated within a single wrapper, this system had static functionality which made future system enhancements much more difficult.

Aversano's case study system was similar to De Lucia. His system was a COBOL legacy system - a banking application that had clerks using traditional dumb terminals – that was migrated to the Web and a cloud computing environment. Like De Lucia, most of the original legacy system and its underlying business processes remained intact. The goal of this migration was to provide a standardised user interface, based on the Web browser, to their users and to enable their legacy system to be accessed across the enterprise regardless of the accessing platform. Their strategy was to migrate this system using a minimum effort and time – the migration team consisted of 8 persons, including an expert user who guided their migration efforts, and it took eight man-months to complete the migration. This team focused on developing Web services, wrappers, and the Web interface. Using tools, the legacy screens were migrated to HTML forms with client-side scripts to provide client-side functionality such as validation. If a Web interface invoked a method, these client-side scripts also extracted data from the Web forms and passed them as function parameters to their corresponding server-side functions that implemented the called function along with information that identified the user and the Web session that invoked the function call. On the server side, the application logic and database layers of the legacy system were put in a single component that was enclosed by a single wrapper, written in Microfocus Object COBOL. Because this wrapper was written in COBOL, any problems integrating this wrapper with the existing COBOL legacy system or with data format conversion were minimized. (Aversano, 2001). Like De Lucia, using a single server wrapper made future modifications to the system difficult. Furthermore, the migration of this system to the Web was designed to make its employees able to access the system via the Web rather than enable its bank customers to perform online banking through this system.

Zoufaly's case study was another banking system, the Central Bank of Costa Rica. Unlike previous banking systems which were designed to work only within a particular bank, this system had a high degree of interaction, of up to 100 000 transactions per day, with 65 outside financial institutions across the country. The system performed check clearing, wire transfers, and account debit and credit accounting for their financial institution partners. The architecture consisted of 1.3 million lines of Visual Basic 6 code, in 250 components, interacting with 250 workstations and 1 200 unique users. When migrating this system to the Web, the goals of this migration were to improve the degree of integration among Costa Rican financial institutions, reduce maintenance costs, and develop a platform that can be used to support new business models and services in the future (Zoufaly, 2002).

In order to achieve this migration, tools were used that automatically migrated up to 90% of the code with the remaining 10% requiring manual re-coding. Ten full-time software engineers were required for five calendar months in order to complete the migration. Unlike the previous legacy systems, the migrated target system was reengineered to a n-tier componentialized architecture interacting with a relational database. Because the reengineered target system used .NET technology, the built-in functionality of .NET allowed the use of standardized protocols such as SOAP and XML data that enabled the sending, receiving, and processing of data amongst different proprietary systems. This built-in functionality, particularly the use of XML, enabled a more seamless integration of their system with the systems of their partners resulting in a higher partner participation rate and lower costs of transactions. In addition, the use of .NET technology with its built-in functionalities

for different platforms enabled the development and integration of new services within this system, such as services for mobile devices and portals for third-party clients. The built-in functionalities of .NET were used or easily adapted to provide the system with operational reliability, availability, and security (Zoufaly, 2002).

Although both Zoufaly and Aversano's case study legacy systems were based on the financial sector, their approaches to legacy system migration differed. Aversano wanted to provide a Web-based interface to his legacy system, in the minimum amount of time, while retaining as much of the legacy system intact as possible. The legacy system, minus the user interface, was wrapped in a single wrapper which handled the interaction between the new Web-based user interface and the legacy system. However, Aversano does not mention how, or if, the wrapper handled the unique challenges of a Web environment relative to the original mainframe environment such as issues of connectivity, authentication, and security. Zoufaly's legacy system was not a monolithic legacy system but component-based. Hence, the work of analysing the legacy system and dividing it up into a logic set of loosely-coupled components had already been done. Furthermore, rather than wrap an entire legacy server system in a single wrapper forming a client-server architecture, tools were used to wrap individual components to form a component-based, n-tier architecture. These wrappers made use of Web technologies such as SOAP and XML to ensure security and platform independence in a migrated Web environment. Furthermore, this migration legacy system made use of their new host language, .NET, functionalities in order to address issues, within a Web environment, of reliability, availability, and security.

RECOMMENDED MIGRATION APPROACH

The type of and stages required for the migration process depends on the type of legacy system to be migrated. An unstructured COBOL mainframe system would require more steps in the migration process, such as object clustering, than an existing object-oriented, componentialised system. Regardless of the type of system, certain steps in the migration, such as migrating the user interface to the web and web wrapping, must be conducted on almost all types of legacy systems when migrating to the cloud computing paradigm.

The cloud computing paradigm presents unique challenges in terms of its migration such as a strict separation of user interface and server components, network latency, and scalability. Network latency is compounded in data intensive systems that previously relied heavily on a fast local network to minimize data transfer times. Once these legacy systems are migrated to the cloud where available network bandwidth is much reduced, the problems of the data intensive nature of some legacy systems are compounded.

In our migration strategy, we argue that analysis of the legacy system must include examination of additional factors besides inter-procedural coupling. Besides determining the degree of coupling between potential objects through inter-procedural and data dependency coupling, analysis can determine which data structures and elements are redundant and which ones are associated with a particular component. Through a dynamic trace under varying conditions, the load between the identified user interface and server components can be measured. This load measurement is useful in determining the best method to handle the scalability factor in data transfers and in client-server requests.

Because most of the methods to help resolve the data intensivity of legacy systems concentrate on utilizing local bandwidth and optimal distribution of data fragments among local nodes to counter-act Internet latency problems, object clustering must take these methods into account. Bodhuin suggested clustering objects around data stores (Bodhuin, 2002). However, Web service identification requires that service components, created through clustering, must be grouped according to the services that they provide rather than the data that they manipulate. Besides grouping by service (business processes), Zoufaly argues that there are special components that perform common system utility functions such as error reporting or transaction logging (Zoufaly, 2002). In order to reconcile these two different views of objects, we propose a two-tier system of object clustering. The first tier of object clustering would be based on persistent data stores in order to maximize the data throughput of that store, minimize required network bandwidth, optimize data locality, and minimize cross-object data transfers. The second tier of object clustering would be based on inter-procedural and data dependency coupling, with separate objects for procedures and their data with high fan-in or fan-out. These second tier objects would interact with the first tier objects but because they are based on coupling, rather than data stores, the objects identified would possess some commonality of purpose and be distinguished amongst each other by the separateness of their functionality. This functionality, in most cases, would represent a business process modeled in the system; by utilizing these objects, it is possible to group these objects into common clusters by functionality, where they would represent a service feature. In addition, because objects with high fan-in (often error reporting) would be placed in separate objects, these objects can be easily separated from the others and be used to operate as system utilities on the server. In order to minimize inter-node communications, the "feature" upper-level object, along with its lower-level data store object, must be located on the same node.

Analysis of dependencies and coupling between data and potential objects could also be used to identify features and services in the legacy system. Often, objects manipulate common data structures in order to create features and services; identifying which objects perform this manipulation serves as a guide in feature identification. Another useful method, in the absence of user expertise and system documentation, is to perform domain analysis on the system in order to derive some semantic meaning as to the data elements that are being implemented and as to the purpose of various functions. Millham presented one method of domain analysis through the parsing and correlation of programmer comments in relation to function purpose and data element semantics with existing data elements and procedures (Millham, 2009a).

Migration of thick client systems (where the client performed some processing) to a thin client system where clients simply accept and display information is difficult. Many of the approaches outlined in the user client interface migration adopted a thin, dumb terminal approach. However, this approach is not workable where the migrated system relies on embedded procedures within the client to validate data or perform some other functionality. Cosimo suggests using manual intervention to handle these embedded client procedure while Arsano suggests transferring these embedded procedures to the server components (Cosimo, 2006; Arsano, 2001). These approaches involve a more lengthy and costly conversion process, as in Cosimo's approach, or a time-consuming round-trip to the server, as in Arsano's approach. Bodhuin uses tools to convert most of these embedded procedures, other than the procedures invoking special functionalities via function keys which are best implemented within the server components, to client-side scripted functions (Bodhuin, 2002). In migrating legacy client interfaces to the web and migrating their embedded client functions, Bodhuin's approach is the most feasible because it performs most of the functionalities needed, such as data validation, without consuming time and Internet bandwidth by

transferring these functions to the server. Some of these functions, such as those that require access to server-held data, must be deployed on the server side. However, by minimizing these server-side functions and relying mostly on client-side functions, precious Internet bandwidth and time can be minimized for optimal functioning of a migrated legacy system in a cloud computing environment.

Because the user interface and server components are now separated during the migration process, each component side must utilize a middleware layer to redirect requests from the other side to their appropriate component functionality and to format responses to be acceptable to the new client interface.

Different methods have been proposed to deal with data intensive systems. Liu suggested locating data on internal network nodes to reduce Internet bandwidth limitations; his method relies on programmer expertise on distributing the data rather than proposing an algorithm for data distribution (Liu, 2008). Logan's objects serve to reduce file contention, which contributes to slow data access times, but Logan does not provide an algorithm to distribute data optimally (Logan, 2007). Chang proposes data striping to help parallelize data access from distributed data in order to reduce data access times (Chang, 2005). However, applications often require fragments of data rather than entire files (striping often distributes files rather than fragments) so Chang proposes the use of on-demand fetching of data fragments as they are required by the application (Chang, 2007). An algorithm to optimally distribute these data fragments in a cohesive manner, along with an algorithm to handle on-demand access of these fragments, needs to be developed and verified.

Analysis of the legacy system, in terms of the type and number of data accesses, is required due to the different natures of different legacy systems. An example, DeLucia found that in his legacy system, the time needed to perform read/write operations from the database in order to display and accept data from the client interfaces required more time than the time to perform internal data processing itself (DeLucia, 2006). Analysis of data usage per legacy system, via a dynamic trace that measures the type and number of calls to the database under varying usage conditions, is necessary to determine the type and number of data manipulations on a particular set of data. Bianchi uses this trace analysis to help determine redundant data and the underlying structure of legacy data for data reengineering (Bianchi, 2000). This analysis is very useful in determining the optimal distribution of data, whether fragments or files, in order to perform the most common data manipulation operations optimally. In other words, if a particular query operates often on a specific subset of data, it is necessary to determine this information so that the specific subset of data could be distributed optimally within the internal network in order to take advantage of parallel reading of this data distributed among parallel drives/nodes and, using locality of nodes holding the data, determine the best and fastest method to perform a query or join on these newly-read fragments for use in the migrated system.

A web environment poses unique challenges to systems designed for a local networked or standalone environment. Systems that function in a web environment require specialized mechanisms to handle sessions and message handling. Redesigning and redeveloping server and client side components to manage these specialized mechanisms are quite costly. It is much more cost effective to wrap them with specialized classes that contain web-specific functionality, such as Session or Cache Duration. In keeping with the cloud's ideal of locational transparency of service, these wrapping classes must contain functionality that, upon a client request, looks up the location of the particular service within the cloud. The client request is then redirected to the location of the particular service. In order to avoid functional staticity, wrapping of legacy components, especially at a high degree of granularity, should be minimized. The legacy system

should be transformed into a system of services implemented by wrapped components, rather than services provided by a wrapped system-wide single server component.

FUTURE RESEARCH DIRECTIONS

Part of this chapter focused on enabling legacy systems to adapt to new technology; in particular, demonstrating methods, such as wrapping of these systems, to enable legacy systems to migrate to the cloud paradigm. However, enabling legacy system migration is only part of the solution in software evolution. Legacy systems, whether in their original or migrated paradigm, must be able to adapt to business changes that their legacy system models as well. Jarzabek and Atkinson estimate that up to 50% of a legacy system's maintenance costs can be attributed to changing business rules rather than technological changes (Jarzabek, 1998; Atkinson, 1994). Consequently, there is a need to develop new techniques in reengineering that embrace both technological and business changes in order to reduce maintenance costs. Furthermore, encapsulating whole legacy systems with a single wrapper to enable a quick migration to the cloud but which entails static functionality of the migrated system seldom works.

This chapter also deals with methods of migrating the legacy system, notably the application and database layers, to the cloud. However, Klein argues that these application and database layers require specialized user expertise, constitute core intellectual property of a business, contain high value to stakeholders, provide crucial differentiation for businesses in the same sector, and pose the highest risk to outsource to cloud providers. Consequently, companies face high risk and inadequate solutions if they rely on cloud vendors to provide generic software solutions to replace their existing systems (Klein, 2010). Hence, the need to develop methods for companies to enable them to migrate their existing critical business systems to the cloud.

Rather than provide software-as-a-service provision in the cloud, Klein views the independent cloud vendor as offering infrastructure provision to support these migrated proprietary systems. These vendors would provide the hardware and lower-level software infrastructure with their expert ability to manage its underlying reliability, scalability, and security challenges (Klein, 2010). Mikkileni, on the other hand, views migration of legacy systems to the Web as part of the first phase of the cloud computing evolution where new distributing computing models are provided, in part, using Web services and the Software-As-a-Service paradigm (Mikkileni, 2009).

One possible market for vendors providing software-as-a-service, in addition to the provision of their underlying cloud layers, is small-to-medium sized enterprises. These businesses have little or no in-house expertise, limited IT budgets, and insignificant business systems that are not worthwhile migrating to the cloud paradigm. Cloud computing offers these businesses additional advantages and the ability to compete with larger business with more developed business systems through the use of vendor software services. These advantages include access to software services that these businesses currently have no access to, access to the most current infrastructure, backup services, reliable power sources, and round-the-clock expertise on call (Yee, 2010). Coffee also recognizes the benefits of cloud computing to small-to-medium sized enterprises in terms of lower costs of application deployment and faster return on development costs. Coffee views the future of cloud computing as relying on specialized vendors rather than companies utilizing the cloud to enable their clients to access their particular systems. These vendors concentrate on providing business systems that focus on a particular set of customers in order to help them improve their business processes rather than supporting, through infrastructure, non-cloud specialised companies that have migrated their existing company legacy systems to the Web for

use by their company clients (Coffee, 2010). However, Yee recognizes that in order to exploit this cloud computing advantage, bandwidth capacity of the Internet must increase greatly. (Yee, 2010)

Another trend within cloud computing is the establishment of standards. Although clients initially may be attracted to cloud computing due to their software and infrastructure provision, one of the main attractions to cloud computing is the offloading to the vendors of many of management practices, such as those of fault, configuration, accounting, performance, and security, which are vendor-specific; soon standards will be needed in order to enable interoperability of these proprietary solutions among cloud computing clients. These standards will enable clients to quickly move from one cloud computing solution to another, as their needs change. (Mikkilineni, 2009)

Mei also sees the need for standards and differentiates the standards existing for cloud computing versus service-oriented computing. Mei defines service-oriented computing as a model to develop, operate, and manage business services. Services publish themselves, discover peer services, and bind them to these services using standardized protocols. Cloud computing is more loosely-defined as a massive collection of network nodes that provide infrastructure and services to clients behind a "cloud" of transparency. Mei sees storage provided by service-oriented architectures as within a specific host while storage in the cloud is stored collectively; this distinction permits cloud computing to scale up as demand for storage increases. Services in the service oriented model are performed by individual Web services while cloud services are provided through a combination of intra and inter cloud services. Service-oriented computing uses a service interface, communicates via XML using standard protocols such as SOAP, and provides both asynchronous and synchronous communication. Cloud computing, due to its youth, has no defined interface, no clear communications means, and no formally-defined method for synchronous or asynchronous communication. Like Mikkilineni, Mei sees the need for standards to emerge in these areas of cloud computing. Mei draws a distinction between service-oriented and cloud computing in the way that services are provided; having cloud computing adopt a service-oriented approach may be antithetical to its model. An example, service-oriented computing utilizes a WSDL approach for its Web services where services are coded explicitly using a URL. The cloud, on the other hand, may provide the same service but because it utilizes the notion of locational transparency, coded URLs for its services may be infeasible. Different methods to handle cloud services while maintaining its advantage of locational transparency need to be found (Mei, 2008).

CONCLUSION

This chapter concentrates on business migrating their critical business legacy systems to the cloud computing paradigm, as a software-as-a-service model, rather than focusing on independent vendors providing their generic software solutions for business clients. In this chapter, we first examined some of the reasons why a business might want to migrate their business critical legacy systems to the cloud computing paradigm. We then outlined a migration approach, for the software-as-a-service model, for the application and data layers of these legacy systems. The type of migration approach to be taken is highly dependent on the type of legacy system that is being migrated. As our case studies demonstrate, the specific type of legacy system dictates a number of factors such as the granularity of Web wrapping, the use of client-side scripted functions on the Web interface, and the use of object clustering for componentialisation. Because the direction of the migration process is highly dependent on the type of legacy system, a more thorough pre-migration analysis of the legacy system must occur in order to determine the degree of component coupling, redundant data,

underlying data structures, data access patterns, and load requirements.

The Web environment poses special challenges to migration such as location transparency, network latency, and security. Possible solutions such as the use of specialized proxy classes within the Web wrappers, look up tables of services along with the corresponding current nodes on which they reside, and optimized distribution of data fragments within the server local area network have been proposed. Future directions such as developing new reengineering techniques in reengineering that are able to manage both technological and business changes and the development of cloud computing standards have been discussed.

REFERENCES

Aebi, D. (1997). *Data engineering: A case study. Proceedings in Advances in Databases and Information Systems*. Berlin, Germany: Springer-Verlag.

Aebi, D., & Largo, R. (1994). Methods and tools for data value re-engineering, *International Conference on Applications of Databases, Lecture Notes in Computer Science 819*, (pp. 1-9). Berlin, Germany: Springer-Verlag.

Aiken, P., & Muntz, A. (1993). *A framework for reverse engineering DoD legacy information systems. WCRE*. Los Alamos, NM: IEEE Press.

Arsanjani, A., Zhang, J.-L., & Ellis, M. (2007). A service-oriented reference architecture. *IT Professional, 9*(3), 10–17. doi:10.1109/MITP.2007.53

Atkinson, S., Bailes, P. A., Chapman, M., Chilvers, M., & Peake, I. (1994). A re-engineering evaluation of software refinery: Architecture, process and technology. *Proceedings of the Third Symposium on Assessment of Quality Software Development Tools*. Los Alamos, NM: IEEE Press.

Aversano, L., Canfora, G., Cimitile, A., & De Lucia, A. (2001). Migrating legacy systems to the Web: An experience report. *Proceedings of European Conference on Software Maintenance and Reengineering.* Los Alamos, NM: IEEE Press.

Beaty, K., Kochut, A., & Shaikh, H. (2009). *Desktop to cloud transformation planning.* IEEE International Symposium on Parallel & Distributed Processing. Los Alamos, NM: IEEE Press.

Behm, A., Geppert, A., & Diettrich, K. R. (1997). *On the migration of relational schemas and data to object-oriented database systems. Proceedings of Re-Technologies in Information Systems, Klagenfurt, Austria.* Los Alamos, NM: IEEE Press.

Bianchi, A., Caivano, D., & Visaggio, G. (2000). *Method and process for iterative reengineering of data in a legacy system. WCRE.* Los Alamos, NM: IEEE Press.

Bieber, G. (2001). *Introduction to service-oriented programming.* Presented at Sun's Worldwide Java Development Conference.

Bisbal, J., Lawless, D., Wu, B., & Grimson, J. (1999). *Legacy information systems: Issues and directions. IEEE Software.* Los Alamos, NM: IEEE Press.

Bodhium, T., Guardabascio, E., & Tortorella, M. (2002). *Migrating COBOL systems to the Web by using the MCV design pattern. WCRE.* Los Alamos, NM: IEEE Press.

Bohm, C., & Jacopini, G. (1966). *Flow diagrams, turing machines, and languages with only two formation rules. Computer Assisted Collaborative Memory, 9(5), 266.* New York, NY: ACM Press.

Borstlap, G. (2006). *Understanding the technical barriers of retargeting ISAM to RDBMS.* Retrieved June 30, 2010, from http://www.anubex.com/anugenio!technicalbarriers1.asp

Bovenzi, D., Canfora, G., & Fasolina, A. R. (2003). Enabling legacy system accessibility by Web heterogeneous clients. *Working Conference on Reverse Engineering,* (pp. 73-81). Los Alamos, NM: IEE Press.

Brodie, M. L., & Stonebraker, M. (1995). *Migrating legacy systems: Gateways, interfaces, and the incremental approach.* Upper Saddle River, NJ: Morgan Kaufmann.

Chang, R.-S., & Chen, P. H. (2007). Complete and fragmented replica selection and retrieval in data grids. *Future Generation Computer Systems, 23,* 536–546. doi:10.1016/j.future.2006.09.006

Chang, R.-S., Wang, C.-M., & Chen, P. M. (2005). *Replica selection on co-allocation data grids, parallel and distributed processing and applications* (pp. 584–593). New York, NY: Springer-Verlag.

Chen, F., & Shaoyun, L. (2005). *Feature analysis for service-oriented reengineering. APSEC.* Los Alamos, NM: IEEE Press.

Chen, P.-Y., Chiang, J., et al. (2009). Memory-mapped file approach for on-demand data co-allocation on grids. *IEEE International Symposium on Cluster Computing and the Grid,* Los Alamos: IEEE Computer Society Press.

Cleve, A., Henrard, J., & Hainaut, J.-L. (2006). *Data reverse engineering using system dependency graphs. WCRE.* Los Alamos, NM: IEEE Press.

Coffee, P. (2009, January 18). The future of cloud computing. *Cloud Computing Journal.* Retrieved November 2, 2010, from http://cloudcomputing.sys-con.com/node/771947

Colosimo, M., De Lucia, A., et al. (2007). Assessing legacy system migration technologies through controlled experiments. *International Conference on Software Maintenance,* (pp. 365-374). Los Alamos, NM: IEEE Press.

De Lucia, A., Francese, R., et al. (2006). A strategy and an eclipse based environment for the migration of legacy systems to multi-tier web-based architectures. *International Conference on Software Maintenance*, (pp. 438-447). Los Alamos, NM: IEEE Press.

Dugan, E. (2010). *ICST and SMEs: Theories, practices, and challenges.* Presented at IRMA Conference, Hershey, PA: IRMA International.

Eisenbarth, T., Koschke, R., & Simon, D. (2001). *Aiding program comprehension by static and dynamic feature analysis.* International Conference on Software Maintenance. Los Alamos, NM: IEEE Press.

Fergen, H., et al. (1994). Bringing objects into COBOL: Moore – a tool for migration from COBOL to object-oriented COBOL. *Proceedings of Conference of Technology of Object-Oriented Languages and Systems*, (pp. 435-556). Los Alamos, NM: IEEE Press.

Gall, H. W., Eixelsberger, M., Kalan, M., Ogris, H., & Beckman, B. (1988). *Recovery of architectural structure: A case study. Development and Evolution of Software Architectures for Product Families (ARES II), LNCS 1429* (pp. 89–96). New York: Springer-Verlag.

Glatard, T., Emsellem, D., & Montagnat, J. (2006). *Generic web service wrapper for efficient embedding of legacy codes in service-based workflows. Technical Report, I3SC, CNRS.* France: University of Nice.

Grossman, R. L. (2009). The case for cloud computing. *IT Professional, 11*(2), 23–27. doi:10.1109/MITP.2009.40

Guo, H., Guo, C., Chen, F., & Yang, H. (2005). *Wrapping client-server application to Web services for internet computing.* PDCAT.

Hainaut, J.-L., Chandelon, M., Tonneau, C., & Joris, M. (1993a). *Contribution to a theory of database reverse engineering. WCRE.* Los Alamos, NM: IEEE Press.

Hainaut, J.-L., Chandelon, M., Tonneau, C., & Joris, M. (1993b). Transformation-based database reverse engineering. *Proceedings of the 12th International Conference on Entity-Relationship Approach*, (pp. 1-12). London, UK: Springer-Verlag.

Henrard, J., Hick, J. M., Thiran, P., & Hainaut, J. L. (2002). Strategies for data reengineering. *Working Conference on Reverse Engineering*, (pp. 211-222). Los Alamos, NM: IEEE Press.

Janke, J.-H., & Wadsack, J. P. (1999). *Varlet: Human-centered tool for database reengineering. WCRE.* Los Alamos, NM: IEEE Press.

Jarazabek, S., & Hitz, M. (1998). *Business-oriented component-based software development and evolution.* DEXXA Workshop. Los Alamos, NM: IEEE Press.

Jeusfeld, M. A., & Johnen, U. A. (1994). An executable meta model for reengineering of database schemas. *Proceedings of Conference on the Entity-Relationship Approach.* London, UK: Springer-Verlag.

Jiang, Y., & Stroulia, E. (2004). *Towards reengineering web sites to web-services providers. CSMR.* Los Alamos, NM: IEEE Press.

Joris, M. (1992). Phenix: Methods and tools for database reverse engineering. *Proceedings 5th International Conference on Software Engineering and Applications.* Los Alamos, NM: IEEE Press.

Klein, M. (2010). *SaaS value added and risk management.* Retrieved September 15, 2010, from http://resource.onlinetech.com/

Kumar, A., Neogi, A., & Pragallapati, S. (2007). *Raising programming abstraction from objects to services. ICWS.* Los Alamos, NM: IEEE Press.

Law, K., Ip, H., & Wei, F. (1998). *Web-enabling legacy applications. ICPADS*. Los Alamos, NM: IEEE Press.

Lecue, F., Salibi, S., et al. (2008). Semantic and syntactic data flow in web service composition. *Proceedings of IEEE Conference on Web Services*. Los Alamos, NM: IEEE Press.

Li, S., & Chen, F. (2005). *Using feature-oriented analysis to recover legacy software design for software evolution. SEKE*. Los Alamos, NM: IEEE Press.

Liu, H., & Orban, D. (2008). GridBatch: Cloud computing for large-scale data-intensive batch applications. *International Symposium on Cluster, Cloud, and Grid Computing*, (pp. 295-305). Los Alamos, NM: IEEE Press.

Logan, J., & Dickens, P. M. (2007). *Using object based files for high performance parallel I/O. Intelligent Data Acquisition and Advanced Computing Systems* (pp. 149–154). Los Alamos, NM: IEEE Press.

McRobb, S., Pu, J., Yang, H., & Millham, R. (2005). Visualising COBOL legacy systems with UML: An Experimental report. In Yang, H. (Ed.), *Advances in UML-based software engineering*. Hershey, PA: Idea Group. doi:10.4018/978-1-59140-621-1.ch010

Mehoudj, K., & Ou-Halima, M. (1995). Migrating data-oriented applications to a relational database management system. *Proceedings of the Third International Workshop on Advances in Databases and Object-Oriented Databases*, (pp. 102-108). Los Alamos, NM: IEEE Press.

Mei, L., Chan, W. K., & Tse, T. H. (2008). *A tale of clouds: Paradigm comparisons and some thoughts on research issues. APSCC*. Los Alamos, NM: IEEE Press.

Merlo, E., & Gagn, P. Y. (1995). Reengineering user interfaces. *IEEE Software*, *12*, 64–73. doi:10.1109/52.363164

Mikkilineni, R., & Sarathy, V. (2009). *Cloud computing and lessons from the past. WETICE*. Los Alamos, NM: IEEE Press.

Millham, R. (2002). *An investigation: Reengineering sequential procedure-driven software into object-oriented event-driven software through UML diagrams. COMPSAC*. Los Alamos, NM: IEEE Press.

Millham, R. (2005). *Evolution of batch-oriented COBOL systems into object-oriented systems through unified modelling language*. Unpublished doctoral dissertation, De Montfort University, Leicester, UK.

Millham, R. (2009a). *Domain analysis in the reengineering process of a COBOL system. COMPSAC*. Los Alamos, NM: IEEE Press.

Millham, R. (2010). *Migration of a legacy procedural system to service-oriented computing using feature analysis. ECDS-CISIS*. Los Alamos, NM: IEEE Press.

Millham, R., & Yang, H. (2009b). *Industrial report: Data reengineering of COBOL sequential legacy systems. COMPSAC*. Los Alamos, NM: IEEE Press.

Millham, R., Yang, H., & Ward, M. (2003). *Determining granularity of independent tasks for reengineering a legacy system into an OO system. COMPSAC*. Los Alamos, NM: IEEE Press.

Mirzaei, N. (200, January 9). *Cloud computing independent study report.*

Moore, M., & Moshkina, L. (2000). Migrating legacy user interfaces to the internet: Shifting dialogue initiative. *Working Conference on Reverse Engineering*, (pp. 52-58). Los Alamos, NM: IEEE Computer Press.

Newcomb, P. (1999). *Reengineering procedural into object-oriented systems. WCRE.* Los Alamos, NM: IEEE Press.

Newcomb, P., & Kotik, G. (1995). Reengineering procedural into object-oriented systems. *Second Working Conference on Reverse Engineering,* (pp. 237-249). Los Alamos, NM: IEEE Press.

Papazoglou, M., & Traverso, P. (2007). Service-oriented computing: State of the art and research challenges. *Computer, 40*(11). Los Alamos, NM: IEEE Press.

Pomerlani, W. J., & Blaha, M. R. (1993). *An approach for reverse engineering of relational databases. WCRE.* Los Alamos, NM: IEEE Press.

Rob, P., & Coronel, C. (2002). *Database systems: Design, implementation, and management* (pp. 1–800). Boston, MA: Thomas Learning.

Sabanis, N., & Stevenson, N. (1992). Tools and techniques for data remodeling COBOL applications. *Proceedings 5th International Conference on Software Engineering and Applications.* Los Alamos, NM: IEEE Press.

Saradhi, V., & Akula, N. (2002, August). Understanding requirements of large data-intensive applications. *Information Management Direct.*

Schluting, C. (2010). *Sorting out the many faces of cloud computing.* Retrieved September 9, 2010, from http://www.internet.com/IT/NetworkingAndCommunications/VirtualInfrastructure/Article/42644

Smith, D., O'Brien, L., & Kontogiannis, K. (2006). *Program comprehension and migration strategies for web service and service-oriented architectures. Working Session: ICPC.* Los Alamos, NM: IEEE Press.

Sneed, H. M. (1996). *Encapsulating legacy software for use in client/server systems,* (pp. 104-109). WCRE. Los Alamos, NM: IEEE Press.

Sneed, H. M. (2008). *COB2WEB: A toolset for migrating to Web services. WSE.* Los Alamos, NM: IEEE Press.

Spruth, W. (2007). *The future of the mainframe. EuroCMG.* Philadephia, PA: CMG Group.

Strobl, S., Bernhardt, M., & Grechenig, T. (2009). *Digging deep: Software reengineering supported by database reverse engineering of a system with 30+ years of legacy. ICSM.* Los Alamos, NM: IEEE Press.

Tan, K., Ip, H. H. S., & Wei, F. (1998). *Web-enabling legacy applications. ICPADS.* Los Alamos, NM: IEEE Press.

Teng, T., Huang, G., & Hong, M. (2006). *Interference problem between web services caused by data dependencies. CEC/EEE.* Los Alamos, NM: IEEE Press.

Tilley, S. R., & Smith, D. B. (1995). *Perspectives on legacy system reengineering. Technical Report.* Pittsburgh, USA: Software Engineering Institute, Carnegie Mellon University.

van Deursen, A., & Kuipers, T. (1999). Identifying objects using cluster and concepts analysis. *Proceedings 21st International Conference on Software Engineering.* Los Alamos, NM: IEEE Press.

Vemuri, P. (2008). *Modernizing a legacy system to SOA – Feature analysis approach. IEEE TENCON.* Los Alamos, NM: IEEE Press.

Weber, C. (2006). *Assessing security risk in legacy systems.* Cigital, Inc. Retrieved August 26, 2010, from https://buildsecurityin.us-cert.gov/bsi/articles/best-practices/legacy/624-BSI.html

Weiderhold, G. (1995). Modelling and system maintenance. *Proceedings of the International Conference on Object-Orientation and Entity-Relationship Modeling.* London, UK: Springer-Verlag.

Wilde, N., & Scully, M. C. (1995). *Software reconnaissance: Mapping features to code. Software Maintenance: Research and Practice, 7*. Hoboken, NJ: John Wiley.

Wong, K., & Sun, D. (2006). On evaluating the layout of UML diagrams for program comprehension. *Software Quality Journal, 14*(3), 233–259. doi:10.1007/s11219-006-9218-2

Yee, G. (2010). Cloud computing bandwidth requirements - Trends and future. Retrieved September 7, 2010, from http://EzineArticles.com/?expert=George_Yee

Zhang, Z., & Yang, H. (2004). *Incubating services in legacy systems for architectural migration. APSEC*. Los Alamos, NM: IEEE Press.

Zhou, Y., & Kontogiannis, K. (2003). *Incremental transformation of procedural systems to object-oriented platform. COMPSAC*. Los Alamos, NM: IEEE Press.

Zou, Y. (2001). Towards a Web-centric legacy system migration framework. *Proceedings of the 3rd International Workshop on Net-Centric Computing: Migrating to the Web, ICSE*. Los Alamos, NM: IEEE Press.

Zoufaly, F. (2002). *Issues and challenges facing legacy systems*. Retrieved May 23, 2010, from http://www.developer.com/mgmt/article.php/1492531/Issues-and-Challenges-Facing-Legacy-Systems.htm

ADDITIONAL READING

Ahson, S., & Ilyas, M. (2010). *Cloud computing and software services: Theory and techniques*. London, UK: CRC Press. doi:10.1201/EBK1439803158

Amajad, U. (1997). *Application reengineering: Building web-based applications and dealing with legacies*. Upper Saddle River, NJ: Prentice-Hall.

Chorafas, D. (2010). *Cloud computing strategies*. London, UK: Routledge. doi:10.1201/9781439834541

Heuvel, W.-J. (2007). *Aligning modern business processes and legacy systems: A component-based perspective (cooperative information systems)*. Boston, MA: MIT Press.

Hugos, M., & Hulitzky, D. (2010). *Business in the cloud: What every business needs to know about cloud computing*. Hoboken, NJ: John Wiley and Sons.

Krutz, R., & Vines, R. (2010). *Cloud security: A comprehensive guide to secure cloud computing*. Hoboken, NJ: John Wiley and Sons.

Linthicum, D. S. (2009). *Cloud computing and SOA convergence in your enterprise: A step-by-step guide*. Upper Saddle River, NJ: Addison-Wesley.

McDaniel, W. D. (2001). *Wrestling legacy data to the web & beyond: Practical solutions for managers & technicians*. New York, NY: McGraw.

Miller, H. (1998). *Reengineering legacy software systems*. New York, NY: ACM Digital Press.

Secord, R., Plakosh, D., & Lewis, G. (2003). *Modernizing legacy systems: Software technologies, engineering processes, and business practices*. Upper Saddle River, NJ: Addison-Wesley.

Ulrich, W. (2002). *Legacy systems: Transformation strategies*. Upper Saddle River, NJ: Prentice-Hall.

KEY TERMS AND DEFINITIONS

Cloud Computing: An emerging model of data and computation sharing over a scalable network of nodes ("the cloud"). Unlike service-oriented computing which focuses on the provision of software services via the Web, cloud computing is more embracing. It includes infrastructure to support their software, such as datacenters, over a loosely-coupled network of nodes that can shrink and expand with client demand.

Data-Intensive Applications: Applications that retain and manipulate huge amounts of data for their system functionalities. Data intensive applications pose a problem for cloud computing because many of these applications were designed for use within local high-speed networks but when these same applications are migrated to the cloud, they are bottlenecked by the limited Internet bandwidth that cloud computing is based upon.

Data Reengineering Conceptual Conversion: A method that attempts, through a variety of means, to derive the semantic meaning of legacy source database. Using this meaning, a more logical grouping of data by their meaning into their appropriate data constructs in the target database can be performed.

Data Reengineering Physical Conversion: A method that simply extracts the existing legacy data constructs of the source database and converts them to the closest corresponding data construct of the target database, without consideration of the semantic meaning of the data that is being transferred. An example, a record structure of the legacy database is transferred to the target database without considering if all of their record fields should be grouped logically within that record.

Feature Identification: An approach to extract features and services from a selected system. A feature is a logical operation of the system, such as updating a customer's details, while a service is a logical grouping of one or more of these features. Usually, a service corresponds to a business process, such as customer management, that is being modeled by this particular system.

Location Transparency: In cloud computing, the ability to relocate web and other services to any particular node within its cloud cluster of network nodes. This ability provides cloud computing with the capability to relocate services to maintain service continuity even as network nodes fail.

Multi-valued Attribute: Consists of a file or table's attribute that may contain multiple values. An example, a COBOL record may have a field, Status, with several permittable values, such as Y,N, or U. In order to translate this multi-valued attribute to its corresponding relational database equivalent, the multi-valued attribute is connected to a linked list or linked table in the relational database that contains all of its permitted values

Web Wrapping: A wrapper is a type of interface that encapsulates legacy components that have been migrated into a new paradigm. Other components interact with the wrapper via message passing; the wrapper accepts request messages from these components and redirects these messages to the proper legacy component for implementation. In order to have the required functionality performed, the wrapper then converts the request message into a method invocation of the encapsulated legacy component. If the invoked method produces an output, the wrapper then converts this output into a response message which is redirected to the requesting component. The purpose of using wrappers is to allow components of new applications to interact easily with legacy components without the need for special coding within these components.

Chapter 2
Model Expansion in Model-Driven Architectures

Tsung Lee
National Sun Yat-Sen University, Taiwan

Jhih-Syan Hou
National Sun Yat-Sen University, Taiwan

ABSTRACT

In this chapter, the authors introduce a model expansion method that is used in a new methodology of model composition and evolution for broad design domains. In the methodology, hierarchical model compositional relationships are captured in a model composition graph (MCG) as a schema of designs. An MCG schema can be used as a blueprint for systematic and flexible evolution of designs with three hierarchical model refinement operations: expansion, synthesis, and configuration. In this methodology, due to the need of hierarchical sharing in software and hardware domains, the authors designed an algorithm to achieve conditional and recursive model expansion with hierarchical model instance sharing that is not achievable in other expansion methods. Hierarchical model instance sharing complicates the design structure from tree structures to graph structures. The model expansion algorithm was thus designed with enhanced features of maintenance of MCG instance consistency, path-based search of shared submodel instances, and dependency preserving expansion ordering. The expansion specification and the expansion process are integrated with the MCG-based methodology. Model parameters set by designers and other refinement operations can be used to guide each expansion step of design models iteratively.

DOI: 10.4018/978-1-4666-0897-9.ch002

INTRODUCTION

In the coming era of cloud computing, vast amount of applications will be employed to provide a rich set of cloud services to various users. Such applications can be designed off-the-shelf or synthesized on-the-fly. Hence, there is a problem to enhance design productivity of tremendous amount of application services. Design reuse is considered extremely important to meet such need.

With kinds of support of design reuse, applications can be freely synthesized and deployed in cloud environments. Application designs can be synthesized at static time or on-the-fly. Model-driven architectures (MDA) (Majkut, 2003; Miller & Mukerji, 2003; Trujillo, Batory, & Diaz, 2007; Bhati & Malik, 2009; Perovich, Bastarrica, & Rojas, 2009) play a key role in reusing existing designs to generate application designs. Aspect-oriented programming (AOP) (Kuhlemann, Rosenmuller, Apel, & Leich, 2007; Ubayashi & Nakajima, 2007) joins clustered design aspects together with application-specific code into a main design. Aspects can be clustered in advance and reused dynamically. Feature-oriented programming (FOP) (Batory, 2004; Kuhlemann et al., 2007; Trujillo et al., 2007; Ubayashi & Nakajima, 2007; Apel, 2008; Apel, Kastner, & Lengauer, 2009) forms reusable features in advance and applies them to transform design via stepwise refinement.

In this chapter, we focus on introducing a design methodology that can support methodologies of MDA, FOP, and AOP. A model composition graph (MCG) representation was designed to represent hierarchically composed design models. It naturally reflects the model-driven architectures. We also designed the blueprint representation of model composition graph instances, called model composition graph schema (MCG schema). It can capture feasible design feature composition rules at static time and at dynamic time. Needed hierarchical feature composition models can be provided to compose features at any instant and thus support FOP and AOP models.

A design represented by a model composition graph instance (MCG instance) can be dynamically refined via three kinds of refinements: expansion, synthesis, and configuration. When MCG schemas are formed manually or automatically, designers can utilize these refinement operations to iteratively evolve a partial design or the initial design gradually into a desirable target design. Operations in the MDA methodology can be supported by our three refinement operations. Since all design steps can be classified in such three categories and integrated in this design methodology, it can thus support all design tasks in the life cycle of MDA designs.

In this chapter, we focus on introducing the techniques for one of the model refinement operations, namely, the model expansion method. Model expansion utilizes an MCG schema as a blueprint. Each model schema in the MCG schema specifies how submodels compose the model. Designers can specify the model composition in a procedure with conditional, repetitive, and recursive expansion of submodels. Multiple hierarchically composed model schemas thus form an MCG schema of a design domain.

In software and hardware system designs, we observed the need of hierarchical model instance sharing. Hierarchical model instance sharing exhibits that certain lower level submodel instance may be shared by intermediate model instances under certain higher level model instance's scope. In practical designs, hierarchical model instance sharing can be classified into two types: sharing pure mechanisms without shared states and sharing non-pure mechanisms with state sharing. For example, a divider may be shared among multiple processors for the first kind of sharing in a processor chip. A level-2 cache may be shared among multiple processors for the second kind of sharing. Such hierarchical model instance sharing is not supported by previous expansion techniques.

We introduce a model expansion method with hierarchical model instance sharing and integrated the method with the MCG design process.

Expansion with hierarchical sharing results in graph-restructured (not tree-structured) expansion that complicates the expansion algorithm design. We designed the expansion algorithm with maintenance of MCG instance consistency to handle such complication. In order to achieve hierarchical model instance sharing, we support hierarchical model instance sharing with path-based searching of shared submodel instances and dependency-preserving ordering of expansion steps. Conditional and recursive expansions are also supported in the algorithm.

In the following, we first briefly introduce related work. It is followed by a description of the schema-based model refinement design methodology. Then, we specify the model expansion approach. We describe algorithm design of model expansion in four parts: the main algorithm, maintenance of MCG instance consistency, path-based search of shared submodel instances, and dependency-preserving ordering of model expansion. We then introduce the implementation and design examples. Lastly, we conclude the chapter and specify some future directions.

BACKGROUND

Related Work

Nowadays, in software field, a number of paradigms emerge and provide new vision and methodologies to enhance software design process from the modeling level to programming level. They include design patterns, aspect-oriented programming (AOP) and design, feature-oriented programming (FOP) and design, and model-driven architectures (MDA).

Their main concerns lie in design reuse and flexible design methodology to effectively support design process. They try to crosscut designs into reusable parts and assemble such parts into a design in various ways. MDA captures a design at the modeling level at static time and transforms

decisions into final design. It utilizes a fixed model structure. AOP joins clustered design aspects together with application-specific code into a main design. Aspects can be clustered in advance and reused dynamically. FOP forms reusable features in advance and applies them to transform design via stepwise refinement. On current state of these methodologies, MDA is top-down with static time captured models, AOP and FOP are more bottom-up. AOP focuses on joining of aspects. But, FOP focuses on stepwise refinement via layers of features.

Model-driven architecture (MDA) (Miller & Mukerji, 2003) enhances software design process from the modeling level to programming level. Main considerations of MDA methodology are separation and composition of concerns for design reuse and systematic design synthesis. They try to crosscut designs into reusable models and assemble such models into a design in various ways. MDA captures a design at the modeling level at static time and transforms models through computation independent model (CIM), platform independent model (PIM), and platform specific model (PSM) into a final design . It utilizes a fixed manually specified model structure. In MDA, CIM is utilized to capture a (sub)problem with domain-specific requirements. PIM specifies functional design of a (sub)problem but is independent of any platforms. PSM further specifies platform-specific design decisions and details in the model. Models are connected statically and are applied model transformations to evolve into final designs.

Current design issues focus on providing good crosscutting and facilitating suitable refinement of target designs on reuse and variability (Mezini & Ostermann, 2004). Suitability of design methodologies in various application development depends on the domain characteristics and requirements of target applications. Some work (Leich, Apel, Marnitz, & Saake, 2005; Kastner et al., 2009) focuses on providing integrated environment for corresponding methodologies.

In our work (Lee, Chuang, & Hou, 2009), we designed a representation of model composition graph (MCG) to naturally reflects the hierarchical model composition relationships in model-driven architectures. We designed a model schema to specify feasible model composition rules of each hierarchical model instance utilized at static time and at dynamic time. Multiple model schemas of hierarchically composed models thus form the model composition graph schema (MCG schema) of a design domain. This is similar to specify fixed syntax tree (Majkut, 2003) of a model. But our approach is more general in two ways: (1) model compositions can be at CIM, PIM, and PSM levels, and (2) model compositions can be recursively composed and expanded with or without shared submodels.

In the methodology, a design represented by a model composition graph instance (MCG instance) can be dynamically refined via iteratively applying three kinds of model refinement operations: expansion, synthesis, and configuration on an MCG instance. When an MCG schema is formed manually or automatically, designers can utilize these refinement operations to iteratively evolve an initial design into a desirable target design. Since all design steps can be classified in such three refinement categories and can be integrated in this design methodology, it can thus support all design tasks in the life cycle of MDA designs.

Expansion and instantiation of design instances were developed in various forms. Macro expansion (Chiba, 1998; Ward, 2000; Flatt, 2002) is usually utilized in preprocessing of designs. Constant definitions, macro functions, conditional expansion, and recursive expansion are utilized for pre-instantiation of designs with macros. It does not support expansion with shared subcomponents. Template instantiation (D. Gregor & J. Järvi, 2007; Spiegel, Frye, & Day, 2008; Axelsen & Krogdahl, 2009) is utilized in programming languages. It is also utilized for pre-instantiation. It utilizes template parameter substitution and derivation to instantiate functions and classes.

Existing design entities are shared and reused via matching signatures only. Parameterized module generation (Kicinger, Arciszewski, & De Jong, 2005; Zhou, Gao, & Huo, 2008) is utilized in computer-aided designs of software and hardware designs. Ad hoc techniques are utilized in different work and mainly utilize procedural instantiation of design components and submodels with/without signature-based sharing. In object-oriented languages such as C++, static data members are shared among object instances of the same class as a form of global instance sharing. All of above techniques cannot be integrated in an iterative design refinement process of hierarchically composed designs. Only some of them support global instance sharing and/or sharing with signature matching. During expansion, they only handle tree-structured expansion relationships.

Schema-Based Model Refinement

In this section, we firstly introduce the design methodology of model composition graph of our previous work. Then, we introduce the approach of the model expansion method.

Our design methodology (Lee, Chuang, & Hou, 2009) supports defining the design schema of possible target designs. As shown in Figure 1, an MCG schema as a design schema specifies how a target design model can be hierarchically composed and refined. Each model in the design hierarchy can be specified as a model schema. Multiple hierarchically composed model schemas thus form an MCG schema of a design domain.

As shown in Figure 2, as a high level view of an example, its MCG schema is composed of model schema represented as a node. In an MCG schema, designers can specify composition constraints as conjunctive, disjunctive, or subset composition represented with an arc mark, no mark, or line mark on the composition fan-out, respectively. After certain successive refinement operations, an MCG instance representing an intermediate or final design is created. It is hier-

Figure 1. MCG-based design methodology

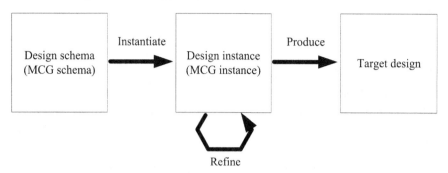

archically composed of model instances represented as a node. Designers can specify design, analysis, verification, and management components in a model schema to support the refinement of a model iteratively.

As shown in Figure 3(a), a model consists of a number of model components, several model decisions, and certain number of submodels. Decisions determine adoption of model components, selection of submodels, and parameters that can be substituted into adopted components and selected submodels. Model schema of a model instance serves as its blueprints and can be reused to create multiple model instances. As shown in Figure 3(b), during instantiation of a model instance, a model schema's components, submodels, and design constraints are reused. By determining decisions via setting manually, executing its expansion program, or executing overall synthesis program, a model instance is

created with adopted components, selected submodels, and substituted parameters.

As shown in Figure 4, an MCG instance can be instantiated from a given MCG schema. The instantiation process is an expansion process that consists of a number of model instance expansion steps from corresponding model schemas hierarchically.

As shown in Figure 5, we planned a design methodology that supports designers to perform design refinement according to an MCG schema. An MCG schema can be analyzed and defined/reused to effectively support the MCG instance refinement process. Three MCG instance refinement operations are supported for designers to iteratively refine a design manually, semi-automatically, or even automatically to reflect designer's intent of a flexible, detailed, and powerful design process.

Figure 2. A hierarchical MCG schema and its MCG instance

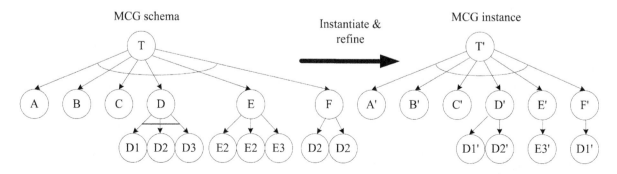

Figure 3. Model schema and model instance; (a) The composition of a model; (b) Instantiation from a model schema to a model instance

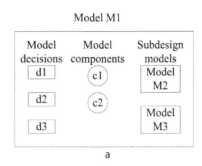

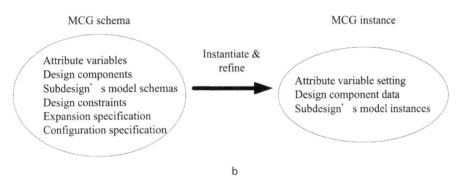

Figure 4. Instantiation of an MCG instance

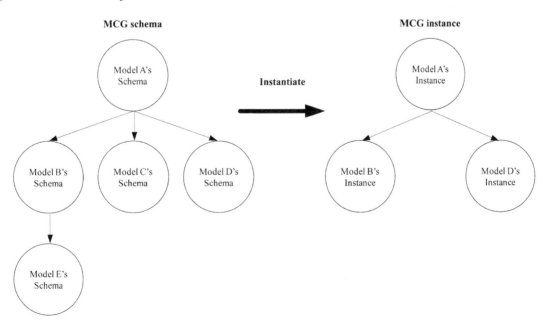

Figure 5. Design process based on model composition graph

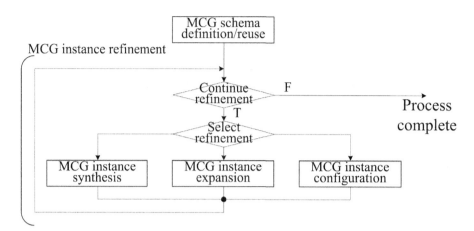

Model refinement of an MCG instance represents a task of iteratively performing various design refinement subtasks including synthesis, expansion, and configuration of the design. During the refinement of an MCG instance, there are many design decisions to be made iteratively or in a clustered way. Such tasks are called design synthesis tasks. Both manual and automatic design synthesis is supported for designer's application iteratively. An MCG instance can be hierarchically composed and expanded into more refined design with lower level design submodel instances. A design expansion operation substitutes some subdesigns into an upper level designs. When a model instance is synthesized and expanded, more implementation-specific designs can be generated via specifying their design configuration. Local configuration performs model transformations via fixed template substitution and module generation. Global configuration of a number of model instances performs design integration with propagation of common settings and generation of systematic design organizations.

As shown in Figure 6, by successively performing model refinement steps according to a design schema, partial and complete design instances can be evolved via design refinement steps across the design space. Such design exploration can

be performed manually, automatically, or semi-automatically.

In MDA, model transformations are utilized to transform designs across CIM, PIM, and PSM levels. Actual model transformations can be composed as iterative combinations of the three model refinement operations proposed in this work.

SCHEMA-BASED MODEL EXPANSION

Issues, Controversies, Problems

With model expansion, lower level model instances can be instantiated and connected as composition of an upper level model instance. The hierarchical model composition structure of a system design can thus be evolved with model expansion manually or automatically at any model of the model composition hierarchy. Such design composition process corresponds to a sequence of MCG instance expansion operations. Independent MCG instance expansion operations can even be done in parallel. As shown in Figure 7, by determining decision variables via executing its expansion control program, a model instance

Figure 6. Design exploration with successive MCG refinements

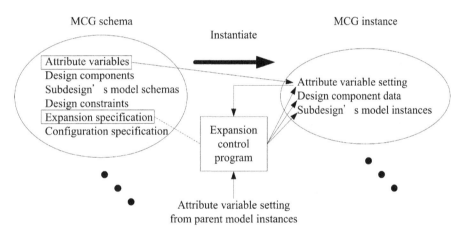

Design schema

Instantiate

Design space

Evolved
designs

Design evolution

Refine

Design
i
Design
j
Design
k

Figure 7. Model expansion via executing of an expansion program

MCG schema

MCG instance

Instantiate

Attribute variables
Design components
Subdesign's model schemas
Design constraints
Expansion specification
Configuration specification

Expansion
control
program

Attribute variable setting
Design component data
Subdesign's model instances

Attribute variable setting
from parent model instances

is created with adopted components, selected submodels, and substituted parameters.

In this work, we firstly support sharing of model schema. Some model instances may share the same model schema but in their enclosing MCG instance, such model instances are distinct model instances. This is shown in Figure 8. The model instances *B1'* and *C1'* only share the common model schema *E*. They actually instantiate their own submodel instances *E1'* and *E2'*, respectively. This in effect is reuse model in the same MCG schema. Such model sharing can be

achieved directly in MCG schema representation marked by the label *SS*.

We also designed model expansion with hierarchical model instance sharing for the design need in software and hardware design domains. This is shown in Figure 9. In the MCG schema, an instance of model *E* is shared by instances of model *B* and *C* under instance of model *A*. A link with label *IS* denotes such hierarchical model instance sharing. In a corresponding expanded MCG instance, *E1'* is shared by *B1'* and *C1'* under *A1'*. There will be at most one *E1'* model instance under the *A1'* model instance to be shared

Figure 8. Sharing of model schema

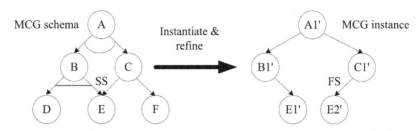

Figure 9. Sharing of model instance

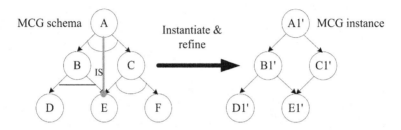

Figure 10. Recursive MCG expansion

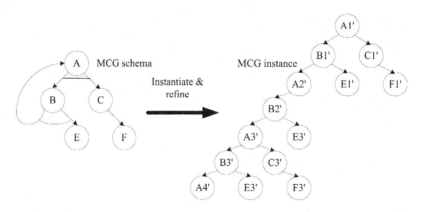

by existing *B1'* and *C1'*. When the MCG schema in Fig 9. is only part of the overall MCG schema, model *A* can be instantiated into another *A2'* model instance. *A2'* will have its own *E2'* model instance to be shared by its submodel instances *B2'* and *C2'*. Such hierarchical model instance sharing thus only is effective within its own specified hierarchical scope.

We allow designers to specify conditional and recursive expansion definitions at each model schema. As shown in Figure 10, model *A* and *B* forms a recursive composition relationships. Model *A* can have conditional subset selection of model *B* and *C*. Thus, model instance composition is recursively expanded from model instance *A1'* through *A4'*. At model instance *A2'*, it expands only submodel instance of *B2'* only. At model instance *A4'*, it expands none of its submodels at all.

Figure 11. Skeleton of model expansion algorithm

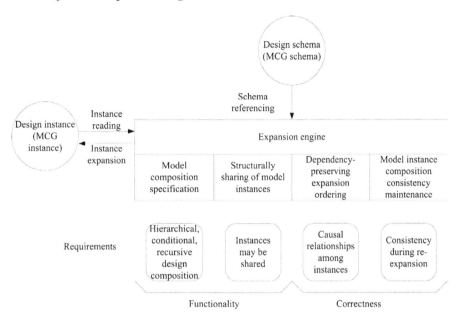

Approach

In this section, we introduce the algorithm design of the model expansion method. As shown in Figure 11, it includes the main algorithm design, structurally sharing of model instances, maintenance of MCG instance consistency, path-based search of shared submodel instances, and dependency preserving expansion ordering. The second and the third tasks were designed to satisfy corresponding functional requirements. The last two tasks were designed to satisfy corresponding correctness requirements.

In the main algorithm of model expansion, initially, all user-specified model instances are inserted into an expansion queue from which model instances are fetched for performing model expansion (see Algorithm 1). Such starting model instances may be leaf or internal model instances in current MCG instance for expansion and re-expansion. Users can firstly perform manual or automatic synthesis and configuration on current MCG instances, then select these model instances for model expansion.

Model expansion is then iteratively performed by fetching model instance and expanding the fetched model instance. Expansion procedures are given by MCG schema designers on corresponding model schemas on the MCG schema. During expanding a model, corresponding expansion procedure is invoked. Such procedure then accesses its own and parent model instances' variables, and sets its own variables and its submodel expansion setting on control variables. According to the submodel expansion setting, links should be added and removed to the submodel instances. After expansion, non-used model instances kept in a removal list can be removed recursively.

During expansion and re-expansion of model instances in an MCG instance, existing and new links/model instances should be maintained consistently. When shared model instances exist, they should be reused instead of creating new model instances according to the MCG schema. Due to the shared model instances, an expanding MCG instance is graph-structured, not tree-structured. The expansion order of model instances cannot be

Algorithm 1.

```
Algorithm Model_Expansion()
begin
  for each selected model instance inst for start expansion
    store inst in expansion_queue
  while expansion_queue is non-empty
    expanded_inst = dequeue from expansion_queue
    // compute control&state variables of the instance
    if expanded_inst.expansion_proc is valid
      perform expanded_inst.expansion_proc()
    for each submodel.control_variable = true
    Add_Link(expanded_inst, sub_inst)
    for each submodel.control_variable = false
    Remove_Link(expanded_inst, submodel)
  Remove_Instance();
end.
```

Figure 12. Model expansion

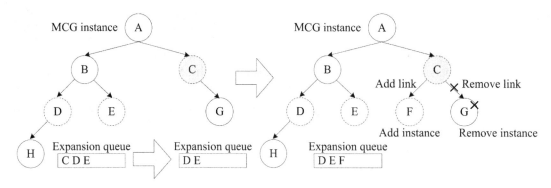

in arbitrary order, nor in the FIFO order. Causal expansion dependencies among model instances to be expanded should be detected. The expansion queue following such detected dependencies is dependency-preserving. Handling of these design issues are described in the following subsections.

As shown in Figure 12, during the model expansion process, a model instance C not yet expanded is selected for expansion from the expansion queue. Then, model instance C's expansion program is executed. It decides to create a new model instance F that is inserted into the expansion queue. It also decides to eliminate an existing model instance G.

Sharing of Expanded Model Instances

In an MCG instance, when a shared submodel instance is to be linked, we need to find it. This can be accomplished with path-based searches in both the MCG instance and its MCG schema. As shown in Figure 13, this can be handled in two cases.

Figure 13. Search of shared instance

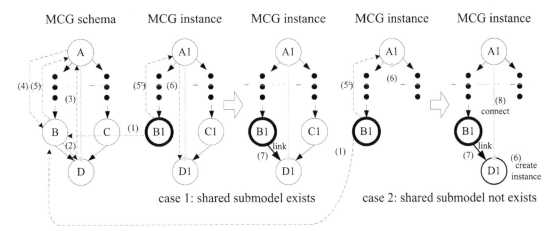

(1) When a shared submodel instance exists, we can perform steps 1 to 6 to find the shared submodel instance. For the model instance *B1*, step 1 finds its model *B* in the MCG schema. Step 2 traces from the model *B* to the immediate shared submodel *D*. Step 3 traces from model *D* to the model *A* enclosing the hierarchical sharing scope. Step 4 traces from model *A* to model *B* in the MCG schema. Step 5 and 5' synchronously trace from *B* back from model *B* to model *A* in the MCG schema and from model instance *B1* to model instance *A1* in the MCG instance, respectively. Step 6 finds the shared model instance *D1* from the model instance *A1*. Then, step 7 creates a link from the instance *B1* to the shared submodel instance *D1*. The instance is then inserted into the expansion queue for re-expansion.

(2) When a shared submodel instance does not exist, steps 1 to 6 can be performed similarly. Since no shared submodel instance is found, a new submodel instance *D1* can be created and a link is created from the instance *B1* to the instance *D1*. The instance is then inserted into the expansion queue for expansion.

Preserving Causal Dependencies of Expanded Model Instances

In the main algorithm, when new model instances are inserted into the expansion queue, each is fetched for expansion from such model instances. Since the MCG instance can be a complicated graph with shared model instances, model instances inserted in the expansion queue cannot be expanded in arbitrary order. As an example, in Figure 14, when a model instance *B1* is probably an ancestor model instance of a model instance *C1*, *B1* should be expanded before *C1* such that *C1*'s expansion can get B1's expansion effect causally. In this case, there is an expansion order dependency from *B1* to *C1*. The expansion queue should maintain such detected dependencies in its expansion order.

As shown in Figure 14, when a new model instance *B1* is to be created. We can find if there is certain existing model instance *C1* that has not yet expanded is probably dependent on the model instance *B1*. When we insert *B1* into the expansion queue, such dependency is detected. The inserted *B1* is preceded before *C1* in the expansion queue. This is similar when *C1* is created after *B1*.

The dependency detection requires 4 steps. Step1 finds its model *B* in the MCG schema.

Figure 14. Dependency preserving expansion order

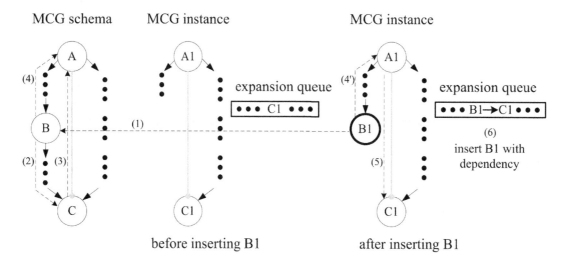

Step 2 traces from the model *B* to the descendant shared submodel *C*. Step 3 traces from model *C* to the model *A* enclosing the hierarchical sharing scope. Step 4 and 4' synchronously trace from *B* back from model *B* to model *A* in the MCG schema and from model instance *B1* to model instance *A1* in the MCG instance, respectively. Step 5 finds the shared model instance *C1* from the model instance *A1*.

Consistency Maintenance of Expanded Model Instances

During iterative MCG instance evolution, links and model instances may be inserted, removed, and re-expanded. We should maintain a consistent MCG instance along the design process. No non-used links and model instances should exist in an MCG instance. However, when a shared model instance exists, a new link from an upper level model instance should be bound to the existing model instance. In the graph-structured MCG instance, the consistency maintenance is complex. As shown in Figure 15, we handle the consistency maintenance with classified handling.

1. In order to link to a lower-level non-shared model instance, the instance should be inserted and linked. This is the same for a found lower-level shared model instance. For a non-found lower-level shared model instance, only the instance is linked. When an instance to be removed is found, it is linked and reused, and is deleted from the removal list. This is shown in Figure 15(a) and the *Add_Link* algorithm (see Algorithm 2).

2. In order to unlink to a lower-level non-shared model instance, the link is removed and the instance is moved to a removal list to be removed later. This is the same for a found lower-level shared model instance with its reference count = 0. For a found lower-level shared model instance with its reference count > 0, only the link is removed. This is shown in Figure 15(b) and the *Remove_Link* algorithm (see Algorithm 3).

3. In order to remove all model instances in the removal list, a model instance is fetched for removal. It is then deleted together with its outgoing links. This utilizes above unlinking function and may cause recursive model instance removal of its lower level model

instances. This is shown in Figure 15(c) and the *Remove_Instance* algorithm (see Algorithm 4).

Implementation and Design Examples

In this section, we introduce the software implementation and usages of the model expansion method. Then, several examples are shown to illustrate the functionality of the model expansion method.

As shown in Table 1, in this work, the model expansion software is implemented in C#. Model schemas and model instances are represented in XML externally and in DOM internally. User-specified model expansion procedures for each model schema can be written in Perl-Twig. Such model expansion procedures can be written in any other languages that can access model instances in XML.

Figure 15. MCG instance consistency; (a) Add a link to a model instance; (b) Remove a link to a model instance; (c) Delete a model instance

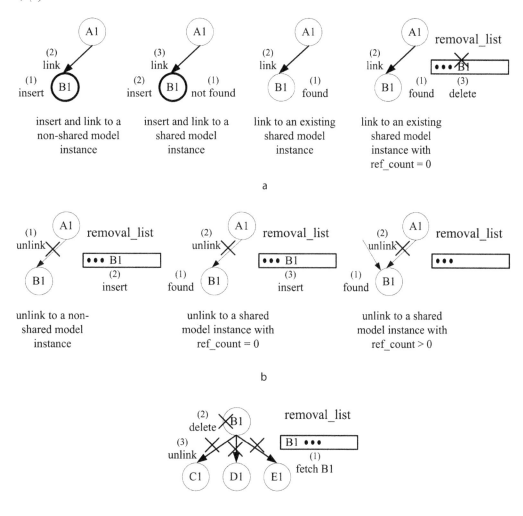

Algorithm 2.

```
Algorithm Add_Link(inst, submodel)
begin
  if link from inst to the submodel exists
    return
  if submodel instance is not shared
    create new_inst for the submodel instance
    insert new_inst in expansion_queue
    link from inst to new_inst
    new_inst.ref_count = 1
    return
  shared_inst = find_submodel(MCG, inst, submodel)
  if shared_inst is not exist
    shared_inst for the submodel instance
  insert new_inst in expansion_queue
  link from inst to shared_inst
  increment shared_inst.ref_count
  if shared_inst in removal_list
    delete shared_inst from removal_list
end.
```

Algorithm 3.

```
Algorithm Remove_Link(inst, submodel)
begin
  if submodel instance is not shared
    remove link to the submodel instance
    submodel instance's ref_count = 0
    store the submodel instance into removal_list
    return
  shared_inst = find_submodel(MCG, inst, submodel)
  remove link to shared_inst
  decrement shared_inst.ref_count
  if shared_inst.ref_count is 0
    store shared_inst into removal_list
end.
```

Algorithm 4.

```
Algorithm Remove_Instance()
begin
  for each removal_inst in removal_list
    for each (link, submode) of removal_inst
      Remove_Link(removal_list, submodel)
    remove removal_inst
end.
```

Table 1. Implementation languages

Design entities	Implementation
Representation of models, MCG schema, and MCG instances	XML files, DOM
Framework design	C#, .NET
Model expansion program	C#
Model expansion specification in model schemas	Perl/Twig

1. Users writing an MCG schema should provide model expansion procedures for each model schema in the MCG schema. Such procedures determine expansion functionality specific to corresponding design models.
2. Users perform model expansion with an MCG schema can set custom model expansion procedures for model instances, set model instance variables accessed by model expansion procedures of the corresponding model instance and next lower model instances, select model instances from which model expansion starts, and start the model expansion process with above setting.
3. In overall, users can write procedures that iteratively perform model expansion, model synthesis, local model configuration, and global model configuration. They can also perform steps of these refinement operations manually and semi-automatically.

As shown in Figure 16, the first example has an MCG schema with two model schemas. Model *A1* recursively composed of *A1* and *A2*

Figure 16. Recursive expansion

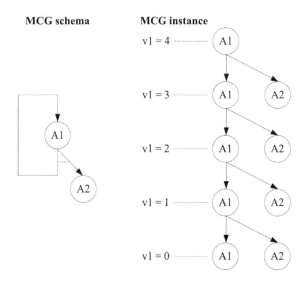

as its submodels. Subset composition constraints relax the selection of submodel instances based on condition evaluation only. A down-count state *v1* is utilized in the model instances of model *A1*. The expansion procedure set in the model *A1* consists of conditional expansion of next lower level's model instance of *A1* with condition "*v1* > *0*", setting the value of *v1* of the expanded

Figure 17. Recursive expansion with model instance sharing

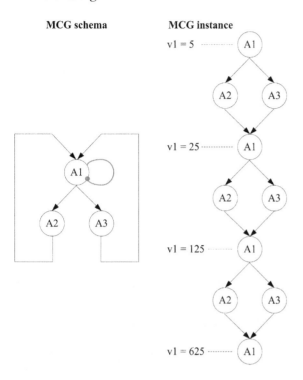

Figure 18. Expansion of a simplified configurable operating system; (a) MCG schema; (b) MCG instance with local caches; (c) MCG instance with a shared buffer cache

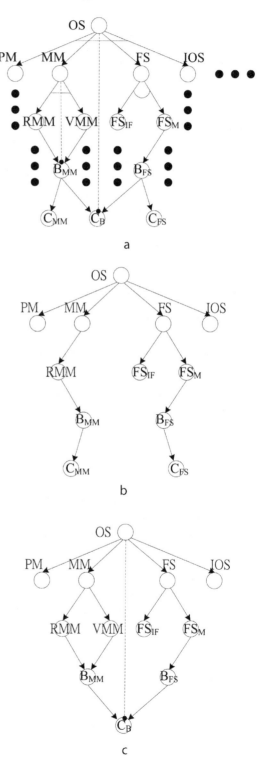

model instance of *A1* as the decremented value of *v1* of the upper level model instance of *A1*, and unconditional expansion of model instance of *A2*.

As shown in Figure 17, the example has an MCG schema with two model schemas with recursive composition. A link labeled from model *A1* to itself denotes hierarchical model instance sharing from an upper level *A1*'s instance to a lower level *A1*'s instance. Recursively expanded model instances of *A2* and *A3* under each *A1* instance's hierarchical range thus shares the same next lower model instance of *A1*. The expansion procedure at the model schema of *A1* has similar setting of the first example except that *v1*'s state is updated by multiplying by 5, and expansion condition are set as "*v1 < 500*".

As shown in Figure 18, configurable operating system designs can be specified with an MCG schema. By providing design decisions initially, various instances of configured operating systems can be expanded. In the illustrated model schemas and model instances, buffer designs (B_{MM} and B_{FS}) utilized in real memory management (RMM), virtual memory management (VMM), and file system mechanisms (FS_M) can alternatively be composed of each own local caches (C_{MM} and C_{FS}) or the shared model instance of buffer cache (C_B).

FUTURE RESEARCH DIRECTIONS

In the future, current model instance sharing can be extended to other structural instance sharing patterns including conditional and unconditional transitive model instance sharing patterns. Non-structural model instance sharing can also be supported. The overall methodology can further be extended with hybrid model evolution with manual and procedural control, and mixed top-down and bottom-up model evolution. The methodology can be applied to application synthesis and deployment at static time or dynamic time in the cloud environments.

CONCLUSION

In this chapter, we introduce a model expansion method to be utilized in the design methodology to evolve hierarchically composed designs with model composition graph schema. In the expansion method, a model schema can be shared to instantiate multiple model instances from the same model schema. Considering the need of hierarchical subdesign sharing, the expansion method supports hierarchical model instance sharing that complicates design composition structures from tree structures to graph structures. The model expansion algorithm was designed to maintain MCG instance consistency, search shared submodel instances, and order expansion in dependency. It can perform conditional and recursive model expansion with hierarchical model instance sharing as a new capability. It can be utilized in model-driven architecture to transform designs across CIM, PIM, and PSM levels.

REFERENCES

Apel, S. (2008). An algebra for features and feature composition. In M. Johnson (Ed.), *The Twelfth International Conference on Algebraic Methodology and Software Technology* (pp. 36-50). Berlin, Germany: Springer-Verlag.

Apel, S., Kastner, C., & Lengauer, C. (2009). FEATUREHOUSE: Language-independent, automated software composition. In S. Fickas (Ed.), *The 2009 IEEE International Conference on Software Engineering* (pp. 221-231). Washington, DC: IEEE Computer Society.

Axelsen, E. W., & Krogdahl, S. (2009). Groovy package templates: Supporting reuse and runtime adaption of class hierarchies. In J. Noble (Ed.), *The Fifth Symposium on Dynamic Languages* (pp. 15-26). New York, NY: ACM.

Batory, D. (2004). Feature-oriented programming and the AHEAD tool suite. In A. Finkelstein (Ed.), *The Twenty-Sixth Conference on Software Engineering* (pp. 702-703). Washington, DC: IEEE Computer Society.

Bhati, S. N., & Malik, A. M. (2009). An XML-based framework for bidirectional transformation in model-driven architecture (MDA). *SIGSOFT Software Engineering Notes, 34*(3).

Chiba, S. (1998). Macro processing in object-oriented languages. In C. Mingins (Ed.), *The Twenty-Seventh International Conference of the Technology of Object-Oriented Languages and Systems* (pp. 113-126). Washington, DC: IEEE Computer Society.

Flatt, M. (2002). Composable and compilable macros: You want it when? In M. Wand (Ed.), *The Seventh ACM SIGPLAN International Conference on Functional Programming* (pp. 72-83). New York, NY: ACM.

Gregor, D., & Järvi, J. (2007). Variadic templates for C++. In Y. Cho (Ed.), *The 2007 ACM Symposium on Applied Computing* (pp. 1101-1108). New York, NY: ACM.

Kastner, C., et al. (2009). FeatureIDE: A tool framework for feature-oriented software development. In S. Fickas (Ed.), *The 2009 IEEE International Conference on Software Engineering* (pp. 611-614). Washington, DC: IEEE Computer Society.

Kicinger, R., Arciszewski, T., & De Jong, K. (2005). Parameterized versus generative representations in structural design: An empirical comparison. In H.G. Beyer (Ed.), *The 2005 International Conference on Genetic and Evolutionary Computation* (pp. 2007-2014). New York, NY: ACM.

Kuhlemann, M., Rosenmuller, M., Apel, S., & Leich, T. (2007). On the duality of aspect-oriented and feature-oriented design patterns. In Y. Coady, et al. (Eds.), *The Sixth Workshop on Aspects, Components, and Patterns for Infrastructure Software*. New York, NY: ACM.

Lee, T., Chuang, C. H., & Hou, J. S. (2009). Schema-based model composition and evolution. In H. D. Chen (Ed.), *The Twentieth Workshop on Object-Oriented Technology and Applications*. Taichung, Taiwan: Computer Society of the Republic of China.

Leich, T., Apel, S., Marnitz, L., & Saake, G. (2005). Tool support for feature-oriented software development featureIDE: An Eclipse-based approach. In M. N. Storey, M. G. Burke, L. T. Cheng, & A. ven der Hoek (Eds.), *The 2005 Object-Oriented Programming, Systems, Languages, and Applications Workshop on Eclipse Technology Exchange* (pp. 55-59). New York, NY: ACM.

Majkut, M. (2003). Generation of implementations for the model driven architecture with syntactic unit trees. In M. G. Burke (Ed.), *The Second Object-Oriented Programming, Systems, Languages, and Applications Workshop on Generative Techniques in the Context of Model Driven Architecture*. New York, NY: ACM.

Mezini, M., & Ostermann, K. (2004). Variability management with feature-oriented programming and aspects. In R.N. Taylor (Ed.) *The Twelfth ACM SIGSOFT Internationl Symposium on Foundations of Software Engineering* (pp. 127-136). New York, NY: ACM.

Miller, J., & Mukerji, J. (Eds.). (2003). *MDA guide version 1.0.1*. OMG. Retrieved May 5, 2011, from http://www.omg.org/cgi-bin/doc?omg/03-06-01.pdf.

Perovich, P., Bastarrica, M. C., & Rojas, C. (2009). Model-driven approach to software architecture design. In P. Lago, P. Avgeriou, & P. Kruchten (Eds.), *The 2009 ICSE Workshop on Sharing and Reusing Architectural Knowledge* (pp. 1-8). Washington, DC: IEEE Computer Society.

Spiegel, D. S., Frye, L. M., & Day, L. L. (2008). Issues in the instantiation of template classes. *ACM SIGCSE Bulletin, 40*(2), 48–51. doi:10.1145/1383602.1383633

Trujillo, S., Batory, D., & Diaz, O. (2007). Feature oriented model driven development: A case study for portlets. In J. Knight (Ed.), *The Twenty-Ninth International Conference on Software Engineering* (pp. 44-53). Washington, DC: IEEE Computer Society.

Ubayashi, N., & Nakajima, S. (2007). Context-aware feature-oriented modeling with an aspect extension of VDM. In Y. Cho (Ed.), *The 2007 ACM Symposium on Applied Computing* (pp. 1269-1274). New York, NY: ACM.

Ward, W. A. Jr. (2000). Algorithm 803: a simpler macro processor. *ACM Transactions on Mathematical Software, 26*(2), 310–319. doi:10.1145/353474.353484

Zhou, M., Gao, M., & Hou, X. (2008). Design method for parameterized IP generator using structural and creational design patterns. In D. Guo (Ed.), *The Second International Conference on Anti-counterfeiting, Security and Identification* (pp. 378-381). Chengdu, China: IEEE Chengdu Section.

ADDITIONAL READING

Aly, M., Morsillo, N., Chrysanthis, P. K., & Pruhs, K. (2005). Zone sharing: A hot-spots decomposition scheme for data-centric storage in sensor networks. In A. Labrinidis, & S. R. Madden (Eds.), *The Second International Workshop on Data Management for Sensor Networks* (pp. 21-26). New York, NY: ACM.

Basu, A. (2010). Rigorous component-based system design using the BIP framework. *IEEE Software, 28*(3), 41–48. doi:10.1109/MS.2011.27

Bendraou, R., Jézéquel, J.-M., Gervais, M.-P., & Blanc, X. (2010). A comparison of six UML-based languages for software process modeling. *IEEE Transactions on Software Engineering, 36*(5), 662–675. doi:10.1109/TSE.2009.85

Bukhari, S., & Waheed, T. (2010). Model driven transformation between design models to system test models using UML: A survey. In F. Arif (Ed.), *The 2010 National Software Engineering Conference*. New York, NY: ACM.

Buschmann, F. (2010). On architecture styles and paradigms. *IEEE Software, 27*(5), 92–94. doi:10.1109/MS.2010.122

Cortellessa, V., Marco, A. D., & Inverardi, P. (2006). Software performance model-driven architecture. In H. M. Haddad (Ed.), *The 2006 ACM Symposium on Applied Computing* (pp. 1218-1223). New York, NY: ACM.

Crnkovic, I., Stafford, J., & Szyperski, C. (2011). Software components beyond programming: From routines to services. *IEEE Software, 28*(3), 22–26. doi:10.1109/MS.2011.62

Dahiya, D., & Dahiya, S. (2008). Software reuse in design and development of aspects. In J. Bosch, & J. Wong (Eds.), *The Thirty-Second Annual IEEE Computer Software Applications Conference* (pp. 745-750). Washington, DC: IEEE Computer Society.

Dantas, F., & Garcia, A. (2010). Software reuse versus stability: Evaluating advanced programming techniques. In T. Baista (Ed.), *The 2010 Brazilian Symposium on Software Engineering* (pp. 40-49). Washington, DC: IEEE Computer Society.

de Boer, R. C., Lago, P., Telea, A., & van Vliet, H. (2010). Ontology-driven visualization of architectural design decisions. In R. Kazman (Ed.), *The 2009 European Conference on Software Architecture* (pp. 51-60). Washington, DC: IEEE Computer Society.

Edwards, G., & Medvidoic, N. (2008). Rhizome: A feature modeling and generation platform. In S. Fickas (Ed.), *The 2008 Twenty-Third IEEE/ACM International Conference on Automated Software Engineering* (pp. 375-378). Washington, DC: IEEE Computer Society.

Elleuch, N., Khalfallah, A., & Ben Ahmed, S. (2007). Software architecture in model driven architecture. In M. Sugeno (Ed.), *The Third International Symposium on Computational Intelligence and Intelligent Informatics* (pp. 219-223). Washington, DC: IEEE Computer Society.

Ge, G., & Whitehead, E. J. (2008). A methodology and framework for creating domain-specific development infrastructures. In P. Inverardi (Ed.), *The 2008 Twenty-Third IEEE/ACM International Conference on Automated Software Engineering* (pp. 168-177). Washington, DC: IEEE Computer Society.

Gonzalez-Huerta, J., Blanes, D., & Insfran, E. E., & Abrahão, S. (2010). Towards an architecture for ensuring product quality in model-driven software development. In M. Oivo (Ed.), *The Eleventh International Conference on Product Focused Software* (pp. 28-31). New York, NY: ACM.

Hovsepyan, A., Scandariato, R., Baelen, S. V., Berbers, Y., & Joosen, W. (2010). From aspect-oriented models to aspect-oriented code? The maintenance perspective. In J. M. Jézéquel (Ed.), *The Ninth International Conference on Aspect-Oriented Software Development* (pp. 85-96). New York, NY: ACM.

Ispir, M., & Betin Can, A. (2008). An assume guarantee verification methodology for aspect-oriented programming. In P. Inverardi (Ed.), *The 2008 Twenty-Third IEEE/ACM International Conference on Automated Software Engineering* (pp. 391-394). Washington, DC: IEEE Computer Society.

Kiczales, G., & Mezini, M. (2005). Aspect-oriented programming and modular reasoning. In G. C. Roman (Ed.), *The Twenty-Seventh International Conference on Software Engineering* (pp. 49-58). New York, NY: ACM.

Kim, H., Zhang, Y., Oussena, S., & Clark, T. (2009). A case study on model driven data integration for data centric software development. In P. Chen, W. Li, & S. Wang (Eds.), *The ACM First International Workshop on Data-Intensive Software Management and Mining* (pp. 1-6). New York, NY: ACM.

Kim, S., Park, S., Yun, J., & Lee, Y. (2008). Automated continuous integration of component-based software: An industrial experience. In P. Inverardi (Ed.), *The 2008 Twenty-Third IEEE/ACM International Conference on Automated Software Engineering* (pp. 423-426). Washington, DC: IEEE Computer Society.

Lewis, G., Morris, E., Simanta, S., & Smith, D. (2011). Service orientation and systems of systems. *IEEE Software, 28*(1), 58–63. doi:10.1109/MS.2011.15

Liang, Y. (2008). An instance-based approach for domain-independent schema matching. In J. Cross, & H. Narang (Eds.), *The Forty-Sixth Annual Southeast Regional Conference on Database Systems* (pp. 268-271). New York, NY: ACM.

Malavolta, I. (2010). A model-driven approach for managing software architectures with multiple evolving concerns. In I. Gorton (Ed.), *The Fourth European Conference on Software Architecture* (pp. 4-8). New York, NY: ACM.

Mattsson, A., Lundell, B., Lings, B., & Fitzgerald, B. (2007). *Experiences from representing software architecture in a large industrial project using model driven development*. In The Second Workshop on Sharing and Reusing Architectural Knowledge Architecture, Rationale, and Design Intent. Washington, DC: IEEE Computer Society.

McNeile, A., & Roubtsova, E. (2009). Composition semantics for executable and evolvable behavioral modeling in MDA. In M. Aksit, E. Kindler, E. Roubtsova, & A. McNeile (Eds.), *The First Workshop on Behavioural Modelling in Model-Driven Architecture*. New York, NY: ACM.

Meng, Y., Meng, X., & Yang, W. (2009). Component based software reuse key technology research and design. In Zhou, Q. (Ed.), *The 2009 International Forum on Information Technology and Applications* (pp. 89–92). Washington, DC: IEEE Computer Society.

Parichehreh, A., Javadi, B., & Jafarzadeh, O. (2010). Multi-level zone based hybrid service discovery protocol for mobile ad-hoc grid. In L. Kleinrock (Ed.), *The 2010 Second International Conference on Future Computer and Communication, 1,* (V1-391-V1-395). Washington, DC: IEEE Computer Society.

Peng, X., Wu, Y., & Zhao, W. (2007). A feature-oriented adaptive component model for dynamic evolution. In R. Krikhaar (Ed.), *The 2007 Eleventh European Conference on Software Maintenance and Reengineering* (pp. 49-57). Washington, DC: IEEE Computer Society.

Ramachandran, M. (2005). Software reuse guidelines. *ACM SIGSOFT Software Engineering Notes, 30*(3), 1–8. doi:10.1145/1061874.1061889

Salay, R., Mylopoulos, S., & Easterbrook, S. (2008). Managing models through macromodeling. In P. Inverardi (Ed.), *The 2008 Twenty-Third IEEE/ACM International Conference on Automated Software Engineering* (pp. 447-450). Washington, DC: IEEE Computer Society.

Santos, R., & Werner, C. (2010). Revisiting the concept of components in software engineering from a software ecosystem perspective. In I. Gorton (Ed.), *The Fourth European Conference on Software Architecture* (pp. 135-142). New York, NY: ACM.

Singh, Y., & Sood, M. (2009). Model driven architecture: A perspective. In D. Garg (Ed.), *The 2009 IEEE International Advance Computing Conference* (pp. 1644-1652). Washington, DC: IEEE Computer Society.

Störrle, H. (2010). Structuring very large domain models: experiences from industrial MDSD projects. In I. Gorton (Ed.), *The Fourth European Conference on Software Architecture* (pp. 49-54). New York, NY: ACM.

Trujillo, S., Zubizarreta, A., Mendialdua, X., & Sosa, J. D. (2009). Feature-oriented refinement of models, metamodels and model transformations. In S. Apel, et al. (Eds.), *The First International Workshop on Feature-Oriented Software Development* (pp. 87-94). New York, NY: ACM.

Wang, R., Mao, X.-G., Dai, Z.-Y., & Wang, Y.-N. (2010). Extending UML for aspect-oriented architecture modeling. In Q. Li, F. Yu, Y. Liu, & M. Russell (Eds.), *The Second International Workshop on Computer Science and Engineering* (pp. 362-366). Washington, DC: IEEE Computer Society.

Woods, E., & Rozanski, N. (2010). Unifying software architecture with its implementation. In I. Gorton (Ed.), *The Fourth European Conference on Software Architecture* (pp. 55-58). New York, NY: ACM.

Xu, K., & Feng, J. (2010). A new look at schema instance recoverability with the notion of information carrying. In X. Tian (Ed.), *The 2009 International Conference on Research Challenges in Computer Science* (pp. 15-17). Washington, DC: IEEE Computer Society.

Zhang, J., Chen, Y., Zhang, Y., & Li, H. (2009). Aspect-oriented modeling and mapping driven by model driven architecture. In S. Xubang, S. Misra, & L. Fernando (Eds.), *The 2009 Second IEEE International Conference on Computer Science and Information Technology* (pp. 180-184). Washington, DC: IEEE Computer Society.

Zhang, J., & Fei, W. (2010). Research of the improved traditional MDA. In F. Chin, A. Sachenko, & C. Yang (Eds.), *The 2010 Second International Conference on Networks Security, Wireless Communications and Trusted Computing* (pp. 475-478). Washington, DC: IEEE Computer Society.

Zhang, L. L., Ying, S., Ni, Y.-C., Wen, J., & Zhao, K. (2009). An approach for multi-dimensional separation concerns at architecture Level. In W. Zheng (Ed.), *The 2008 Workshop on Power Electronics and Intelligent Transportation Systems* (pp. 541-545). Washington, DC: IEEE Computer Society.

Zhu, Z. (2009). Study and application of patterns in software reuse. In *The 2009 International Conference on Control, Automation, and Software Engineering* (pp. 550-553). Washington, DC: IEEE Computer Society.

KEY TERMS AND DEFINITIONS

Model Composition: A description of entity composition that is captured in a model of the entity.

Model Composition Graph Instance: Generated hierarchically composed entity instances of corresponding model schemas by hierarchical model expansion.

Model Composition Graph Schema: A specification of hierarchical model composition that consists of hierarchically composed model schemas.

Model-Driven Architecture: A software design approach to transform software designs by incrementally adding implementation details.

Model Expansion: A process to generate entity instance composition according to model composition specified in corresponding model schema and given expansion parameters.

Model Instance: Generated entity instance of corresponding model schema by model expansion.

Model Schema: A specification of model composition of certain entities together with model refinement data and behaviors.

Chapter 3
Components and Frameworks in the Cloud Era

Dino Konstantopoulos
The MITRE Corporation, USA

Mike Pinkerton
Northrop Grumman Corporation, USA

Eric Braude
Boston University, USA

ABSTRACT

The emergence and popularity of Cloud computing could not have happened were it not for the massive amount of underlying software reuse, as reuse of services and applications is what saves development dollars and allows IT infrastructure to adapt more nimbly to the changing environment. Software fosters two reuse syntaxes: Sharing and reuse of human-readable source code (open source), or sharing and reuse of machine-readable binary code (proprietary). Software also caters to two reuse semantics: where the software is either prepackaged as components or as frameworks. In this chapter, the authors examine software reuse in the Cloud. By categorizing it in these dual categories, they glimpse the practices that prime Cloud-based software for massive reuse.

INTRODUCTION

Source code, binary code, components, and frameworks are the currencies and exchange mechanisms of software reuse. This reuse occurs at different points on the production line of new software. For components, it's early in the production line, and for frameworks it is late in the production line of new software: Before a software

program can be executed, it needs be converted from source code to binary code, and so sharing and reuse can occur upstream of the software production line (as source code), when the software may not even be complete, or downstream, when it is packaged and ready for download and execution (as binary code). Components are mature products on their own right but they're most often leveraged early in the software production line of other software applications: The application is built around them. Frameworks on the other

DOI: 10.4018/978-1-4666-0897-9.ch003

hand host software products as add-ins, and these add-ins extend their host's functionality. And so frameworks represent the end of the production line for those software products. Moreover, much like there are two currencies, or syntaxes, of software reuse (source code and binary code), and two exchange mechanisms, or semantics (components and frameworks), there are also two communities of interest that promote the reuse: The free software and open source movements promote "no-cost" sharing of source code, while the proprietary world promotes market mechanisms through exclusive rights of ownership to binary code, protected by licenses and copy protection mechanisms. Currencies, exchange mechanisms, and communities of interest are well represented in today's public Clouds. Let's examine the exchange mechanisms a bit closer. It is important to note that when we talk about sharing and reusing code, it is in the context of (third party) developers sharing and reusing code originally written by other developers, in order to incorporate original functionality into a new program or extend the original functionality with new features. Software users don't really reuse or share software: They "use" it in the sense that they execute it. And so the exchange mechanism is between developers. When source code is exchanged between developers, it is packaged in the form of a "source tree" that can be loaded into a development environment and compiled into a binary executable. Source code functionality can be easily uncovered by reading the source code. It is easily modifiable, and so there need not be a standard architecture for the source tree. Third-party developers extend it with new functionality in various and multifaceted ways. In contrast, when binary code is reused, it is packaged in standard architectures, which are either software components or software frameworks, abstractions in which common binary code providing generic functionality can be most easily leveraged, extended, and specialized by third-party developers. Let's take a closer look

at the technical differences between components and frameworks.

When developers reuse software components, they write code that calls the components' code. Software components are often called component "libraries", and software that uses component libraries is often known as "component-oriented architectures". In contrast, when third-party developers reuse software frameworks, they write "callback" code that is called by framework code. In other words, third-party developers implement interfaces dictated by the architecture of the software framework. When the framework is executed, it calls the new third-party implementations which it discovers by a registration mechanism specified by the framework's developers. And so, framework reuse consists of both implementation and design reuse, while component reuse is usually just an implementation reuse. Perhaps the most notable example of this distinction consists in how software programs are hosted today: One can either write programs that are self-hosted and run as standalone components on an operating system like Microsoft Windows, Linux, or Apple iOS, or one can write programs that are hosted by browsers like Microsoft Explorer, Firefox, or Apple Safari. In the latter case, the programs are reusing very popular frameworks that consist of implementation (internet browsers) and architecture (for writing add-ins and enhancing the browser's functionality). We first examine the origins of these two types of software abstractions, and then we concentrate on their best principles, in the sense that they facilitate software reuse on the Cloud and guide the design of the building blocks of Cloud computing.

A SHORT HISTORY OF COMPONENTS

The original vision of software reuse was based on components: Units of software re-use across independent parties. Component-oriented software may also be object-oriented, although the internal objects may not be accessible by the reusing party if the software is binary code. The main motivation underlying component-oriented software was an economic one: By building applications from pre-fabricated components, companies would decrease the time to market. To make this possible, component-oriented software emphasizes separation of concern over the total functionality in the software. Components relate parts of the system that are functionally related. Not only does this allow components to be sold in software marketplaces, this has also been proven to improve maintenance through division of labor and system evolution through cohesiveness.

Component-based source code was promoted by open source practitioners very early on, and a form of component-based binary code was popularized soon after the commercial success of personal computing packages like Visicalc (Bricklin, VisiCalc: Information from its creators) and Lotus 1-2-3: Companies would wrap functionality into component libraries that could be reused through their Application Programming Interfaces (APIs). Examples of such packages consisted of communication components such as Winsock libraries for Windows-based operating systems (Heng, Free Sockets and Winsock Libraries), But component-based binary code had to wait until integration standards such as CORBA and COM were established before widespread adoption. These standards enabled a more easily instrumented and automated reuse of these components, since they leveraged operating system subsystems for uncovering functionality and more seamlessly integrating objects outside and inside the component.

There is now a boundless marketplace of software components that can be reused to assist development efforts on all the different computing platforms available today (Windows-based, Linux-based, Apple, mobile platforms like the iPhone, Android, and Windows phone), targeting all existing binary integration standards (e.g.

ActiveX, .NET, J2EE), and source code languages (e.g. C#, Java, ObjectiveC, Ruby).

A SHORT HISTORY OF FRAMEWORKS

For frameworks, the underlying idea was to invert the production line: A framework developer writes the software application (the final product, which may also include component libraries popular to 3rd party developers), and defines interfaces that framework extension developers implement to extend the framework with new functionality. Frameworks typically provide a blueprint for how to develop new components, as well as a way to manage a system of interacting components. New components developed to extend a framework share consistent design attributes with the framework and potentially even common implementations. This in turn results in more consistent, more maintainable systems, and through separation of concerns minimizes the amount of code that is duplicated in a system. For example, a framework may provide a standard system-wide methodology for components to handle errors, exchange data, discover each other's functionality, and invoke operations on each other. And so, frameworks are a skeleton of an application that can be extended and specialized, a context for developing new components with little effort, and a baseline of functionality that can be immediately reused. Reusing a framework consists in adopting a design, a large-scale pattern for component development and interaction, and a baseline of prefabricated components. In contrast to the software component approach to software reuse, which is built on the paradigm of assembling small building blocks of components to build bigger ones, frameworks allow the highest common abstraction level in a system to be captured in terms of general concepts and structures and design that can be inherited by each new framework component. Both components and frameworks reuse functionality, but in the case of the framework, architecture and design are reused as well. Very popular frameworks in use today consist of all Internet browsers, the .NET common language runtime for developing Windows-based applications, and Flash and Ruby on Rails for developing rich internet applications. The architectural pattern that underlies the vast majority of these frameworks is the Inversion of Control (IoC) pattern (an "inversion" because the final product is architected and developed first) (Fowler, Inversion of Control). What are the origins of this pattern? A little bit of history is in order.

The introduction of graphical user interfaces on Apple, Microsoft, and Linux platforms, revolutionized programming. Console programs (programs targeting ASCII I/O interfaces) were batch-driven, with instruction-flow determined by the programmer. Programs targeting graphical user interfaces are event-driven: with instruction flow determined by events such as sensor outputs, user actions like mouse clicks, as well as messages from other programs. Event-driven programs are extensible, with new event detection algorithms and new event-handling routines defined by end-users. These extensible event-driven programs gave rise to new architectural styles of programming like Inversion of Control and dependency injection (Fowler, Inversion of Control), which supplanted legacy batch-driven programs.

To provide value-added functionality by leveraging batch-driven component libraries and Software Development Kits (SDK), a value-added programmer (hereafter denoted as *end-users*[1]) writes a new batch-driven program that calls each component one by one in order to access their functionality: The flow of the program is dictated by end-users. In contrast, to provide value-added functionality by leveraging an Inversion of Control (IoC) framework, the end-user extends the original framework by writing a new module according to a pre-defined template dictated by the framework, and it is the framework that calls the new module according to a predefined convention. The flow

of the integrated framework plus extension is not dictated by the end-user anymore; it is determined by the framework and the new module is called at the convenience of the framework. That is the reason why this new architectural style of integration is called Inversion of Control: Extension of functionality by an end-user comes at the cost of the loss of program flow control, which is retained by the IoC framework. But the benefits of this architectural style are bountiful, including reducing the cost of software integration by implementing a common architecture and extensibility template instead of reinventing new ones, and reducing the overall cost of software development for all end-users as features that that are desired by end-users are developed only once and included with the IoC framework. An IoC architecture instills complexity and responsibility on its architects because they have to predict and accommodate all end-user requirements by either offering them out of the box as framework components, or making them attainable by extensibility of the framework through pre-defined templates.

Dependency injection (Fowler, Inversion of Control) is the most common implementation pattern for an IoC architecture today: The IoC framework defines interfaces that value-added extension modules written by end-users implement. These extension modules are then called by convention by the framework.

And so frameworks and their Inversion of Control architectures owe their existence to graphical user interfaces, event-based programming, and the great graphical interfaces of Apple, Microsoft Windows, and Linux. Without the Inversion of Control pattern, it would be almost impossible to leverage a single framework program across a varied community of reuse and be able to extend it in many different ways.

CLOUD COMPUTING FRAMEWORKS AND COMPONENTS

From its mainframe roots, to the reality of personal computers, to the brave new world of Cloud computing, we are in the third generation of computing paradigms (fourth if one considers Web computing as the third paradigm), and almost back to our roots as computation is once again delivered from central locations, albeit through the Web. But the delivery model is completely modern: Software is delivered like a utility to multiple customers; it stretches and shrinks elastically on demand by rapidly bootstrapping virtual operating systems, load balancing applications across them, provisioning duplicate copies of any application across distinct virtual operating systems and transferring over to a working copy when an application fails. The end result is applications that go into production more quickly, scale linearly, and at an order of magnitude less cost than traditional IT approaches. All of that essentially started with *Amazon* (Amazon), a company that sold books over the Web and expanded its computing infrastructure to sell many other things. The infrastructure worked so well, that Amazon decided it could sell those services that helped it sell services, and *Amazon Web Services* (Amazon Web Services) in tandem with the *Elastic Cloud* (Amazon Elastic Cloud) infrastructure was born. Microsoft and Google soon followed suit with their own platform offerings: *Azure* (Microsoft Windows Azure) and *App Engine* (Google App Engine). Traditional Internet service providers like *Rackspace* (Rackspace.com) rebranded themselves to match the Cloud model. Enterprises like *SalesForce* (Salesforce.com) that were already delivering services over the Web adopted the Cloud model and gave customers the option to pay only for computing resources used, and to pool, provision, and release these in real time based on demand. That model probably would not have been possible were it not for companies like *VMware* (EMC VMWare), which worked to enable full-fledged operating systems

to run as applications on a host operating system, and almost as efficiently as the host operating system itself. This in turn made it possible to easily and rapidly create multi-tenant environments on a single piece of hardware. Provisioning computer resources became a matter of switching on an operating system, instead of buying, shipping, and installing hardware. A new economy of scale was born. This economy fostered rapid innovation in the software industry, and legacy software products adapted to the Cloud while new Cloud-based software products started making their appearance as well. Some of these proved so popular that they were reused over and over, and gave rise to new products based on them. In the next two paragraphs, we explore some of these popular components and frameworks. Later, we gather lessons learned in terms of the qualities it takes to become a building block of software innovation.

POPULAR COMPONENTS

We find that most component-based software reuse on the Cloud concerns data tier or middleware (business logic) tier components. These components are used as value-added capabilities by applications targeting the Cloud. There is reuse of presentation tier software as well, but it mostly concerns software frameworks and we will address those in the next paragraph. There is perhaps no more important component for the Cloud than that which helps persist data on the Cloud, so that it can be mined and combined. In the traditional world this is the domain of the relational database. The story of the implementation of the relational database model on the Cloud is a very interesting one, and the Cloud is the primary driver of database research and innovation today. It is noteworthy that the only two widespread *relational* database offerings on the Cloud are SQLAzure (Microsoft SQLAzure) (based on *Microsoft SQLServer*) and Amazon's Relational Database Service (RDS)

(Amazon Relational Database Service) (based on ex-open source *MySQL*, now owned by Oracle)[2]. Both SQLAzure and RDS are limited in size to no more than 50 GB for SQLAzure and 1 TB for RDS. This is a major roadblock for enterprise databases, which often exceed terabytes in size. An example of the migrating pains of enterprise databases to the cloud is the story of the Sloan digital Sky Survey, a public dataset of astronomical data with a medium-complexity schema (Thakar, Migrating a (Large) Science Database to the Cloud). There is a reason for this restricting upper limit in size, and it is one that will be hard to overcome. The reason is that improvement of data transfer rates severely lags that of hard drive storage capacity: Data transfer rates have improved by a couple of orders of magnitude in the last decade, while storage drive capacity has improved by over five orders of magnitude, and this proportion is likely to remain the same in the foreseeable future. In other words, the network and the speed of electrons within it is the limiting factor[3]. Since the Cloud relies on data and process duplication (most often, three copies are generated, across distinct hardware failure zones), it must actively replicate data across its copies. If the data grows in size, the transfer load does as well, and being able to do the requisite data transfer in the background while guaranteeing seamless switch-over from one copy to another in the eventuality that one of them fails implies a hard limit on the size of the database. Being able to ration the data transfer over time and leave parts of the database in an inconsistent state across copies would be the principal mitigating strategy for this limitation. However relational databases have this one essential feature that characterizes them: They are *relational* and at any moment in time queries may be run against them that aggregate data across the entire database. And so consistency cannot ever be sacrificed. And that is the reason underlying the hard limitation in size for Cloud-based relational databases.

The non-relational database offerings on the Cloud, of which there are many, sacrifice instantaneous consistency in favor of eventual consistency. Examples are *BigTable* (Google BigTable), and *SimpleDB* (Amazon SimpleDB). There is also a new breed of databases whose adoption rate is increasing exponentially: This breed is known as the *No-SQL movement*[4] (No-SQL movement), and it essentially espouses the viewpoint that SQL *Joins* (the ability to create intersections and unions of database rows based on mathematical relations on their fields) are not appropriate operations for the Cloud. Instead, alternative strategies for aggregating data are leveraged, and one of the most popular ones is based on the highly acclaimed *MapReduce* (Google MapReduce) algorithm, which is described in the Frameworks section further below. Examples of popular No-SQL databases include *MongoDB* (Mongodb.org) and *CouchDB* (Apache CouchDB). Since relations over fields are not allowed, fields need not be predefined before data is persisted. In other words, new fields can be added and legacy fields can be deleted as new data is stored and old data deleted. That is not to say that schema (how the persisted data is structured) is not important, only that the schema is allowed to be fluid and change over time. And so it is not just computation or storage that is of "elastic" nature on the Cloud, but data organization as well. The ability to constantly refactor how data is stored so that it can be better mined, archived, and combined with new data is a key feature of popular data storage components on the Cloud. Schema is also important in computation, not just data storage, and schema in computation is often referred to as the "object model" of a computation. Whereas schemas in storage are more often relational (relational databases) in order to organize large amounts of data, schemas in computation are most often hierarchical in order to compute as fast as possible, and thus object inheritance and parameterized classes (also called generics or templates) play an important role. Although the mapping between how data is persisted and how it is loaded into a computation is often custom tailored by the computing application, best of breed components that excel at this object-relational mapping are often reused. One of these popular components is *Hibernate* (http://www.hibernate.org), an object-relational mapping library for the Java language. Another such component is *Entity Framework* (Microsoft, Entity Framework)), an object-relational mapping library for the .NET family of languages, which includes C#. Yet another option for applications is to persist objects in a hierarchical format, in the same format as they are being used in the computation. These strategies alleviate network bottlenecks, as virtual machines are continuously forced to wait for data to be transferred to or from the network. There are popular components that do just that: They serialize objects across the Cloud in an optimal fashion so that they're closest to the applications that need them. They are most often referred to as "caches", and one of these is the *Velocity* (Microsoft, Velocity) cache. The Velocity runtime pools together individual distributed caches to present a unified view to the application. *Memcached* (Memcached.org) is another such cache. Whereas Velocity is proprietary, memcached is open source. Velocity is a managed component[5] targeting .NET applications, while memcached is a binary component implemented in C, originally written for Linux and now ported to both Mac and Windows.

Finally, storage components for objects of small sizes, like music files, pictures, or videos, are available from many Cloud vendors, including Microsoft, Amazon, and Google. These storage components are available as queues, simple tables for small objects, and directories for larger binary objects. Popular uses of these components are for backing up data, or as temporary store-and-forward repositories. Cloud-based online services like *Google Docs* (Google Docs) and *SkyDrive* (Microsoft, SkyDrive) leverage these components to allow users to store a minimal amount of in-

formation for free, and past a certain threshold, charge based on storage space and bandwidth.

In the middleware tier, domain of specialized business logic software that applications can use, the most leveraged Cloud-based components relate to deploying applications on the Cloud, scaling applications on the Cloud, payment services for application on the Cloud, authentication and authorization of users accessing applications on the Cloud, and managing connectivity between applications. *Elastic Beanstalk* (http://aws.amazon.com/elasticbeanstalk/) is Amazon's component to help deploy applications to the Amazon Cloud, while *Visual Studio*[6] (Microsoft Visual Studio) is the component that deploys applications to the Microsoft Cloud.

Dynamically scaling applications based on demand is probably one of the most actively researched topics on the Cloud. Dynamic scaling refers to the ability to add capacity into and remove capacity from a Cloud infrastructure based on actual usage. It is most often implemented by scaling applications out. *Scaling out* of applications refers to the ability to host multiple instances of the same applications on multiple virtual machines, and load-balancing demand across the virtual machines. *Scaling up* of applications is the opposite model, whereby a single application is enabled with the capability to acquire hardware resources in proportion to demand. Scaling applications up is the most natural model for agile computation, and in a certain sense, opting to scale out instead of scaling up represents in the authors' opinion the most glaring failure of today's generation of operating systems. A single operating system should be able to coordinate with a single application in order to earmark a dynamically varying amount of computing resources like CPU, hard disk, memory, and network. But that is not the model underlying today's Cloud. Instead, it consists of operating systems essentially cloning themselves in memory (the virtual machines) while a central supervisor directs the spawning of new copies of an application in virtual machines hosted in distinct (across hardware failure lines) hardware, and a load balancer dispatching demand across these copies. Although this might appear as a technical failure for today's operating systems, it is more an issue of economy of scale than the adoption of an elegant technical model: It is cheaper overall to provide computing power in the guise of many instances of cheap hardware, than in the guise of fewer instances of better performing and more expensive hardware. It is also, in the end, a reflection of the *Pareto principle* which states that for many events, roughly 80% of the effects come from 20% of the causes. Reworded, it says that it takes 80% more effort to provide 20% more computing power per unit of hardware. Settling on many copies of minimum effort is more economical, and so most dynamic scaling components leverage the *scaling out* implementation. There are many proprietary solutions to this and few widely embraced ones. Elastic Beanstalk (Amazon Elastic Beanstalk) is one such choice for the Amazon Cloud.

Digital payment components represent the bleeding edge of financial innovation. *PayPal* (Paypal.com) is a leading provider of digital payments, and they have componentized their architecture so that vendors can incorporate it as value-add into their solutions. The hardest part of digital payment is authentication and authorization, and this is a popular software reuse topic. A leading component is the *AppFabric Access Control service* (Microsoft AppFabric). It enables authorization decisions to be pulled out of applications and into a set of declarative rules that can simplify incoming security claims for applications. The Access Control service component lives on the Microsoft Cloud, but it may be accessed by any application, even those that are not Cloud-based. Microsoft's AppFabric also provides a *Service Bus* (Microsoft Azure Service Bus) component, which enables secure communications between applications, whether they are on the Cloud or not. It provides many options to leverage popular communication and messaging protocols and patterns and also takes care of delivery assurance,

reliable messaging and scale. Finally, it provides patterns that allow applications to bypass corporate firewall and Network Address Translation table limitations so that any two applications behind firewalls and Address Translation tables can tunnel through and securely communicate both as talker and listener. It is essentially a *Skype®* (http://www.skype.com) for applications, and in that light it may not be surprising that Microsoft has recently acquired Skype itself, in order to consolidate on that capability.

We conclude the discussion on Cloud-based components with a component that is almost a blueprint as to how to integrate computers and manpower in a globalized economy and thus almost blurs the boundaries between components and frameworks. It is one with far-reaching implications, whose popularity in our opinion will continue to increase: Amazon's *Mechanical Turk* (Amazon Mechanical Turk). Mechanical Turk is a component that applications can integrate with in order to leverage a global market of cheap human workforce to perform tasks for which computers are not well suited for, such as complex image and video processing. By combining two popular modern concepts: Micro-loans such as those offered by Nobel-prize winning *Grammeen Bank* (Grameen Bank), and Web-based Want-ads such as *Craig's list* (Craig's List), one could leverage Mechanical Turk to decompose an application into small independent parts and outsource the development of these small parts to a cheaply available workforce. This would be an extreme form of IT globalization. It is interesting to note that most Cloud-based components with high rates of reuse are binary components that are free: In other words components that adhere to well-defined but mostly proprietary standards of interoperability, and yet completely free to use. The utility of the component (exclusively for use on a proprietary public Cloud) is leveraged by Cloud providers to attract customers to their proprietary Cloud. Today, even Open Source components, whether Cloud-based or not, adhere to this utility model (as a pathway to proprietary adoptions or fee-based services), and that is far removed from the original "free-speech based" ideals of the Open Source movement (Gnu.org, Free Software Definition).

POPULAR FRAMEWORKS

In the last paragraph we mentioned popular Cloud-based components and noted that most of them relate to either the data or middleware tier. In the presentation tier however, most software reuse concerns frameworks and not components. In contrast to components, which are used as value-added capabilities by applications, the framework is the application and reuse consists in extending the framework by providing it with custom add-in implementations. In contrast to components that are mostly reused as proprietary binary code, we will see that a sizable percentage of Cloud-based frameworks are provided in both binary and source code formats.

Probably the most foundational piece of Cloud-based source code is the *MapReduce* (Google, MapReduce) framework. It is the framework behind their very successful implementation of a strategy to rank Web sites according to the number of hyperlinks that direct users to them, called *PageRank* (Google PageRank). This ranking is what popularized Google as a search engine to users, and it is their main source of revenue as it brings in billions of dollars in advertising revenue. Google has described the MapReduce computation framework in detail, and researchers from the Apache project have adopted it and produced a version of it as an open source framework called *Hadoop* (Apache Hadoop). Hadoop is used by academia, the financial industry, pharmaceutical companies, advertising agencies, and any organization that needs to process massive amounts of data economically and efficiently. Hadoop is trusted by users and resilient to hardware failures. When computations run across thousands of computing servers built economically with commodity hardware, failures happen often. Hadoop has built-in software logic to handle these, recover gracefully, and resume the computation. It can scale out from a few computing servers to thousands of them in order to accommodate the problem at hand. Hadoop is open in that it can be configured and extended in many ways, and it complies with the latest Java standard on which it is based. Hadoop is a framework because users implement predefined interfaces to specialize the computation to the problem at hand, and they run the Hadoop executable to get results. If one could only name a few frameworks behind the extensive adoption of Cloud computing by researchers and industry, this would be one of them.

All computers in use today are based on the von Neumann architecture, whereby the same memory is used for both data and program instructions. Because program instructions need to be critically close to computing registers for fast calculations, data was moved to the memory locations for program instructions. This trend continued with the appearance of network and distributed computing: the data is transferred to the server overseeing the calculation. Cloud computing has introduced caches that accelerate this transfer, but sometimes even that is not enough. The data is often so massive, and the calculating algorithm so simple, that is often more expedient to send the calculation to the network location where the data resides. This principle is at the basis of Cloud computing frameworks like Hadoop and other frameworks for execution of data parallel applications. A very promising approach for computing with massive data sets involve modeling the dataflow of an application as a directed graph, with the vertices of the graph defining the operations that are to be performed on the data without specifying concurrency or mutual exclusion semantics, and leaving that up to specialized runtimes. Two popular such computational frameworks are *Pregel* (Google, Large Scale Graph Computing at Google) and *Dryad* (Microsoft, Dryad).

Software architectures are the blueprint behind software products, but some of these blueprints have had such successful implementations that the blueprints have become a kind of framework in their own right: Even though software products that abide by these blueprints will be their own hosts and not reuse a framework host, the flow and logic of execution is so tightly dictated by the architecture and so similar across all implementations that these can be thought of as being hosted by an abstract framework. At that point, the abstract framework remains abstract and is called a *pattern*. Automated engines that translate the abstract frameworks into concrete implementations spring up and become *factory frameworks*, helping applications along to develop implementations based on the abstract framework. Factory frameworks are not like frameworks in that they don't host applications at runtime, but they host the development process for such an application. In other words, they host the application at design-time. There are a number of such factory frameworks that are popular with Cloud-based applications. One of these is *Model View Controller* (Fowler, GUI Achitectures), a pattern developed for the Smalltalk language and popularized by the open source Ruby-based *Ruby on Rails* (Ruby On Rails) factory framework and the similarly open source .NET-based MVC (Microsoft Model-View-Controller) framework by Microsoft. Ruby on Rails includes tools to simplify development tasks and scaffolding that can automatically construct some of the models and views needed for a basic Website. Microsoft's MVC3 framework integrates with Microsoft's flagship Integrated Development Environment (Microsoft Visual Studio) and assists the developer in creating basic models, views, and controller needed for a basic Website. Two other popular abstract frameworks are the *Model-View-ViewModel* framework (Microsoft, Model-View-ViewModel), a pattern spun off from MVC that is enjoying immense a great degree of adoption with *Silverlight* and *WPF* based applications[7], and *Reactive extensions (Rx)* (Microsoft,

Reactive Extensions), a programming pattern based on LINQ[8] that simplifies asynchronous event-based programming. A common feature of MVVM and Rx is that they produce very terse and easy to understand code that results in very high productivity rates for developers.

We conclude this section with the most venerable of all frameworks: The Web browser itself. No other framework has done so much in so little time and revolutionized the software industry as deeply. It has created an entirely new modality for familiar user interfaces based on a transducer state-machine[9] concept, the thin client, and then ushered a flurry of asynchronous programming development to improve it using techniques now commonly known as *Asynchronous Javascript And XML* (AJAX) (W3 Schools, Ajax). Its add-in extensibility model has fostered highly capable and compact proprietary runtimes such as *Flash* and *Silverlight*. These are desktop-like environments running on the client browser and allowing server-based applications to offload all user interface processing to the client so they can concentrate on what they do best: compute centrally and distribute results to the clients. As a result, a new highly capable and open standard with open source implementations, HTML5 (W3 Schools, HTML5), is at the brink of being released by a standards committee with extensive industry participation and buy in. HTML 5 is expected to be a disruptive technology, and it will play an important role in the new generation of Web browsers, middleware, and Operating Systems (Microsoft Windows, Windows 8). The Web browser throughout its history has been very much a von Neumann product: It emits data and code in tandem as HTML and Javascript, the "Esperanto" of all technologies as it is understood and spoken by all browsers. There are many factory frameworks that translate proprietary server-side technologies such as Microsoft's ASP.NET, Oracle's JSP, and open source PHP, to HTML and Javascript, enabling developers to code with compiled languages and in managed environments. The software delivery model of the Cloud relies centrally on the Web browser, and the Web browser has become the de-facto user interface of the Cloud. A large part of the migration of an application to the Cloud is about porting its user interface so that it can run within a browser. And so it may not be surprising that frameworks dominate presentation tier software reuse on the Cloud.

BEST PRACTICES

In the last two sections, we described some of the most popular software reuse on the Cloud, in the form of components and frameworks, and as source or binary code. In this section, we examine ten best practices and principles, and conclude with what it takes to create a component, framework, source, and binary code that are building blocks of reuse and innovation.

Accountable

One of the biggest challenges in software engineering today concerns the issue of trust: Developing techniques that demonstrate that software can be trusted by developers that integrate with it. Software frameworks, as showcased by the Linux operating system, may be composed of thousands of integrated software extensions that have implemented operating system-defined software interfaces. What happens when developers build a new component by implementing a framework interface and an end-user executes the software framework and the new component, only to run into a software bug caused by another component implementing a completely different interface which crashes the entire program? To the user, the software framework or the new component is the party at fault because these two implementations were viewed by the user as the dying act of the program! The situation is much less obscure with component libraries: caller code can segregate a component API call within an exception

block. The exception block's catch handler will reveal if the bug is in the library or in the caller's code, and the user can be appropriately notified. Software frameworks need to work harder to implement accountability by providing absolute transparency about which interface implementation and what component caused the program to crash. Software frameworks need to implement a general exception handling mechanism by encapsulating public interfaces within exception blocks and defining another public interface that callers can implement and which can return and multicast exceptions to any caller that implements that interface. Callers can then be informed of any bug that is not caught and appropriately handled within a third party extension, and to divest responsibility from an ungraceful crash by notifying the user in case the user is exercising a caller's module at the time of the crash. With accountability in hand, trust in the aggregate of software framework plus extensions is a much more straightforward affair, and similar to trust mechanisms for software libraries. Software that works hard to gain the trust of its users includes Model View Controller frameworks, which by the very nature of a decomposable architecture allows users to test each part independently. In fact, most of these frameworks include templates for automatic unit test generation, and they are very popular with the test-driven development community, which firmly believe that application requirements should be captured into unit tests and that tests should be developed prior to any application implementation. A popular option for increasing the accountability of a framework or a component without adding any out of band mechanisms for increasing accountability is to provide it as source code, even if it may be downloaded as binary code. Many traditionally proprietary software shops have chosen this route to increase the accountability of software that they provide for free and which is meant to increase the utility of related for-pay services or software. Even though accountability is an important topic for any component and framework, it is even more important for cloud-based components and frameworks since the largest obstacle standing today between public Clouds and their evolution to vast accepted integration nexuses is the issue of trust.

Resilient

Resilience when confronted to hardware failures is one of the defining characteristics of today's Cloud infrastructure. But the resilience is not implemented in the hardware, but rather in the software. When Cloud providers bring thousands of servers together under one gigantic roof, the statistics of commodity hardware failures are inescapable. When hardware failures are expected and not exceptional conditions, failures are mitigated with software: components, frameworks, and virtualized operating systems are duplicated or even tripled and kept synchronized so that a failure on one of the copies can be mitigated by replacing that instance with one of the duplicated. With the bar on resiliency set so high by native Cloud infrastructure, components and frameworks need to follow suit and provide high degrees of resiliency to all kinds of error conditions. Examples of software that works hard at providing resiliency are MapReduce (Google, MapReduce) implementations like Hadoop (Apache, Hadoop) and Graph-based frameworks like Pregel (Google, Pregel) and Dryad (Microsoft, Dryad), but also data tier components like relational and non-relational databases, simple queues and tables, object relational mappings, and caches.

Segmented

Many components and frameworks suffer from feature creep. This often results in code bloat and problems maintaining and evolving the software baseline. The best defensive strategy against code bloat is to decompose components and frameworks into distinct segments and to integrate these segments at runtime instead of maintaining

a single source code tree. There can be no better documentation about components or frameworks than actually decomposing them into units of distinct functionality. This is even more relevant for Open Source components and frameworks: When decomposed into distinct source code trees, each tree is smaller in size and tends to be more maintainable, and easier to document and understand. Components and frameworks that are clearly segmented experience a considerably higher amount of reuse.

Service Oriented

In the previous paragraph, we stated that segmentation is an important issue for components and frameworks. Is there a way to segment that is better than others? It turns out there is, and it is the service oriented way, which emphasizes a clear separation of concern between services so that they may be comprehensively deconstructed and recomposed into new business solutions. Frameworks are usually composed of many segments, and so achieving separation of concern for frameworks is more of a challenge than for individual components. Frameworks, over the course of many revisions, often need to refactor internal segments to minimize linkage between them. Minimal linkage, also known as loose coupling, benefits system maintainability by imbuing flexibility into the system, a key characteristic of service oriented architectures. One of the easiest ways to achieve this is to implement framework logic by fulfilling sub-goals in a simple accumulating manner so that the code fulfilling each sub-goal keeps invariant all fulfilled sub-goals. The following are key properties driving the implementation of the sub-goals of a service oriented framework:

1. (Implementation Independence) Using or extending a sub-goal through a call is independent of the manner in which the sub-goal was implemented

2. (Invariance) Using or extending a sub-goal does not compromise (make inconsistent) the prior use or extension of any other sub-goals
3. (Loose coupling) The fulfillment ordering of sub-goals should confer on the state diagram of the framework the weakest possible partial order

The third property may sound a bit obscure. All it says is that execution of the framework plus extensions, as it proceeds from one state to another, must be as stateless as possible (past states should have minimal influence on future states). Naturally, some states necessarily precede some other states (e.g. one needs to read a file before one can plot its data), and this forms an ordering relation between states. However, as much as possible, the framework should be able to move from one state to another irrespective of any order. In other words, some states do not have to be ordered with respect to other states. And this is why the ordering is a partial order (some states need to be ordered, some don't have to be). If the number of states that need to be ordered is minimized, then the weakest possible partial ordering of states is achieved. This represents the loosest possible coupling between states, and is a hallmark of service oriented architectures. The second property is inherent to software frameworks: Because a framework retains program flow control, the internal logic of a framework needs to remain consistent. It should not be possible, through use or extension, to move to a state that is logically inconsistent. It has been recognized that invariance is a central notion for software construction (Liskov, Data Abstraction and Hierarchy). A service oriented framework can also be called a cumulative framework (Braude, Cumulative Subgoal Fulfillment in Software Development). Examples of service oriented frameworks include Model View ViewModel (Microsoft, Model-View-ViewModel), which is experiencing a high rate of reuse amongst applications because of its

high degree of loose coupling between presentation tier and business logic.

Open and Extensible

Extensible frameworks (e.g. the Web browser) have proved more popular than non-extensible ones with similar functionality. By predefining interfaces to be implemented by callers, extensible frameworks enable new capabilities and allow select ones to be extended. However core functionality in frameworks often cannot be modified. In other words, frameworks are designed with selected capabilities that can be extended and others that cannot. It is the responsibility of the framework designer to predict the nature and measure of extensibility required in order to provide the necessary public interfaces that will need to be implemented. This responsibility draws on the creative talents of the framework development team. Add-ins at the end of the software development production line are often developed by integrators, who have the additional responsibility of testing and packaging all add-ins with a version of the framework and installing them for end-users. Integrators become the accountable party in the eyes of end-users: If something doesn't work right, integrators are responsible for coordinating the fix. Fixing the problem may require intervention upstream of the production line and may even involve modification to the framework itself. And so, when the resulting user experience does not entirely conform to expectations, it seems logical to give integrators the option of replacing core framework components over just extending some of them. In other words, core software components need to be wrapped by public interfaces whose implementations allow callers to override base implementations. Core components in best of breed frameworks are modifiable, or overridable to use a more precise technical term. Overriding core framework capabilities taps into creative solution-oriented talents along the entire production line and thus enables parties other than just the framework developer to participate in the process of developing a framework composed of best-of-breed components. This opens up the framework to a communitarian ideal: that of cooperation, which can only help to increase software reuse. Open source operating systems such as the ones in the Linux family have actively experienced creativity efforts of this type in the last decade. But frameworks don't need to be Open Source in order for their core components to be overridable. They just need to be sufficiently *open*. Frameworks with core components that can be overridden are also more testable, since those core components can be replaced with mock components that can be instrumented and tested. Even though it is not the only way, the easiest way to open up a framework is to provide its source code, and many frameworks opt to do that, including Hadoop and Microsoft's MVC framework (Microsoft, Model-View-Controller). Microsoft, that champion of proprietary software, has been posting the source code for software it wants to see reused on its Open Source (Microsoft Codeplex) website, and this has vastly increased the amount of reuse.

Minimalist

For frameworks and components, it is important to provide just enough function for the business at hand and no more. Only the functionality that is absolutely needed should be provided. The rest should be a matter of reusing and extending. It is also important to provide a single and consistent way to do things rather than multiple ways, as this creates confusion and more code to maintain. It is also important for software components and frameworks to seek to minimize loading time. This can be accomplished by lazy-loading subcomponents: References can be instantiated but memory is not claimed and associated processor use is deferred until the subcomponent is actually used for the first time. This allows callers that only a use a fraction of the software's capabilities to only

incur the resource cost for the resources that they actually require. So-called minimalist components include non-relational databases like *SimpleDB* (Amazon, SimpleDB), *MongoDB* (Mongodb.org), and *CouchDB* (Apache CouchDB). Most Cloud-based components offered on Amazon's Cloud and on Google App Engine are minimalist, and that may be a key ingredient in their rapid adoption. Components and frameworks on the Microsoft Cloud tend to offer more features out of the box and tend to be less minimalist. A good example is Microsoft's promotion of the *SOAP* (W3 Schools, Simple Object Access Protocol) protocol for Web-based services, which is much less minimalist than the alternative *REST*-based protocol (W3 Schools, REST Protocol). Microsoft is now supporting both protocols, recognizing the attractive minimalist features of REST.

Simple and Easy-to-Use

Another principle that is related to the minimalist principle concerns frameworks that produce source code to be reused by the developer, such as Microsoft's *MVC* (Microsoft, Model-View-Controller), but also component APIs that are minimally chatty, such as Google's App Engine (Google, AppEngine). Minimalism concerns capabilities, while the simple principle concerns how these capabilities are integrated and reused. The integration mechanisms need to be as simple as possible, and it is interesting to note how the evolution of each product always follows the track of simplifying integration. Integration mechanisms are often referred to as "plumbing". As Web services have evolved from SOAP implementation to REST implementations, plumbing has considerably decreased, even sometimes at the price of reducing the feature set. One of the longest-living Object communication and integration models in the industry, Microsoft's evolution from COM, to .NET, and onto WCF (Microsoft, Windows Communication Framework), has considerably minimized the required plumbing or chattiness between remote objects, implementing simple object decorators to reduce the need for boilerplate imperative code that is just overhead to the developer. Microsoft's MVC framework has undergone three major releases, and the last release incorporates a new View engine called Razor, which simplifies the syntax for mixing up client-side mark-up and server-side managed code. The object relational mapping Hibernate essentially came into being by simplifying the complexities of EJB2-style entity beans. Simple also applies to source code. Source code packages that are most reused are those that are as simple as possible for the feature set they expose.

Component and framework design is hard. But it is harder to use frameworks than it is to use components, because effective reuse of frameworks often implies intimate knowledge of framework internals: understanding architecture, implementation details, and the framework-codified pattern of interaction between internal components and add-in components. Best of breed frameworks set many conventions, including and not limited to how errors are handled, how data is exchanged, and how inter-component operations are invoked. Framework object instantiations, event sequencing, and thread assumptions often make a difference with how they are extended and reused. All this needs to be learned before the framework can be reused and extended. That is why adequate documentation is critical to a framework. Learning by example is another training tool. To this end, it is important to provide a set of examples and test cases with frameworks and components which clearly show intended use. Hadoop (Apache, Hadoop) for example includes an extensive library of examples that the user can exercise in order to get familiar with capabilities, and many components from Amazon's, Microsoft's, and Google's Clouds include example source code that exercise them.

Configurable

In the section on open frameworks, it was mentioned that core framework capabilities should be overridable, as this affords callers more flexibility over just extending and specializing a framework. However, there may be a middle ground between extending/specializing and replacing: It may be possible for callers to reconfigure the start-up process of the framework, or even its steady-state operation, by eschewing certain operations which the caller does not require and thus represent a wasteful cost in resource use. This can be achieved, for example, through the use of a configuration database that gives callers, and specifically integrators since they are the last party in the software manufacturing chain, to pick which operations should be eschewed in order to speed up start-up or steady-state operations. This results in software frameworks that are more flexible, and better adapted to the particular uses that callers and integrators may require and to the nature of the targeted end-user community. Hadoop (Apache, Hadoop) for example is a highly configurable framework, and optimizing performance is often a matter of fine tuning configuration. The other side of the coin is that configuration often requires extensive effort from the developer, and so some components and frameworks offer default configuration out of the box. Visual Studio is known to do this explicitly and extensively, and other frameworks like MVC do that implicitly by relying on convention over configuration[10].

Elastic

Scalability is a hallmark of Cloud-based software, as it should be able to grow and shrink on demand. Scalability that is dynamic in time is often referred to as "elastic". But scalability also implies performance, which should be optimal prior to scaling out or scaling in and remain optimal thereafter. Scaling out on the Cloud usually implies many-fold software duplication on distinct virtual machines. If the underlying software underperforms, it will underperform many times over on many virtual machines, and underperformance will be scale linearly with demand. Thus, performance and scalability are twin characteristics, and elasticity implies both. Heavily reused elastic Cloud-based software is scalable and highly performing.

Standards Compliant

Standards are the rules for industry interoperability. To give companies the opportunity to outsource or partially outsource their Information Technology (IT) infrastructures by taking advantage of Cloud-based IT infrastructures, Cloud-based components and frameworks need to comply with the latest standards, possibly with many offerings when there are many standards. For example, the SOAP and REST standards which we mentioned previously actively compete in the arena of Web services. SOAP is a transport neutral technology stack with automated code generation features that facilitate integration, and which provides a number of industry standard protocol implementations (e.g. security, transactions, identity etc.) out of the box. REST is an HTTP-specific technology stack that emphasizes separation of concerns and takes advantage of the CRUD[11]-based HTTP programming model to make it easy to build service oriented architectures. REST is very popular with direct-to-public software because of the broad reach of the HTTP protocol, while SOAP is popular with business-to-business software due to its proven built-in capabilities and integration features. In the arena of Web services, there are many use cases, and a sets of standards applicable to each. Components and frameworks that aspire to become best of breed on public Clouds need to subscribe to all use cases and all widely acknowledged standards. Amazon components subscribe to both SOAP and REST based standards, and even that Goliath software company that used to be well known for creating

its own de-facto standards is attentive today to provide implementations that accommodate all standards, even those that compete with standards it helped to develop.

CONCLUSION

In this chapter we examined popular Cloud-based components and frameworks, in Open Source and proprietary binary format, and ten of the principles behind their high rates of reuse. These were found to be their high degree of accountability, resiliency, segmentation, service orientation, openness and extensibility, minimalism, simplicity and ease of use, configurability, elasticity, and standards compliance. For frameworks, all these principles are equally important. For components, simplicity and ease of use, resilience, and elasticity are crucial. For binary code, accountability, openness and extensibility, configurability, elasticity, resilience, and standards compliance are pivotal. For source code, segmentation, and simplicity and ease of use are essential. It is harder to reuse frameworks than components because intimate knowledge of framework internals is required for effective reuse. However, frameworks offer many distinct runtime advantages over components because design as well as implementation is reused, whereas only implementation is reused for components. Developers abdicate a certain measure of control when they reuse software frameworks over software components, but they inherit a proven execution environment. It is generally easier to reuse binary code, but in some cases it can be harder as source code offers more possibilities since it can be easily reengineered. Binary code must be very configurable to be easily reusable. But providing both binary as well as source code to users, with binary code as the basic reuse mechanism and source code as an accountability and enhanced configurability mechanism has proven to be the most successful model for software reuse. Cloud computing will deliver on its business model promise when the integration nexus that is the public Cloud grows to be bigger than the sum of its parts, and that implies high rates of software reuse. For Cloud-based software components and software frameworks, some of the basic enabling principles are listed in this chapter.

REFERENCES

W3 Schools, HTML5. (n.d.). Retrieved from http://www.w3schools.com/html5/default.asp

W3 Schools, REST Protocol. (n.d.). Retrieved from http://www.xfront.com/REST-Web-Services.html

W3 Schools, Simple Object Access Protocol. (n.d.). Retrieved from http://www.w3schools.com/soap/default.asp

W3Schools, Ajax. (n.d.). Retrieved from http://www.w3schools.com/ajax/default.asp

Amazon Elastic Beanstalk. (n.d.). Retrieved from http://aws.amazon.com/elasticbeanstalk/

Amazon Elastic Cloud. (n.d.). Retrieved from http://aws.amazon.com/ec2/

Amazon Mechanical Turk. (n.d.). Retrieved from http://aws.amazon.com/mturk

Amazon. (n.d.). Retrieved from http://www.amazon.com/

Amazon Relational Database Service. (n.d.). Retrieved from http://aws.amazon.com/rds/

Amazon SimpleDB. (n.d.). Retrieved from http://aws.amazon.com/simpledb/

Amazon Web Services. (n.d.). Retrieved from http://aws.amazon.com/

Apache CouchDB. (n.d.). Retrieved from http://couchdb.apache.org

Apache Hadoop. (n.d.). Retrieved from http://hadoop.apache.org

Azure, M. (n.d.). *Service Business.* Retrieved from http://msdn.microsoft.com/en-us/library/ee732537.aspx

Braude, E. (2007). Cumulative subgoal fulfillment in software development. *Proceedings of the 11th IASTED International Conference on Software Engineering and Applications*, (pp. 480-485).

Bricklin, D. (n.d.). *VisiCalc: Information from its creators, Dan Bricklin and Bob Frankston.* Retrieved from http://www.danbricklin.com/visicalc.htm

Craig's List. (n.d.). Retrieved from http://www.craigslist.com

EMC VMWare. (n.d.). Retrieved from http://www.vmware.com

Fowler, M. (2005). *Inversion of control.* Retrieved from http://martinfowler.com/bliki/InversionOfControl.html

Fowler, M. (2005). *Inversion of control containers and the dependency injection pattern.* Retrieved from http://www.martinfowler.com/articles/injection.html

Fowler, M. (n.d.). *GUI architectures.* Retrieved from http://www.martinfowler.com/eaaDev/uiArchs.html

Gnu.org. (n.d.). *Free software definition.* Retrieved from http://www.gnu.org/philosophy/free-sw.html

Googe PageRank. (n.d.). Retrieved from http://www.google.com/about/corporate/company/tech.html

Google AppEngine. (n.d.). Retrieved from http://code.google.com/appengine/

Google BigTable. (n.d.). Retrieved from http://labs.google.com/papers/bigtable.html

Google Docs. (n.d.). Retrieved from http://docs.google.com

Google, Large Scale Graph Computing at Google. (n.d.). Retrieved from http://googleresearch. blogspot.com/2009/06/large-scale-graph-computing-at-google.html

Google, MapReduce. (n.d.). Retrieved from http:// labs.google.com/papers/mapreduce.html

Grameen Bank. (n.d.). Retrieved from http://www. grameen-info.org

Heng, C. (1999). Free sockets and winsock libraries. Retrieved from http://www.thefreecountry. com/sourcecode/sockets.shtml

Liskov, B. (1987). Data abstraction and hierarchy. *OOPSLA 87: Conference on Object Oriented Programming Systems Languages and Applications*, Keynote Address.

Memcached.org. (n.d.). Retrieved from http:// memcached.org

Microsoft AppFabric Access Control Service. (n.d.). Retrieved from http://msdn.microsoft.com/ en-us/library/ee732536.aspx

Microsoft Codeplex. (n.d.). Retrieved from http:// www.codeplex.com

Microsoft Dryad. (n.d.). Retrieved from http:// research.microsoft.com/jump/50745

Microsoft, Entity Framework. (n.d.). Retrieved from http://msdn.microsoft.com/en-us/library/ aa697427(v=vs.80).aspx

Microsoft Model-View-Controller. (n.d.). Retrieved from http://www.asp.net/mvc

Microsoft, Model-View-ViewModel. (n.d.). Retrieved from http://msdn.microsoft.com/en-us/ magazine/dd419663.aspx

Microsoft, Reactive Extensions. (n.d.). Retrieved from http://msdn.microsoft.com/en-us/data/ gg577609

Microsoft SkyDrive. (n.d.). Retrieved from http:// explore.live.com/windows-live-skydrive

Microsoft Skype. (n.d.). Retrieved from http:// www.skype.com

Microsoft SQL Azure. (n.d.). Retrieved from http:// www.microsoft.com/windowsazure/sqlazure/

Microsoft, Velocity. (n.d.). Retrieved from http:// msdn.microsoft.com/en-us/magazine/dd861287. aspx

Microsoft Visual Studio. (n.d.). Retrieved from http://www.microsoft.com/VisualStudio

Microsoft Windows Azure. (n.d.). Retrieved from http://www.microsoft.com/windowsazure/

Microsoft Windows Communications Framework (WCF). (n.d.). Retrieved from http://msdn.microsoft.com/en-us/netframework/aa663324

Microsoft Windows, Windows 8. (n.d.). Retrieved from http://msdn.microsoft.com/en-us/library/ windows/apps/br211386.aspx

MongoDB.org. (n.d.). Retrieved from http://www. mongodb.org

No-SQL Movement. (n.d.). Retrieved from http:// nosql-database.org/

PayPal.com. (n.d.). Retrieved from http://www. paypal.com

Rackspace.com. (n.d.). Retrieved from http:// www.rackspace.com

Redhat Hibernate. (n.d.). Retrieved from http:// www.hibernate.org

Ruby on Rails. (n.d.). Retrieved from http://www. rubyonrails.org/

Salesforce.com. (n.d.). Retrieved from http://www. salesforce.com

Thakar, A., & Szalay, A. (2010). *Migrating a (large) science database to the cloud.* Center for Astrophysical Sciences and Institute for Data Intensive Engineering and Science (IDIES), The Johns Hopkins University. Retrieved from http://dsl.cs.uchicago.edu/ScienceCloud2010/s08.pdf

ENDNOTES

[1] These are the developers that reuse software and the focus of this chapter. Not to be confused with the end-users of the resulting software application.

[2] A Cloud-based version of *Oracle 11g* is expected to be available on Amazon by the second quarter of 2011 (Amazon Web Services, http://aws.amazon.com/rds/#legal).

[3] This is essentially the Cloud version of the von Neumann bottleneck, the limited data transfer rate between the CPU and memory compared to the amount of memory. This throughput is much smaller than the rate at which the CPU can work, limiting the effective processing speed when the CPU is required to perform minimal processing on large amounts of data: The CPU is continuously forced to wait for needed data to be transferred to or from memory. In the Cloud version of the von Neumann bottleneck, virtual machines are forced to wait for data to be transferred through the Internet. Alleviating strategies to the traditional von Neumann bottleneck consist of processor caches between the CPU and main memory, and similar strategies have become best practices on the Cloud. We explore these caches later on in the same paragraph.

[4] These databases are also known as *document-oriented* databases.

[5] A managed component is one that is hosted by a managed environment like a Java virtual machine or the .NET Common Language Runtime (CLR). Velocity is hosted by the .NET CLR.

[6] Visual Studio is primarily an Integrated Development Environment (IDE) for .NET-based applications. It can be extended with a Software Development Kit (SDK) from Microsoft so that it can create pre-canned templates for Cloud-based applications targeting the Microsoft Cloud (Azure), and it can even create all the packages required to deploy them onto Azure.

[7] Silverlight is Microsoft's client-based Web development paradigm that relies on a streamlined version of its Common Language Runtime that runs as an add-in to all popular Web browsers and enables developers to write .NET-based add-ins that run on all Web browsers. WPF is Microsoft's desktop-based development paradigm that uses an XML based description language for user interfaces called XAML.

[8] LINQ, or Language INtegrated Query, is a relational query language that uses recent advances in .NET-based languages to implement a SQL-like interface to mining object oriented and hierarchical data. It is the other side of the coin to object-relational mappings like Hibernate: instead of mapping objects to relations in order to persist objects in a relational database, it maps objects and hierarchies to query expressions in order to mine their structure and data in memory.

[9] A Transducer state machine generates output based on a given input and/or a state.

[10] This implies more training required for the developer, in order to learn and abide by all conventions.

[11] CRUD: Create – Read – Update – Delete, the standard persistent storage software serialization operations.

Chapter 4
Service–Oriented Architecture:
Adoption Challenges

Qusay F. Hassan
Mansoura University, Egypt

ABSTRACT

Since the emergence of Service-Oriented Architecture (SOA), many organizations have thought they should migrate to it as a strategic solution that would enable higher agility in meeting fluctuating needs. However, SOA is not a "silver bullet" as many might think. SOA implementation is not a trivial task as it is facing a number of adoption challenges that should be addressed and accounted for before delving into the migration process. Paying close attention to these challenges would enable adopters to successfully reap the inherent benefits. This chapter lists the most important challenges that might prevent adopters from successfully implementing SOA in their organizations, with the help of some recommended solutions. Furthermore, it presents a step-by-step implementation case study in order to teach beginners the best ways to apply SOA to their organizations.

INTRODUCTION

Service-Oriented Architecture (SOA) is one of the topics being talked about in the IT field. It has been grabbing the eyes and ears of both IT and business professionals since the beginning of this century. This widespread hype is due to the fact that SOA is a promising paradigm with a number of accompanying benefits for its adopters. Some of these benefits include (Hassan, 2009; Kobielus, 2005):

- **Reusability:** Technical components and business functionalities are abstracted, after removing redundancy and inconsistencies, in a reusable form so they could be used again and again by different systems and business units.

DOI: 10.4018/978-1-4666-0897-9.ch004

- **Data Sharing:** Underlying data could be shared between different systems, by wrapping data sources with joint data service.
- **Location/Platform Independence:** Greater interoperability is enabled between different systems and business partners. This is achieved by allowing access to services regardless of their physical locations or used platforms.
- **Business Alignment:** Since the *"service"* is originally a business term, SOA enables better alignment between IT and business professionals.

The ability to realize the aforementioned benefits depends on properly addressing the challenges that SOA adopters might face. These challenges range from a prior understanding of SOA terms through implementation obstacles to management strategies. The lack of awareness of these challenges could place SOA implementations at risk and could lead to complete failure among its adopters.

CHALLENGES

During the migration process to SOA, adopters face up to nine key challenges:

1. **Misconception.** What is SOA? Is it another name for XML web service? Is it a product that an organization can buy? What are its key elements?
2. **Lack of Education.** How is SOA different from other software methodologies? Is it essential to educate and train prospective adopters on the "nuts and bolts" of SOA? If so, what do they need to learn in order to effectively deploy SOA?
3. **Over Expectations.** Is SOA a panacea to all of the organization's problems? Does it fit all needs? In which scenarios should the adopters avoid SOA?
4. **High Up-front Budgets.** What about the initial budgets needed for the migration process? One of the benefits of adopting SOA is cost reduction, so, how is that possible if high budgets are required during the initial migration phases?
5. **Lack of Trust.** How essential is the trust between SOA parties? Since trust is a human term as well as a technical term, how can the adopters build and guarantee it?
6. **Inappropriate Implementation Technologies.** How critical are the chosen implementation technologies to the success of the SOA migration process? Is XML the only available technology for SOA implementations? Is it always better to use standards-based technologies rather than the vendors-based ones?
7. **Lack of Security Terms.** How can the providers secure their services and the underlying resources against key security breaches and malicious attacks? How can confidential and sensitive information be secured against leaks either while moving between nodes or when saved at any end?
8. **Slow Performance.** How can implementers overcome the slow application performance that may occur due to the extensive use of document-oriented messages in SOA? Are there recommended techniques to enhance the overall performance of both services and client applications?
9. **Lack of Governance Framework.** How will the adoption and operation phases be monitored and audited? How will the services be controlled? Who is responsible for defining the management policies?

In the subsequent sections below, the paper will discuss the key adoption challenges in detail and introduce approaches that organizations can follow to help ensure successful SOA implementation.

Challenge #1: Misconceptions

SOA has different meanings to different people. Some of these misconceptions about SOA include (CIO Magazine, 2007):

- **A product.** Organizations usually think that SOA is a product that can be purchased from software vendors. This belief comes from the fact that software vendors put the label of SOA on their websites and in their brochures.
- **A synonym to XML Web Services.** SOA is a design methodology that aims to build software systems in a way that makes them easy to reuse and integrate. XML Web Services, on the other hand, is simply a modern technology that enables access to remote objects. People widely use the two terms interchangeably because many (if not most) SOA implementations are built with XML Web Services.
- **A business goal.** SOA itself is not a goal that can be achieved by business stakeholders. Rather, it is a way to build software systems in terms of abstract and callable components known as *services*. These services can be flexibly used/reused whenever needed. This is attained by wrapping (bundling) business and technical complexities to enable different systems to have unified, cohesive, and easy access to them.

To better understand SOA, readers may consider services offered by one of the cell phone companies as analogous to SOA services. In this model, subscribers only concern themselves with the service provider, offered services, the way to subscribe and use services they are interested in, QoS, and cost of using these services. Subscribers do all of that without bothering themselves with technical aspects such as infrastructure components, services location, network structure,

updates, etc. All these terms are handled by service providers behind the scenes, thus allowing subscribers to focus on their needs. Moreover, it enables them to easily have access to new services whenever offered by providers.

In the context of software, SOA is a design model that tends to package functionalities as a collection of accessible and loosely-coupled services. These services can communicate with each other to pass information, and/or coordinate business workflows while abstracting technical details.

A service is a well-defined, self-contained block composed of a set of operations and components, built in a way that lets them be dynamically integrated to cover technical and/or business needs. The functionality that the service performs may range from a simple task such as calculating a loan interest rate, to a complete business workflow such as granting a loan.

As illustrated in Figure 1, each service has three constituent elements:

- **Contract:** Provides informal specifications of the purpose, functionality, constraints and usage of the service. It may also contain formal definition based on a description language such as IDL or WSDL that provides information about programing language, middleware, network protocols, and runtime environment.
- **Interface:** Acts as a stub/proxy class that exposes available operations.
- **Implementation:** Contains the physical implementation of the service logic which may be encapsulated internally within the service itself or provided by external components. Service implementation may come from legacy components, modern components, object-oriented code, and/or databases. Separation between service interface and implementation offers a "clean" model that enables designers/developers to

Figure 1. Basic service elements

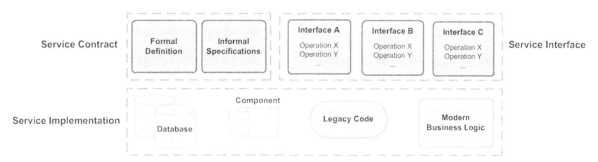

change underlying logic without affecting callers.

As illustrated in figure 2, work in SOA is done collaboratively by three distinct parties (Papazoglou, 2003):

- **Service Provider:** Creates, publishes, and maintains/supports services. A part of the service provider's job is to buy, install and manage the infrastructures needed to offer the services. This includes the physical assets, human resources, hardware components, networks, Internet connections, operating systems, database engines, and development frameworks and tools.
- **Service Broker:** Enables access to the registered services. The service registration process refers to publishing services (either internally within the organization or externally via the Internet) with information that enables clients to discover and bound to them. It is worth mentioning that in many cases, the service provider plays the role of the service broker in addition to his original role.
- **Service Client:** Looks for services that meet its specifications, and follows the instructions to test and use them. Interaction between clients and services normally deploys the request/reply model where a

service receives requests from clients and forwards back the returned results.

Different services can be combined together to form a composite service, again while hiding underlying complexities. However, in real SOA models, each service must not depend on the state of other services. That is, calls between individual services must not be embedded inside them, but rather, composition and "glue" logic must remain outside of the services. Orchestration tools or custom code can be used to associate separate services together either in new composite services or directly in client applications.

It is clear that this perspective is quite different from traditional methods that depend on creating a myriad of (mostly redundant) software systems for business silos. These systems are usually created to meet today's needs without considering unforeseen requirements (Papazoglou, 2003). Modifying (or integration with) these systems is a burden that IT executives face in organizations making them less *agile* in meeting business needs. For instance, a legacy system is usually composed of a number of statefull and tightly-coupled objects that do not separate between operations, interfaces, and business processes. This model results in spaghetti architectures that are hard and time-consuming to modify. Conversely, leveraging SOA to turn software systems into a set of tested infrastructure common services that would be built upon to meet

Figure 2. Collaboration between SOA parties

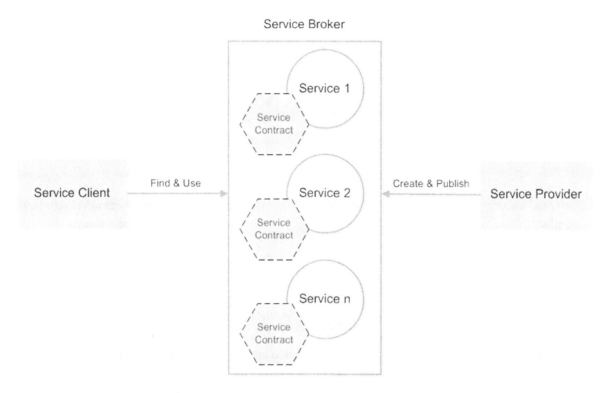

business fluctuations can improve agility levels in organizations (Krafzig et al., 2004).

Challenge #2: Lack of Education

Most software specialists are knowledgeable about traditional software methodologies and terms, including, for example, functions, classes, modules, libraries, Object-Oriented Programming (OOP), and Component-Based Development (CBD). This knowledge allows software specialists to accomplish their regular tasks efficiently. However, these skills are not sufficient when dealing with SOA.

To enable people to professionally deal with SOA, they should first learn about the basics. This should include the aspects of SOA lifecycle which includes analysis, modeling, design, implementation and testing (Tsai et al, unpublished).

The following sections briefly list the main differences between these aspects in SOA and traditional paradigms.

Traditional Paradigms

- **Analysis:** Requirements are given in a natural language to system analysts who convert them to technical specifications in order to enable developers, designers, and architects to understand them.

- **Modeling:** Analysts and developers use various models such as use cases diagrams, sequence diagrams, data flow diagrams, state flow diagrams and flowcharts to represent requirements, relationships, and specifications. However, keeping these models updated to reflect technical changes is challenging. That is to say, developers sometimes are faced with circumstances (e.g., during the testing and maintenance phases) that require them to deviate from design models during implementation phases, but without reflecting these changes in original models.

- **Design:** Relationships between underlying objects are statically defined so they cannot be changed once created. UML and word processors are usually used to create system models.
- **Implementation:** Development is performed by a single, virtual or physical, party that creates functions, classes, modules, components and libraries. Object-oriented languages such as java, c++, c# are usually used to develop system constructs.
- **Testing:** Testing is performed by testers in the same organization. Validation and verification (V&V) is performed based on the source code and functional specifications. Test cases are defined by developers/testers, usually from within the same organization. Test scripts are defined by developers/testers also from within the same organization.

SOA Paradigm

- **Analysis:** Domain analysis is solely done by providers, enabling application builders to focus only on finding and combining services that meet their business/technical specifications.
- **Modeling:** Models are represented in both human-readable and machine-readable forms, associated with policies and specifications that enable service builders to automatically translate them into executable code.
- **Design:** Bindings and relationships in SOA are dynamically defined at runtime instead of static definition at design/development time. Hence, new services can be dynamically created using existing ones. Sophisticated tools and languages such as MS.NET, BizTalk, WebSphere, Oracle SOA Suite, and BPEL are used to design services and workflows.

- **Implementation:** Development is divided between a service provider and an application builder. A service provider writes and exclusively owns the code of offered services, whereas an application builder develops client applications that make use of offered services. This separation enables application builders to focus on business logic while leaving technical details to service providers. Open standards such as XML, WSDL, SOAP, XSD XSLT, RSS and JSON are usually used to build and call services. Common software packages as those used for designing services offer great support for open standards.
- **Testing:** Testing is divided between the service provider, the broker and the client, with little or no interaction between them. The Service provider tests services based on the functional specification and source code, and it then creates test cases for other parties. Service Providers give test cases to brokers and clients, and therefore services can be tested before their registration and usage, respectively. Moreover, test scripts can be automatically generated on the spot by both brokers and clients during the V&V process based on service metadata and specifications.

In addition to educating software specialists about the basics of SOA, decision makers should learn about SOA, so they can harness its power and know exactly in which scenarios it can be leveraged. In this regard, software and business schools should offer courses and curriculums about SOA (Tsai et al., 2006). This would permit IT and business professionals to gain missing knowledge and skills that allow them to apply SOA methods in situations where doing so makes sense.

Challenge #3: Over Expectations

Adopters should always remember that SOA is not a panacea that can solve all organization problems (Pizette et al., 2009). Hence, they should know exactly why to migrate to SOA and what to expect from that switch. This is crucial because in many cases it might be the wrong move. Some cases for which SOA might not be suitable include (Lewis et al., 2005):

- Organizations cannot afford abandoning their investments in existing systems to re-develop them as services from scratch.
- Although the ability to migrate existing systems to SOA is one of the SOA benefits, the technical specifications of these systems such as age, architecture, technologies, and documentation, can complicate this process.
- Lack of information about existing systems.
- High costs, risks, and efforts linked with migration process.
- Big gap between the state of existing systems and future state of the targeted services.
- Lack of clear vision and migration strategy.

In such cases, leveraging SOA would be counterproductive and might lead to negative results to the organization. Thus, knowing exactly why, when and how to use SOA is critical for successful adoption.

One way in which organizations can support their decision about SOA adoption is to read about others' prior experience. This would provide initiatives with details about conditions for the use of SOA as well as a deeper understanding of distinct implementation challenges, obstacles and best solutions. Then, initiatives can start the adoption journey by migrating a small, non-critical application. Following a "think big, start small" approach will give adopters the chance to better understand the value of SOA while minimizing risks.

Another helpful recommendation is to plan an adoption roadmap. This roadmap involves: understanding the business domain; gathering information about current processes, applications, integrations, security, data and governance; and reducing the SOA gap readiness (Bieberstein et al., 2005). Such a roadmap might also include an impact analysis to forecast the extent of change to existing resources affected by SOA, transition plans, and approximate estimates for the future growth of services.

Challenge #4: High up-Front Budgets

One of the benefits linked with using SOA is the reduction of development and integration costs. However, this reduction is difficult to accomplish during the initial stages of SOA implementation (Raines, 2009). During these stages, adopters can expect to expend significant resources in order to procure the necessary hardware and software tools, train users, and convert traditional software systems to SOA-enabled systems. They should also expect that these stages might last for a few months or even years until they reach maturity point. Figure 3 illustrates the inverse relationship between the rate of expenses and the learning curve during the SOA implementation phases.

In fact, successful adoption of SOA is threatened by the lack of awareness of funding that should be dedicated during the initial phases. This inattention to the fiscal aspect could lead adopters to think that SOA is simply a bad methodology that causes them to spend too much money rather than saving overall costs. To mitigate these budgetary concerns, adopters should always remember that SOA is like any business in which stakeholders choose to incur limited up-front costs in order to realize an even greater windfall in the future. Also, it is important for businesses to conduct a thorough cost/benefit analysis before beginning the design phase, so that implementa-

Figure 3. Inverse relationship between Initial expenses and learning curve

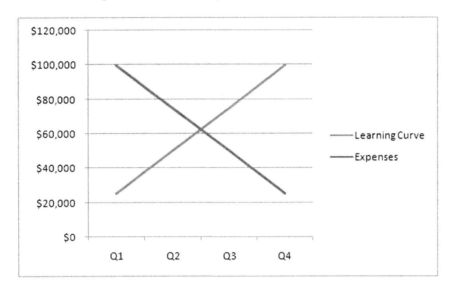

tion costs are well understood. Furthermore, since SOA benefits are broadly shared, it is important to identify all potential stakeholders early in the design process so that costs are equitably shared.

Again, initiatives should not follow a "big-bang" approach to realize successful implementation (Schmelzer, 2005). Rather, adopters should use iterative and incremental implementations especially when constrained by the availability of resources. The incremental approach tends to allow new adopters to start small and grow over time. Such an approach can give adopters the chance to learn, enjoying hands-on experience to SOA terms while minimizing both risk and expenditures.

Challenge #5: Lack of Trust

Different applications have different requirements regarding reliability, security, and scalability. The applicable requirements for each application should be identified early in the design process. Having trust that the service provider will offer services that meet clients' needs and expectations as stated, and their information will be safe are examples to trust issues of the service clients. On the other side, guaranteeing that the clients will pay their dues on time and they will not use the offered services for malicious purposes are two main concerns of the service providers. Some of questions that adopters may ask when considering trust include:

- How is the reliability and correctness of the offered services guaranteed when providers and clients belong to the same organization?
- How will the secrecy of sensitive information be assured when providers and clients belong to different organizations?
- What if clients depend of providers who decide to leave the market?
- How is support and updates going to be applied and maintained?

Trust is an intangible value which cannot be included in the service level agreement (SLA), for that reason, it is one of the hardest challenges to overcome. Nevertheless, building trust between service clients and providers is possible, yet not achieved overnight –it is similar to trust between people. That is, it could take time and effort to build strong relationships between clients and providers.

Challenge #6: Inappropriate Implementation Technologies

In principle, different technologies can be used to create needed services. This includes Message Queues, COM/DCOM/COM+, EJB, Jini, CORBA and Web Services. Each of these technologies has its own strengths and limitations; thus, each has its own comparative advantages that best fit particular scenarios and requirements.

The question for adopters when thinking about using a specific technology is: to what extent is that technology supported by software vendors? Is that technology vendor-based or standards-based? Using vendor-based technologies will definitely prohibit loose-coupling between service providers and clients. The ultimate goal of this loose-coupling is to allow clients to use services offered by providers no matter what technology was utilized to achieve them. Furthermore, loose-coupling enables clients to change used services or even providers with little or no effect on their applications.

Generally, adopters are highly encouraged to utilize standards-based solutions to be able to gain optimum benefits offered by SOA. However, adopters should be careful that the support to standard-based approaches varies from one vendor to another and from one tool to another. The extension of support to standards in products depends on different circumstances such as implementation challenges and marketing issues. In some cases, a vendor misinterprets standards to an extent that it just offers vendor-based solutions disguised as standards-based ones. Preserving loose-coupling and interoperability between service providers and clients in such cases might be problematic due to inconsistencies in the data types/formats, for example. To avoid such scenarios, both providers and clients are advised to read the original specifications, and current implementations of adopted

standards in the offered solutions. Understanding these specifications would enable SOA parties to abstract services and calls with wrappers that assure the use of original standards only instead of masked vendor-based offerings.

Examples to standards that could be used in SOA-based projects include CORBA, JSON, RSS, REST, and XML.

XML Web Services represents the head of the pyramid of standards-based technologies available in the software field for realizing SOA applications (W3C, 2004). Preferences to XML Web Services in SOA implementations are attributed to its benefits, including (Endrei et al., 2004):

- **Ease-of-use:** It is easy to learn and use by both service providers and clients.
- **Acceptance and Support:** It has broad support from almost all key software vendors.
- **Affordability:** It is affordable vis-à-vis proprietary technologies.
- **Readability:** XML syntax is easy to understand by both computers and humans, enabling different nodes to easily interpret transmitted data.
- **Modularity:** It is modular by nature making it possible for implementers to encapsulate their logic into separate operations and services.
- **Composability:** Implementers can easily combine and aggregate different services together.

Although using XML Web Services in building SOA-based implementations have been of increasing interest in the past few years, XML is not the answer to all problems. XML is just a rich tool that will fit some requirements. Some of the examples where other technologies may be more suitable when compared with services entirely based on XML (such as SOAP web services), include:

- **JavaScript Object Notation (JSON):** JSON is a lightweight, text-based, open-standard data format designed for data interchange between different parties (Crockford, 2009). JSON is derived from JavaScript as an easy to read (both by computers and humans) and parse serialization format for transmitting data over network between nodes. JSON offers a number of basic data types that enable its users to simply formulate and structure their information. These types are: Number; String; Boolean; Array; Object (an unordered collection of key/value pairs); and null. Applications can use JSON Schema to define and validate the structure of the data objects –similar to DOM and XSD in XML. Due to the simplicity and nimbleness of the generated information, JSON is being referred to as a strong alternative to XML in serializing information. A number of JSON-derived standards are also available, making it possible for SOA implementers to find exactly what fits their needs. For example, some implementations use JSON-RPC as a remote procedure call protocol based on JSON to enable bidirectional communications and data interchange between clients and services (Kollhof, 2009). BSON, or Binary JSON, is also available so that developers can lightly and more efficiently serialize data using the binary format. Support for JSON and the derived standards are given through both commercial and open-source products in different languages and development frameworks such as c, c++, Visual Basic, Java, Delphi, Python, ASP, Perl, PHP, Ruby, ColdFusion, and .NET.
- **Representational State Transfer (REST):** REST has gained global acceptance in the Web design and development community as an architecture model for building web applications (Fielding, 2000). Being an architectural style means that there is no official standard for building RESTful services; however, recommendations and best practices are available (He, 2004). Some modern SOA-based implementations use REST style to responsively return (representation) information in different data format such as HTML, MIME, and plaintext. Typically, as in the Web, anything in REST is a resource with a unique resource identifier (URI) that can be easily accessed via HTTP protocol from traditional browsers. A Service provider is responsible for providing one or more resource representations that reflect the state of the resource when the client requests it. On the other side, a client has four verbs (or operations) to deal with services and resources: POST (to create a resource); GET (to retrieve a resource); PUT (to replace a resource or change its state); and Delete (to remove a resource). Access to RESTful services occurs in a stateless form where the server (or a cluster of servers) does not store any state or context between requests. Thus, every request must embody, in HTTP headers, all information needed by the service in order to process it. This statelessness, of course, improves the scalability and performance of the designed services, and simplifies the design of the implemented services as well (Rodriguez, 2008). RESTful web services have no default formal description documents to guide clients through the right ways to use the offered services, as WSDL does in XML Web Services. There is no built-in validation for passed information, either. Due to these limitations, explicit creation of the formal documents for the offered services and validation of the information passed with client's requests are the responsibility of the service provider. The client also should explicitly validate data passed to and from the service to make

sure that these services are being properly invoked and errors are avoided. Examples to REST adopters include Amazon, Yahoo, YouTube, Facebook, Twitter and PayPal.

Challenge #7: Lack of Security Terms

Implementers should note that due to the nature of SOA, where computing resources are represented in terms of remote operations offered by service providers, information is susceptible to distributed systems risks as well as to message risks (Peterson. et al., 2006). In this context, it is worth mentioning that while SSL is widely used to secure web applications, it is not enough for securing SOA-based projects. Adopters should pay attention to general security standards and practices such as those listed in OWASP Top Ten Project as well as special concerns related to the used technologies (OWASP, 2010). This would enable implementers to build services that are immune against the main six security threats: spoofing, tampering, repudiation, information disclosure, denial of service, and elevation of privileges (STRIDE) (Hernan et al., 2006). STRIDE is a security approach, developed by Microsoft, which aims at enabling software builders to discover and correct design-level security problems. The following list gives readers brief information on STRIDE threats, and the recommended solutions, in the context of SOA:

- **Spoofing:** Spoofing refers to the ability to pretend as an authorized service client or service provider (by means of offered services), by falsifying data to gain access to restricted resources and information. The lack of an authentication mechanism that checks the identity of both the callers and providers usually tempts hackers to forge information in order to impersonate. Likewise, attackers may take advantage of the absence of integrity protection for the messages traversing intermediaries and nodes (different services, or the service and the client) to steal confidential information. Implementers should exploit the power of security tokens (such as username/password, Kerberos, and SAML) to protect their applications against spoofs at both service and message levels.

- **Tampering:** Illegal alteration of the information hosted on the providers' servers or in transit. Attackers usually take advantage of the absence of data validation in the offered services and client applications to deploy injections flaws such as malicious scripts, SQL, XML/XPath, OS and LDAP injections that could lead to complete system failures. Therefore, both service providers and application builders should validate the data before using or saving them into databases. Digital signature solutions (such as SSL and XML Signature) can also mitigate the tampering threat by making sure that data has not been illegally altered in transit.

- **Repudiation:** A service client may claim that he/she did not perform a specific action against the service. This problem may occur if each service does not properly keep track of its calls. Services makers are highly advised to deploy strong audit trail and logging components that can record all actions and activities being performed by the clients.

- **Information Disclosure:** The ability to reveal information, especially sensitive ones, which the service deals with, puts both the service provider and the client at risk. Therefore, protecting information from eavesdropping is the responsibility of both parties. What makes SOA-based implementations harder to protect against information disclosure is that the access to services' contracts and description documents is made open in order to enable clients to correctly make their calls. Attackers can take advantage of this technical information to design their attacks against the services. Furthermore, because service requests and responses may participate in multiple-hops transactions, the probability of caching such information at any node is extremely high. To prevent information from illegal disclosure, service providers should deploy strong controls such as encryption at both service and database levels. Digital signatures should also be leveraged to make sure that data has not been illegally altered on the transport layer. Disabling or minimizing contents caching is another action that implementers can take to thwart insider and outsider threats. On the other side, service invokers should make sure that no sensitive information is left behind or cached in the client applications. These countermeasures should be deployed with the least negative impact on the applications performance.

- **Denial of Service (DoS):** A service could be overwhelmed with a number of calls that is more than it can deal with, or could handle requests that would drain the underlying resources such as hard disk, memory and/or processor. For example, an attacker may inject malicious code that yields infinite loops or stack overflows which in turn would cause the service to freeze. Such scenarios can easily lead to the inability to receive new calls or even total service failure. Digital signatures, authentication, and limitation of calls or messages received from each client during a certain length of time would inhibit DoS attackers from doing their job. Additionally, conventional monitoring of the offered services, bandwidth, and hardware utilization can help systems administrators protect their implementations against DoS attacks.
- **Elevation of Privileges:** It refers to gaining more privileges in order to have access

to resources or information that are protected from the service caller. An attacker may exploit a design defect of a service that is not developed to give the least privileges to its clients. He may also inject a malicious code or attach a harmful object such as an unsafe executable or virus to steal information or cause systems instability. Implementers should always check and validate data against tampering threats. They also should scan attachments (if any) to make sure that no viruses were embedded in the call messages. Finally, systems administrators should rectify their systems by installing up-to-date patches to the reported vulnerabilities in operating systems, networks and applications.

Challenge #8: Slow Performance

In fact, performance is one of the most important non-functional requirements in all software systems. Creating a software application that suffers from slow performance in processing end users' requests puts that application at risk that it will not be used.

As mentioned, communication between SOA parties depends on messages to send requests and receive responses. As mentioned in the technology section, many of the contemporary implementations of SOA heavily use XML Web Service and other text-based technologies to realize needed services. This with no question leads to bigger data files when compared with binary messages being used in other client-server technologies such as RMI, RPC, etc.

Many studies have focused on the slow performance of modern SOA implementations in order to produce a list of best practices that could help in overcoming this problem, including (Riad et al., 2009):

- **Non-SOAP Formats:** Requests and responses in XML Web Services can take different formats. SOAP (Simple Object Access Protocol) is the basic and most used communication protocol for transferring data between service nodes. The original specifications of SOAP state that it is a simple, lightweight and neutral protocol for formulating and transferring requests and responses between service callers and providers and vice versa. However, SOAP is no longer simple or lightweight. Due to high acceptance to SOAP, key software players such as Microsoft and IBM have added a number of enhancements and new specifications that enables implementers to meet complex requirements such as transaction support, session management, and complex security features. These enhancements have led to the slow performance in handling requests and responses. Not only that, but also SOAP payload can be bloated and drain on network and hardware resources. Modern SOA-based implementations should only use SOAP if such specifications are really needed. As mentioned before, other standards such as REST, JSON, RSS and RPC web services are available in the industry so that implementers can take advantage of them while avoiding the limited performance of SOAP.

- **Binary Format:** Traditional XML syntax is originally lengthy as it is composed of many angle bracket tags that use plaintext data format. This makes both request and response files larger in size and more complex in structure; processing such files is neither an easy nor a fast process. One way to make generated data files smaller and simpler is to use Binary XML (Geer, 2005).

- **Efficient XML Parsers:** Most of XML parsers such as SAX and DOM depend on opening and reading files more than once, paging, and caching data before parsing

them. This makes these techniques slow and inefficient when parsing files, especially those that are large in size. To save parsing time and resources, fast and non-extractive techniques should be utilized. VTD-XML (Virtual Token Descriptor XML) is one of the popular examples for non-extractive tokenization approaches available in the market (Zhang, 2004; Zhang, 2008). With similar products, adopters can have light and fast parsing for their XML data.

- **Schema-Specific Parsers:** Many XML-based implementations of SOA use general-purpose parsers to understand documents being exchanged between nodes. This makes the parsing process runs slowly due to the need to extract and understand the structure of files prior to the parsing phase itself. Parsers can run faster by generating and caching serialization assemblies of available data objects at providers and clients for later use.

- **Silicon-based XML engines:** Many hardware engines and parsers are available in the market to process XML data at higher speeds. These hardware elements might be embedded into different components including switches, routers, PCI-cards, and servers.

- **Break Large Messages:** Some implementers prefer those service operations that can accomplish all tasks with only a few large messages instead of many operations with smaller logic. Depending on the technique often leads to having large and complex data files being transmitted between nodes. As a result, the probability of network clogs is very high. To avoid similar scenarios, implementers should divide logic embedded in one complex operation into a set of simpler operations. This could yield messages that are smaller, thus allowing them to move faster on the network. Also, this approach would enable better a utilization

Figure 4. Aspects of SOA governance

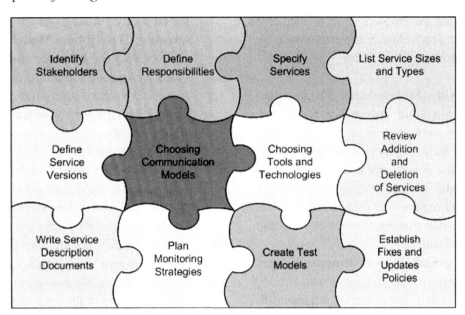

of network resources. Of course, following this approach does not mean breaking service operations into a large number of extremely small operations as this would drain the installed networks. Determining the granularity of services being constructed is not an easy mission. This mostly depends on the level of understanding of the business domain for those services which are being generated.

• **Compression Algorithms:** ZIP/GZIP algorithms might be applied on data being transmitted between nodes. This technique could allow implementers to eliminate white spaces and additional sizes making data files smaller.

• **High Speed Networks:** Fast network technologies such as Gigabit Ethernets, and fiber channels and links can be used to speed up the transmission rate between nodes. These advanced technologies are now available in the market making it possible for implementers to build powerful infrastructures to meet the complex needs of SOA applications.

To this end, adopters can mix and match these techniques according to their needs and available budgets. This would lead to successful and fruitful implementations for SOA both in small-to-medium and medium-to-large scale organizations.

Challenge #9: Lack of Governance Framework

Governance is probably the most important aspect for a smooth and fruitful implementation of SOA. The broad definition of SOA governance refers to the processes, policies, principles and best practices that an organization applies to ensure the successful implementation of SOA. The purpose of having a solid governance framework is to efficiently control different aspects related to the services (OASIS, 2009; Anne, 2005). Without efficient governance, SOA implementation could be chaotic: the total adoption process could easily fail. Governance policies and strategies should be planned and defined before the implementation phase, not afterwards. This can be achieved by constructing an internal governing committee that will manage all aspects of services. As illustrated in Figure 4, the governance aspects are like a puzzle that is composed of various elements complementing each other. Some of the important elements of governance include:

- **Identifying Stakeholders.** Proper planning for a solid governance framework typically starts with identifying all stakeholders including those who will participate in the governance body. Stakeholders list should include people with different roles and experiences (e.g., business owners, decision makers, domain experts, and technical staffs).
- **Defining Stakeholders Responsibilities.** Each member in the governance body should clearly know his/her responsibilities so that he/she can appropriately play the assigned roles.
- **Defining Ownership.** Since work in SOA is done collaboratively by three parties (providers, brokers and clients), and they usually belong to different boundaries (such as departments, subsidiaries, or even different organizations) it is important to define the ownership of each party to avoid future conflicts.
- **Identifying Services.** The governance body should clearly define the services to be generated and offered/used. This definition is often based on factors such as: cost/benefit analysis, business domain and needs, available technical skills, etc.
- **Specifying Services.** After the general identification of the needed services, the governance body will be responsible for listing the type, granularity level, communication models and message patterns of each service.
- **Controlling Services Versions.** Defining different versions and uses of each service.
- **Selecting Realization Technologies.** Choosing the tools and technologies that will be used to create and manage services

is one of the most important steps towards the creation of the identified services.

- **Creating Description Models.** As mentioned earlier, each service should be provided with enough description documents for callers to make appropriate use of. One of the roles of governance teams is to design these formal specifications and description documents.
- **Controlling Services Proliferation.** The governance body should review the addition and deletion of services to make sure that no redundant services are created and no essential services are removed.
- **Validation and Verification.** Creating validation, verification and test models to assure the quality of the generated services.
- **Defining Update Policies.** Establishing policies for fixes, and changes and updates.
- **Planning Audit Strategies.** Planning auditing strategies to monitor performance and ensure that both business and technical objectives are successfully achieved.

CASE STUDY

This section introduces a hypothetical case study of a supply management system (SCM) for a manufacturing company with two plants. The purpose of this case study is to give readers an insight into the main phases through which implementers can apply SOA to their projects.

Problem Definition

Figure 5 illustrates a high level overview of the different systems available in the company. Figure 6 illustrates the business process which dictates that when one plant runs out of a particular item, its enterprise resource planning (ERP) system starts sending a notification message to the headquarter (HQ) system, which, in turn, starts to query the ERP system at the other plant. If the other plant does not have the requested item, then the HQ

Figure 5. Enterprise architecture

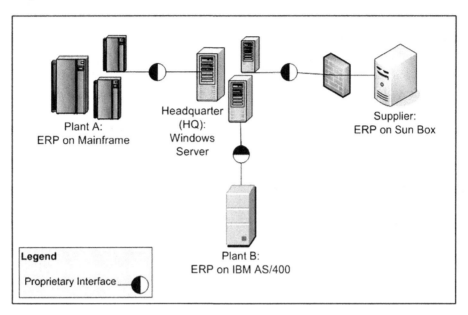

Figure 6. Business process

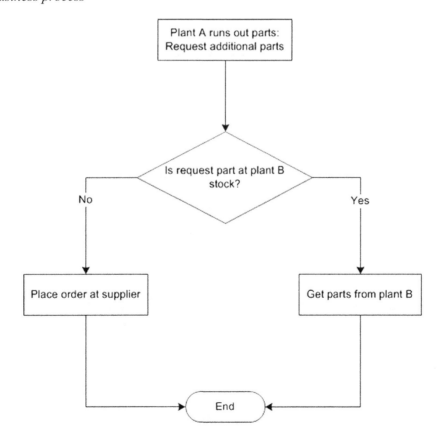

issues a purchase order (PO) to the suppliers' ERP system.

The presented systems are hosted on different operating systems and platforms. For example, the first plant is hosted on a mainframe that is connected to a windows-based server on the HQ site, which is connected to a machine hosted on IBM AS/400 at the other plant, and a Sun Box at the suppliers'. To complicate our scenario, let us assume that the manufacturing company wishes to expand and have one more plant. Let us also assume that the company wants to allow new suppliers to be integrated with them to provide the needed materials and speed up the manufacturing process. In order to connect these different systems together, the point-to-point (P2P) integration methods use many proprietary interfaces. This means that one proprietary interface could be used as a wrapper for different data formats being transmitted between each two points (systems).

Due to the high implementation costs, time and effort, choosing proprietary interfaces for integrating the presented systems is not the optimum solution for our scenario. Long implementation time will be needed either in the case of adding new plants or suppliers, or when modifying existing systems required for meeting changes in business processes. Such forms of tight coupling could prevent enterprises from restructuring the architecture to fulfill the fluctuating business requirements. This limitation, with no doubt, will prevent the enterprise from hunting for new business chances.

Proposed Architecture

The proposed solution aims to allow the integration between different (homogeneous, heterogeneous) systems provided by participating partners and suppliers. To meet this need effectively, implementers intend to convert traditional integration methods that mainly depend on P2P interfaces to service-oriented integration (SOI) methods. This

conversion process to a SOA-based implementation, which is known as *servicetization*, refers to turning existing systems into a set of flexible, usable and reusable services. Basically, "service-orientation", in our context, means keeping the existing software assets and investments to act as core systems, and building a set of wrappers (shells) around them. The purpose of having these wrappers is to expose the entire functionalities in a form of standardized services that are easy to use and modify whenever needed.

Figure 7 illustrates the proposed solution that simply builds a new service layer above existing systems at each participating node, and a central service hub that enables new participants to easily plug into the system. This service hub could be considered a central point through which distributed services are monitored, managed, and secured.

Approaching SOA

To effectively apply SOA terms to our architecture, implementers are advised to leverage Service-Oriented Analysis and Design (SOAD) methods. SOAD helps implementers to determine functional areas that need to be transformed to services, their size, and how they are going to interact with each other (Zimmermann et al., 2004). In the subsequent sections below I will try to list some of the SOAD methodologies in order to enable effective integration between the different systems apparent in our scenario.

Step #1: Domain Decomposition

During this phase the analysts try to understand the business domain in order to identify its functional areas, use cases, and business processes. Table 1 lists the key functional areas of the demonstrated scenario.

As described in Table 2, analysts can start defining the systems' use cases after understanding the business domain and defining its functional areas.

Figure 7. Proposed enterprise architecture

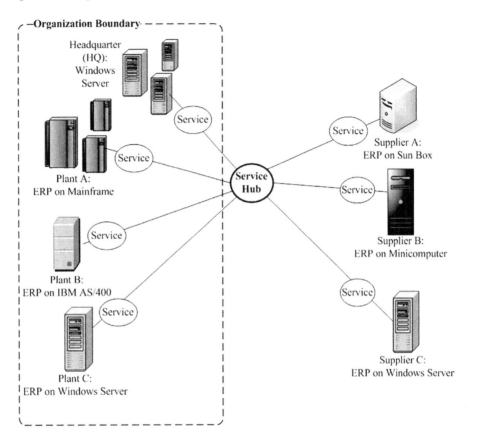

Table 1. Functional areas of demonstrated scenario

Functional Area Name	Description
Manufacturer HQ	Acts as both, a service provider and a service requestor. A service provider for plants that require items when the predefined threshold value is reached. A service requestor for other plants that have demanded items or for suppliers who will provide its plants with the needed raw materials.
Plant	Acts as both, a service provider and a service requestor. A service provider for other plants that have a low inventory level for some items. A service requestor for the HQ in case they are in need of items that are below a threshold.
Supplier	Acts as a service provider for the HQ allowing it to issue purchase orders for some raw materials.
Shipping Companies	They are third-party partners who act as service providers for both suppliers and the manufacturer, enabling them to transfer both issued and returned items respectively.
Banking Services	They are third-party partners who act as service providers for both suppliers and the manufacturer, enabling them to transfer the needed funds and fees from one account to another.

Table 2.

Use Case Number	UC2
Use Case Name	Query Plants
Description	When one plant runs out of some items, it sends notification messages to the HQ to start querying other plants' stocks.
Invoker	Plant
Implemented By	HQ

Use Case Number	UC1
Use Case Name	Alert HQ
Description	It is an internal use case that describes how the HQ looks for needed items at all available plants.
Invoker	HQ
Implemented By	Plant

Use Case Number	UC3
Use Case Name	Move Items
Description	When the HQ finds the needed items at one of its plants, it sends a message to that plant to start transferring items to the requesting one.
Invoker	HQ
Implemented By	Plant

Use Case Number	UC4
Use Case Name	Move Items
Description	It is an internal use case that enables the HQ to look for suppliers who could provide needed items.
Invoker	HQ
Implemented By	HQ

Use Case Number	UC5
Use Case Name	Sign Contract
Description	It is an optional use case that could probably be executed between the HQ and new suppliers.
Invoker	HQ
Implemented By	Supplier

Use Case Number	UC6
Use Case Name	Order Items
Description	If the HQ does not find the needed items at any of its plants, it starts to place orders at one or more of its raw material suppliers.
Invoker	HQ
Implemented By	Supplier

Use Case Number	UC7
Use Case Name	Prepare Items

continued on following page

Table 2. Continued

Description	It is an internal use case that is implemented and invoked by suppliers. It simply allows suppliers to prepare issued items by making, assembling, packaging, and finally delivering them to the shipping company. A shipment company is a third-party partner which is responsible for transferring items, from suppliers to their final destinations.
Invoker	Supplier
Implemented By	Supplier
Use Case Number	UC8
Use Case Name	Cancel Orders
Description	Enables the HQ to cancel issued orders for specific items.
Invoker	HQ
Implemented By	Supplier
Use Case Number	UC9
Use Case Name	Reject Items
Description	Enables the HQ to reject items that may be damaged or do not conform to the defined standards.
Invoker	HQ
Implemented By	Supplier
Use Case Number	UC10
Use Case Name	Receive Items
Description	Enables the HQ to notify the contracted supplier that the requested items were successfully received.
Invoker	HQ
Implemented By	Supplier
Use Case Number	UC11
Use Case Name	Transfer Funds
Description	Enables the manufacturer to pay the fees to their suppliers by transferring money from its bank accounts to the suppliers'. It is also responsible for allowing suppliers to pay for contracted shipping companies.
Invoker	HQ/Supplier
Implemented By	Bank Services
Use Case Number	UC12
Use Case Name	Transfer Items
Description	Enables the supplier to hand over issued items to the shipping company that will be responsible for delivering them to their final destinations. It may also be used by the manufacturer to return rejected items back to their suppliers.
Invoker	Supplier/HQ
Implemented By	Shipping Company

continued on following page

Table 2. Continued

Use Case Number	UC13
Use Case Name	Receive Returned Items
Description	Enables the shipping company to deliver rejected items to their suppliers.
Invoker	Shipping Company
Implemented By	Supplier
Use Case Number	UC14
Use Case Name	Track Items
Description	Enables both the manufacturer and suppliers to track items that are being moved between them via shipping companies.
Invoker	HQ/Supplier
Implemented By	Shipping Company

Figure 8. Use case model

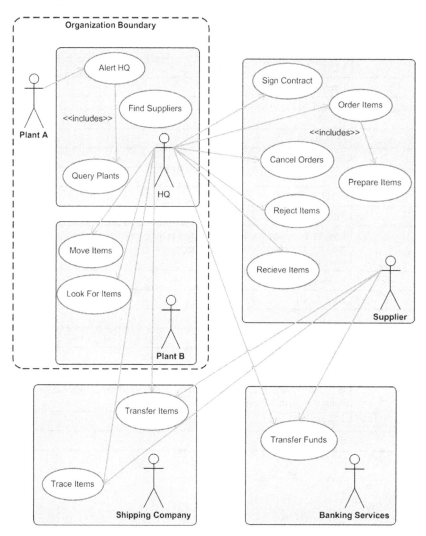

Figure 8 illustrates the interaction between the generated use cases.

As described in Table 3, analysts can start defining business processes soon after having a list of business use cases.

Figure 9 illustrates the relationships between different processes included in our scenario and the way they could be implemented using use cases yielded during the domain decomposition phase.

Step #2: Subsystem Analysis

Technically, this phase is responsible for achieving two main goals: first, turning defined use cases into services in order to publish them; second, identifying subsystems and components that will be used for realizing defined services.

In our scenario, the three main identified subsystems are: *Plants, Manufacturer HQ*, and *Suppliers*. In addition, two optional third parties are included: *Banking Services*, and *Shipping Companies*. Each of these subsystems must implement

Table 3.

Process Number	P1
Process Name	Demand Items
Description	Enables plants to order items that fall under certain thresholds. This process encapsulates the following logic: • When one plant runs out of some items, it notifies the HQ to take appropriate action. • The HQ queries all other plants in order to get the missing items (if available). • If the needed items are found at one of the queried plants, that plant transfers them to the targeted one. If the items are not found, the HQ issues purchase orders to one or more of the available suppliers.
Included Use Cases	• **UC1:** Alert HQ • **UC2:** Query Plants • **UC3: Move Items**

Process Number	P2
Process Name	Issue Purchase Orders
Description	Allows the HQ to buy needed items from suppliers. This process encapsulates the following logic: • The HQ searches for suppliers from which it can buy the required materials. • After locating the suppliers, the HQ places their orders for the needed items. • Then the HQ transfers funds to suppliers via the agreed-upon banking services and forms. • After paying the fees, material suppliers ship the items to the HQ via the shipping company which provides a facility to track shipped items. • After the arrival of the issued items, the HQ starts checking them, and if everything is ok it receives them and notifies the suppliers that the items are approved. • If the items are not at the desired quality, the HQ has the right to return them back to their suppliers. • If the items arrived too late, the HQ has the right to reject them and notify the suppliers that the deal has failed.
Included Use Cases	• **UC4:** Find Suppliers • **UC6:** Order Items • **UC11:** Transfer Funds • **UC14:** Track Items • **UC10:** Receive Items • **UC9:** Reject Items

continued on following page

Table 3. Continued

Process Number	P3
Process Name	Supply Items
Description	Allows material suppliers to meet the manufacturer's orders. This process encapsulates the following logic: • When the supplier gets a purchase order from any manufacturer, it starts the preparation phase for the issued items. • After preparing the items, the supplier hand them over to the shipping company in order to deliver them to the targeted manufacturer. • After delivering the items to the shipping company, the supplier transfers the needed funds to it. • The shipping company gives its suppliers a facility to track items, so they would know the status of the sent items.
Included Use Cases	• **UC7:** Prepare Items • **UC12:** Transfer Items • **UC11:** Transfer Funds • **UC14:** Track Items

Process Number	P4
Process Name	Return Items
Description	Allows the manufacturer to return issued items to suppliers. This process encapsulates the following logic: • If the issued items have some problems, the HQ rejects them and notifies its supplier about it in order to take the appropriate action. • The rejection action forces the shipping company to return those items back to the original supplier. • After transferring the rejected items, the supplier receives them.
Included Use Cases	• **UC9:** Reject Items • **UC12:** Transfer Items • **UC13:** Receive Returned Items

Figure 9. Relationships between processes and use cases

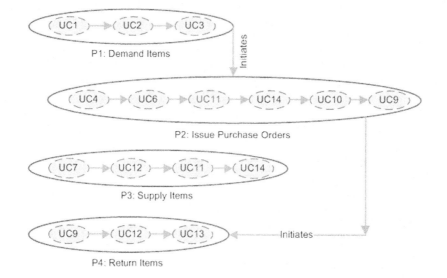

Table 4.

Service Number	S1
Service Name	Plant
Description	Handles plants' transactions such as allowing clients to find, transfer, and receive issued items.
Exposed Functions	• **ListItems:** Enables business partners to list items available on the provider side. • **LookForItem:** Allows business partners (the HQ and other plants) to query plants for specified items with a set of predefined conditions. • **SearchResultsCallback:** Receives detailed notifications from the HQ with the query results. • **ReceiveItems:** Updates plants' stock levels after receiving new items either from other plants or suppliers. • **MoveItems:** Allows the HQ to transfer the needed items from one plant to another, which, in turn, updates related information about their stock levels. • **SummerizePlantsInformation:** Allows the HQ to generate different reports about plants' status including available items, transactions that occurred on them within a quarter, etc.

Service Number	S2
Service Name	Manufacturer
Description	It is a key service that manages most tasks at the manufacturer's side such as looking for needed items at available plants, looking for available suppliers who could provide them, registering new suppliers, and deleting some of the existing ones.
Exposed Functions	• **NotifyHeadquarterCallback:** Receives alert notifications from any plant when it runs out of a specified item in order to allow that plant to take the appropriate action. • **FindSuppliers:** Allows the manufacturer to select one or more of the available suppliers in order to get the needed raw materials. • **RegisterSupplier:** Allows new suppliers to join the manufacturer in order to provide it with the needed raw materials. • **UpdateSuppliersProfile:** Allows existing suppliers to update their profiles. Profile information may include business activities, addresses, fax numbers, and phone numbers. • **DeactivateSupplier:** An internal method that allows manufacturer to stop working with the specified suppliers.

Service Number	S3
Service Name	Supplier
Description	It is a key service that manages almost all important tasks performed by the supplier. These tasks may include showing available products to customers, accepting new purchase orders, preparing issued items, and receiving returned items.
Exposed Functions	• **SignContract:** Allows suppliers to sign contracts with new manufacturers, shipping companies, and other suppliers. • **ViewProducts:** Lists available items and raw materials in order to enable manufacturers to easily find and place orders for needed items. • **AcceptPOs:** Accepts POs issued by manufacturers in order to start its preparation phase. • **PrepareItems:** Allows suppliers to enter the preparation phase for the issued items which includes making and packaging items, and contacting shipping company for transferring them. This function should automatically take place after accepting POs from any manufacturer. • **NotifySuppliersCallback:** Notifies the supplier about the status of the manufacturer's POs. • **CancelPOe:** Enables the manufacturers to cancel issued POs. • **ReturnItems:** Enables the manufacturers to return issued items.

continued on following page

Table 4. Continued

Service Number	S4
Service Name	Shipment
Description	Provides functionalities related to shipment services such as transferring items from one location to another, and allowing customers to track items that are being shipped.
Exposed Functions	• **TransferItems:** Accepts orders to transfer items from one location to another. It could be used by suppliers to move issued items to a manufacturer or another supplier, or it could be used by the manufacturer to return issued items back to the source supplier(s). • **TrackItems:** Enables both the suppliers and manufacturer to track items being transferred between them.

Service Number	S5
Service Name	Banking
Description	Covers payment services that allow customers to pay their service providers.
Exposed Functions	• **DebitAccount:** Enables bank clients (suppliers and shipping companies in this case) to debit some money from specified accounts. • **CreditAccount:** Enables bank clients (manufacturer in this case) to credit some money to specified accounts.

and realize business (functional) use cases that were identified during the domain decomposition phase, plus technical (non-functional) services such as security, performance, audit-trail, etc.

After completing the subsystem analysis phase, implementers end up with a set of large-grained components to be implemented as services. The sections in Table 4 briefly describe the subsystems included in the demonstrated scenario, presented with a set of public functions provided by each one.

The realized services could act as infrastructure (elementary) services that could be easily used by IT specialists to implement business processes identified during the domains' decomposition phase. IT specialists can build a composite services layer above those services in order to provide the needed logic in a loosely-coupled manner. Composite services could be physically constructed using standards like BPEL4WS, orchestration tools available in the market such as MS BizTalk, or even custom code. Figure 10 illustrates a set of composite services dynamically composed to satisfy the business process needs.

The purpose of creating these composite services is to improve the flexibility at the business process level. This flexibility enables IT special-

ists to change the business logic easily by modifying their orchestration structure without having to alter the logic of the underlying services, components, or systems. Altering the orchestration structure/logic refers to changing the composition configuration and execution order of available business processes. Also, composite services could improve the reusability level as they may be used to compose more complicated composite services. For example, the manufacturer may need to create a new service that allows it to handle the whole process for providing items required by one plant. The manufacturer can cover this shortage either by moving items from other plants, or by issuing POs to contracted suppliers. This need could be easily fulfilled by creating a new composite service that is composed of "Demand Items" and "Issue PO" services.

Step #3: Service Categorization

This process starts after identifying system services. The purpose of categorizing identified services is to appropriately assign them to different layers. These services could be categorized according to different aspects including:

Figure 10. Composite services needed for yielded business processes

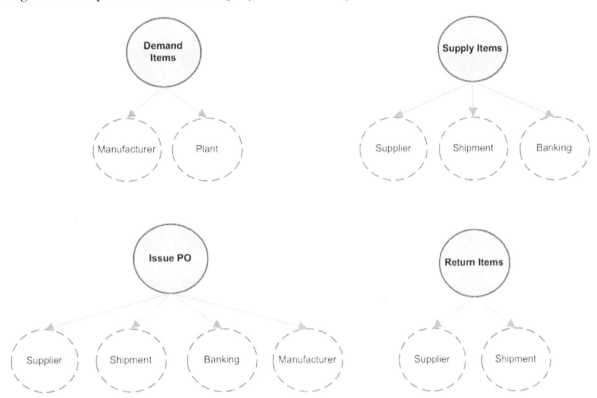

- **Customer Type:** Internal service, customer service or partner service.
- **Service Functionality:** Function service, validation service or process service.
- **Service Type:** Technical services vs. business services.
- **Service Size:** Fine-grained service vs. coarse-grained service.

Step #4: Service Specification

As mentioned earlier, each service should contain a formal contract that defines necessary pre-conditions, post-conditions, invocation syntax, semantics, and quality of service (QoS) terms. All this information is essential for helping consumers use available services effectively.

Step #5: Service Realization

This step specifies technologies and tools to be used in realizing given services. It also determines the realization strategies for those services. Realization strategies may include building services in-house, outsourcing, leasing, or buying them.

For the technology part, we decided to use MS Visual Studio 2008, .NET framework 3.5, c# language, XML Web Services (for the sake of simplicity), and MS SQL 2008 to illustrate how the realization process could take place. The code snippet in Box 1 demonstrates the c# code written to develop our simple *Plant* service. As illustrated in Figure 11, the *Plant* service has a number of operations that handles plants' transactions such as allowing clients to find, transfer, and receive issued items. Figure 12 and 13 illustrates the WSDL document for the *Plant* service and *ListItems* operation, respectively. These WSDL documents were automatically created by Visual Studio 2008, and any changes to the actual implementation will be automatically reflected as well. The code snippets in Box 2 and Box 3 demonstrate a sample SOAP request and response, respectively.

Box 1. Code Snippet 1: Service code

```
using System;
using System.Web;
using System.Web.Services;
using System.Data;
using System.Data.SqlClient;

namespace PlantService
{
    [WebService(Namespace = "http://PlantService.org/")]
    [WebServiceBinding(ConformsTo = WsiProfiles.BasicProfile1_1)]
    public class Plant: System.Web.Services.WebService
    {
        #region Service Operations

         [WebMethod]
        public DataSet ListItems()
        {
            //Inistantiate needed objects
            SqlCommand sqlSelectPlantItems = new SqlCommand();
            SqlDataAdapter sdaListPlantItems = new SqlDataAdapter();
            SqlConnection cnPlant = new SqlConnection();
            DataSet dsPlantItems = new DataSet();

            cnPlant.ConnectionString = "Data Source=(local);Initial
Catalog=Plant;Integrated Security=True";    //Database connection string
            sqlSelectPlantItems.CommandText = "SELECT ItemID, ItemName, Item-
Description FROM Items";                //Select query
            sqlSelectPlantItems.Connection = cnPlant;
            sdaListPlantItems.SelectCommand = sqlSelectPlantItems;
            sdaListPlantItems.Fill(dsPlantItems);
            return dsPlantItems;                //Return resultset
        }

        [WebMethod]
        public DataSet LookForItem()
        {
            //Replace the following line with actual logic
            return null;
        }

        [WebMethod]
        public string SearchResultsCallback()
```

continued on following page

Box 1. Continued

```
    {
        //Replace the following line with actual logic
        return null;
    }
     [WebMethod]
    public int ReceiveItems()
    {
        //Replace the following line with actual logic
        return 0;
    }
    [WebMethod]
    public int MoveItems()
    {
        //Replace the following line with actual logic
        return 0;
    }

    [WebMethod]
    public DataSet SummerizePlantsInformation()
    {
        //Replace the following line with actual logic
        return null;
    }
    #endregion
    }
}
```

Figure 11. Service operations

Plant

The following operations are supported. For a formal definition, please review the Service Description.

- **ListItems**
  Enables business partners to list items available on the provider side.

- **LookForItem**
  Allows business partners (the HQ and other plants) to query plants for specified items with a set of predefined conditions.

- **MoveItems**
  Allows the HQ to transfer needed items from one plant to another, which in turn updates related information about their stock levels.

- **ReceiveItems**
  Updates plants stock levels after receiving new items either from other plants or suppliers.

- **SearchResultsCallback**
  Receives detailed notifications from the HQ with the query results.

- **SummerizePlantsInformation**
  Allows the HQ to generate different reports about plants' status including available items, transactions occurred on them within a quarter, etc.

Figure 12. Service WSDL

```
<?xml version="1.0" encoding="UTF-8"?>
<wsdl:definitions xmlns:wsdl="http://schemas.xmlsoap.org/wsdl/" targetNamespace="http://PlantService.org/"
  xmlns:http="http://schemas.xmlsoap.org/wsdl/http/" xmlns:soap12="http://schemas.xmlsoap.org/wsdl/soap12/"
  xmlns:s="http://www.w3.org/2001/XMLSchema" xmlns:tns="http://PlantService.org/" xmlns:mime="http://schemas.xmlsoap.org/wsdl/mime/"
  xmlns:soapenc="http://schemas.xmlsoap.org/soap/encoding/" xmlns:tm="http://microsoft.com/wsdl/mime/textMatching/"
  xmlns:soap="http://schemas.xmlsoap.org/wsdl/soap/">
  <wsdl:types>
    <s:schema targetNamespace="http://PlantService.org/" elementFormDefault="qualified">
      <s:element name="ListItems">
        <s:complexType/>
      </s:element>
      <s:element name="ListItemsResponse">
        <s:complexType>
          <s:sequence>
            <s:element name="ListItemsResult" maxOccurs="1" minOccurs="0">
              <s:complexType>
                <s:sequence>
                  <s:element ref="s:schema"/>
                  <s:any/>
                </s:sequence>
              </s:complexType>
            </s:element>
          </s:sequence>
        </s:complexType>
      </s:element>
      <s:element name="LookForItem">
        <s:complexType/>
      </s:element>
      <s:element name="LookForItemResponse">
        <s:complexType>
          <s:sequence>
            <s:element name="LookForItemResult" maxOccurs="1" minOccurs="0">
              <s:complexType>
                <s:sequence>
                  <s:element ref="s:schema"/>
                  <s:any/>
                </s:sequence>
              </s:complexType>
            </s:element>
          </s:sequence>
        </s:complexType>
      </s:element>
      <s:element name="SearchResultsCallback">
```

Figure 13. ListItems operation schema

```
<?xml version="1.0" encoding="UTF-8"?>
<DataSet xmlns="http://PlantService.org/">
  <xs:schema xmlns="" xmlns:msdata="urn:schemas-microsoft-com:xml-msdata" xmlns:xs="http://www.w3.org/2001/XMLSchema" id="NewDataSet">
    <xs:element msdata:UseCurrentLocale="true" msdata:IsDataSet="true" name="NewDataSet">
      <xs:complexType>
        <xs:choice maxOccurs="unbounded" minOccurs="0">
          <xs:element name="Table">
            <xs:complexType>
              <xs:sequence>
                <xs:element name="ItemID" minOccurs="0" type="xs:int"/>
                <xs:element name="ItemName" minOccurs="0" type="xs:string"/>
                <xs:element name="ItemDescription" minOccurs="0" type="xs:string"/>
              </xs:sequence>
            </xs:complexType>
          </xs:element>
        </xs:choice>
      </xs:complexType>
    </xs:element>
  </xs:schema>
  <diffgr:diffgram xmlns:msdata="urn:schemas-microsoft-com:xml-msdata" xmlns:diffgr="urn:schemas-microsoft-com:xml-diffgram-v1">
    <NewDataSet xmlns="">
      <Table diffgr:id="Table1" msdata:rowOrder="0">
        <ItemID>1</ItemID>
        <ItemName>Test Item 1</ItemName>
      </Table>
      <Table diffgr:id="Table2" msdata:rowOrder="1">
        <ItemID>2</ItemID>
        <ItemName>Test Item 2</ItemName>
      </Table>
      <Table diffgr:id="Table3" msdata:rowOrder="2">
        <ItemID>3</ItemID>
        <ItemName>Test Item 3</ItemName>
      </Table>
      <Table diffgr:id="Table4" msdata:rowOrder="3">
        <ItemID>4</ItemID>
        <ItemName>Test Item 4</ItemName>
      </Table>
      <Table diffgr:id="Table5" msdata:rowOrder="4">
        <ItemID>5</ItemID>
        <ItemName>Test Item 5</ItemName>
      </Table>
    </NewDataSet>
  </diffgr:diffgram>
</DataSet>
```

Step #6: Service Registry

Service registry, in basic terms, is a special type of database used to register created services in order to allow business partners, both existing and new, to easily discover and use them. During the registration process, metadata information that describes the service is extracted and stored in the service registry. This information includes technical specifications that guide customers so that they can consume published services; quality of service (QoS) terms such as uptimes, downtimes, and estimated response time for each request; and general information about business domain such as business types and contact information.

In fact, service registry can play a great role in our scenario. For example, let us say that our manufacturer intends to simultaneously deal with more than one supplier to get the needed materials quickly in order to speed up the production cycle and meet urgent requests. To accomplish this mission, the IT team on the manufacturer's side can

Box 2. Code Snippet 2: Sample SOAP 1.2 request

```
POST /Plant.asmx HTTP/1.1
Host: localhost
Content-Type: application/soap+xml; charset=utf-8
Content-Length: length
<?xml version="1.0" encoding="utf-8"?>
<soap12:Envelope xmlns:xsi="http://www.w3.org/2001/XMLSchema-instance"
xmlns:xsd="http://www.w3.org/2001/XMLSchema" xmlns:soap12="http://www.
w3.org/2003/05/soap-envelope">
  <soap12:Body>
    <ListItems xmlns="http://PlantService.org/" />
  </soap12:Body>
</soap12:Envelope>
```

Box 3. Code Snippet 3: Sample SOAP 1.2 response

```
HTTP/1.1 200 OK
Content-Type: application/soap+xml; charset=utf-8
Content-Length: length
<?xml version="1.0" encoding="utf-8"?>
<soap12:Envelope xmlns:xsi="http://www.w3.org/2001/XMLSchema-instance"
xmlns:xsd="http://www.w3.org/2001/XMLSchema" xmlns:soap12="http://www.
w3.org/2003/05/soap-envelope">
  <soap12:Body>
    <ListItemsResponse xmlns="http://PlantService.org/">
      <ListItemsResult>
        <xsd:schema>schema</xsd:schema>xml</ListItemsResult>
    </ListItemsResponse>
  </soap12:Body>
</soap12:Envelope>
```

Figure 14. Adding reference to Plant service

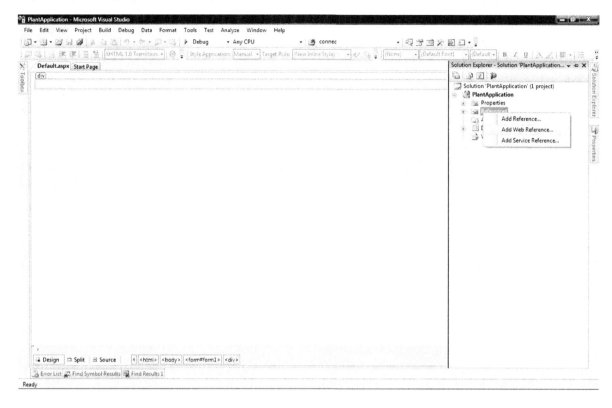

Figure 15. Browsing for the target Web services

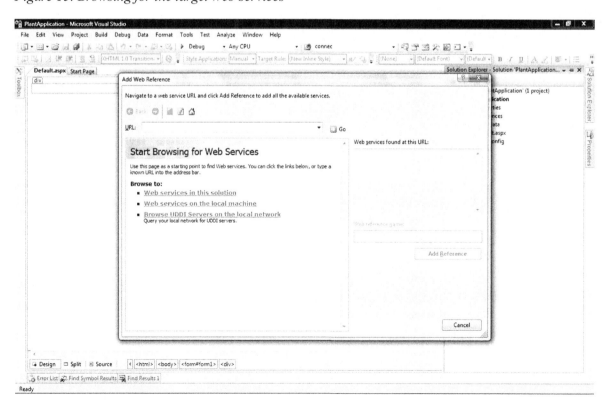

Figure 16. Locating Plant service

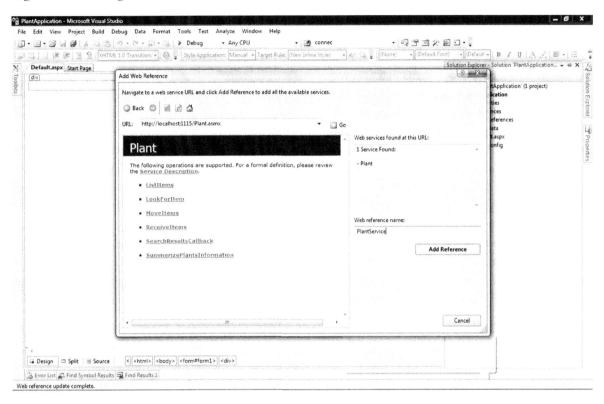

Figure 17. A reference to Plant service has been added

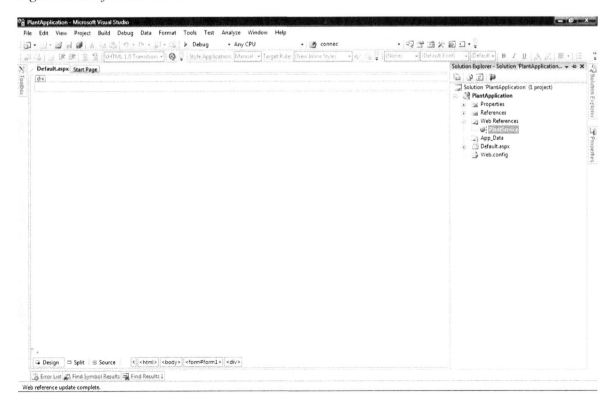

publish the services responsible for monitoring and managing their warehouses in a way that allows new suppliers to detect items that fall under a certain threshold. With this facility, suppliers can bid on providing needed items in a neat way.

Furthermore, service registry enables SOA to scale rapidly. For example, assume that the manufacturer wants to institute an electronic competitive bidding system for its orders. The suppliers who want to bid to win business from the manufacturer can simply search for offered services, extract attached metadata, and connect to the bidding system.

UDDI is a good example for service registry which offers great search tools to enable easy discovery of services. Information documents provided by UDDI can be retrieved either manu-

ally using URLs or programmatically using APIs that come with UDDI registries (UDDI, 2004).

Step #7: Service Call

Once the services are created, registered in the service registry, and made available for internal/external access, clients can start building modules and applications that make use of them. Figure 14, 15, 16 and 17 illustrate the steps that the client application developer performs to add a reference to *Plant* service.

The code snippet in Box 4 demonstrates the c# code written to develop a simple ASP.NET page that adds reference to *Plant* service and call its operations. This code snippet simply calls the *ListItems* operation which returns a list of avail-

Box 4. Code Snippet 4: Calling service operations in an ASP.NET page

```
using System;
using System.Web;
namespace PlantApplication
{
    public partial class _Default: System.Web.UI.Page
    {
        protected void Page_Load(object sender, EventArgs e)
        {
            try
            {
                //Inistantiating Plant Webservice
                PlantService.Plant plant = new PlantService.Plant();
                //Displaying returned data
                gvPlants.DataSource = plant.ListItems();
                gvPlants.DataBind();
            }
            catch (Exception ex)
            {
                Response.Write(ex.Message);
            }
        }
    }
}
```

Figure 18. Adding a GridView control to display data returned from Plant service

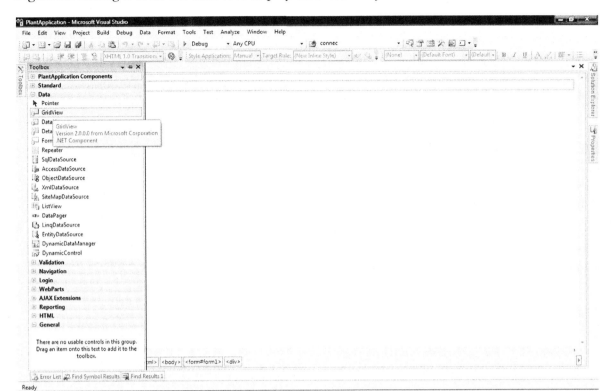

able items in the provider's store. Figure 18 illustrate the way to add a GridView control to display data returned from the *Plant* service. Figure 19 illustrate the client view of the created ASP.NET page.

CONCLUSION

SOA is rapidly being accepted by IT professionals all over the world as a design and architecture model for building, deploying and integrating information systems. However, its adoption is neither easy nor straightforward. This article has introduced a number of issues that new adopters should consider during the adoption and implementation phases. Paying close attention to the challenges that might accompany SOA adoption is important to successful implementation. This success will be clear to adopters once they begin reap-

Figure 19. Displaying data returned from Plant service

ItemID	ItemName	ItemDescription
1	Item 1	Description 1
2	Item 2	Description 2
3	Item 3	Description 3
4	Item 4	Description 4
5	Item 5	Description 5

ing the promised benefits, making organizations feel more secure in having made the right choice. A hypothetical case study was also presented to demonstrate the steps through which beginners can apply SOA principles to their organizations during the migration process.

ACKNOWLEDGMENT

The author would like to thank Jeff T. Goebel and Rana S. Shaker who were abundantly helpful and provided invaluable comments and assistance in proofreading this work.

REFERENCES

ABCs of SOA. (2007). *CIO Magazine*. Retrieved from http://www.cio.com/article/40941

Anne, T. M. (2005). *The elephant has left the building*. Retrieved from http://www.intelligententerprise.com/showArticle.jhtml?articleID=164301126&pgno=3

Bieberstein, N., Bose, S., Fiammante, M., Jones, K., & Shah, R. (2005). *Service-oriented architecture compass: Business value, planning, and enterprise roadmap*. IBM Press.

Crockford, D. (2009). *Introducing JSON*. Retrieved from http://www.json.org/

Endrei, M., Ang, J., Arsanjani, A., Chua, S., Comte, P., & Krogdahl, P. (2004). *Service-oriented architecture and web services* (pp. 83–102). IBM Redbooks.

Erl, T. (2005). *Service-oriented architecture: Concepts, technology, and design*. Prentice Hall.

Fielding, R. T. (2000). Architectural styles and the design of network-based software architectures. In *Representational state transfer*. Retrieved from http://www.ics.uci.edu/~fielding/pubs/dissertation/rest_arch_style.htm

Geer, D. (2005). Will binary XML speed network traffic? *Journal of Computer, 38*(4). IEEE Computer Society Press.

Governance, I. T., & Governance, S. O. A. (n.d.). *OASIS*. Retrieved from http://wiki.oasis-open.org/soa-rm/TheArchitecture/Governance

Hassan, Q. F. (2009). Aspects of SOA: An entry point for starters. *Annals Computer Science Series, 7*(2). Retrieved from http://anale-informatica.tibiscus.ro/download/lucrari/7-2-12-Hassan.pdf

He, H. (2004). Implementing REST Web services: Best practices and guidelines. Retrieved from http://www.xml.com/pub/a/2004/08/11/rest.html

Hernan, S., Lambert, S., Ostwald, T., & Shostack, A. (2000). *Uncover security design flaws using the STRIDE approach*. MSDN Magazine.

JSON-RPC. (n.d.). Retrieved from http://json-rpc.org/

Kobielus, J. (2005). The ROI of SOA: The more you reuse, the more you save. *Network World*. Retrieved from www.networkworld.com/techinsider/2005/101005-roi-of-soa.html

Kollhof, J. (2009). *Welcome to JSON-RPC*. Retrieved from http://json-rpc.org/

Krafzig, D., Banke, K., & Slama, D. (2004). *Enterprise SOA service-oriented architecture best practices*. Prentice Hall. Lewis, G., Morris E. J., Smith, D. B., & Wrage L. (2005). SMART: Service-oriented migration and reuse technique. *Proceedings of the 13th IEEE International Workshop on Software Technology and Engineering Practice*.

Papazoglou, M. P. (2003). Service-oriented computing: Concepts, characteristics and directions. *Proceeding of the Fourth International Conference on Web Information Systems Engineering*.

Peterson, G., & Lipson, H. (2006). *Security concepts, challenges, and design considerations for Web services integration security*.

Pizette, L., Semy, S., Raines, G., & Foote, S. (2009). A perspective on emerging industry SOA best practices. *The Journal of Defense Software Engineering, 22*.

Raines, G. (2009). Leveraging federal IT investment with service-oriented architecture. *The Journal of Defense Software Engineering: CrossTalk, March.*

Riad, A. M., Hassan, A. E., & Hassan, Q. F. (2009). Investigating performance of XML Web services in real-time business systems. *Journal of Computer Science and System Biology*, *2*(5). Retrieved from http://www.omicsonline.com/ArchiveJCSB/2009/October/01/JCSB2.266.pdf

Rodriguez, A. (2008). *RESTful Web services: The basics.* Retrieved from http://www.ibm.com/developerworks/webservices/library/ws-restful/

Schmelzer, R. (2005). Right-sizing services. *ZapThink.* Retrieved from www.zapthink.com/report.html?id=ZAPFLASH-20051115

Top, O. W. A. S. P. 10 – 2010. (2010). *The ten most critical Web application security risks.* Retrieved from http://owasptop10.googlecode.com/files/OWASP%20Top%2010%20-%202010.pdf

Tsai, W. T., Chen, Y., & Paul, R. A. (n.d.). *Service-oriented computing and system engineering.* Unpublished book.

Tsai, W. T., Malek, M., Chen, Y., & Bastani, F. (2006). Perspectives on service-oriented computing and service-oriented system engineering. *Proceedings of the Second IEEE International Symposium on Service-Oriented System Engineering.*

Universal Description. (2004). *Discovery and integration specification,* version 3.0.2. OASIS UDDI Technical Committee. Retrieved from http://uddi.org/pubs/uddi_v3.htm

Web Services Architecture. (2004). *World Wide Web consortium* (W3C). Retrieved from http://www.w3.org/TR/ws-arch

Zhang, J. (2004). *Better, faster XML processing with VTD-XML.* Retrieved from http://www.devx.com/xml/Article/22219/0/page/1

Zhang, J. (2008). *VTD-XML: XML processing for the future* (Part I). Retrieved from http://www.codeproject.com/KB/cs/vtd-xml_examples.aspx

Zimmermann, O., Krogdahl, P., & Gee, C. (2004). *Elements of service-oriented analysis and design: An interdisciplinary modeling approach for SOA projects.* Retrieved from http://www-128.ibm.com/developerworks/webservices/library/ws-soad1/

Section 2
Reuse of Architecture, Infrastructure, Platforms, and Services

Chapter 5
Reuse across Multiple Architectures

Indika Kumara
WSO2 Inc, Sri Lanka

Chandana Gamage
University of Moratuwa, Sri Lanka

ABSTRACT

The commonality across software systems can be exploited to develop multiple heterogeneous systems successfully without undue cost, time, and effort. The systematic reuse across different systems is of paramount importance. With a well-planned reuse approach, a vendor can offer individualized products, which are products tailored to meet the requirements of a particular user effectively, as well as the products constructed to deliver solutions for a greater variety of application domains such as enterprise application integration and business process management. This chapter describes the development of software systems having different architectures reusing most of the implementations of the required functionalities as-is. It presents a systematic process for crafting multi-architecture reusable components and for using those components in formulating software systems. Furthermore, the chapter highlights the significance of the strategic reuse across systems in three contemporary research spheres.

INTRODUCTION

Software reuse has been widely touted as means of amortizing the cost of the software development. Two notable engineering disciplines that have exploited reuse are software product line (SPL) and component-based development (CBD). SPL

has been employing strategic reuse to formulate product families successfully (Bass, Clements, & Kazman, 2003). CBD has incorporated reusability into the software development process to make software reuse a driving force in developing software systems (Crnkovic & Larsson, 2002). Although these reuse paradigms can establish a process for reuse, without purposefully architecting systems, components and other artifacts for

DOI: 10.4018/978-1-4666-0897-9.ch005

reuse, the desired reuse goals would not be attainable (Griss, 1999). For instance, as not every architecture style facilitates reuse, the employed architecture for a particular component-based system may impede the opportunities for reuse. Moreover, a new product can use an existing component; however, the component cannot provide the software qualities that the product expects.

The capability to produce a variety of software systems offers both vendors and customers discernible advantages. A customer can use a tailor-made product that provides minimum yet optimum functionalities required for implementing only her or his own business solutions. In addition, a customer can gain the flexibility to adapt the systems and applications to support the changing business goals of the organization. From a vendor's perspective, the software systems developed to provide solutions for different application domains such as enterprise application integration (EAI), business process management (BPM), etc., can potentially enable a vendor to reach to wideranging customers. However, the heterogeneity of the systems poses grand challenges on how to develop multiple systems cost and time effectively. Typically, software architectures, features, and technologies make systems different. In order to achieve tremendous savings in costs and time in producing multiple different software systems, a systematic reuse across the systems is crucial (Altintas & Cetin, 2008) (Griss, 1999), and the components that are reusable across the systems can provide the required reusability.

A critical issue undermines a sustainability of a software system is *architectural erosion*, a phenomenon in which a system's architecture decays over time to the point that it does not exhibit its key attributes. An eroded architecture is unwieldy and cannot adequately respond to the changes in requirements. Redesigning such architecture from scratch is practical compared with maintaining it (Gurp, 2002). A key reason for *architectural erosion* is that a system has to undergo an evolution to accommodate ever changing customer require-

ments. Architectural erosion can be stemmed if the system can reform its architecture to fulfill the new emerging demands (Bernhard, 2010). Therefore, the capability for changing the architecture of a system with either practical or economical ease is a promising solution for *architectural erosion*. An approach to achieve a systematic reuse across systems having different architectures paves the way for such a solution.

There is no considerable research related to the reuse across multiple architectures, and we observe that previous research has focused merely on functionality reuse and have not taken into account that a reusable component should be capable of supporting quality requirements required by various systems. Furthermore, most of the existing approaches do not provide a suitable solution to prevent *architectural erosion* that weakens the reusability and sustainability of the components and the systems.

The objectives of this chapter are to introduce the reader *Multi-Architecture Reusable Components*, and to discuss the techniques for designing and implementing them. We also present an approach for using them in producing multiple software systems successfully. Our experiment with two middleware systems shows that our approach provides a systematic reuse across different systems effectively.

This chapter is structured as follows. Section *Background* explores the opportunities for exploiting reuse across systems, and highlights related work. Next sections unfold our approach for achieving large scale reuse across multiple architectures. Finally, we present our conclusions and future research directions.

BACKGROUND

Simply stated, software reuse across multiple architectures is systematically creating software systems having diverse architectures from existing software assets. In this context, a strategic reuse precludes the mere functionality reuse and promotes the reuse of functionality with the quality attributes required for a particular software system. Such reuse provides a software vendor with a sheer capability to construct versatile software products to support the requirements of wide-ranging users. On the other hand, a well-planned reuse across systems makes a provision against a kind of software crisis that occurs when the software system cannot meet changing business requirements adequately. In summary, a strategic reuse across systems potentially reinforces the overall agility of an organization.

In next subsections, firstly, we deeply discuss the significance of reuse across systems having different architectures. Secondly, our discussion focuses on the existing approaches that leverage the heterogeneity in software architectures and provide a large scale reuse across systems. Finally, the previous researches pertinent to the reusable asset development are explored.

Importance of Reuse across Multiple Architectures

This section discusses the importance of the systematic reuse across multiple architectures, focusing on the applicability of it in three essential research areas: service-oriented architecture, cloud computing, and multiple product lines.

Service Oriented Architecture Infrastructures

Service Oriented Architecture (SOA) is a paradigm for the realization of business processes, which span over heterogeneous enterprises (Josuttis, 2007). The essence of SOA is the concept of a service which offers a well-defined, self-contained a function without depending on the context or state of other services. In SOA, a business process is basically a collection of services. The adoption of SOA as the application architecture of enterprises has escalated for the past several years. SOA has reached a variety of industries, such as telecommunications, healthcare, travel, and education. Similarly, SOA has succeeded in large enterprises, mid range size businesses, and small organizations.

SOA infrastructure market comprises both proprietary organizations and open source organizations. Most of the SOA vendors offer a SOA platform, which provides customers with the services such as service deployment, service access, service composition, business process management and so on. In order to identify the opportunities for a large-scale reuse in formulating a SOA platform, we analyzed three prime ingredients of a SOA platform: service hosting environment, enterprise service bus, and business process management system.

1. **Service Hosting Environment (SHE):** SHE is a server environment to host and manage services. It primarily performs activities such as service deployment, service life cycle management. A server which is capable of hosting an application and offers the application as a service is an example for a service hosting environment. Although an application can represent diverse technologies, including Java, J2EE (Java 2 Platform Enterprise Edition), WCF (Windows Communication Foundation), dynamic languages, etc., it is exposed as an SOA service.

2. **Enterprise Service Bus (ESB):** An ESB is an infrastructure middleware, which supports the Enterprise Application Integration (EAI). By serving as a communication intermediary, an ESB lowers the coupling between service consumers and providers through providing the virtualization and management of service interactions (Rosen, Lublinsky, Smith, & Balcer, 2008). The ESB architectures can be broadly categorized into four: JBI (Java Business Integration), SCA (Service Component Architecture),

Table 1. Commonality across a SOA platform

Infrastructure Services	Software Systems		
	SHE	**ESB**	**BPMS**
Persistence	Yes	Yes	Yes
Request Routing *Content and Header Based Routing (CBR and HBR)*	No	Yes	No
Data and Message Transform *XML(Extensible Markup Language), EDI(Electronic Data Interchange), etc.*	Yes	Yes	Yes
Transport Services *HTTP / HTTPS, FTP, JMS(Java Message Service), Email, etc.*	Yes	Yes	Yes
Security *LDAP (Lightweight Directory Access Protocol), WS-Security, JAAS(Java Authentication and Authorization Service), etc.*	Yes	Yes	Yes
Load Balance	No	Yes	Yes
Caching *Database Records, Messages, etc.*	Yes	Yes	Yes
Transaction *JTA (Java Transaction API), WS-Transaction, etc.*	Yes	Yes	Yes

MQM (Message Queuing Middleware), and custom-designed. Typically, ESB customers contemplate pros and cons of different ESB architectures based on their application requirements to select the most appropriate ESB for implementing their integration solutions.

3. **Business Process Management System (BPMS):** A BPMS manages the interactions among applications, business partners, and human in a business processes across one or more enterprises. It chiefly focuses on providing a systematic approach to service orchestration and process automation. In the BPM (Business Process Management) sphere, there are several standards such as BPEL (Business Process Execution Language), WSCI (Web Service Choreography Interface), XPDL (XML Process Definition Language), etc., and there are considerable commonalities in the functionalities offered by these standards. BPEL is emerging as the standard that is likely to succeed and WSCI could emerge as part of a W3C Web services choreography specification. XPDL is a workflow-centric standard and does not depend on Web services for application integration (Chang, 2006). In additions to these standards, several custom-designed standards and approaches for BPM can be found in contemporary research literature (Cumberlidge, 2007) (Aalst & Hofstede, 2005).

Table 1 illustrates how several functionalities (infrastructure services) could be shared across the three aforementioned SOA systems. An infrastructure service represents a generic functionality that can possibly be reused by the three products either with the same abstraction or a different abstraction. For instance, the *invoke* activity in a BPEL product employs transport services such as HTTP (Hypertext Transfer Protocol), FTP (File Transfer Protocol). We have only analyzed nine services as the selected services precisely demonstrate the possibility for a large-scale reuse across the three software systems.

As shown in Table 1, most of the services are potentially reusable across the three products. Each product has its own architecture, and a particular architecture represents diverse architectural styles and standards. In order to produce these different systems in a cost-effective manner the systematic reuse across the systems is crucial. Therefore, the services mentioned in Table 1 need to be developed in a way that those can be strategically reused by the three SOA systems and their variations.

Cloud Computing Infrastructures

Cloud computing delivers computational resources as services over the Internet to a greater variety of consumers. Cloud services can be broadly categorized into three types: *Infrastructure-as-a-Service (IaaS)*, *Platform-as-a-Service (PaaS)*, and *Software-as-a-Service (SaaS)*. IaaS makes computational resources such as storages and operating systems available through the Internet to consumers. PaaS exposes application development platforms as services. SaaS is the model in which software resources are delivered as services over the Internet (Velte, Velte, & Elsenpeter, 2010) (Mell & Grance, 2009).

As computational resources are shared by multiple users, cloud computing can be identified as a reuse paradigm. La and Kim (2009) defined reusability as a key characteristic of a SaaS service, and engineered a systematic process for developing SaaS services with the required reusability. By identifying and modularizing the variation points in the SaaS service, and composing them appropriately to the kernel of the SaaS service, Jegadeesan and Balasubramaniam (2009) supported the reuse of a SaaS service across different SaaS service consumers. However, a functional component is only a single reusable asset. The strategic reuse often requires a large-scale reuse of product roadmaps, requirement specifications, domain models, software architectures and designs, people, and so on. In addition, the reuse of artifacts across different SaaS services potentially reduces the cost and effort associated with the service development.

Cloud service consumers are heterogeneous and need the services that can successfully fulfill their own unique business requirements. Mietzner (2008) emphasized the requirements for configurable SaaS applications to support the requirements of different consumers. Sun et al. (2008) also discussed the inevitability of the configuration and customization of SaaS solutions. Furthermore, an empirical study on consumers' preferences for cloud services revealed that customized cloud applications would significantly improve the adoption of SaaS services in enterprises (Koehler, Anandasivam, & Dan, 2010). Moreover, the provision of cloud services should be centered on the service level agreements (SLA) between consumers and providers (Buyya, Yeo, Venugopal, Broberg, & Brandic, 2009). As the software qualities of a system are primarily determined by the system's architecture, the diverse architectural styles potentially allow supporting SLA requirements of wide-ranging SaaS consumers.

Therefore, it is evident that an approach for constructing individualized cloud services with enormous saving in cost and time is crucial. Such an approach allows a vendor to classify customers based on their SLA requirements and create a customized SaaS service instance for each customer class. It would result in great satisfaction for customers and economic advantages for the vendor. The systematic reuse across different SaaS applications can significantly contribute towards attaining this goal.

Multiple Software Product Lines

Software Product Line (SPL) is a set of software-intensive systems sharing a common, managed set of features that satisfies the specific needs of a particular market segment or mission and that are developed from a common set of core assets in a prescribed way (Clements & Northrop, 2001). The core asset base is generally called as the product line platform. By taking economics advantages of commonalities shared by a set of software systems and predicted variability among them, a product line approach for developing software-intensive systems can yield significant improvements in cost, time to market and productivity. The traditional way to build a software product line is the explicit, planned re-use of a common architecture and elements that populate it across similar systems. Therefore, for an organization, a suitable approach to develop different software systems would be multiple product lines. SPL has succeeded due to the large-scale reuse within a single product family. Thus, multiple product lines should provide a systematic reuse within multiple product families (Altintas & Cetin, 2008).

As discussed in section *Service Oriented Architecture Infrastructures*, the customer base of the SOA is diverse in several aspects such as business domains, business scale. We reckon that each customer prefers an individualized SOA platform that can solve his or her business problems in a scalable and robust manner. Moreover, each product in a SOA platform is heterogeneous in terms of architectures and features. Architectures have made each product differ in quality attributes such as performance, reliability, and extensibility. Features have provided customers with the great flexibility for implementing their business solutions. As a reason, each product variation has a separate customer base, which is attributed to the features and architectures of the product. In order to create multiple product variations without undue cost, time and effort, the multiple product lines of products supporting SOA can be employed.

Furthermore, in order to produce individualized SaaS services with vast savings in costs and time, the product line approach can be utilized. SaaS product lines can effectively support the configuration and customization of SaaS Services – the creation of individualized SaaS services. A single SPL can provide a systematic reuse only within a single SaaS service family, whereas multiple product lines can provide a systematic reuse across multiple SaaS service families. Hence, the reuse across multiple architectures empowers

a SaaS service provider to realize SaaS service product lines.

Related Work

This section explores the previous research appertaining to the reuse across systems as well as the approaches for taking advantages of different architectural styles and the development of components to be reused by a great variety of users.

Large Scale Reuse across Systems

Altintas and Cetin (2008) proposed the concept of Software Factory Automation (SFA) to manage reusable assets across distinct software product lines based on Domain Specific Kits (DSK) and Software Asset Model (SAM). DSK is to encapsulate reusable domain artifacts abstractly. It consists of a domain specific language (DSL), a runtime to execute the DSL, and the development environment to construct the domain artifacts of the DSL. DSKs are reusable across multiple product lines and can be plugged into the reference architecture of a SPL, which employs a choreography model to compose domain-specific artifacts in deriving products from the core assets. SAM is to define an asset modeling language tailored for a particular product family. Our approach differs from the foregoing research on several aspects. We propose a pragmatic approach to develop a component that is reusable in different products with adequate quality attributes. In addition, every component is developed to be reused and there are no product-specific components because any product should be capable of changing its architecture and produce a new variation from the existing assets. More importantly, our work enables a vendor to construct products reusing not only components but also concrete solutions formed by composing various components.

Griss (1999) maintained that the large-scale component reuse should be employed in building complex software systems, and both components and systems should be carefully designed for reuse. In his view, a successful large-scale reuse effort is ascribed to four factors: business driven, architected, process oriented, and organized. The author asserted that business goals should guide the reuse strategy, and the artifacts, including applications, systems and components should be thoughtfully designed and implemented for reuse. Furthermore, a development and maintenance process for artifacts should be devised. More importantly, all these efforts should be supported by the organization's leadership through activities such as training people appropriately. His approach has leveraged object-oriented methodologies to model components, systems and business process. The system architecture for reuse is a layered architecture, which consists of three layers of components and the application systems at the top layer. Below the application layer are components reusable only for the specific business, such as healthcare. The cross-business middleware components constitute the third layer. The lowest layer of system software components includes interfaces to hardware, such as an operating system interfacing to the computer. We also employed a layered architecture (solution space) with two layers: abstract solution space and concrete solution space. The abstract solution space consists of different products and reuses the concrete solution space 'as-is' in formulating products.

Medvidovic, Oreizy, and Taylor (1997) have assessed the flexibility in using *off the shelf components* for developing applications designed in accordance with the C2 software architectural style. C2 is a component- and message-based architectural style where a hierarchical network of concurrent components linked together by connectors governed by a set of rules. They created an application family by reusing two user-interface constraints solvers, two graphics toolkits, a World Wide Web browser, and a persistent object manager. Each application used architecture that adheres to the rules of C2. Their research outcomes concluded that the C2 style offers significant reuse potential to application developers. As our approach inherently supports using different architectures for a particular software system, the C2 architecture style can also be employed for structuring components with our approach.

Microsoft Enterprise Library (MEL) (Newton, 2007) has attempted to capture enterprise wide concerns to enable reuse of them within a great variety of applications. MEL consists of designs and implementations of widely used concerns in the enterprise applications, including logging, caching, security, validation, police injection, data access, and exception handling. Each concern has been implemented as a reusable and configurable software component. The component library developed in this research project has drawn many architectural tactics, best practices, etc., from the work of MEL. However, our research focuses on devising a systematic process for developing components reusable across architecturally heterogeneous systems. Moreover, we proposed a reuse architecture that makes a strong context for a strategic reuse.

Reusable Component Development

In this section, we consider only the development of components that are to be reused by different users to satisfy their own unique requirements.

La and Kim (2009) have devised a systematic process for developing SaaS services with pre-defined attributes in which the reusability is one prime attribute. In their opinion, if a large number of consumers reuse the cloud services, a service provider would be able to obtain a high return on the investment. As a reason, it is highly desirable for cloud services to embed a high level of reusability. The authors have leveraged the commonality and variability analysis in order to identity reusable functions. Moreover, a theoretical foundation for SaaS has been provided via a meta-model and a variability and commonality model (V & C model). Our research also engineered a pragmatic approach to create reusable components and aptly employed a feature model which serves as a V & C model. Additionally, in our approach, a component is reusable in diverse architectures.

Jegadeesan and Balasubramaniam (2009) have employed the aspect-oriented programming (AOP) to produce the variations of a SaaS service. In the authors' view, supporting service variability in a cloud environment is a crucial requirement for SaaS services because in a multi-tenant cloud environment a single shared instance of an enterprise service must support customer specific variations. In their approach, a kernel of the service is formulated, and the variability features are incorporated into the kernel using the aspect weaving. This approach has offered the provider with tremendous configurability and reusability of services so that the same SaaS service can be configured to serve diverse consumers. In our work, a reusable component used a stable kernel as its foundation design. However, we decoupled a product and its architecture to make it possible to change the architecture appropriately to utilize the diversity in the strengths of different architectural styles.

Leveraging Architectural Diversity

Dynamic software architectures changes during system's operation to accommodate modifications in functional and non-functional requirements. A dominant scenario of a modification is reorganizing the software's architecture in response to the changed quality requirements for a system. As the quality attributes of the system are mostly attributed to the system's architecture, the changes in the quality requirements can be supported with a suitable variation in the architecture. In the process of the dynamic reconfiguration of architecture, the first step is to identify how the dynamic updates and reconfigurations are initiated. Secondly, an appropriate configuration is selected, and a reconfiguration procedure is formulated. Finally, the required changes are applied to the system, and the resultant system is assessed to ensure the

consistency and correctness of the changes (Andersson, 2000). Architecture has been employed as a basis for reconfiguration of self-healing systems, which support runtime management and reconfiguration of the systems without human interference (Qun, Xian-Chun, & Man-Wu, 2005). They expressed the reconfiguration of the architecture using a graph transformation technique. A graph has been used as the meta-model of the architecture to capture the structural information of the architecture. This meta-model guided the validation of changes introduced to the system. Moreover, they have employed the high-level system architecture to detect system anomalies and to identity architectural constraints which aid in governing the changes in architecture.

Harrison and Avgeriou (2007) proposed the systematic use of architecture patterns to help the architect satisfy changing quality attributes, and thus reduce the risk of later rework of systems. They have analyzed a set of architectural patterns, including pipe and filers, layered, and blackboard. The impacts on quality attributes that each architecture pattern can cause concisely were presented in order to aid software architects in understanding the implications of the architectural decisions. According to their work, each architecture style possesses strengths and weakness, and the selection a particular architectural style for a system should be ascribed to the quality attributes that the system should meet. Therefore, the capability of changing the architecture of a system, either dynamically or statically can enable the system to support the requirements of a greater variety of users. Menasce, Sousa, Malek, and Gomaa (2010) have also emphasized the role of architectural patterns in formulating an architecture that maximizes a utility function for a software system. They implemented autonomic system adaptation based on QoS (Quality of Service) patterns, where the system continuously monitors QoS goals and takes action automatically based on the attainment the QoS goals. Their work emphasized the importance of supporting multiple architectures for a system, especially the capability to change the architecture of the system with practical ease.

The research presented in this chapter also focuses on leveraging different architectural styles for several purposes. One reason is to support diverse quality attributes requirements of a wide range of users. Another reason is to counter and prevent *architectural erosion*. More importantly, it is to enhance the overall agility of a vendor.

A SYSTEMATIC APPROACH TO ACHIEVE LARGE SCALE REUSE ACROSS MULTIPLE ARCHITECTURES

In this section, we introduce a novel approach for attaining the goal of a well-planned reuse across software systems having different architectures. Firstly, we define the essential characteristics that make a component reusable in multiple systems. Secondly, we discuss the design principles and strategies that can be employed to construct a component with those characteristics. Next, we unfold a process for crafting such components. Finally, a new reuse architecture for building systems from reusable components is presented.

Although this research will only focus on component-based systems, we believe that most of the research's outcomes are applicable to various kinds of software systems. As the component based engineering has been employed successfully to create complex software systems such as middleware, application servers, we reckon our contribution is timely and valuable.

Multi-Architecture Reusable Components

We coined the term *Multi-Architecture Reusable Components* for the components which can be reused across multiple architectures. The very strict requirement for a well-planned reuse across different systems poses many requirements on a

Multi-Architecture Reusable Component in additions to the requirements for a component in a typical component-based system. In order to elicit them precisely, it is crucial to discover technical barriers to large-scale reuse. In this chapter, we consider two key barriers: *architectural mismatch* and *design (architectural) erosion.*

Architectural mismatch is primarily caused due to incompatibilities in assumptions about the nature of components, the nature of connectors, the global architectural structure, and the component construction process (Garlan, Allen, & John, 1995).The authors have suggested that careful consideration should go into building components, and have discussed four necessary aspects for a long-term solution: (1) making architectural assumptions explicit, (2) constructing large pieces of software using orthogonal sub-components, (3) providing techniques for bridging mismatches, and (4) developing sources of design guidance. We agreed with the last three solutions and employed them in this research. However, regarding the first solution, our view is the same as Shaw's (Shaw, 1995). We expected to utilize the diversity in the strengths of different architecture styles, the diversity in application domains, the diversity in the standards for component packaging, etc.

Design (architectural) erosion is the phenomenon in which the design of a system degrades gradually and finally becomes incompetent in responding adequately to the changing requirements. As the longevity of a reusable asset is paramount, it is crucial to address *design (architectural) erosion* successfully. It occurs chiefly because of four reasons: (1) inability to extract design decisions from the system (2) increasing maintenance cost, (3) conflicts in design decisions, and (4) incorporating unforeseen requirements. The separation of concerns, a model to express the design adequately, a stepwise process for refining designs, and effective refactoring can contribute to counter or prevent *design (architectural) erosion* (Gurp, 2002).

To be able to prevent both *architectural mismatch* and *design (architectural) erosion*, we devised a set of requirements for a reusable component. Among them, we consider following six requirements essential. The requirements are carefully selected so that a component can evolve independently, and can be reused 'as-is' in different architectures with the required quality attributes in addition to counter the aforementioned technical bottlenecks to systematic reuse.

1. **Autonomous:** Because a *Multi-Architecture Reusable Component* is to be reused 'as-is' in different architectures, it should be well-defined, self-contained, and should not depend on the context or state of other components or the systems that would use it. The autonomy of a component can also enhance modifiability dramatically, and is inevitable to better support reuse (Medvidovic, Oreizy, & Taylor, 1997).

2. **Strict Modifiability:** As many different systems possibly use a particular *Multi-Architecture Reusable Component*, the functional changes introduced to the component for supporting requirements of one or more products, cannot affect most of the other products. The very strict modifiability of a *Multi-Architecture Reusable Component* can make modifying systems transparent to each other.

3. **Adaptable to Multiple Architectures:** A component to be used in a particular architecture, it should be a type of the component that the architecture expects. As a *Multi-Architecture Reusable Component* is a generic component, to use it in systems having different architectures, it should be transformed transparently into a component of a target system's architecture. Moreover, the component adaptation should be simple, and should not incur negative effects on a system's quality attributes.

4. **Composable with Multiple Architectures:** Component-based systems have component models to assemble their components, and their architectures determine the component models. As *Multi-Architecture Reusable Components* are to be used in different architectures, the flexibility to assemble them based on a variety of architectural styles is inevitable. This requirement allows a particular product to use either the same component model of the product or a different component model to structure the *Multi-Architecture Reusable Components*. More importantly, it allows changing the architecture of a product with ease, making it possible to deal with *architectural erosion* successfully.

5. **Software Quality Attributes Configurable:** Developing multiple products reusing the *Multi-Architecture Reusable Components* may not be successful if a *Multi-Architecture Reusable Component* cannot provide the qualities required by each product. It is vital to support the qualities such as performance, scalability, etc., required by different products in various granularities and mixes such as low performance - high scalability, high performance - high reliability, and so on. The requirement is to have a design that can be configured to achieve the desired qualities in appropriate levels. Supporting this requirement for a *Multi-Architecture Reusable Component* is challenging due to the conflicts in qualities. For example, some tactics used to provide a high reliability may lower performance and make achieving the combination of high performance - high reliability impossible.

6. **Strict Extensibility:** A design of a *Multi-Architecture Reusable Component* should be flexible to incorporate variation points, which are the places that can be tailored to a particular product in preplanned ways. The strict extensibility promotes additive

Figure 1. The high-level design of a multi-architecture reusable component

changes and can support to preclude invasive changes.

Developing Multi-Architecture Reusable Components

This section discusses our approach for designing and implementing the *Multi-Architecture Reusable Components* in a manner that their primary requirements presented in the previous section are successfully met. In our research, we developed eight components namely log, crypto, caching, load balance, exception handling, monitoring, persistence, and proxy. The log component is used in our discussion of the component development process, and the cache component will be described separately in detail in chapter *Reuse across ESB Systems*.

Design Principles

Among design strategies and principles for supporting the requirements for a *Multi-Architecture Reusable Component*, we consider the following two essential.

Strict Separation of Concerns (SoC)

The principles of SoC can be leveraged to support most of the requirements of a *Multi-Architecture Reusable Component*. Additionally, SoC can potentially counter *design erosion* (Gurp, 2002). The coupling between a component and systems determines the component's reusability in the systems. By eliminating this coupling, a component can be made autonomous, adaptable to

and composable with multiple architectures, and reusable in any system variation.

For a long-term reuse of a *Multi-Architecture Reusable Component*, its foundation design should be sustainable. It should allow additive changes and avoid invasive changes. The tactics to support the long-term reuse can be identified from the relationship between two well-known concepts: abstraction and concrete implementation. An abstract separates an object's essential behavior from its implementation, and allows changing its implementation transparently (Booch, 1994). Therefore, by identifying an abstraction that represents the *Multi-Architecture Reusable Component* as *a whole*, and by incorporating concrete functionalities as the implementations of the abstraction, the design of a *Multi-Architecture Reusable Component* can be made durable. The idea is to separate the functionalities of the *Multi-Architecture Reusable Component* into two layers: abstract and concrete. Moreover, we have the same view as Bass, Clements, and Kazman's (2003) about the quality attributes and functionalities. They are orthogonal and the design decisions taken for implementing functionality will determine the relative level of quality. The quality attributes should be incorporated into the concrete layer of a component's functionalities. For that purpose, the concrete layer was divided into two orthogonal segments. Figure 1 depicts the high-level design for a *Multi-Architecture Reusable Component*.

The foundation design encapsulates the minimum requirements for supporting the simplest yet a complete behavior of a *Multi-Architecture Reusable Component*. It does not contain any concrete functionality. All design strategies for supporting the requirements of quality attributes or concrete functionality should be incorporated into the design as the implementations of the abstractions provided in the foundation design. More precisely, there are extensibility points to the foundational design. The clean separation among the abstraction that represents the component as a whole, its concrete functionalities, and its qualities, supports achieving a great deal of modifiability for a component. Moreover, the foundation design forms the abstraction for the kernel of a component and acts as the high level architecture for a component.

Although some software qualities such as performance and reliability have conflicts, we observed that it is possible to separate the architectural tactics, which are taken to support each quality, from each other. The clean separation between the tactics supporting qualities significantly underpins dealing with the conflicts in qualities successfully. Moreover, multiple tactics for supporting the same quality attribute should be implemented as it allows selecting the most suitable set of tactics to deal with conflicting qualities.

Incorporating required changes around a stable kernel has been employed in some research. Jegadeesan and Balasubramaniam (2009) support the configurability and reusability of a SaaS service by integrating additional requirements as variation points into the kernel of the service. Furthermore, dynamic architecture based approaches for adapting a system for supporting new requirements use a high level architecture of the system to govern the modifications to the system (Crnkovic & Larsson, 2002). We leveraged the same concept - the foundation design of the *Multi-Architecture Reusable Component* is to guide its implementations. The foundation design merely mandates the abstractions that should be implemented to provide a complete behavior for a component. It does not hinder in achieving any software quality attribute, but support to deal with tradeoffs among qualities by aptly employing SoC principles.

Feature Model

Feature modeling is a domain analysis technique, which analyzes the commonality and variability in a particular domain. A feature model visually represents the commonality and variability of the domain (Beuche, Papajewski, & Schröder-Preikschat, 2004). The usage of the feature model in our approach can be broadly divided into two use cases: variability and commonality model (V & C model) and dealing with the feature interaction.

1. **Variability and Commonality Model (V & C model):** A feature model concisely defines the requirements of a *Multi-Architecture Reusable Component* in terms of features. In the component design process, it facilitates separating the abstractions from their concrete variations distinctly. In the product development process, it facilitates creating individualized products. A feature model can also facilitate tracing design decisions from the design. Furthermore, a V & C model can maximize the reusability of a component and can serve as a meta-model for modeling a component (La & Kim, 2009).

2. **Dealing with the Feature Interaction:** The feature interaction is the interference between features, and it occurs when the behavior of one feature is affected by the behavior of another feature or another instance of the same feature (Calder & Magill, 2000). A feature interaction can possibly impact negatively on either the software development or the customer satisfaction. As discussed in the high-level design for a *Multi-Architecture Reusable Component* (Figure 1), the abstraction that represents the component as *a whole*, its concrete functionalities, and its qualities are clearly separated from each other. Furthermore, a particular functionality is divided into discrete and orthogonal functions. These design decisions make it possible to reduce

Figure 2. Feature model notations

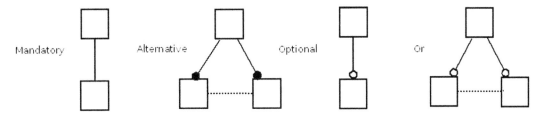

negative effects on the system development due to the feature interaction.

To reduce the negative effects of the feature interaction on the customer satisfaction, the feature models of the *Multi-Architecture Reusable Components* can be used. In the feature models, the complex interactions among features are visible. Furthermore, the abstraction and the concrete variations of a feature are distinguishable. The strategy is to identify conflicting features of a *Multi-Architecture Reusable Component* using its feature model. If the feature interaction results in the conflicts in quality attributes, as discussed in the previous subsection, the strategy of separating the architectural tactics, which are taken to support each quality, can be applied. If the feature interaction results in the conflicts in functionalities, a feasible approach is to avoid selecting those features. It can be done partly when an instance of a *Multi-Architecture Reusable Component* is created and configured. Further research is required to enforce the correct selection of features.

Figure 2 shows the notations we use in the feature models this chapter presents.

Mandatory – child feature is required. *Alternative* – one of the sub-features must be selected. *Optional* – child feature is optional. *Or* – at least one of the sub-features must be selected.

Feature modeling has been used in some research in constructing reusable components. FORM (Feature-Oriented Reuse Method) (Kang, Kim, Lee, Kim, Shin, & Huh, 1998) is a systematic method that employs the feature model to capture commonalties and differences of applications, and to formulate domain artifacts including reusable functional components and the applications using the domain artifacts. It also has used feature models to identify complex feature interactions. For the same purposes, we employed feature models in the components and systems formulation processes presented in this chapter.

Design Concepts

This section explores two design concepts introduced to form the foundation for implementing *Multi-Architecture Reusable Components*.

Data Access Model

By separating a component from the target systems' architectures, it is possible to make the component autonomous. For that purpose, based on the work of Crnkovic and Larsson (2002), we studied the essential behavior of a component in a component-based system. A component provides some kinds of service, which is configurable through the component' configuration, and is accessible through a well-defined interface. When a set of components are collaborating, a particular component performs a specific operation(s) based on the request received from another component, and produces a result and calls another component with the result. This behavior of a component-based system can be viewed as a transit of a data context among the components where each component modifies the data context. This observation led us to select the abstraction of a data processor for a *Multi-Architecture Reusable Component*. The

Figure 3. The design of the data access model

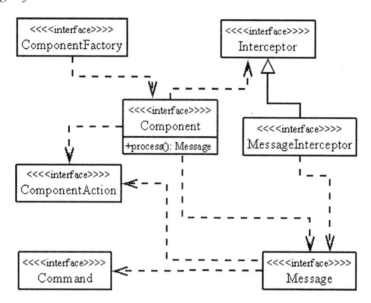

functionality of the *Multi-Architecture Reusable Component* can be distinctly divided into two discrete operations: data access operation and component operation. A concept of a data access model was introduced to design the data access operation. By making the *Multi-Architecture Reusable Component* depending only on the data access model (data access operation) to provide its service (component operation), the *Multi-Architecture Reusable Component* can be made autonomous. The design of the data access model is shown in Figure 3.

The data access model is chiefly based on two concepts: *Message* and *Interceptors*. Next sections discuss each ingredient of the data access model shown in Figure 3.

Message is to exchange the data among components and to make them loosely coupled. It leverages the Message pattern (Buschmann, Henney, & Schmidt, 2007), which provides a means of exchanging pieces of information without introducing dependencies on concrete component types and their interfaces. Message is also analogous to the asynchronous messages used in communicating among components in C2-style architectures (Medvidovic, Oreizy, &

Taylor, 1997). It is self-contained and is an independent unit of communication similar to the message concept used in the service-oriented architecture to model the communication among services (Erl, 2005).

The stability of the API of the data access model determines the reusability and the modifiability of a *Multi-Architecture Reusable Component*. A modification to the API can potentially make the functionalities of most components broken, and systems to suffer a ripple effect, whereby a modification in some part has unexpected and possibly dangerous effects overall. In order to extend transparently the functionalities already provided by the data access layer, we introduced the concept of *Interceptors*. It is based on the Extension Interface pattern (Buschmann, Henney, & Schmidt, 2007), which supports exporting multiple interfaces by a component, and preventing bloating of interfaces and breaking of client code when developers extend or modify the functionality of an existing component. The already developed API is mostly not changed, and by a means of *Interceptors*, new APIs are added to the data access model.

Typically, the *Command* shown in Figure 3 encapsulates a retryable operation such as database access. It is used to exchange internal requests among *Multi-Architecture Reusable Components* in a loosely coupled manner. For example, to retry for failures in database access, the persistence component can send a database access operation as a *Command* to the error handler component. The *Command* allows achieving a desired level of separation of concerns and reuse.

The data access model provides two categories of data: runtime and static. The runtime data is provided by a means of a *Message*, whereas the static data is populated when the *ComponentFactory* creates an instance of a *Multi-Architecture Reusable Component* using the component's configuration. The *ComponentAction* shown in Figure 3 encapsulates an operation of a *Component* in terms of the operation name and the parameters to be used in the operation. Although the *ComponentAction* for a *Multi-Architecture Reusable Component* is specified in its configuration, it can also be provided through the *Message*. The latter option for providing the *ComponentAction* allows changing the operation of the *Multi-Architecture Reusable Component* dynamically. By leveraging the *ComponentAction* and the *Command*, with the help of the other *Multi-Architecture Reusable Components*, a particular component can perform the operations that it cannot do itself alone.

The data access model provides the autonomy and a considerable level of modifiability and adaptability for a component.

Intuitive Requirement

As per the discussion in section *Design Principles*, the modifiability of a *Multi-Architecture Reusable Component* is largely attributed to the stability and extensibility of its foundation design. To achieve that, our strategy was to identify an abstraction representing the component as *a whole*, and to model all behaviors as concrete implementations of the abstraction. In order to identify the abstraction for a component, we introduced the concept of *Intuitive Requirement*. By *Intuitive*

Requirement, we mean the high-level requirements of a particular *Multi-Architecture Reusable Component* that obviously can be identified as the minimal requirements to provide a useful service for at least one system from a set of systems. It represents the simplest yet a complete behavior of a component, and captures the mandatory features of a component. More precisely, it captures invariant commonalities that must be in any variation of a particular component.

Multi-Architecture Reusable Component Development Methodology

This section discusses the development methodology for *Multi-Architecture Reusable Components*. The primary outcomes of the process are a design, a feature model, and an implementation. Figure 4 depicts the process.

Next subsections discuss each step in the process shown in Figure 4 in detail.

Identifying and Refining Intuitive Requirement

We observed that eliciting *Intuitive Requirement* for a *Multi-Architecture Reusable Component* requires an abstract reasoning about the behaviors of the component in the target context. The gathered *Intuitive Requirement* should be refined until it represents the simplest yet a complete behavior, and does not contain any concrete information. The process of identifying and refining the *Intuitive Requirement* for the log component is discussed in the following. The initial *Intuitive Requirement* for the log component can be stated as follows.

"Generates logs and saves the generated logs"

The above requirement is complete and is the simplest behavior for a logging component for most systems. However, it contains a concrete term – *save*. The saving is only a single operation that can be applied on the generated logs. For example, the logs can be sent to remote log

Figure 4. Multi-architecture reusable component development methodology

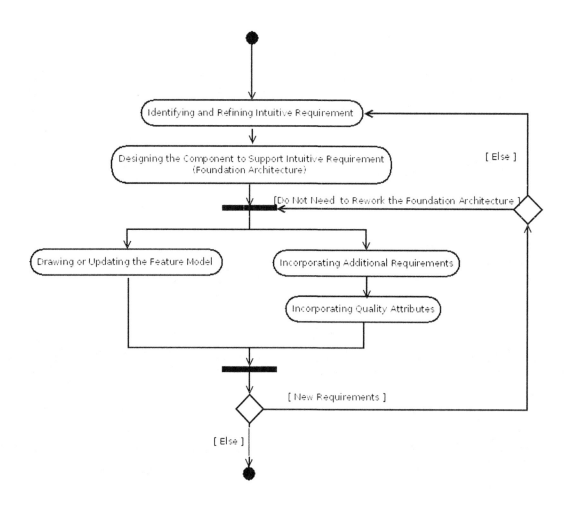

analyzers. The concrete term *"save"* should be replaced by an abstract term (here *"process"*).

"Generates logs and processes the generated logs"

The next step in the refinement process is to apply the principles of separation of concerns to divide the requirement into orthogonal functionalities. The above requirement clearly has two orthogonal functionalities: the generation of logs and the processing of the generated logs. The final step in the refinement process is to compose the orthogonal functionalities in a loosely coupled manner. The foregoing strategy makes it possible

to derive loosely coupled abstractions for the foundation design from the *Intuitive Requirement*.

"Logs are generated and the generated logs are transported into the destinations, which process the logs."

In the above requirement, we have used the concept of a transport to compose the generation of logs and the processing of the generated logs in a loosely coupled manner. The above *Intuitive Requirement* is the abstraction for the log component, and represents the invariant commonality or the mandatory features for it.

Designing the Component to Support its Intuitive Requirement

Based on the *Intuitive Requirement*, the foundation design for a *Multi-Architecture Reusable Component* is formulated. To achieve a desired level of modifiability for the component, the principles of information hiding and separation of concerns should be employed. As the *Intuitive Requirement* is simple and considerably stable, the foundation design of a component is simple and sustainable. Moreover, because the foundation design consisted of loosely coupled and orthogonal abstractions, changing the design is economically and practically feasible.

Drawing or Updating the Feature Model

A feature model can be used to present the commonality and variability of a *Multi-Architecture Reusable Component*. The component design process uses the feature model appropriately to identify the variation points for the design. When creating the feature model for a *Multi-Architecture Reusable Component*, the first step is to identify the mandatory features based on the *Intuitive Requirement*. Secondly, based on a domain analysis for the component, the feature model is updated. The domain analysis is an iterative process. The new features added to the main abstraction of the component are always optional. The design of a component should support the realization of the feature model of the component. Moreover, incorporating quality attributes or additional requirements (next steps) may result in a new feature or updating an existing feature.

Incorporating Additional Requirements

The abstraction for a *Multi-Architecture Reusable Component* represents the *Intuitive Requirement*, and we identify any modification to it as a concrete variation of the abstraction. For example, the replacing of the verb *"processes"* with *"saves"* in the log component's *Intuitive Requirement* forms a concrete variation.

"Logs are generated and the generated logs are transported into the destinations, which saves the logs."

As discussed in the previous sections, any concrete variation is incorporated into the foundation design as an extensibility point. Therefore, the *"saves"* is added to the design as a variation of the abstraction that presents *"processes"* in the design.

Incorporating Quality Attributes

Another challenge in designing a core asset for multiple products is supporting quality attributes requirements of different products. For example, a system designed for providing a high reliability may require the *Multi-Architecture Reusable Components* designed for providing a high reliability; a system designed for supporting a high performance may require the *Multi-Architecture Reusable Components* designed for supporting a high performance. The conflicts in the quality requirements for a component are obvious. As per the discussion in previous sections, our strategy to deal with conflicting qualities is to identify orthogonal architectural strategies to provide the qualities, and to incorporate them into the foundation design as extension points. To identify the required qualities, the foundation design is refined using a quality attribute analysis. As a particular component has to support quality requirements of many products, we defined a comprehensive set of quality attributes based on the work by Bass, Clements, and Kaman (2003). The procedure for refining the design can be intuitively divided into two steps. The first step is to select a set of applicable qualities from the complete quality attributes list. Secondly, for each quality attribute in the selected list, the architectural tactics that can be used to support the quality with wide-ranging levels such as low, high, etc., are identified and implemented. This process is performed whenever a requirement is changed or added, to ensure that

Figure 5. The basic design of the log component

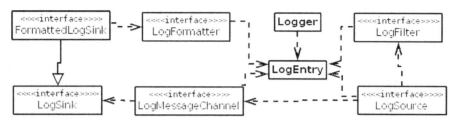

the software qualities would not be negatively affected by the changes.

When adding a new requirement, the first step is to examine carefully whether the changes in the foundation architecture are required. Secondly, based on the outcome of the aforementioned evaluation, the development process is reinitiated from either the first step or the third step. By developing eight components and using 'as-is' them in two middleware systems, we observed that the foundation design resulted from the *Intuitive Requirement* is stable. It is ascribed to the fact that the foundation design reflects the minimum yet complete behavior and does not impede achieving any quality attribute. Moreover, our strategy of adding a new requirement as a part of a concrete implementation or extension of the foundation design is also contributed to the sustainability of the design.

The resultant artifacts from the development process of the log component are shown in Figure 5 and Figure 6.

Figure 5 shows only the primary abstractions used in the design of the log component. *Logger*

generates *LogEntries*, and then performs the filtering on the generated logs. *LogEntry* represents a log message. *LogSource* is a destination for raw *LogEntries* and routes them to log sinks through a *LogMessageChannel*. *LogSinks* are the destinations for raw *LogEntries*, and uses *LogFormatters* to format the content of the *LogEntries* before doing its operations such as saving a log entry in a database.

The abstractions of *LogSink, LogMessageChannel, LogSource,* and *LogEntry* were derived from the *Intuitive Requirement*, and collectively form the foundation design for the log component. In the quality attribute analysis phase, to support desired performance, we implemented the log generation as a staged process where each stage performs a filtering log records based on the content of the raw *LogEntries*. For that purpose, we introduced *LogFilter* abstraction. As *LogEntries* should be presented in a format suitable to analyze, the *LogFormatter* was also incorporated into the log component's design.

Figure 6 shows the feature diagram for the log component. As per the *Intuitive Requirement*

Figure 6. The feature diagram of the log component

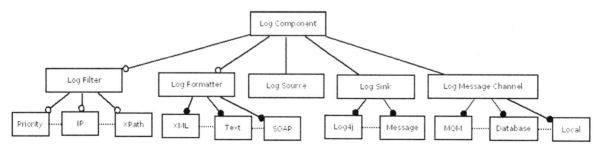

of the log component, the mandatory features of the log component are log sources that generate logs, a medium to transport the generated logs, and destinations, which process the logs. Based on a domain analysis for a logging, we chose the variation points for the log component as log sources, log filters, log sinks, log formatters, and log message channels. The feature diagram and the design are so similar that both artifacts can be derived from each other. As shown in Figure 6 there are two log sinks: *Log4J* and *Message*. The *log4J*-based log sink is used an open source logger library called Log4J. The message log sink enables the log component to send log messages to the other components in the system. For example, in order to implement secure logging, a log component can send the log records to a security component.

In order to demonstrate how the conflicts in quality attributes of the log component can be surmounted, we consider two software qualities: security and performance. These qualities inevitably inhibit each other. For instance, applying security operation such as encryption on a log message negatively affects on the runtime performance of the system. However, in our approach, as the architectural tactics for supporting qualities are clearly separated from each other, the tradeoff among qualities can be successfully confronted. For example, by using a queue-based *LogMessageChannel* to transport raw log messages, it is possible to implement the passive logging to minimize logging overhead. In the passive logging, the processing of the log messages is performed in a different thread or a process, reducing the negative effects of the runtime performance. The passive logging makes supporting security without hindering the performance is a trivial task.

Building Systems Using Multi-Architecture Reusable Components

In this section, we discuss the development and evolution of different component-based systems reusing the *Multi-Architecture Reusable Components*.

Solution Space: Reuse Architecture

A software system provides some kinds of solutions. An EAI middleware provides application integration solutions; A BPM middleware supports the automation of business processes. Multiple systems collectively form a solution space, which can provide wide-ranging solutions, compared with a single system. Based on the concept of the solution space, this section presents an approach for building multiple systems using the *Multi-Architecture Reusable Components*. The primary goal of the approach is to enable a large-scale reuse across multiple systems and to provide the flexibility to develop and evolve the systems cost and time effectively. The solution space builds a strong context for reuse and enforces the development of any component as a reusable component, even if the component would only be used by a single system. With our process for developing reusable components, formulating a component for a well-planned reuse does not incur any cost. Indeed, it saves cost and time if the component would be reused by new systems as time pass. Moreover, a component reusable across systems dramatically increases the agility of the organization as it makes practicable reforming an existing system or building a new system to meet changing requirements.

The solution space is separated into two subspaces (layers): abstract solution space and concrete solution space. The abstract solution space is built top on the concrete solution space. The main goal of this division is to achieve a total reuse of concrete functionalities, which typically is the largest part of the source code of a system. Additionally, all other artifacts associated with concrete components (solutions), including documents, designs, and people are reusable across systems. More precisely, the main goal is to develop and evolve different systems only reusing the concrete

Figure 7. The architecture of the solution space

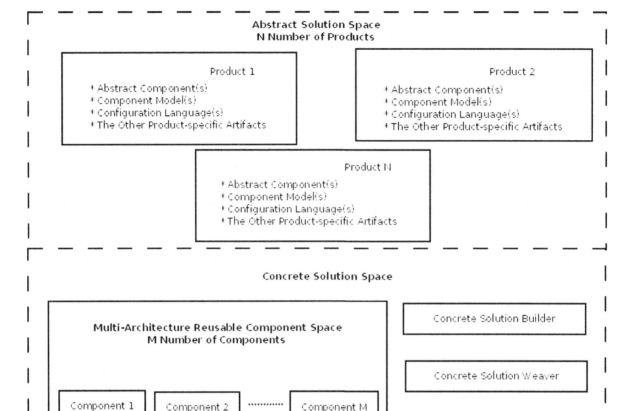

solution space. Furthermore, the division of the solution space allows evolving each sub-space independently. The high-level structure of the solution space is shown in Figure 7. The solution space can be implemented with different technologies. The chapter *Reuse across ESB Systems* will discuss an implementation for the ESB domain to formulate ESB products reusing the same set of ESB services.

As shown in Figure 7, a product, which is the main ingredient of the abstract solution space, primarily consists of a component model, an abstract component, and a configuration language for defining the solutions offered by the product. A product may also have product-specific artifacts

such as documents describing the configuration language of the product. The abstract solution space can have an arbitrary number of products. An arbitrary number of *Multi-Architecture Reusable Components*, a concrete solution definition language, a concrete solution builder and a concrete solution weaver constitute the concrete solution space. Next sections discuss each ingredient of the solution space in detail.

Abstract Solution Space

The abstract solution space consists of a set of products. The mandatory artifacts for each product are an abstract component, a component model, and a configuration language. However, a product may consist of several modules where each module may have a separate component model and a configuration. A particular product or module creates a skeleton of a solution by assembling the instances of the abstract components according to the component model of the product or module. The solution is declaratively defined by the product or module's configuration. In other words, the abstraction solution space is to be used for modeling end-user solutions.

Abstract Component (Skeleton Component)

An abstract component defines a particular functionality abstractly. It should be a type of the component of the target system (or module). We named the abstract component as *Skeleton Component*. A skeleton component implements the interfaces mandated by the target product's (module) architecture but does nothing in the implementation. Typically, an ideal skeleton component has empty functions but in practice, it may have internal or generic functions that are mandated by the architecture. Mostly, a particular product variation only needs a single skeleton component. A JBI skeleton component for a JBI based ESB; a SCA skeleton component for a SCA based ESB and so on.

At runtime or startup time, a skeleton component is augmented with the required functionality to provide a meaningful service. It is achieved through replacing a skeleton component's instance with a concrete solution. The first step in the replacement process is to locate the correct instance of the skeleton component. For that purpose, the skeleton component should be addressable. This can be easily done using the configuration of a product (module). As a skeleton component does not contain any functionality, and mostly, the configuration of the skeleton component only specifies the information required to identify it uniquely, such as "*name*", "*type*", etc.

Component Model

A component-based system uses a component model to assemble its components and the architecture of the system determines the component model. Typically, the implementation of the architecture is the implementation of the component model. For a JBI based ESB, it is the JBI component model; for a SCA based ESB, it is the SCA component model, and so on.

Configuration Language

Both skeleton components and their compositions should be declarative as it enables to define a solution using a configuration mechanism. Therefore, each system should have a configuration language. If systems are based on open standards such as BPEL (Business Process Execution Language), SCA (Service Component Architecture), etc., the configuration languages should be the corresponding standards.

Concrete Solution Space

The main ingredients of the concrete solution space are *Multi-Architecture Reusable Components*, a concrete solution builder, a concrete solution weaver, and a language for defining concrete solutions.

Identifying Multi-Architecture Reusable Components

The identification of *Multi-Architecture Reusable Components* should consider new products as well as exiting products. For that purpose, the feature model and the principles of separation of concerns (SoC) can be employed. Figure 8 depicts the *Multi-Architecture Reusable Component* identification process. It is an iterative process and is performed for each product. The goal of the process is to identify the foundation services that a particular product is built upon.

As per Figure 8, a feature model for a product is created using either its feature list or its require-

Figure 8. The multi-architecture reusable component identification process

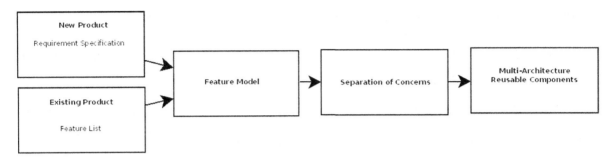

Figure 9. A part of a feature diagram for an ESB

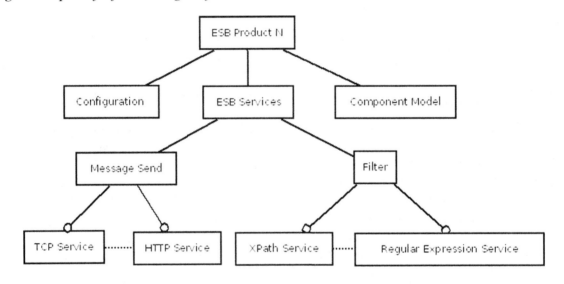

ment specification. In a feature model of a particular product, it is possible to identity product-specific abstractions and the foundation services that the product-specific abstractions are built upon. This separation is typically not visible in a feature list, and for that reason, we use a feature model. Figure 9 shows part of a feature model for an ESB.

In Figure 9, the feature *Message Send* is an ESB-specific feature and employs communication services such as HTTP, TCP, etc. Those communication services are foundation services that can be possibly reused by many products. We encapsulate the foundation services as *Multi-Architecture Reusable Components*. From the *Filter* feature, regular expression and XPath (XML Path Language) foundation services can be identified as *Multi-Architecture Reusable Components*. It is important to note that the abstraction for a foundation service is ascribed to the systems that are built upon the foundation services. For instance, although the HTTP service is a foundation service for an ESB, it is not a foundation service for a system that implements HTTP; instead, the foundation services for such a product would be byte buffering, string parsing, socket connection pooling, and so on. Irrespective of the type of products, a feature model offers an apt means of discerning foundation services in suitable abstractions.

Upon the completion of the *Multi-Architecture Reusable Component* identification process for each product, the concrete solution space is populated with the implementation of each identified unique component. The feature model of a product is also saved into the abstract solution space so that it can be used later to customize the product based on features.

Concrete Solution Builder

This component is responsible for the formation of concrete solutions, which are composites of the instances of the *Multi-Architecture Reusable Components*. Since in our approach, the products in the abstract solution space are component-based systems, employing a component-based approach in building concrete solutions is most appropriate. The solution builder can structure *Multi-Architecture Reusable Components* based on a component model, which can be explicitly given. The main advantage is the capability to use the component model of the product to compose *Multi-Architecture Reusable Components*. Furthermore, the strengths of different architectural styles can be leveraged. Moreover, the flexibility to change the system architecture makes it possible to counter *architectural erosion*. The chapter *Reuse across ESB Systems* will discuss an implementation of a concrete solution builder.

Concrete Solution Weaver

The required end-user solution is formed by weaving its concrete solutions to its abstract solutions transparently at runtime or startup time. A concrete solution should not be aware of the target products and should be reusable 'as-is' in different systems. Since this composition should also be suitable for a component-based system, the most adequate approach for it should be a component-based approach. For attaining that goal, the design decision was to modify the component model of the product transparently. For that purpose, we introduced the concept of a *Proxy* based on the Proxy design pattern, to transform an instance of a skeleton (abstract) component into a functional

component of the target product. The *Proxy* exports the same interfaces as the skeleton component and the logic inside the proxy is merely the execution of the *Multi-Architecture Reusable Components'* composites formulated by the concrete solution builder. The functionality of the solution weaver can be broadly divided into three steps: locating an instance of the skeleton component, creating an instance of the *Proxy*, replacing the skeleton component's instance with the *Proxy*'s instance. This composition is transparent as the *Proxy* and the skeleton component implement the same interfaces. Upon the completion of the solution weaving, the component model of a product consists of the instances of the *Proxy*, instead of the instances of the skeleton component.

Concrete Solution Definition Language

A definition for a *Multi-Architecture Reusable Component* is a meta-data describing the resources need to implement its functionality. For example, the configuration information for a logging component would include the log filtering mechanism, the destination for log records, etc. As a concrete solution can be a single component or a composite of components, the language should be capable of expressing composition semantics declaratively. Moreover, as a final (required) solution is formulated by merging its concrete solutions and its abstraction solutions, the language should also be able to express merging semantics. Furthermore, because the language is to be used by every product, it should not reflect the abstractions related to a particular product.

Implementing Solutions

The first step in implementing a particular end-user solution is to identify and to separate its abstract solution from its concrete solution. Secondly, both the abstract solution and the concrete solution are implemented. Finally, the required solution is formed by composing the concrete solution to the abstract solution transparently. Although, an end-user solution may involve more than one product, in this section, we only consider a single product.

Step 1: Selecting a Suitable Product(s)

In implementing a solution, the first step is to select a suitable product(s). For instance, a BPM system is for implementing a business process; an ESB is for implementing an EAI solution; a Web Service engine is for exposing an application as a Web Service and so on.

Step 2: Building Abstract Solutions

An abstract ESB solution consists of one or more instances of the skeleton (abstract) component of a product. Each instance defines a particular functionality abstractly and the solution would be a composition of the instances according to the component model of the product. The configuration language of the product defined the instances of the skeleton component and their compositions. As discussed in section *Abstract Solution Space*, a skeleton component only needs to define some means that can be used to identify uniquely the instances of the skeleton component. For instance, if the product uses an XML configuration, then the abstraction solution for accessing a database can be defined as in Figure 10.

In Figure 10, the *component* tag is the configuration of the skeleton component, and is used to define the abstract solutions. By only changing the *name* attribute, a set of different solutions abstractly can be defined. The *DataAccessor* may be a complex service – it may be a composition of cache, security and persistence. Mostly, to define each service, several parameters such as database driver, connection URL, cache storage, etc., are required. In our approach, those details are not part of the abstraction solutions; those are in the concrete solutions. Therefore, our approach abstracts out not only the concrete functionalities but also the concrete configuration information. That allows non-technical stakeholders such as

Figure 10. An example for an abstract solution

```
<component name="DataAccessor" />
```

business analysts, to participate in modeling end-user solutions.

Step 3: Building Concrete Solutions

The building block of a concrete solution is the *Multi-Architectures Reusable Component*; the instances of components are composed according to a given component model to form a concrete solution. The concrete solution definition language is used to define concrete solutions. As discussed in section *Concrete Solution Space*, the language specifies components, how they should be composed to form concrete solutions, and how concrete solutions should be weaved into abstraction solutions. The first step in building concrete solutions is to define the required concrete solutions using the language. Secondly, by executing the concrete solution builder with the configuration of the concrete solutions, the concrete solutions are formulated.

Step 4: Weaving Concrete Solutions to Abstract Solutions

After the formation of the concrete solutions is completed, the concrete solution weaver composes the abstraction solutions and the concrete solutions to form the required end-user solution. Firstly, the weaver parses the concrete solution definition language and extracts the identifiers for the abstraction solutions. Secondly, using the extracted identifiers, the weaver locates the correct instances of the skeleton component from the instance of the component model of the product that has implemented the abstraction solutions. Finally, it creates *Proxies* encapsulating concrete solutions, and replaces the instances of the skeleton component with the created *Proxy*'s instances appropriately. It is important to note that an identifier is a text value, and is typically the name of an instance of the skeleton component. For example, the identifier to locate the *DataAccessor* skeleton component shown in Figure 10 should be *DataAccessor*.

As concrete solutions are independent of the products in the abstract solution space, and use only the identifiers of skeleton components' instances, a particular concrete solution can be reused 'as-is' in another product. For example, a concrete solution formed for a JBI based ESB is reusable 'as-is' in another ESB. This capability of our approach makes it possible to change the products with practical and economical ease.

Product Development and Evolution

Since with the approach proposed in this chapter, the artifacts in the concrete solution space are reusable 'as-is', mostly, the development of a new product will be economically feasible. A new product requires the mandatory artifacts in the abstract solution space: a skeleton (abstract) component, a component model, and the configuration language. The implementations of a *Proxy* and the data access model, and the code to perform the concrete solution building and weaving programmatically are also required. We observed that implementing the foregoing artifacts is only a trivial task. If the product should conform to a specification such as BPEL (Business Process Execution Language), the development of the configuration language and component model of the product may require some efforts. However, it is possible to leverage open source products to reduce such efforts. For example, it may be practical to take an open source BPEL engine and to refractor it.

The evolution of a product can be done by modifying the artifacts in either the abstract or the concrete solution spaces. A product can change its architecture and the configuration language, or

(and) it can evolve merely with the enhancements in the *Multi-Architecture Reusable components*.

Evaluation

We implemented the solution space discussed in this chapter and will present our implementation in chapter *Reuse across ESB Systems*. For the evaluation of the implementation, we did two case studies, which employ the proposed approach in two open source middleware systems: Apache Synapse ESB (2008) and Apache Axis2 Web Service engine (2009). To use our approach in those products, each product only needed the implementations of the data access model, a proxy and a skeleton component. There was no refactoring in either product. The case study with Synapse involved twenty-two scenarios, and the chapter *Reuse across ESB Systems* presents and discusses those.

The case study with Axis2 involved the scenarios 1, 2, 3, 4, 5, 7, 8, 11, and 12 of the case study done for Synapse ESB. As other scenarios used a few synapse native components, we could not implement those scenarios with Axis2. Furthermore, some ESB specific scenarios were unsuitable for Axis2. The key observation from the case studies was that we could reuse not only *Multi-Architecture Reusable Components* but also the concrete solutions formulated for Synapse ESB in Axis2.

Reusability

Multi-Architecture Reusable Components and most of the concrete solutions were reused in two different products 'as-is'. We used the same component in multiple scenarios with different types of the other components. Furthermore, we reused the architectures, the languages of both Axis2 and Synapse, and some Synapse components 'as-is'.

Modifiability

The concrete solution space and the abstract solution space are orthogonal to each other, and due to that, each can evolve independently. The two case studies manifest that. The concrete solutions were reused 'as-is' in two different products, which implies that our approach enables to change products (the abstract solution space) without affecting the concrete solution space. Furthermore, most of the *Multi-Architecture Reusable Components* have provided diverse features. All these features have implemented as extensibility points for the foundation design. They are orthogonal and the modifications are local to a particular feature implementation. All of these design decisions are attributed to our *Multi-Architecture Reusable Component* development methodology, including design principles, concepts, and the process.

Flexibility

From the case studies, it is apparent that by developing all functionalities Synapse and Axis2 need as *Multi-Architecture Reusable Components*, our approach can support the solutions they provide. It implies that both products can be refactored or re-implemented as new products to use our approach. As discussed in this chapter, with our approach, developing a new system or evolving an existing system is significantly cost and time effective. Hence, our approach can aptly offer the flexibility required to produce a new product and to change an existing product with economic and practical ease.

CONCLUSION

A systematic reuse across systems will be the driving force in the development of products that are heterogeneous yet sharing significant commonality. For that matter, a strategic software reuse will remain the prime factor that decides the success in developing software systems.

This chapter has discussed a novel approach for developing and evolving multiple component-based systems reusing the same set of concrete functionalities. It is centered on the components reusable 'as-is' in component-based systems having different architectures. We coined the term *Multi-Architecture Reusable Components* for such components. We defined the essential characteristics which such a component must exhibit in order to underpin a systematic reuse across different systems, and discussed the design principles and strategies for supporting those characteristics. Moreover, a component development methodology was introduced to design and implement a *Multi-Architecture Reusable Component* in a way that its key properties are preserved. Our approach for reusing the *Multi-Architecture Reusable Components* in developing multiple component-based systems (products) is based on the concept of a *solution space*, which is further divided into two sub-spaces (layers): abstract solution space and concrete solution space. Products are in the abstract solution space. The concrete solution space mostly consists of the *Multi-Architecture Reusable Components*, a concrete solution definition language, a concrete solution builder, and a concrete solution weaver. The products can be developed and evolved by reusing the concrete solution space. An experiment with two middleware systems showed that our approach provided a systematic reuse across different component-based systems effectively.

FUTURE RESEARCH DIRECTIONS

As the section *Importance of Reuse across Multiple Architectures* indicated, there are considerable opportunities of exercising our work or any other work that addresses the systematic reuse across different systems in various research areas. We maintained that with our approach, a middleware platform supporting SOA (service-oriented architecture) can be developed with significant saving in time and cost. Furthermore, a developing a set of SaaS (software as a service) services in which each service focuses on a particular application domain is another research topic where the reuse across architectures can be employed. More importantly, multiple product lines, especially multiple product lines of SaaS services and SOA platforms inevitably require a well-planned reuse across systems having different architectures. As in contemporary research, the focus on SOA and cloud computing is increasingly high, the application of the software product line (SPL) in those spheres is promising.

The evaluation of the results of this research must also come to the forefront. Our component development methodology has to be tested in a considerable number of real word applications because we have only employed it to build eight components, and have used the components in two middleware systems. The reuse architecture we proposed in this research can be used in developing different types of software systems. The separation of concrete and abstraction solutions, developing each component for a strategic reuse, etc., must be validated by employing those concepts in different application domains. Moreover, how our approach for formulating reusable components can counter and prevent *architectural mismatch* and *design erosion* have to be systematically evaluated. More importantly, it would be a prime future work to enhance our platform for a production environment and to use it as a software product line platform.

In the final analysis, while many positive steps have been made in achieving a systematic reuse across software systems having diverse architectures, several research aspects remain open and must adequately be addressed in order to reduce the cost associated with the software development from existing components, and to increase an organization's overall agility.

REFERENCES

Aalst, W. M., & Hofstede, A. H. (2005). YAWL: Yet another workflow language. *Information Systems*, *30*(4), 245–275. doi:10.1016/j.is.2004.02.002

Altintas, N. I., & Cetin, S. (2008). Managing large scale reuse across multiple software product lines. *ICSR '08 Proceedings of the 10th International Conference on Software Reuse: High Confidence Software Reuse in Large Systems* (pp. 166 - 177). Heidelberg, Germany: Springer-Verlag Berlin.

Andersson, J. (2000). Issues in dynamic software architectures. In *Proceedings of the 4th International Software Architecture Workshop*, (pp. 111–114).

Axis2 Homepage. (2009). *Apache Axis2*. Retrieved June 8, 2010, from http://ws.apache.org/axis2/

Bass, L., Clements, P., & Kazman, R. (2003). *Software architecture in practice*. Addison-Wesley.

Bernhard, M. (2010). Stop the software architecture erosion: building better software systems. *SPLASH '10 Proceedings of the ACM International Conference Companion on Object Oriented Programming Systems Languages and Applications Companion* (pp. 129-138). New York, NY: ACM.

Beuche, D., Papajewski, H., & Schröder-Preikschat, W. (2004). Variability management with feature models. *Science of Computer Programming - Special Issue: Software Variability management*, 333-352.

Booch, G. (1994). *Object-oriented analysis and design*. Boston, MA: Addison-Wesley.

Buschmann, F., Henney, K., & Schmidt, D. C. (2007). *Pattern-oriented software architecture: A pattern language for distributed computing*. Boston, MA: Wiley & Sons.

Buyya, R., Yeo, C. S., Venugopal, S., Broberg, J., & Brandic, I. (2009). Cloud computing and emerging IT platforms: Vision, hype, and reality for delivering computing as the 5th utility. *Future Generation Computer Systems*, 599–616. doi:10.1016/j.future.2008.12.001

Calder, M., & Magill, E. (2000). *Feature interactions in telecommunications and software systems V*. Amsterdam, The Netherlands: IOS Press.

Chang, J. F. (2006). *Business process management systems*. New York: NY Auerbach.

Clements, P., & Northrop, L. (2001). *Software product lines: Practices and patterns*. Boston, MA: Addison-Wesley Professional.

Crnkovic, I., & Larsson, M. (2002). *Building reliable component-based software systems*. Norwood, NJ: Artech House.

Cumberlidge, M. (2007). *Business process management with JBoss jBPM: A practical guide for business analysts*. Olton, TX: Packt Publishing.

Erl, T. (2005). *Service-oriented architecture: Concepts, technology, and design*. Pearson Education.

Garlan, D., Allen, R., & John, O. (1995). Architectural mismatch: Why reuse is so hard. *IEEE Software*, *12*(6), 17–26. doi:10.1109/52.469757

Griss, M. L. (1999). Architecting for large-scale systematic component reuse. *ICSE '99 Proceedings of the 21st International Conference on Software Engineering* (pp. 615 - 616). New York, NY: ACM.

Gurp, J. (2002). Design erosion: Problems and causes. *Journal of Systems and Software*, *61*(2), 105–119. doi:10.1016/S0164-1212(01)00152-2

Harrison, N. B., & Avgeriou, P. (2007). *Leveraging architecture patterns to satisfy quality attributes*. University of Groningen. Research Institute for Mathematics and Computing Science.

Jegadeesan, H., & Balasubramaniam, S. (2009). A method to support variability of enterprise services on the cloud. *CLOUD '09 Proceedings of the 2009 IEEE International Conference on Cloud Computing* (pp. 117-124). Washington, DC: IEEE Computer Society.

Josuttis, N. M. (2007). *OA in practice: The art of distributed system design*. Sebastopol, CA: O'Reilly Media.

Kang, K. C., Kim, S., Lee, J., Kim, K., Shin, E., & Huh, M. (1998). FORM: A feature-oriented reuse method with domain-specific reference architectures. *Annals of Software Engineering*, 5.

Koehler, P., Anandasivam, A., & Dan, M. (2010). Cloud services from a consumer perspective. *AMCIS 2010 Proceedings*, (p. 329).

La, H. J., & Kim, S. D. (2009). A systematic process for developing high quality SaaS cloud services. *CloudCom '09 Proceedings of the 1st International Conference on Cloud Computing* (pp. 278 - 289). Heidelberg, Germany: Springer-Verlag.

Medvidovic, N., Oreizy, P., & Taylor, R. N. (1997). Reuse of off-the-shelf components in C2-style architectures. *SSR '97 Proceedings of the 1997 Symposium on Software Reusability* (pp. 190 - 198). New York, NY: ACM.

Mell, P., & Grance, T. (2009). *The NIST definition of cloud computing*. National Institute of Standards and Technology.

Menasce, D. A., Sousa, J. P., Malek, S., & Gomaa, H. (2010). Qos architectural patterns for self-architecting software systems. *ICAC '10 Proceeding of the 7th International Conference on Autonomic Computing* (pp. 195-204). New York, NY: ACM.

Mietzner, R. (2008). *Using variability descriptors to describe customizable SaaS application templates*. Fakultät Informatik: Universität Stuttgart.

Newton, K. (2007). *The definitive guide to the Microsoft enterprise library*. Berkeley, CA: Apress. doi:10.1007/978-1-4302-0315-5

Qun, Y., Xian-Chun, Y., & Man-Wu, X. (2005). A framework for dynamic software architecture-based self-healing. *ACM SIGSOFT Software Engineering Notes, 30*(4), 1–4. doi:10.1145/1082983.1083007

Rosen, M., Lublinsky, B., Smith, K. T., & Balcer, M. J. (2008). *Applied SOA: Service-oriented architecture and design strategies*. Indianapolis, IN: Wiley.

Shaw, M. (1995). Architectural issues in software reuse: it's not just the functionality, it's the packaging. *SSR '95 Proceedings of the 1995 Symposium on Software Reusability* (pp. 3-6). New York, NY: ACM.

Sun, W., Zhang, X., Guo, C. J., Sun, P., & Su, H. (2008). Software as a service: Configuration and customization perspectives. *SERVICES-2 '08 Proceedings of the 2008 IEEE Congress on Services Part II* (pp. 18-25). Washington, DC: IEEE Computer Society.

Synapse, E. S. B. Homepage. (2008). *Apache Synapse - The lightweight ESB*. Retrieved October 8, 2009, from http://synapse.apache.org/

Velte, T., Velte, A., & Elsenpeter, R. (2010). *Cloud computing: A practical approach*. New York, NY: McGraw-Hill.

ADDITIONAL READING

Clements, P., & Northrop, L. (2001). *Software product lines: Practices and patterns*. Boston, MA: Addison-Wesley Professional.

Crnkovic, I., & Larsson, M. (2002). *Building reliable component-based software systems*. Norwood, NJ: Artech House.

Erl, T. (2005). *Service-oriented architecture: Concepts, technology, and design*. Pearson Education.

Griss, M. L. (1999). Architecting for large-scale systematic component reuse. *ICSE '99 Proceedings of the 21st International Conference on Software Engineering* (pp. 615 - 616). New York, NY: ACM.

Harrison, N. B., & Avgeriou, P. (2007). *Leveraging architecture patterns to satisfy quality attributes*. University of Groningen. Research Institute for Mathematics and Computing Science.

Shaw, M. (1995). Architectural issues in software reuse: it's not just the functionality, it's the packaging. *SSR '95 Proceedings of the 1995 Symposium on Software Reusability* (pp. 3-6). New York, NY: ACM.

Sun, W., Zhang, X., Guo, C. J., Sun, P., & Su, H. (2008). Software as a service: Configuration and customization perspectives. *SERVICES-2 '08 Proceedings of the 2008 IEEE Congress on Services Part II* (pp. 18-25). Washington, DC: IEEE Computer Society.

Chapter 6

Software Development Using Service Syndication Based on API Handshake Approach between Cloud–Based and SOA–Based Reusable Services

Vishav Vir Singh
Intersil Corporation, USA

ABSTRACT

Reusability in the software development realm is a momentous cornerstone in deciding the success of an organization. The quantum leap in reusability was provided by object-orientation, which fundamentally altered the manner of thinking of software architects. The notion of the object and the installation of reusability as one of the central tenets is a critical requisite. Components that represented bigger and better software aggregates easily utilized by businesses to gain instant execution for their business services have made great strides. This gave way to the ultimate notion of a service which took software aggregates in components to fine and sharpened streams of software execution called services. This has been another inflection point in the overall curve of reusability, and most importantly, in agility and turnaround time for software production. The notion of services mandated the birth of a secure and trusted public interface to a service, which is called the Application Programming Interface (API). APIs represent a directory of services that a given enterprise offers.

DOI: 10.4018/978-1-4666-0897-9.ch006

INTRODUCTION

Upon fulfillment of contractual obligations between the service provider and consumer, a process known as API Handshake ensues and brings the two parties onto a common collaboration plane. On the enterprise side many infant services may be amalgamated to constitute composite services, a process known as Service Syndication. Syndication obviates the need to create new services from scratch and greatly boosts reusability in an organization. This chapter follows the contours of evolution from object orientation to Cloud Computing and Service-oriented Architecture (SOA) to understand reusability in the context of service syndication based on the API handshake approach between diverse systems.

The transcendence of massive, rigid and uniform systems into co-acting, flexible and interconnected systems has been an evolutionary requisite. Almost two decades ago, the notion of object-orientation found its genesis in the software development paradigms. And a decade later, in came the messiahs of technology-neutral pluggability – components. This was the cornerstone of the very concept of reusability of an information asset so that it could be aggregated into any solution targeting a problem domain. The more recent advances in research into architectures and their orientation around services is a direct derivative of these initial baseline agents.

The two primary doctrines of code reusability and technology independence paved the way for the formation of a new generation computing platform that addressed these two golden principles with its own hallmark design paradigms, solution models, and technology deployment archetypes. It was the advent of the Software Oriented Architecture (SOA). SOA aims to carve and sculpt solution logic in a way that is very clean-cut, definitive and highly targeted towards the problem domain in the form of discrete and spearheaded streams of functionality. Such solution code representation is the service-orientation of architecture. This way of organizing solution model is greatly focused on the principles of loose coupling, reusability and interoperability.

A great chance of failure awaits organizations trying to share and expose services or components via SOA without furnishing a homogeneous programming framework with a very clear-cut and well-defined array of rules, constraints and principle of behavior. The public designations of such a model constitute the Application Programming Interface (API). An API lays out the syntax and semantics of declaration of objects, methods, classes, protocols and invoking mechanisms through exposed interfaces that are used as a communication medium between the provider and consumer of services.

A subsequent endeavor went underway to provide on-demand access to not just services aspired by SOA, but to any IT resource including assets that publish processes, databases, services and hardware. This approach was named Cloud Computing. While SOA concentrates on providing solution models oriented around services within the confines of an enterprise, cloud computing aims at graduating SOA to outside enterprise firewalls catering to the on-demand provisioning of any IT resource available as a service over the Internet. When the cloud-based software services are to be aggregated into a solution logic unit by the consumers, a handshake occurs between the consumer solution module and the cloud provider API which allows the consumer to leverage all the power of the service in its environment.

This chapter delves into a study of this orchestration of services and their APIs within the purview of disparate cloud-based systems using the notion of reusability via syndication. This powerful composition principle can be applied to render a well-adaptive, time-efficient and agile software development process using third-party services.

BACKGROUND

History serves as a great guide when it comes to understanding the current ecosystem of technologies and architectures. It also serves as a great bread-crumb trail to understand how the evolution of computing paradigms occurred and the motivations and justifications of arriving on these decisions.

We had one computing paradigm revolution after the other initiating with the object-oriented programming model followed by the component-oriented software which led the basis of how code can be reused in a technology independent way. In succession to this came the notion of a service, which was a lightweight and highly maneuverable pathway of functionality that could be driven to serve any heterogeneous software problem domain by its reusability and syndication. Software architectures that were built around this core of a service became known as Service-oriented Architectures.

This was followed by a revolution that is still considered by some to be in its nascent stages: Cloud Computing. This is the revolution that promises to change the understanding and the very landscape behind IT asset usage. While orienting software around services was a spectacular offering by every yardstick, applying the same principles to any IT asset in general globally over Internet is a big leap forward for cloud computing. It serves to foster cost effectiveness and robustness of use of resources like databases, hardware, storage etc.

There are myriad challenges in how the service oriented offerings by cloud or SOA providers are to be federated and reused in the technical environment of the service consumer. There has to be a strong and consistent intermediate interface that serves as a high-level abstraction for the consumer without any visibility of the underlying complexity and technology of the provider and one that also defines a uniform set of rules and constraints of how consumers will access providers' logic components. This set of specifications is collectively known as the Application Programming Interface (API). API essentially represents a public contract by the service publisher that defines how the different programmatic constructs are to be used and reused across multiple consumers.

This chapter follows this vision of delineating how computing platforms can build agile solutions by the API handshakes between individually shaped, multi-source and reusable services through a technique known as service syndication. A special coverage is provided for cloud computing and SOA platforms as these form the crux of a majority of systems that have services as their operating medium.

This chapter illustrates the subject matter by including an elaborate case-study. This case-study demonstrates and elucidates on real world issues with service reuse in such a usage scenario and clarifies some of the major dilemmas on solution strategy design decisions when it comes to advancing with cloud computing or SOA based solutions.

OBJECT: THE SEED OF DATA MODEL

An object is the most fundamental stratum in the entire strata of service-oriented architectural models. It is the chief enabler of reusability of capabilities across higher enclosing software artifacts. The motivation behind the proposal of an 'object' at the time of the genesis of this notion was to simulate in a technology environment the two main descriptors that define real-world 'objects' – state and behavior. The 'state' part represented a feature that the object carried and the 'behavior' would let an object attach action to it. Cutting through to the deepest level of detail behind the notion of an object, the bifurcation of the object description into state and behavior was the setting of the foundation behind reusability of an omnipresent object. This in a technology environment symbolized 'variables' and 'methods'.

When everything is thought of as an object, as is the case in object-oriented architectures, we essentially imply aggregation of structures that are alike in that each carries state and behavior. This alikeness produces reusability of the notion of an object. The entire establishment of SOA and cloud computing rests on this cardinal concept.

The other central concept behind the notion of object orientation is the advancement of the notion of abstraction. In essence, with every programming language from assembly to high level languages, the level of abstraction has risen further and further. By abstraction, we mean creating a plane of programming constructs that hide machine-specific details from the programmer and allow for a convenient mechanism to focus on the computing solutions instead of machine details. This was the road from assembly to high level languages. Nevertheless, each level of abstraction that computing has witnessed inevitably bore some burden of accounting for machine or platform specific details. Objects take this level of abstraction to a whole another level where a person trying to solve a problem can think in terms of the structure as it pertains to the problem domain instead of accounting for machine related details or dependencies.

Alan Kay listed five basic tenets of object orientation as it applied to Smalltalk, the first successful object-oriented language (Eckel, 2002, Ch. 1: Introduction to Objects):

1. **Everything is an object**. Think of an object as a fancy variable; it stores data, but you can "make requests" to that object, asking it to perform operations on itself. In theory, you can take any conceptual component in the problem you're trying to solve (dogs, buildings, services, etc.) and represent it as an object in your program.

2. **A program is a bunch of objects telling each other what to do by sending messages**. To make a request of an object, you "send a message" to that object. More concretely, you can think of a message as a request to call a method that belongs to a particular object.

3. **Each object has its own memory made up of other objects**. Put another way, you create a new kind of object by making a package containing existing objects. Thus, you can build complexity into a program while hiding it behind the simplicity of objects.

4. **Every object has a type**. Using the parlance, each object is an instance of a class, in which "class" is synonymous with "type." The most important distinguishing characteristic of a class is "What messages can you send to it?"

5. **All objects of a particular type can receive the same messages**. This is actually a loaded statement, as you will see later. Because an object of type "circle" is also an object of type "shape," a circle is guaranteed to accept shape messages. This means you can write code that talks to shapes and automatically handle anything that fits the description of a shape. This substitutability is a powerful concept in OOP.

COMPONENT: THE NUCLEUS OF REUSE AND THE AGENT OF LIBERATION FROM TECHNOLOGY DEPENDENCIES

As the idea of objects afforded strict focus on the problem domain, object orientation tasted significant success in some of the most reusable and well-abstracted software development practices. Over the years, this successful model ran into a set of challenges that led to the rise of the notion of a 'component'. While object orientation worked very well in a singleton and single source problem domains, when it came to multi-party problem representation and solution designing, pure objects had their restrictions. Objects had no comprehension of a business contract as it applied to consumption of functionality by a third party.

This limitation was magnified by the businesses' insistence on contractual and legal conformance when using third party software.

Components lent a true business dimension to the process of building software. Discussions on how to materialize collaborations and business reuse of existing components led to "contractual" discussions. Not only were the components supposed to interact with other components, the technology dependencies between them began to fade as the immense potential of truly reusable and technology independent components was realized.

Szyperski in (Szyperski, 1997) defines four orthogonal properties that any basic reusable component must possess:

P1 contractually specified interfaces,
P2 fully explicit context dependencies,
P3 independent deployment,
P4 third party composition.

It follows that a component has well defined interfaces that are ready for 'contractual' exchanges. Components have well specified dependencies under which they operate which acts as a disclaimer for the component service consumer. A component is supposed to fulfill its entire obligation in isolation as well as in concert. And lastly, a component may become a part of array of other heterogeneous components to form a solution composition for a particular consumer.

As the Software Engineering Institute so well defines:

In the same way that early subroutines liberated the programmer from thinking about details, component-based (or service-oriented) software development shifts the emphasis from programming software to composing software systems.

Due to the context in which components were born and were rounded, they have come to serve as the nucleus of reuse and agents of technology independent software architecture. Further up the abstraction strata, the notion of Web Services are essentially domain specific representations of software architecture compositions comprised of interplaying components.

SERVICE: THE MOBILE MESSENGER OF BEHAVIOR

One of the biggest challenges for software architects has been to boost the turnaround time involved in the development of software. Although components completely reformed the way software could be thought to be developed and composed, component-based software development didn't quite get as much traction and acceptance. There were undercurrents among software developers that derived their relevance from practical and day to day scenarios that were repeated. It turned out that when it came to composing software functionalities, it was far easier for them to write their own components than study the integration of third-party components as well as the obscure contractual guidelines and dependencies that usually accompanied such external components. This alternate convenience in building software architectures despite the availability of external components that operated in the same solution space was a big deterrent for software teams to think in terms of integrating packaged external components into their designs.

This lukewarm acceptance of component based software development led to the rise of the concept of a Service. A portrayal of the component basis and the service basis is presented in Figure 1. The World Wide Web consortium defines a service as (Booth et al., 2004):

A service is an abstract resource that represents a capability of performing tasks that represents a coherent functionality from the point of view of provider entities and requester entities. To be used, a service must be realized by a concrete provider agent.

Figure 1. Evolution from a component to a service

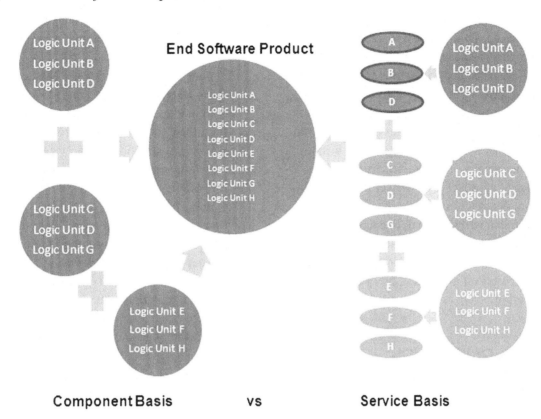

A service, being a very nimble and agile stream of functionality was designed to be collectively and repeatedly used to represent a solution for the problem domain that is being targeted. By this definition, a service is a unit of behavior of the software. And service streams act as the mobile messengers of behavior across the pipeline of software control flow.

The rise of service obviated the difficulty that the software architects and developers faced, that being of colossal efforts required for trying to integrate these big pieces of components together. Service gave the software architects and developers very fine-tuned and individually shaped units of logic that can be reused in software in the blink of an eye, given a quick set of identifiers. The end result is that trying to integrate a lightweight part is far easier than trying to integrate a relatively mammoth component.

A service in the empirical environment has three distinct characteristics:

1. Scope
2. Visibility
3. Granularity

The scope of a service defines the intended consumer context and its confines. For instance, there can be services that can only be embedded as a part of a packaged component. Similarly, there can be a service that will be available to an entire organization. Scope can define the size of the solution space that it is intended to address.

The visibility aspect of a service caters to the accessibility and discoverability facets. There can broadly be public, private or somewhat in the middle (protected) visibility levels for a service. As is self explanatory, private services are meant only to attend to the user base that knows about its existence through some arranged pre-determination. Public services are discoverable through registries accessible by anyone. Protected services are listed in the registries as public items but may impose further level of access restriction.

Finally, the granularity characteristic addresses the fineness and 'lightweightness' of an exposed service. What's the atomicity of the business logic functionality that the service performs? Granularity approaches to answer the preceding question. A service consisting of an aggregate of other services will have to define granularity for its underlying services unless there is a consistent scale for measuring the granularity for composite services based on a business process within an organization.

SERVICE ORIENTATION: FUNDAMENTAL ARCHITECTURE FOR A STANDARDIZED SOLUTION DESIGN DEDICATED TO FULL ABSORBABILITY OF SERVICES WITH AN EYE ON TARGET ENVIRONMENT

Service Orientation is the philosophy of composing and reusing services. In essence, service orientation is the mechanism of creating and aligning services around business processes to achieve a set of defined functions. In principle, business processes use business services to achieve enterprise goals. Service orientation is all about achieving a specified solution state targeted towards a particular business aspect.

The pivotal aim in understanding service orientation is the notion of designing business logic in a uniform way whereby all instances of the logic follow a structure that ultimately serves to achieve a specified solution state.

Thomas Erl (Erl. 2008) defined eight distinct principles of service-orientation along with their official definitions:

- Standardized Service Contract – "Services within the same service inventory are in compliance with the same contract design standards."
- Service Loose Coupling – "Service contracts impose low consumer coupling requirements and are themselves decoupled from their surrounding environment."
- Service Abstraction – "Service contracts only contain essential information and information about services is limited to what is published in service contracts." Service Reusability – Logic is divided into services with the intention of promoting reuse.
- Service Autonomy – "Services exercise a high level of control over their underlying runtime execution environment."
- Service Statelessness - "Services minimize resource consumption by deferring the management of state information when necessary."
- Service Discoverability – "Services are supplemented with communicative meta data by which they can be effectively discovered and interpreted."
- Service Composability – "Services are effective composition participants, regardless of the size and complexity of the composition."

Service-orientation has a rich bag of benefits that an organization gets to tap into once the basic principles of this approach have been applied to the business processes. The first benefit is a fostered alignment between the business community and IT community. Service orientation lets you define your business processes with an eye and awareness about how it would translate into a set of services for your customers.

The second benefit that is derived is that service-orientation is marked by vendor independence. No matter which vendor supplies the framework to go with your set of services, you have always the choice to change your vendor.

A third benefit is the enhanced federation of services. Federation implies a provision whereby different parties can agree on contractual requirements without worrying about the brokering and the mediation that has to ensue at the middle level. This includes things like identity management.

SERVICE-ORIENTED ARCHITECTURE (SOA): MANIFESTATION OF SERVICE-ORIENTED SOLUTION DESIGN

Service-oriented Architecture (SOA) lends a physical manifestation to the idea of service-oriented design paradigm. Thomas Erl (Erl. 2008) defines SOA as 'an architectural model that aims to enhance the efficiency, agility and productivity of an enterprise by positioning services as the primary means through which solution logic is represented in support of the realization of strategic goals associated with service-oriented computing'.

A great deal of confusion has surrounded the introduction to SOA and more often than not it is thought to be synonymous to service-oriented computing. What is important to distinguish and point out on a fundamental basis is that SOA is an architecture and service-orientation is a guiding concept. SOA is just one form of technology architecture to achieve service-oriented computing. The actual implementation of SOA can be constituent of diverse technologies, coding mediums and combination of other technology constructs. This is shown in Figure 2.

Nicolai Josuttis (2007) describes three technical concepts of SOA which I elaborated on in (Singh, 2010):

1. *Service*: We defined service earlier. To revisit, a service is just a technological capability of a business which is executable. With the marked characteristics of visibility, granularity and scope, services are carriers of executed functionality that form a coherent

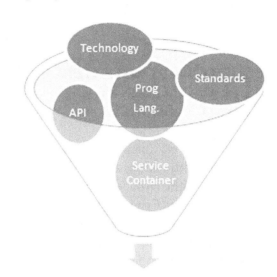

Figure 2. SOA as a combination of various technological flavors

SOA Implementation

unit of execution from a broader view of the business technology perspective.

2. *Interoperability*: The term 'interoperability' refers to the notion of plug-and-play by principles of which the underlying technical architectures are neutralized and treated transparently by the operating services in a heterogeneous environment. It is impossible to characterize the underlying technical framework just by looking at a service because interoperable services can function through any level of dissimilarity of technical framework.

3. *Loose coupling*: Loose coupling is all about boosting independence and hence curbing dependencies and intertwining. A salient feature of loose coupling is that it is exercisable at different levels of interaction in a system – physical, database, model-based, etc. The core concept still remains – decouple various agents to form autonomous assemblies that can function without dependencies. The data sources of a WSS need to be loosely coupled

so fault-tolerance is achieved through transfer of load to alternate systems in case of a disaster.

CLOUD COMPUTING: EXTENDING THE SERVICE ORIENTATION TO ANY IT RESOURCE

The notion of Cloud Computing has gained a lot of acclaim recently and possesses the potential to transform the entire layout of IT resource access architectures. Cloud Computing essentially is the leveraging of any IT resource like database, file system, application hosting and development, physical server etc by an organization over the Internet using pay-per-use basis which can be juxtaposed from a financial standpoint to the traditional model of resource acquisition and procurement as a whole. Put very simply, Cloud Computing represents the protocol of renting an IT resource.

The National Institute of Standards and Technology(NIST) defines Cloud Computing as:

"Cloud computing is a model for enabling convenient, on-demand network access to a shared pool of configurable computing resources (e.g., networks, servers, storage, applications, and services) that can be rapidly provisioned and released with minimal management effort or service provider interaction."

NIST also defines five essential characteristics that the cloud model possesses:

- *On-demand self-service.* A cloud computing consumer is able to dispatch a resource access model based on its needs in an individual manner without requiring any human intervention from the provider.
- *Broad network access.* Cloud computing works over the network and supports all the major types of networks as well as the end devices that are commonly in use. (e.g., mobile phones, laptops, and PDAs).
- *Resource pooling.* The provider's computing resources are pooled to serve multiple consumers using a multi-tenant model, with different physical and virtual resources dynamically assigned and reassigned according to consumer demand. To the end consumer, the resource location is opaque and the resource itself is available in infinite capacities until there is a constraint on the provider's side.
- *Rapid elasticity.* Resources are made adept by the provider to meet the increasing or decreasing needs of the consumer on an on-demand basis. The hosting models allow the infrastructure to quickly release or acquire resources as and when they are needed without impacting the consumer's operations. So in essence, the resources appear endlessly elastic to the consumer.
- *Measured Service.* Cloud systems implicitly attach calibration and measuring mechanisms that feed data about the resource use on the part of the consumer to the provider. This is very similar to the residential utilities like gas and electricity which are monitored my metered systems. There can be many well-defined parameters with which to measure resource usage in the cloud (e.g., storage, processing, bandwidth and active user accounts).

While the above characteristics define guidelines that every cloud system must possess, there are different cloud ownership models that exist. These ownership models define the confines and boundaries of ownership of different constituents of the cloud. The most common types are private, community, hybrid and public clouds. The discussion of these types of cloud systems is outside the scope of this chapter.

SOA AND CLOUD COMPUTING: WELL-GOVERNED INFRASTRUCTURE TO LEVERAGE SERVICES

The interplay between SOA and Cloud Computing is a crossroad in research domains which is not too well traveled. There is not much existing delineation on how these two powerful concepts work hand in hand. By definition, Cloud Computing shares the same principle of service orientation as SOA. Let's now understand the relationship between SOA and Cloud Computing.

As defined previously, cloud computing is the leveraging of IT resources through a third-party vendor over the internet on a subscription model. The IT resources may include physical server, virtual machines, application hosting infrastructure, database etc. SOA is an architecture that is deployed using these IT resources. So Cloud Computing and SOA are complementary to each other and are based on the single common pillar of service orientation. While SOA embodies the business processes offered as services, Cloud Computing represents logical and physical IT resources as services.

If an organization leverages IT resources through the strengths of a vendor, the same is true for SOA. For SOA to be deployable on an organization's IT infrastructure, it is going to have to reside on cloud-based resources. This means that the resource limitations of an organization that would have constrained SOA implementations no longer apply to cloud based resources because by definition the resources in the cloud are infinite. All that matters is the pay-per-use basis and other contractual details.

Another aspect of the relationship is the introduction of virtualization of SOA implementations which is a huge benefit in itself. Virtualization is a very well-grounded concept in computing deployment that has proven advantages like scalability, efficiency, low operational cost, choice of technologies and security. SOA plugs into the virtualization domain very well and is further powered by the thrust offered by virtualization in the cloud. The servers sit with the vendor and can host multiple SOA implementations for multiple tenants.

Figure 3 captures this subtle relationship. We have the business processes of an enterprise that are converted to services through an exhaustive process of business and service modeling. These services sit in an inventory. The inventory itself along with deployment context has to sit on hardware. The hardware comes from the cloud domain and houses the services, deployment context along with all the other common aspects and technology pieces. It is through this cloud infrastructure that the services are exposed to the outside world.

APPLICATION PROGRAMMING INTERFACE (API): THE PUBLIC FACE OF SERVICE-CENTERED PROGRAMMING ENVIRONMENTS AND EMBODIMENT OF REUSE

An Application Programming Interface (API) is an abstraction layer that defines a consistent set of interfaces to expose the services to the consumer. As mentioned in the chapter introduction, an API lays out the syntax and semantics of declaration of objects, methods, classes, protocols and invoking mechanisms through exposed interfaces that are used as a communication medium between the provider and consumer of services.

An API defines 3 levels of details pertaining to the protocol of access:

- Input and Output Values: These values are also called the 'passed values' or function arguments and return values. These values define the metadata regarding the data that the API accepts as well as the return type. Anything above and beyond these prescribed norms will be rejected. The metadata could include information like number

Figure 3. SOA and cloud computing interplay

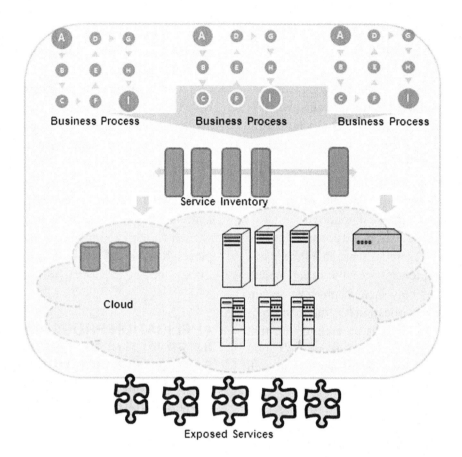

of parameters, the data type of parameters, defined value ranges for parameters etc.

- Invocation mechanisms: APIs also come with specifications as to how it may be invoked from an external program or service. This could include information like query strings vs. REST style. The Representational State Transfer(REST) is a protocol of invocation of an API that has been quite popular owing to its implementation by some of the renowned social networking companies of late.
- Boundaries of usage: Every API comes with a set of rules that must be followed and conformed to in order to avail its services. These rules span from security specifications to authorization and authen-

tication protocol to specifying clearly the terms of execution of functionality and its subsequent use by the consuming party.

A representation of the API operation with respect to the service provider and consumer is presented in Figure 4.

APIs, by their very structure, foster reusability. One way to look at this is that APIs are wrappers around defined set of business logic that can be embedded and reused by any number of clients in a consistent way. This is a great reuse of the code that the APIs embed. In a service oriented environment, this translates to making service available in the form of invokable APIs. If the service oriented environment is based around the Web and extends to outside customers, a technique

Figure 4. API with respect to service provider and consumer

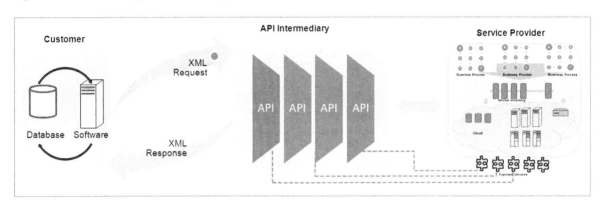

known as Software-as-a-service(SaaS), then the services are called Web Services and are represented and accessed through APIs.

One of the other characteristics about the reuse of APIs is that APIs are valuable corporate assets. There are companies dominating the Web today that are based purely on APIs as their operating and business medium. Twitter is a great example. To the consumers of a service API, it is a dependable and core part of the business plan. API is the entity that facilitates business deals and allows for a contractual agreement which essentially in itself is the livelihood for a company. Through their immense reuse, APIs push themselves to a whole greater plain of imperativeness whereby you may have millions of customers depending on API requests to satisfy the demands and needs of their customers.

It is very important to understand that the notion of an API takes form primarily in Web based environments where a provider wants to expose and offer its services to the outside world. This could be a business-oriented decision or could be completely open source. The relationship between SOA, API and Cloud Computing is that SOA is an architectural style that fosters service oriented software architecture primarily within the confines of an organization. This software architecture when implemented sits on resources extended by Cloud Computing. These resources could be in-house or located completely in the cloud implying that hosting and resource services are being consumed from a third party. An API takes up a service which is designed and composed in SOA phase and puts it out to be consumed by another party outside the organization. So APIs provided a public face to an organization's services.

SERVICE SYNDICATION: THE BIRTH OF COMPOSITION-CENTRIC SOLUTION SPACE AND REPEATED SERVICE AGGREGATION

Service syndication has received much enthusiasm in the B2B(business-to-business) domain. Service syndication is synonymous to the service composability principle mentioned earlier. Moreover software composition has a very close-knot relationship with reusability. Service syndication essentially implies that services don't act in isolation. They interact and operate in concert with other services. Smaller, lower-level services may aggregate to form a composite service which provides a composite unit of functionality to the consumer.

Also to be noted is that service syndication is synonymous to a more popular term called Orchestration. Orchestration basically defines the "workflow of how services interact, including the

Figure 5. Syndicated services in a federated SOA

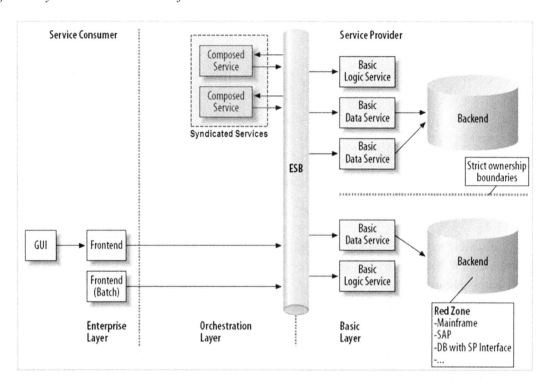

business logic and order of interactions" (Rosen, M et al. 2008). Syndication and orchestration attempt to define the context and semantics of how existing services interplay and achieve a specified target solution.

Let's define another term that is quite popular in SOA context. It's called Federated SOA. Federated SOA is SOA that contains interplay of basic and composed services in its operation. Josuttis in (Josuttis, N. 2007) provides a great diagram to illustrate Federated SOA (see Figure 5).

In Federated SOA, there are primarily 3 subsystems(Josuttis, N. 2007) – Service Consumer(or Enterprise Layer), Orchestration layer and Service Provider(Basic layer). The service consumer could be any external system consisting of GUI and frontends that provide presentation layer support. In the orchestration layer, we have a battery of composed services operating in the same frame of reference. The next most important component to be introduced

here is an Enterprise Service Bus(ESB). The Enterprise Service Bus (ESB) is the communication headquarters for a service in SOA. It is the broker medium which places an intelligent agent to mitigate problems like different messaging formats, varying sources and destinations, different data structures as well as security and reliability. Hence, we can say that the central role of an ESB is to provide interoperability.

The chief responsibilities of an ESB are as follows (Singh, 2010):

- Impart connectivity
- Smart routing of services
- Service brokership
- Infrastructure services such as security, quality of service, etc.
- Record of participating services and channels

Figure 6. API handshake principle

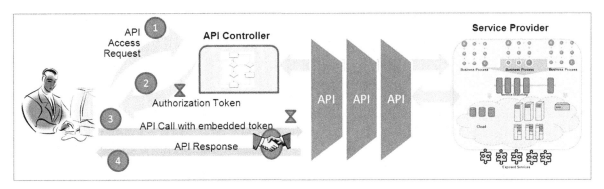

The third layer in a Federated SOA is the Service Provider layer or the Basic Layer. This layer interfaces with the different sources of services originating out of backend subsystems and provides a common stream of access to the service functionality. The glory of this approach is that an ESB is the magical component that performs all these transformation functions in an opaque manner without bothering the involved parties as to the details of this conversion and brokering. An ESB is composed of four major subcomponents – Translation Component, Interface Service Component, Routing Component and Security component (Singh, 2010). The discussion of these components is outside the scope of this chapter. For more details, please refer to my publication (Singh, 2010).

API HANDSHAKE PRINCIPLE: MEDIATION OF CONVERSATION BETWEEN REUSABLE SERVICES

An API handshake is supposed to occur between a service provider and a service consumer when the consumer has fulfilled the protocol of conforming to the API specification – input and output values, invocation mechanism and boundaries of usage. In this scenario, a consumer is fully entitled to utilize the services offered by the API. An important point here is that an API, depend-

ing on its sensitivity level, may enforce certain mechanisms of authentication and authorization to make sure the service consumer is traceable and recordable. Some of the most commercially popular APIs nowadays like Amazon and PayPal have authentication and authorization assemblies that need to be adhered to in order to use the APIs. This could range from acquiring an authorization token and passing in a unique identifier into the API as an input.

Figure 6 depicts a sample scenario where the API Handshake principle is described. Here are the steps:

1. The service consumer submits a request with the Service Provider asking for access to the API. Although the consumer can never see it, the request gets handled by a special module of the provider called the API Controller. The role of an API controller is to mediate exchange of access request and responses with the consumer. The API controller keeps a track of all existing consumers and also handles the registration of first time consumers.

2. In any case, ultimately the API controller dispatches an authorization token to the consumer empowering him to access the API. If for any reason the obligations aren't met by the consumer, then the API control-

Figure 7. Reuse through APIs

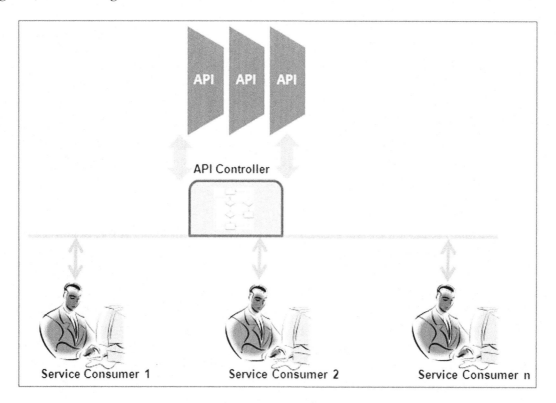

ler denies access and the communication is terminated.

3. The consumer uses the dispatched Authorization Token from the API controller to make direct calls on the API. It is here that the consumer fulfills all rules of the API calls and with the right combination of input/output parameters and invocation mechanism, the API call goes to the service provider and an appropriate response is sent back. At this juncture, an API handshake is said to have occurred.
4. Once the API handshake occurs, a response is sent back to the consumer.

The infusion of true reusability is easy to see at this point. The same set of APIs on the service consumer's side caters to all requests by multiple consumers. The above mentioned steps are repeated per consumer and APIs are invoked

and executed with full reuse. This is illustrated in Figure 7.

SERVICE SYNDICATION BASED ON API HANDSHAKE APPROACH

Let's now understand how API Handshake principle positions itself in a syndicated services scenario, particularly in the Federated SOA context. This is depicted in Figure 8. The API handshake occurs in the orchestration layer of the Federated SOA. The API controller module sends and receive messages using the Enterprise Service Bus. In Figure 8, you see the user submitting a request for API access. The API controller basically routes this request through the ESB which maps this request to the appropriate data service. For example, ESB would route the request to a data service that interfaces with the databases consisting of all the login information. The service fetches the data, returns it to the ESB which stores the caller information which in this case is the API controller. The controller then uses its logic to make a decision and enforces the authentication and authorization policy.

Another point to be noted is that the API controller also uses a "push" data operation when it assigns an authorization token to a consumer. The push data operation is submitted to the ESB which then takes on the task of discovering the data service responsible for storing authorization tokens. This data service handles the push and pull

Figure 8. Service syndication based on API handshake approach

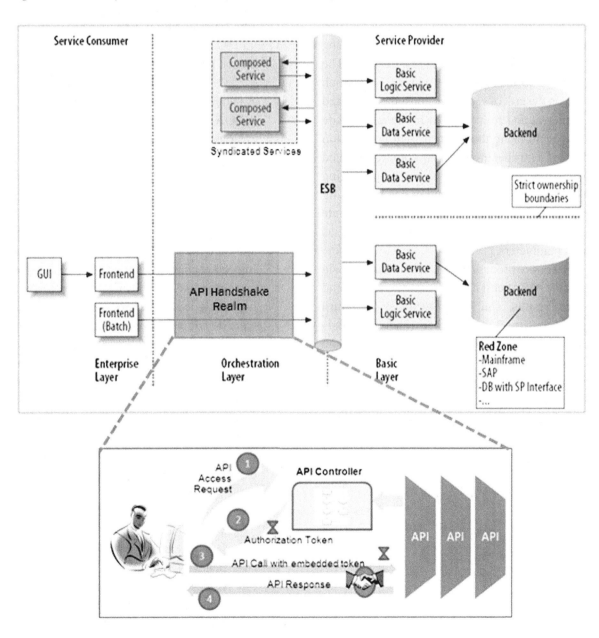

of data from the appropriate database. In addition, the API controller is responsible for logging all API handshakes that this consumer executes and logs them in the appropriate place. In SaaS environments, this logging and recording data becomes critical owing to the subscription costs and on-demand service invocation. This monitoring information constitutes the billing basis for the service provider.

As can be seen clearly from Figure 8, the API controller essentially is never interfacing directly with the APIs of services. This would be a bad architectural decision. A myriad concerns including security would call against such a decision. The Controller instead interfaces with the ESB which takes on the task of accepting consumer input and parameters and routing them to the appropriate service API using the identification information that the Controller includes. This process is called marshalling of the data. This entails packaging of information in such a manner that the routing broker (ESB) has all the directives it needs to route the request as well as feed in data to the API as input parameters.

The entire process repeats upon return of data from the API after it has executed the service and returns results. The ESB then traces the return data back to the API controller which then hands it off to the consumer. A point to note is that the service logic may well have presentation logic included as a separate module in which case the consumer output GUI is rendered and updated accordingly. This also signifies a successful API call to the consumer.

TYING IT ALL TOGETHER: A MODEL ARCHITECTURE ILLUSTRATING SERVICE SYNDICATION BASED ON API HANDSHAKE APPROACH BETWEEN MULTIPLE CLOUD-BASED AND SOA-BASED SYSTEMS

Let's consolidate our acquired knowledge so far and explore what an architecture involving both SOA-based and Cloud-based models would look like operating on the principles of service syndication based on API handshake. This is shown in Figure 9.

We have three systems in this model study:

1. A Cloud-based service provider system
2. A SOA-based service provider system
3. A Consumer system

Let's elaborate on these to better understand the various nuances of this model:

1. Cloud-based service provider system: Let's examine the cloud-based system first. One important characteristic in our cloud-based system is that for illustration purposes we have included all the levels in strata of software development i.e. objects, components and services. This aids in a better grasp of the hierarchy. The baseline layer for the system comprises of supporting cloud-based infrastructure to host the software service. This may be an on-site or third-party software. Regardless of the hosting model, it has a few core constituents that build on top of the cloud infrastructure. The constituents are:
    ◦ *Objects*: As explained earlier in this chapter, an object is a fundamental level of abstraction that the state and behavior aspect to it. Objects may represent anything from business entities to documents. Objects are positioned at the bottom most place in the

Figure 9. Model architecture comprising of a service consumer, a cloud-based system, and a SOA based system

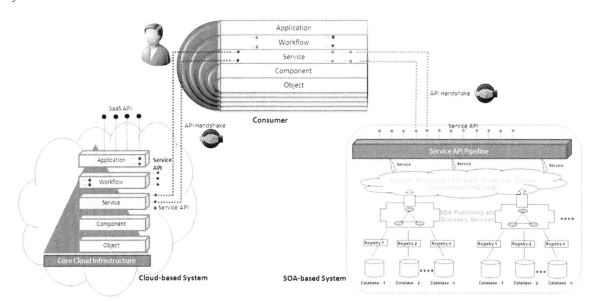

hierarchy of the software service on the cloud.

○ *Components*: Components transform the notion of single-organizational objects into business power blocks. With well-defined and contractually specified interfaces, well-mentioned context dependencies, potential for isolated deployment and their third-party composability, components lend the software development incredible mobility from the perspective of involvement of multiple parties.

○ *Services*: Services lend a mobile abstraction to the notion of reusing existing logic units in the form of services vs. the notion of aggregating bigger chunks into hefty components. With the characteristics of scope, granularity and visibility, services are absorption ready with very low turnaround time for preparing a production software. Services can be single-organization context based

(SOA) or multi-client business context based (SaaS or cloud-based). In the latter case, services expose themselves in form of APIs which are controlled hooks to the outside world to access the service. In our model, the consumer uses these APIs through the Handshake principle to achieve service collaboration.

○ *Workflow*: This is a concept new to this chapter but not too obscure to understand. A set of composed services designed to execute in a particular order to achieve a business goal with the data provided are said to be executed and forming a workflow. A typical example might be the checkout process in any online transaction by a client. The steps of entering payment info, payment info verification, authorization and checkout completion form a workflow. Now a service provider may decide it makes business sense to expose an entire workflow through a single API. This actually may be quite a lucrative proposition considering the commonality of use of such a workflow. In such case, the client calls the workflow API, provides it the requisite inputs and the workflow executes its steps and returns the result back to the client.

- ○ *Application*: An application sits on top of the software development stack providing the ultimate interface to the actual client. An application can be thought of a collection of workflows. It doesn't have to be but any logical bunch of steps executed to mimic a business process can be thought of as a workflow. A workflow further utilizes services for its execution. An important distinction here is that application in itself can be exposed in the form of APIs in which case the APIs are called by the very popular term Software as a Service (SaaS). These are hooks at the application level that the customer can tie into and can derive application level reusability through embedding these application points in their enterprise application.

2. SOA-based service provider system: In the SOA-based service provider system portrayed, we start with the bottom-most layer – the database layer. Let's imagine multiple databases for illustration purposes. These database could house different kinds of data or multiple instances of the same data sets. This really depends on the type of application. Sitting on top of the database and interfacing is a SOA subsystem called the SOA Publishing and Discovery Services (SPDS) (Singh, 2010). No detailed understanding of this subsystem is required for grasping this

model nor is it in the scope of the current subject material. SPDS is responsible for 'reservoiring' services, their publishing in a registry (which is searchable by consumers) and their discovery by the consumers through a discovery process. The services are exposed to the network and they form a series of APIs that are accessible to the outside consumer.

3. The Consumer: The consumer like any other client system is composed of the same hierarchy of technologies and concepts as the cloud-based systems – objects, components, services, workflow sand finally the applications.

Let's discuss the operation of this model architecture. A view is provided in Figure 10.

Step 1: The consumer discovers the two systems that it wants to use the APIs of. The detailed information on systems and their offered APIs can be found in several web service registries that are hosted by different providers. Once the consumer discovers this information, they can utilize this information by employing it in different usage and invocation channels. For example, a user can embed this information ready to fire up API calls in the application code hosted on a server.

Step 2: Once the consumer has recognized a service provider to collaborate with, the consumer undertakes the steps depicted in Figure 6 to initiate an API Handshake. The API controller sends an authentication token back to the consumer to proceed with making the API call.

Step 3: The consumer now submits an API invocation request to the service provider. The request is intercepted by the API Controller which then examines the attached authen-

Figure 10. Glimpse into operation of the model architecture

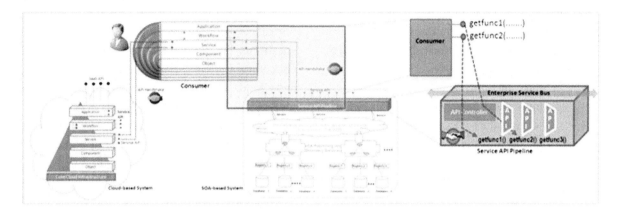

tication token to establish the accurate authorization policies.

Step 4: Once the API controller reaffirms the API access, it then looks at the metadata provided in the consumer request to figure out which API to send this request to.

Step 5: The controller then passes in the input data and the method invocation metadata to the right API.

Step 6: The API executes the request using its business logic and returns the data back to the API controller. It is to be remembered that the message, request and data brokering throughout this entire exchange is handled implicitly by the Enterprise Service Bus (ESB).

Step 7: The API controller then hands off the returned data back to the consumer who then usually has a response handling mechanism and application logic that confirms the success of the operation through the GUI through some suitable user prompt.

The role of the ESB in this process cannot be stressed more. The messaging, request-response mechanism and data brokering forms a big chunk of the complexity of this process.

CHALLENGES BEHIND SOFTWARE DEVELOPMENT IN A SERVICE-CENTRIC SOFTWARE SOLUTION DESIGN ESTABLISHED AROUND REUSABILITY

As with every technology paradigm, service-centric computing has its share of challenges:

1. Service-centric computing entails a paradigm shift in a business organization. This approach can be tenacious enough to demand organizational changes so as to suit the business case to the services offered. In other words, not only does it provide a technology face to its business operations but it also allows for introspection as well. One aspect of this approach that drives this change is the cross-function involvement in designing service-centric solutions for the enterprise. When functional boundaries fade, it leads to tighter integration and immersion of the organization as a whole.

2. The second challenge in service-centric computing is the return on investment(ROI) context within an organization. The ROI computation in SOA environments is not immediately clear to many organizations who must understand that the real value can only be calculated after the deployment. This

scenario of trying to calculate the ROI is compounded by the following two factors:

a. Failure to do a size of organization vs. ROI study of historical data: Usually the size of the organization is not taken into account when looking at ROI numbers. It's the number and design of services that is considered. Emphasis is put on straight ROI numbers.

b. Failure to study the cost and ROI basis for both SOA and non-SOA solutions: Usually the entire focus is primarily on "what is SOA going to fetch me ?" instead of also accounting for "what if we go for a non-SOA solution?"(Alluri, 2009).

3. The third and biggest challenge is security. Conventional and age-old security standards don't apply to SOA as they would on traditional software solution development. This situation is aggravated by the shortage of skilled professionals specializing in security aspects in a service-oriented environment.

4. The fourth challenge is the evolution of standards. SOA standards are still fairly new but quite formidable from a learning curve standpoint. The credit goes to organizations like OASIS who have put their shoulder to this wheel. Evolving standards demand maturity before adoption can begin and SOA has had this challenge for quite some now. Although there are myriad success stories surrounding SOA penetration, the industry wants to see some maturity of standards before SOA can be called the order of the day.

CONCLUSION

The advent of object-orientation followed by the business commoditization of software packages into components and then followed by evolution into lightweight services has greatly redefined the basic tenets of software development – reuse. This continuum has opened up the reach and impact of software development on both end of spectrums- business and the consumer. The two architectural styles of Service-oriented Architecture and Cloud Computing strive to make sure that the idea of wasted development effort is deprecated by aligning reuse of services to business ROI through adoption of these architecture paradigms. A great actor in this play has been the API which is the public face of services and the apotheosis of reusability. These are the pivotal entities that steer the ROI of a business by appealing to the consumer community subsequent to presenting themselves as convincing and secure forms of information exchange. This is what's called the Handshake Principle. APIs are polymorphic in nature. They hide the implementation of services which essentially drives decisions to either compose smaller services into composite ones or use the smaller ones by themselves. The composition lends itself to the notion of service syndication. The doctrine of repeated service aggregation is a vital thrust behind reusability of existing services in the neo-age SOA and Cloud-based systems.

Of course, service-oriented computing is not without its share of challenges. Although it has tasted exquisite success so far in its implementations in some of the world's largest and most respected organizations, it still has a long way to go to assuage many lingering concerns. These are concerns centered on the maturity of evolving standards, security and adoption of the need to revisit business processes and fundamentally realign, if needed, the business model structure. The ultimate goal for an enterprise should be to open up to the customer on the Internet waiting to utilize the services through these liberating architectures.

REFERENCES

Alluri, R. (2009). SOA adoption challenges. *BPTrends*.

Bean, J. (2010). *SOA and Web services interface design: Principles, techniques and standards*. Burlington, MA: Morgan Kaufmann Publishing.

Booch, G. (2007). *Object-oriented analysis and design with applications* (3rd ed.). Addison-Wesley.

Booth, D., et al. (Eds.). (2004). *W3C working group note 11: Web services architecture*. World Wide Web Consortium (W3C), February. Retrieved from www.w3.org/TR/ws-arch/#stakeholder

Eckel, B. (2002). *Thinking in Java* (3rd Edition). Boston, MA: Prentice Hall, Pearson. Retrieved from http://www.mindview.net/Books/TIJ/

Erl, T. (2008). *SOA design patterns*. Boston, MA: Prentice Hall, Pearson.

Erl, T. (2008). *SOA: Principles of service design*. Boston, MA: Prentice Hall, Pearson.

Feilkas, M., & Ratiu, D. (2008). Ensuring well-behaved usage of APIs through syntactic constraints. *The 16th IEEE International Conference on Program Comprehension* (pp. 248-253). IEEE Press.

Gamma, E., Helm, R., Johnson, R., & Vlissides, J. (1995). *Design patterns: Elements of reusable object-oriented software*. Addison-Wesley.

Josuttis, N. (2007). *SOA in practice* (pp. 16–48). O'Reilly Publishing.

Krafzig, D. (2004). *Enterprise SOA: Service-oriented architecture best practices*. Boston, MA: Prentice Hall, Pearson.

Miller, M. (2009). *Cloud computing: Web-based applications that change the way you work and collaborate online*. Indianapolis, IN: Que Publishing.

Rosen, M. (2008). *Applied SOA: Service-oriented architecture and design strategies*. Indianapolis, IN: Wiley.

Roshen, W. (2009). *SOA-based enterprise integration: A step-by-step guide to services-based application integration*. McGraw-Hill.

Singh, V. (2010). Service-oriented architecture (SOA) as a technical framework for web-based support systems (WSS). In Yao, J. T. (Ed.), *Web-based support systems*. London, UK: Springer. doi:10.1007/978-1-84882-628-1_19

Szyperski, C. (1997). *Component software: Beyond object-oriented programming*. Addison-Wesley.

Tulach, J. (2008). *Practical API design: Confessions of a Java framework architect*. Apress.

Chapter 7
Reuse across ESB Systems

Indika Kumara
WSO2 Inc, Sri Lanka

Chandana Gamage
University of Moratuwa, Sri Lanka

ABSTRACT

Enterprise Service Bus (ESB) is a middleware that provides solutions for enterprise application integration. Although the contemporary ESB products exhibit diverse architectural styles and standards such as service component architecture and Java business integration, they mostly provide the same set of ESB services such as data transformation, security, et cetera. The quality attributes of a software system are primarily attributed to the system's architecture, and a set of systems having different architectures can meet the requirements from a great variety of users. To produce several ESB variations successfully, a systematic reuse across ESB systems is crucial. Therefore, the commonality in ESB products, which is comprised mainly of ESB services, should be strategically exploited, and this chapter discusses an approach to realize it. The author presents a platform that can derive architecturally heterogeneous ESB products from reusable ESB services. The approach for building the platform leverages aspect-oriented programming.

INTRODUCTION

Nowadays, enterprises are adopting information technology (IT) to automate their business processes and to simplify their operational activities. A typical business process composes discrete business functions provided by multiple applications. An adaptable and flexible integration of these ap-

plications is vital to execute the business process efficiently, and enterprise application integration (EAI) middleware is to provide robust solutions for application integration. An Enterprise Service Bus (ESB) has been touted as the next generation EAI middleware (Chappell, 2004). The current ESB market encompasses a wide range of ESB products and customers.

The selection of an ESB product for an enterprise is ascribed chiefly to the business domain

DOI: 10.4018/978-1-4666-0897-9.ch007

and business scale of the enterprise. The customer base of an ESB is heterogeneous and consists of business domains such as e-commerce, healthcare, and government. It can also be classified based on the business scale such as large, medium, and small. Moreover, each customer potentially possesses their own unique business requirements. As a reason, an optimum EAI solution for a particular customer would be an individualized ESB, which is an ESB tailored to solve his or her application integration problems in a scalable and robust manner.

The capability to produce ESB variations without incurring excessive cost and time is of paramount importance for an ESB vendor's agility. One reason is that it helps a vendor to respond efficiently to ever changing customer requirements. For instance, an existing ESB cannot meet a particular customer's new software quality requirements, and the ESB architecture should be changed. Another reason is that an ESB already represents a wide range of architectural approaches such as service component architecture, java business integration, etc., and new architectural styles and standards would emerge as time pass. What a vendor requires is to change the architecture of the product with ease. In other words, a vendor needs a potential to produce a new ESB product reusing existing ESB components.

Although the current ESB product space is heterogeneous in terms of architectures, they offer the same set of ESB services such as message routing, message transformation, message and data security, etc. If these ESB services were adaptable for most ESB architectures, then that would allow a vendor to formulate most ESB products from a single ESB service library. This emphasizes the fact that the reusability of an ESB service across the products is critical to develop diverse ESB products. Moreover, as each ESB variation would be for a different market segment, each ESB service's design should be flexible enough to be configured to support a greater variety of software quality attributes.

The significant commonality among ESB products and the variability in their architectures make it plausible that a systematic reuse across multiple ESB architectures is what required for formulating individualized ESB products and ESB variations cost and time effectively. The reuse approach discussed in chapter *Reuse across Multiple Architectures* paves the way for achieving it; each ESB service should be developed as a *Multi-Architecture Reusable Component* and a solution space for an ESB sphere should be the system architecture for reuse. As per the discussion in the aforementioned chapter, the solution space provides a strong context for a well-planned reuse across different systems. Furthermore, the methodology for developing *Multi-Architecture Reusable Components* can ensure that ESB services are reusable in different ESB architectures with the desired quality attributes.

The objectives of this chapter are to present a platform developed for realizing the development and evolution of different ESB products reusing the same set of ESB service implementations. The platform leveraged the reuse approach presented in chapter *Reuse across Multiple Architectures*. As the ESB services are reusable across multiple ESB systems, we identified them as the software elements that encapsulate the concerns that crosscut multiple ESB systems. This observation led us to adopt the principles of Aspect-Oriented Programming (AOP) (Kiczales, et al., 1997), which modularizes crosscutting concerns. Aspects capture crosscutting concerns and in turn, we capture ESB services as aspects. Although, in traditional AOP, an aspect encapsulates concerns such as logging, security, etc., in our approach, an aspect can provide any kind of a self-contained functionality. Our aspect weaver can assemble the aspects (ESB services) in accordance with diverse architectural styles, and employs the component-based development. Throughout this chapter, we use "aspect" and "ESB service" synonymously.

This chapter is structured as follows. Section *Background* describes an enterprise service bus highlighting its commonality and variability. In addition, it outlines the aspect oriented programming, discusses the reason behind the adaptation of AOP, and explores the related work. Next sections unfold our approach for achieving large scale reuse across different ESB systems. Finally, we present our conclusions and potential future research that can leverage this research.

BACKGROUND

This section discusses the enterprise service bus (ESB) and aspect-oriented programming (AOP), and explores previous research that forms the foundation for this research.

Enterprise Service Bus (ESB)

In modern business environments, Information Technology (IT) has become a key success factor. It can assist an enterprise by automating its business processes and simplifying its operational activities. Typically, a business process is implemented by integrating enterprise software applications, which provide a particular set of business functions. For the past decades, enterprises have adopted Enterprise Application Integration (EAI) technologies to underpin integration of applications across enterprises. Enterprise Service Bus (ESB) is the descendant of the race of EAI solutions and is capable of solving a broader range of integration problems comparing to its predecessors (Chappell, 2004). The dominant service of an ESB is the interoperability, which enables loose coupling between service consumers and providers. Additionally, an ESB may provide services such as caching, security, monitoring, etc.

Currently, in the ESB sphere, there are multiple definitions for an ESB, and many of them are conflicting. In the research that this chapter presents, we adhere to the definition provided by Rosen, Lublinsky, Smith, and Balcer (2008).

"An ESB is an enterprise-wide extendable middleware infrastructure providing virtualization and management of service interactions, including support for the communication, mediation, transformation, and integration technologies required by services."

By serving as a communication intermediary, an ESB lowers the coupling between service consumers and providers through providing virtualization and management of the interactions between service consumers and providers.

The architecture of an ESB makes it different from traditional EAI systems (Rosen, Lublinsky, Smith, & Balcer, 2008). An ESB leverages the bus-based architecture, whereas the EAI systems utilize the hub and spoke architecture. In the hub and spoke architecture, the hub is the central processing unit that accepts the requests from heterogeneous applications, which are modeled as the spokes. Although this architecture separates the application logic from the integration logic of the applications, it suffers from limitations of scalability and a single point for failure. The decentralized bus architecture was innovated to overcome these limitations yet providing an efficient centralized control. The components of the bus architecture formulate a logical bus.

Service Oriented Architecture (SOA) is an architectural paradigm for the realization of business processes, which span over heterogeneous enterprises (Josuttis, 2007). The adoption of SOA as the application architecture of enterprises has been increased for the past several years. Many researchers have identified an ESB as an infrastructure to implement SOA-based solutions, which solve application integration problems (Schmidt, Hutchison, Lambros, & Phippen, 2005)(Josuttis, 2007). For that matter, an ESB product variation is an integral part of most currently available SOA platforms. It is evident that SOA has catalyzed the deployment of an ESB in an enterprise's IT architecture.

Variability in ESB

ESB products are available from a great variety of vendors, and these products differ on many aspects such as architecture, base technologies, and features (Majumadar, Dias, Mysore, & Poddar, 2007). As the architecture of a software system generally determines the software qualities offered by the software system, we have focused only on the ESB architecture variation. The ESB architectures can be broadly categorized into four: JBI, SCA, MQM, and custom-designed.

Java Business Integration (JBI) (Sun Microsystems, 2005) is an effort to create a standard-based architecture for integration solutions. It aimed to address the issues with traditional B2B (Business-To-Business) and EAI systems occurred due to their non-standard technologies. In the JBI architecture, the components communicate by a message-based service invocation defined using a standard service description language. The foundation of the JBI architecture is a central mediator providing the loose coupling between the components. The JBI architecture consists of the following three high-level components.

1. **Component Framework:** JBI supports two kinds of primitive components: Service Engines and Binding Components. Service engines implement business logics, and binding components provide a communication infrastructure, including different communication protocols and transports. The JBI component framework allows these components to interact with the JBI runtime environment, which acts as a central mediator.
2. **Normalized Message Router:** Normalized Message Router decouples service consumers and providers, and is responsible for routing message exchanges among service consumers and providers. A message exchange is a JBI specific concept and contains a normalized message.

3. **Management:** Management provides the lifecycle management of the components and the other artifacts.

ServiceMix and Mule belong to the JBI based ESB category (Majumadar, Dias, Mysore, & Poddar, 2007).

Service Component Architecture (SCA) is a set of specifications, which describe a model for building applications and systems using SOA. SCA extends and complements prior approaches to implementing services, and is built on open standards such as Web Services. The primary concepts of the SCA are components and composites. A component implements business logic and provides standard interfaces that describe its services. Furthermore, it consists of service references to consume the services offered by the other components. Moreover, a component implementation can be in any programming language. A composite, which implements a business process, is a collection of components assembled in a prescribed way defined by the Service Component Definition Language (SCDL). In additions to the concept of components and composites, there is a concept of binding, which encapsulates the mechanisms used to communicate among components. SCA provides a wide range of bindings, including web services and messaging standards. Chappell (2007) introduces SCA, highlighting its fundamental concepts and the approaches of realizing it. Web Sphere ESB is based on SCA (Majumadar, Dias, Mysore, & Poddar, 2007).

Message Queuing Middleware (MQM) provides an extensive support for reliable, asynchronous, and loosely coupled communication. In a MQM, applications communicate by inserting messages in specific queues. More importantly, applications can be physically distributed, which makes a MQM based ESB inherently suitable for implementing the business processes that span multiple enterprises. Sonic ESB is an example for a MQM based ESB (Majumadar, Dias, Mysore, & Poddar, 2007).

Table 1. The commonality in ESB products

ESB Services	ESB Products		
	Mule	Synapse	Fiorano
Routing	Content and Header Based Routing (CBR and HBR)	CBR and HBR	CBR and HBR
Transform	XML(Extensible Markup Language) and EDI(Electronic Data Interchange)	XML	XML and EDI
Transport Services	HTTP / HTTPS, FTP, JMS(Java Message Service), Email, Amazon SQS (Simple Queue Service), etc	HTTP/S, FTP, Email, JMS, etc	HTTP/S, FTP, Email, JMS, etc
Security	LDAP (Lightweight Directory Access Protocol), WS-Security, JAAS(Java Authentication and Authorization Service)	WS-Security	WS-Security, LDAP, JAAS
Load Balance	-	support	support
Caching	-	In-memory Caching	In-memory Caching

Custom-designed ESB products exhibit diverse architectural styles, including widely known design and architecture patterns such as Pipe and Filters (Buschmann, Henney, & Schmidt, 2007), Mediator (Gamma, Helm, Johnson, & Vlissides, 1995), and so on. Apache Synapse (2008) is an example for a custom-designed ESB, and leverages both Mediator and Chain of Responsibility (Gamma, Helm, Johnson, & Vlissides, 1995) design patterns. Since there is already a wide spectrum of design pattern and approaches, and many novel patterns and approaches can possibly be innovated in the future, there is a great opportunity to utilize their strengths to support diverse and changing requirements. It is a prime goal of the research that this chapter describes.

Commonality in ESB

The identification of the commonality in appropriate granularity is crucial as it determines the level of reuse and the cost associated with the product development from reusable assets. The primary concerns to be considered are the level of abstraction, coupling, and functional orthogonality. Our approach to identify the commonality is to consider each ESB product as a black box and examine the externally visible features or services they provide. We selected three ESB products: Mule,

Synapse, and Fiorano ESB. Synapse (2008) is an open source ESB and has an architecture that assembles its components in a sequence. Mule ESB is JBI based, and the architecture of Fiorano ESB is based on MQM (Majumadar, Dias, Mysore, & Poddar, 2007). Table 1 summarizes ESB services, which each ESB provides. In this analysis, we have only considered six services as the selected services cover the essentials required to discern the commonality among ESB products.

As shown in Table 1, each ESB provides transformation and routing, and there are services such as load balance, and caching that are provided by more than one ESB. Every ESB provides HTTP, JMS, FTP, and Email transport services. However, there are transport services such as Amazon SQS, etc., offered by only a single ESB product. Apparently, Each ESB provides a sub set of transport services. From our analysis, it is evident that each ESB provides a sub set of ESB services and a sub set of the functionality offered by a particular ESB service. This conclusion can also be traced from the data transformation and security services offered by each ESB. Therefore, each existing ESB can be viewed as a software system that is using a sub set of ESB services from a universal ESB service library with different service composition architectures such as JBI, MQM, etc. This fact motivated us to choose the ESB service abstraction as the unit of reuse.

Aspect Oriented Programming (AOP)

Although the separation of concerns is inevitable for developing sustainable software systems, its achievement is most often difficult due to the crosscutting nature of most concerns of systems. The structure and behavior of a crosscutting concern are scattered across the code base and tangled with the code related to the other concerns (Clarke & Baniassad, 2005). An adequate solution to achieve the separation of concerns is a mechanism to identify, separate, and modularize the crosscutting concerns, and to compose them back to the dependent primary concerns. Aspect-Orientation Programming (AOP) (Kiczales, et al., 1997) offers such a solution. AOP provides a different view of modularity, and modularizes the crosscutting concerns, which are the results of the horizontal decomposition of the system functionality. AOP enables to define the system's base concerns and crosscutting concerns separately and to compose them in a prescribed way to make the final system.

AOP Terminology

In order to prepare the reader for better comprehension of the rest of this chapter, this section outlines the terminology used in AOP.

Components capture the system properties that can be cleanly abstracted out using the Object-Oriented Programming (OOP), and represent the reusable functional units resulted from the vertical decomposition of the system functionality. Components are more generalized and encapsulated.

Aspects are the system properties that cannot be cleanly abstracted out using the OOP. Aspects do not represent the units of the system's functional decomposition, but rather the properties that affect the performance or the overall behavior of the components.

Tangling is taking place in a system that does not use the AOP. In tangling, the aspects are scattered throughout the components, and the resulted tangled code is extremely difficult to maintain.

Join Point belongs to the components, and the aspects are weaved at the join points. This is the location that the main logic and aspects' functionalities are interacted.

Point-cut specifies the join points using a kind of language construct such as annotations and configuration files.

Advice instructs about how an aspect's behaviors should be weaved at the joins points. There are three main types of advices: *before*, *after*, and *around*.

Adopting Aspect Oriented Programming

As per the analysis of three ESB products presented in Table 1, different ESB products offer a great deal of similar functionalities but the source codes of implementations of those are different and kept separately in each product. This situation is a kind of scattering, and AOP is suitable to address it. Therefore, we employed the concepts of AOP to modularize the functionalities that crosscut different ESB products. More precisely, in this research, we exercise the AOP as a programming model for expressing our solutions for formulating diverse ESB systems reusing the same set of ESB services. We employed the principles of AOP, but not the traditional approaches for implementing AOP.

Aspects encapsulate ESB services such as security, logging, cache, HTTP transport service, etc. Those are developed as *Multi Architecture Reusable Components* introduced in chapter *Reuse across Multiple Architectures*, and can be adapted to the components of the different ESB products. To use the functionalities offered by the aspects within a particular ESB product, we developed an aspect weaver, which can structure the aspects based on the architecture styles that are suitable for the products, which uses the aspects. We believe that our approach for the aspect weaving is mostly suitable for the software systems with a component model to assemble their components. The component composition is based on the AOP advices: *after*, *around*, and *before*. AOP advices are defined using the aspect and composition definition language (ACDL) as part of points-cuts definitions. Aspects weaved around ESB components in accordance with the AOP advices, and the aspect weaving transparently modifies the component model of the target ESB. Although, currently, the aspect weaving is done at startup time, by modifying the component model at runtime, it can also be performed easily at runtime.

Related Work

The related work presented in chapter *Reuse across Multiple Architectures* is equally applicable to this chapter. Therefore, in this chapter, our discussion chiefly focuses on the previous research that has employed the AOP on an ESB or a component-based system. Additionally, the approaches for leveraging the diversity in ESB architectures are outlined.

AOP on ESB

A little research has attempted to bring the concepts of the AOP into an ESB. Ermagan, Kruger, and Menarini (2008) have discussed an aspect oriented modeling approach to define routing in an ESB. It leveraged the rich services and Message Sequence Charts (MSC) to control routing capabilities of an ESB in an aspect-oriented manner. MSC defines interactions between components, which communicate with each other via exchanging messages. It has a formal graphical notation somewhat similar to the UML (Unified Modeling Language) sequence diagram. They have addressed crosscutting concerns by modifying the message flow through a router-interceptor layer. At runtime, the interceptor creates an implementation model based on an aspect MSC and observes the

communication among components. If the aspect MSC is applicable, the interceptor modifies the behavior according to the aspect MSC.

Bai and Fitch (2009) have developed an ESB framework for the discovery and delivery of hydrological data to users. In their case study, business logic is implemented by a data approach that primarily consists of two activities: accessing a hydrological data service and converting the response from the data service to a desired format. The chief function of their framework is to provide an interface that users can employ to select data approaches and data translators, and to route messages between the selected data approaches and data translators. They have used an AOP-based approach to implement technical concerns of a business services such as logging and exception management. By using AOP based architecture, the components that provide these technical concerns could traverse easily the implementations of business logic (data modules), providing an adequate solution to confront these crosscutting concerns successfully.

Our research exploited the concepts of the AOP to underpin a systematic approach for reuse across ESB systems by utilizing the AOP as a programming paradigm for aptly providing the basic elements required to build a reuse solution. We leverage the AOP to isolate ESB services from ESB products, and to encapsulate them as aspects. The aspect weaver composes these reusable ESB services each other as well as to ESB products. The AOP terminology forms the language that is used to define ESB services and their compositions.

AOP on Middleware

Spring (Walls & Breidenbach, 2007) provides a rich support for the AOP in its AOP module, which serves as a basis for developing new aspects for any spring-enabled applications. Spring's support for the AOP can be identified in four categories: proxy-based AOP, AspectJ annotation based aspects, pure POJO aspects, and injected AspectJ aspects. AspectJ (Laddad, 2003) is an aspect-oriented extension to the Java programming language, and includes constructs to define the AOP concepts such as *point-cuts* and *advices* and consists of several built-in aspects. Spring provides a set of developed aspects, including caching, exception handling, logging, transaction, and parameter validation. Spring AOP language syntax is an XML-based in which the point-cuts and advices are XML tags. Spring's point-cut model is similar to that of AspectJ. The AOP-oriented platform presented in this research utilizes a proxy-based AOP approach.

To use the spring's AOP in an ESB, the components of the ESB should be spring components (i.e. spring beans). Hence, the qualities such as reliability, performance offered by the ESB architecture mostly cannot be leveraged. With our approach, most ESB architectures and existing ESB components can be used "as is", as we effectively transform a generic ESB service into a component of the target ESB. Furthermore, our aspect weaver is based on the architectural styles, which are suitable for the ESB that uses the aspects. Thus, our approach can preserve the qualities ESB architecture provides, or can further enhance those qualities.

JBoss AOP (Pawlak, Seinturier, & Retaillé, 2005) is a Java framework for the AOP. It can be used in the context of the JBoss application server or standalone. It supports the proxy factory based aspect weaving, AspectJ annotation based AOP weaving, and dynamic weaving. Both XML and Java annotations can be used as the aspect language. JBoss AOP can be identified as an approach to extend the existing J2EE (Java 2 Platform, Enterprise Edition) container services since by developing new aspects and deploying those into the JBoss application server can make them available to all the applications that execute on the server. Moreover, JBoss AOP has made it possible to apply EJB-style (Enterprise Java Beans) services to POJOs (Plain Old Java Objects) without a complex EJB infrastructure code and

deployment descriptors. JBoss AOP also provides a set of built-in aspects, including transactions, security, and caching.

AOP on Component-Based Systems

JAsCo (Suvée, Vanderperren, & Jonckers, 2003) is an infrastructure supporting the execution of dynamically adaptable component-based applications. It is to provide as an aspect oriented implementation language to be used in the component based software development, especially in the Java Beans component model. It treats aspects as first-class entities and provides a separate language for defining the aspect weaving. The main similarity between our approach and JAsCo is the use of a component model for the aspect weaving. The JAsCo component model consists of hooks to support dynamic aspect application and removal. Compared with our approach, the JAsCo component model cannot be changed, whereas our aspect weaver is not coupled to a particular component model and can leverage the strengths of different architectural styles. Furthermore, similar to our approach, JAsCo has used a separate aspect language.

JAC (Pawlak, Seinturier, Duchien, Florin, Legond-Aubry, & Martelli, 2004) is an aspect-oriented framework for supporting dynamic AOP and distributed AOP. They have used the concepts of *Aspect Components* to encapsulate crosscutting concerns, and provided a mechanism for configuring them. In their approach, an application is a collection of base and aspect objects. JAC aspect components provide technical concerns such as persistence, clustering, transactions, etc., and are weaved to base objects in order to augment application logic with technical concerns appropriately. Like JAsCo, JAC allows run-time aspect addition and removal, and embeds hooks at the load-time in base components to be able to interfere with their execution. JAC provides an API to define aspects, point cuts, and pieces of advice code compared with the approaches such as AspectJ that provide a language for the same purpose. Similarly, in our approach, an aspect can be defined via a configuration language as well as an API.

AOKell (Seinturier, Pessemier, Duchien, & Coupaye, 2006) is a framework for developing component-based applications. It provides a component model with two dimensions (layers): the functional and the control dimension, and employs AOP to integrate both dimensions. The functional dimension deals with the functionalities of applications, whereas the control dimension supports managing applications with technical services such as component lifecycle, component binding, etc. The components providing the control functions are reusable, and can be adapted to different application domains. The key similarity between our approach and AOKell is that the clear separation of reusable artifacts from application-specific artifacts. However, we reuse both functional and non-functional concerns, including the control functions.

Leveraging ESB Architectures

An interesting approach to obtain the advantages of different ESB architectures is to embed an implementation of the architecture of one ESB as a component of another ESB. Petals ESB (2010), which is a JBI based ESB, has embedded a SCA service engine as a JBI service component. Our approach is different from that work as we formulates generic ESB services, which can be effectively adapted into the components of most ESB architectures such as SCA, JBI, MQM, etc. When implementing an integration solution, our approach offers a higher flexibility to a software architect for selecting an appropriate ESB, and changing the selected ESB as needed without undue cost and time because the ESB services developed for a one ESB is reusable in another ESB 'as-is'.

FraSCAti (Seinturier, Merle, Fournier, Dolet, Schiavoni, & Stefani, 2009) is a platform for formulating SCA based distributed systems. It utilizes and extends the SCA component model by incorporating runtime adaptation and manageability of SCA applications. FraSCAti is capable of dynamically weaving non-functional services (crosscutting concerns) such as transaction, security to SCA components that implement business logic. It has employed the concept of an interceptor that captures the requests to a particular component, applies its logic, and then forwards the requests to the component. Several AOP frameworks (Pawlak, Seinturier, & Retaillé, Foundations of AOP for J2EE Development, 2005) have used this interceptor mechanism. Similarly, the proxy-based aspect weaving used in this research also leverages the fundamental principles behind the interceptor.

AN AOP-ORIENTED PLATFORM FOR DEVELOPING ESB SYSTEMS

This section discusses the design and implementation of a platform for formulating heterogeneous ESB systems by reusing ESB services across the systems. The platform architecture employs the system architecture for systematic reuse (the solution space) presented in chapter *Reuse across Multiple Architectures*. We leveraged the principles of AOP to construct our platform. In our implementation of the solution space, an aspect (ESB service) is a *Multi Architecture Reusable Component*, and the aspect weaver plays the roles of both concrete solution builder and concrete solution weaver. Similarly, the Aspect and Composition Definition Language (ACDL) serves as the concrete solution definition language. Figure 1 depicts our platform architecture (the solution space) for developing ESB products reusing the same set of ESB services.

As shown in Figure 1, the concrete solution space consists of an M number of aspects (*Multi-Architecture Reusable components*), the aspect weaver, and the aspect and composition definition

Figure 1. The solution space for ESB products

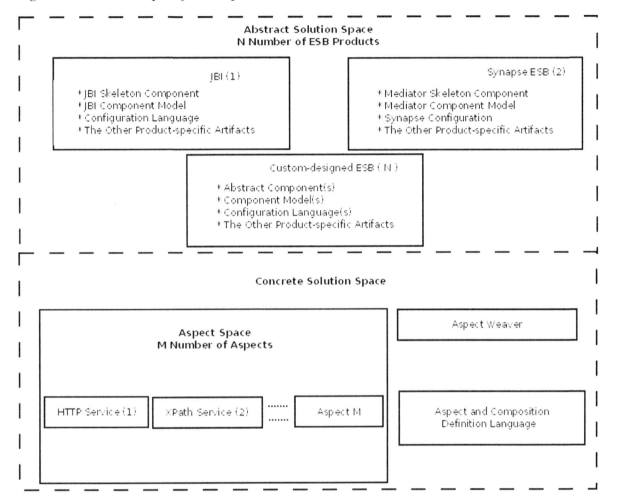

language (ACDL). Similarly, an N number of different ESB systems compromises the abstract solution space. A particular ESB can represent a great variety of ESB architectures, including a standard ESB architecture such as JBI, an architecture employed by another existing ESB product such as Apache Synapse, and an architecture designed to meet the requirements of a specific customer (custom-designed). Each aspect as well as its documents, its designs, and the people employed to develop them are reusable across ESB products. The product-specific artifacts such as product specific documents are kept with each product.

Next sections deeply discuss the aspect space, the aspect weaver and how an ESB solution is built using the solution space. However, we do not present ACDL in this chapter as it is not essential to comprehend our approach for building ESB products. Moreover, we do not describe the functions of some artifacts in the solution space that we have already discussed in chapter *Reuse across Multiple Architectures*.

Aspect Space: Aspect Library

The aspect library (aspect space) is a software library that attempts to implement aspects as reusable and adaptable components. In our prototype

Figure 2. Part of a feature model for Apache Synapse ESB

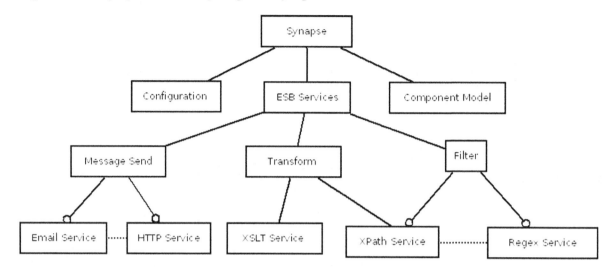

implementation, it consists of eight aspects namely log, crypto, caching, load balance, exception handling, monitoring, persistence, and proxy. An aspect is an autonomous software element and does not depend on the other aspects for providing its service. For that matter, an aspect is a *Multi Architecture Reusable Component*.

In the rest of this section, first we outline the procedure for identifying the candidates for implementing as aspects. Next subsection describes cache aspects in detail following the development process for *Multi-Architecture Reusable Components* discussed in chapter *Reuse across Multiple Architectures*. We have already discussed the log aspect in the aforementioned chapter. However, we do not discuss the other five aspects in this chapter as the selected aspects cover the essentials required to understand our approach for developing aspects.

Identifying Aspects

In section Enterprise Service Bus, we analyzed three ESB products and identified the ESB service as the basic unit of reuse for ESB products. Mostly, an aspect is an ESB service. In order to trace aspects from ESB products, we follow the

Multi-Architecture Reusable Component identification process, which is based on the feature models. A feature mode visually represents the commonality and variability of a particular domain, system, etc. The same notation used in the feature models presented in chapter *Reuse across Multiple Architectures* is used in the feature models that this chapter presents. The first step in the process for identifying aspects is to draw a feature model for each ESB product or the ESB application domain. It was described in the chapter *Reuse across Multiple Architectures* in detail. Secondly, based on a feature model, unique foundation services that form the ESB services are identified. There are the aspects. ESB services that do not exhibit a commonality among them are considered as foundation services. However, if an ESB service has a feature that can be reused by another ESB service, then, that ESB service is itself not a foundation service. Figure 2 shows part of a feature model for Synapse ESB (2008).

In Figure 2, the *Message Sending* service uses transport services such as HTTP service, Email service. Those transport-services are foundation services for an ESB. Although *Transform* and *Filter* services are themselves ESB services, they share a common functionality – XPath (XML Path

Figure 3. Part of the feature model of the cache aspect

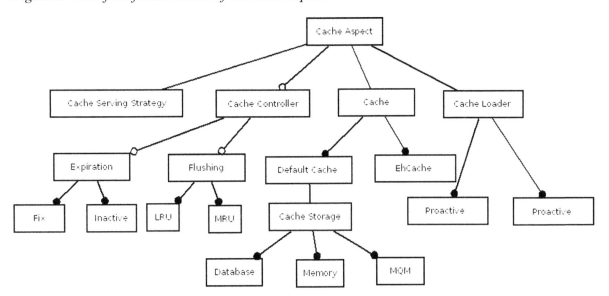

Language) evaluation. Therefore, the *XPath* service is a foundation service, whereas the *Transform* and *Filter* services are high level ESB services built upon the foundation services. Hence, from Figure 2, HTTP service, Email Service, XPath service, XSLT (Extensible Style sheet Language Transformations) service and Regex Service can be identified as aspects (*Multi-Architecture Reusable Component*). It is observable from Figure 2 that the leaf nodes of a feature model mostly become the foundation services. As chapter *Reuse across Multiple Architectures* highlighted, an abstraction for a foundation service (*Multi-Architecture Reusable Component*) is attributed to the product. For instance, although an XSLT service is a foundation service for an ESB, it is not a foundation service for a XSLT engine implementation. Instead, XML (Extensible Markup Language) parsing, XSLT grammar validation, etc., would be the foundation services for a XSLT engine.

Cache Aspect

This section presents the design of the cache aspect following the *Multi-Architecture Reusable Component* development process described in chapter *Reuse across Multiple Architectures*. The design diagram for the cache aspect only reflects key abstractions employed in the cache design.

The resultant artifacts from the development process of the cache aspect are shown in Figure 3 and Figure 4.

In the following, we discuss how the above artifacts are formed from the *Multi-Architecture Reusable Component* development process.

Step 1: Identifying and Refining Intuitive Requirement

The Intuitive Requirement for the cache aspect can be stated as follows.

A cache keeps the data. It should be loaded with the data, and applications' requests should be served from the cache.

Step 2: Designing the Component to Support its Intuitive Requirement

As per the *Intuitive Requirement*, the abstractions for the foundation design are *Cache*, *CacheEntry*,

Figure 4. The high-level design of the cache aspect

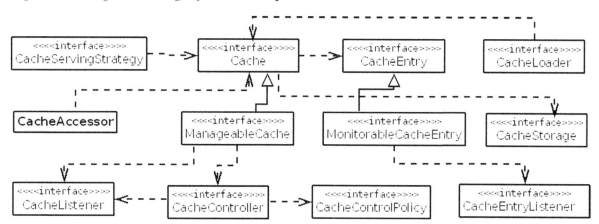

CacheLoader, CacheStorage, and *CacheServing-Strategy.* These abstractions collectively form the abstraction for the cache aspect as a whole. *Cache-ServingStrategy* determines how to serve applications' requests, from the cache, and *CacheLoader* populates the cache with the data. *CacheEntry* represents an item in the cache and contains both data and meta-data such as the last access time of a cache entry. *CacheStorage* is used by *Cache* to keep the instances of *CacheEntry.* Furthermore, we introduced *CacheAccessor,* which is a facade that provides the methods to access the cache. It is an implementation of CacheAccessor (Nock, 2003) pattern, which decouples the caching logic from the data model and data access details to make a consistent, reusable cache for all data types.

Step 3: Drawing or Updating the Feature Model

As per the *Intuitive Requirement,* the mandatory features for the cache aspect are the serving application's requests from the cache, the cache, the cache storage, and the loading the cache with data. The feature model for the cache aspect is drawn based on these mandatory features, and new features are added to it based on a domain analysis for the caching domain. Although we did a comprehensive domain analysis at this step, it is typically an iterative process.

As per our domain analysis, the caching is applicable in any application layer such as communication, data access, etc.; therefore, the cache should have the capability to keep different data types. Additionally, cache coherence should be preserved. It is related with both the cache loading and cache controlling mechanisms, which involve the removing of invalid cache items from the cache. Widely used cache controlling strategies are Least Recently Used (LRU), Most Recently Used (MRU). There are two approaches for the cache loading: *Proactive Loader* and *Reactive Loader.* *Proactive Loader* populates the cache with all data needed usually at the system startup-time. *Reactive Loader* retrieves the data using a synchronous programming model when the application requests for data and then caches it for the future requests. Moreover, the cache uses backup stores such as the file system, the database, etc., to keep the cached data. The feature model in Figure 3 was mainly created based on the domain analysis. However, the next steps in the aspect development process generally modify the feature model by adding or modifying features.

Step 4: Incorporating Additional Requirements

Based on the feature model and the domain analysis done at the Step 3, new functional requirements are identified. The requirement for controlling the cache was implemented by adding a new (optional) abstraction called *CacheController*. Typically, a cache controller requires information such as the last access time of a cache entry. Therefore, we introduced observers (listeners) for the cache and cache entry. To represent the various mechanisms for cache controlling such as LRU, MRU, etc., we introduced *CacheControlPolicy* abstraction. To provide the extension points for different cache loading techniques, *ProactiveCacheLoader*, and *ReactiveCacheLoader* were introduced.

Step 5: Incorporating Quality Attributes

From the standard quality attributes list, we selected the following as the essential qualities for our implementation of the cache aspect. New qualities are added to the list as the aspect evolves.

Quality Attributes: Performance, Reliability, Availability, Security, and Extensibility

In chapter *Reuse across Multiple Architectures*, we emphasized that the strategy for incorporating conflicting software qualities is the separation of the architectural strategies supporting each conflicting quality (i.e. to avoid the conflicts in architectural strategies). Furthermore, we recommended the provision of a set of strategies for achieving the same quality since it allows choosing the best combination of design tactics that can confront the tread offs among qualities successfully.

We introduced two strategies for supporting performance requirements: in-memory cache and proactive cache loader. The asynchronous pull loader, which is a proactive cache loader, runs periodically based on a scheduling policy and retrieves the data from the required places, and keeps those in the cache. For supporting reliability requirement, we selected reliable cache storages such as file system, database, and MQM (message queuing middleware). The cache controlling mechanisms also can contribute to reliability by providing cache coherence. To achieve avail-

ability, non-volatile cache storages and cache replication were used. To support the cache replication, we integrated Ehcache (2010), which is an open source distributed caching system with functionalities such as disk-based caching, cache replication, etc. This integration is an example for the strategic reuse of existing third party products or components within the aspects. The strategy for implementing security requirements of the cache aspect, of any aspect for that matter, is to use the security aspect by a means of the component composition (i.e. a composition of security and cache, and no direct reference to the security aspect in the cache aspect).

In order to support a high performance and a high reliability, which are conflicting software qualities, it is needed to avoid the conflicts in architectural tactics employed to support those qualities. For example, the selection of an in-memory cache (performance) and a file system backed cache (reliability). This cannot be done because both strategies are conflicting as it is only possible to have a single cache type. However, the combination of a proactive cache loader (performance) and a file system backed cache (reliability) can be used for supporting a high performance and a high reliability. Evidently, it is possible to cope with the conflicts in software quality requirements by selecting the architectural tactics, which are not conflicting with each other.

Aspect Weaver

An aspect weaver builds concrete solutions and weaves them to abstract solutions to implement the required end-user solution. More precisely, it acts as both concrete solution builder and concrete solution weaver presented in chapter *Reuse across Multiple Architectures*.

Motivating Example

Our discussion of the aspect weaver flows through two main sections: aspect adaptation and aspect

Figure 5. Secure Logger Example

```
Scenario                     : Logging a message securely
Involved Aspects             : Log aspect and crypto aspect
The Name of the Log Aspect   : log1
The Name of the Crypto Aspect : crypto1
The Name of the ESB Component : secureLogger
Composition                  : log1 before secureLogger and
                               after crypto1
```

composition. It uses a hypothetical example shown in Figure 5 as needed.

The elements in Figure 5 will be discussed as needed during the discussion in the remainder of this chapter.

Design Goals of the Aspect Weaver

The design of the aspect weaver can be chiefly ascribed to two design goals.

- **The aspect weaving must be suited for the ESB that is going to use the aspects.**

An ESB is a component-based middleware, which uses a component model to structure the ESB components. Typically, the ESB architecture determines the component model of a particular ESB. We believe that the runtime of a component-based system should comprise the components assembled according to its component model. Therefore, the aspect weaving should be able to produce the final ESB system as if the ESB system was built using the native ESB components of the ESB. This goal is essential as it ensures that an ESB system provides the same or higher than the software qualities that can be supported by the ESB architecture.

- **The aspect weaving should be transparent.**

The architecture of a software system defines components and the relationships among them. The architecture would be preserved only if the syntaxes and semantics of the components and relationships are not changed, and the transparent aspect weaving allows achieving it.

Aspect Adaptation

A component to be used in a particular architecture, it should be a type of the components that architecture expects. For example, JBI architecture needs JBI components and SCA architecture needs SCA components. Hence, the requirement is to transform transparently an aspect in the aspect space into a component of the product that is going to use the aspect. For this purpose, we employed an aspect adaptation technique, which leveraged the three concepts - *Data Access Model, Skeleton Component (Abstract Component)*, and *Proxy* - which were deeply discussed in chapter *Reuse across Multiple Systems*. However, we briefly look into each of those three concepts in this chapter as well, especially from the implementation perspective.

Skeleton Component (Abstract Component)

A skeleton component implements the interfaces mandated by the target ESB product's architecture but does nothing in the implementation. Typically, an ideal skeleton component has empty functions but in practice, it may have internal or generic functions that are mandated by the architecture. A particular ESB system variation only needs a single skeleton component. A JBI skeleton component is for a JBI based ESB; A SCA skeleton component is for a SCA based ESB and so on. A skeleton

Figure 6. Synapse skeleton component

```
public class SynapseSkeletonComponent implements Mediator {
    private String name;
    private String type;
    public boolean mediate(MessageContext synCtx) {
        return true;
    }
    public String getType() {
        return type;
    }
    public String getName() {
        return name;
    }
    public void setName(String name) {
        this.name = name;
    }
    public void setType(String type) {
        this.type = type;
    }
}
```

component is a type of joint point, which is an AOP construct, and aspects are weaved around it. To be a joint point, it should be addressable. This can be easily done using the configuration of an ESB product. Skeleton component development for Apache Synapse ESB is described in next paragraph. *Mediator* is the primary abstraction for an ESB service in Synapse. Hence, the skeleton component for Synapse is a *Mediator*. It needs two attributes namely the *name* and *type* and the methods to access those attributes. All other methods are ideally empty. Figure 6 shows a code fragment of the skeleton component for Synapse.

In Figure 6, the *mediate* method provides the access to the service the *Mediator* offers. The return value of the *mediate* method indicates whether the mediation flow should be continued or not.

Synapse configuration is an XML-based, and each mediator should have a XML tag name. We named our skeleton component as '*component*'. For the example presented in Figure 5, the skeleton component's configuration (part of Synapse XML) is shown in Figure 7.

As depicted in Figure 7, the configuration of the skeleton component can define an ESB service in an abstract and concise manner. The *secureLog-*

Figure 7. The configuration of the skeleton component for the secureLogger

```
<component name="secureLogger"/>
```

ger is a complex service created through the composition of security and log ESB services (aspects). Each aspect should be configured via giving the properties required for providing its service. For example, the security aspect may need the information such as the key store location, cryptographic operation. Moreover, how the security and log are assembled to form the *secureLogger* should also be given in a declarative manner. However, the configuration in Figure 6, the secure logging service has been defined without such concrete details. In this way, the instances of the skeleton component can be used to define every ESB service involved in an integration solution. In other words, an integration solution can be modeled using the skeleton component. This clear separation of the implementation information from an abstraction solution enables non-technical people such as business analysts,

Figure 8. Synapse proxy

```
public class SynapseProxy implements Mediator {
    private Processable preProcessor;
    private Processable postProcessor;
    private Mediator mediator;
    //here constructor comes
    public boolean mediate(MessageContext synCtx) {
        Message message = messageAdapter.toMessage(synCtx);
        if (preProcessor != null) {
            preProcessor.process(message);
        }
        mediator.mediate(synCtx);
        if(postProcessor != null){
            postProcessor.process(message);
        }
        return true;
    }
}
```

management to involve in the solution formulation process.

Proxy

A *Proxy* is to transform an instance of a skeleton component into a functional component, which provides a functionality such as security, logging. A *Proxy* exposes the same interfaces as the skeleton component. The logic inside the proxy is merely the execution of the concrete solutions, which consist of the instances of aspects assembled according to a component model. Figure 8 shows a code fragment of the *Proxy* for Synapse.

Both *preProcessor* and *postProcessor,* which are types of *Processable*, collectively form a concrete solution. Each *Processable* is a set of aspects structured according to a particular architecture and the procedure for creating those will discuss next sections. In Figure 8, the *mediator* instance can be either a synapse native component or a skeleton component. In the *mediate* method, firstly, the Synapse's *MessageContext* is adapted to the *Message* abstraction in the *Data Access Model*. Next, *preProcessor* is executed with the *Message*. Finally, the *mediator* instance and *postProcessor* are executed sequentially.

When an aspect is weaved into a skeleton component or a native functional ESB compo-

nent, the adaptation process creates an instance of the *Proxy* with references to the aspect chains (*preProcessor* and *postProcessor*) and replaces the skeleton component or the native functional component with the created proxy instance. The proxy creation method can be provided through an implementation of the *Interceptor* discussed in the *Data Access Model* presented in chapter *Reuse across Multiple Architectures*.

The aspect adaption is transparent as the proxy and the skeleton component implement the same interfaces. It is also highly effective, since only a single proxy implementation and an implementation of the data access model are needed to adapt any aspect in the aspect library for a particular ESB architecture. The adapted aspects can be composed using the product architecture. The cost associated with the adaption technique is mainly attributed to the implementation of the *Data Access Model*, especially the *Message*. However, the effect on the performance can be limited to one additional method call by implementing the *Message* as a wrapper around the context object being passed between the components of the ESB product that uses aspects. For Synapse, it is a wrapper around Synapse's *MessageContext*. For a JBI based ESB, it is a wrapper around the *MessageExchange*,

Figure 9. AspectObjectModel interface

```
public interface AspectObjectModel {
    public Processable build(AspectChainPair aspectChainPair, Interceptor interceptor);
}
```

which is the context object being passed between JBI components.

Aspect Composition

Aspect composition is done by the aspect weaver and is divided into two stages: *aspects-to-aspects* and *aspects-to-skeleton components*. The composition is based on the AOP advices: after, around, and before - aspects weaved around the components based on AOP advices. The AOP advices are defined using the aspect and composition definition language (ACDL) as a part of points-cuts that specify the join points, which can be used to locate the instances of both the aspects and the components of the system that uses the aspects.

Aspects to Aspects Composition

Aspects-to-aspects composition implements the functionality of concrete solution builder presented in chapter *Reuse across Multiple Architectures*. It is a merely structuring aspects based on a component model which assembles aspects according to a particular architecture. A concrete solution is an instance of either one aspect or an aspects-composite. A single aspect provides a basic functionality and most often, a particular solution requires a complex functionality. For example, a log aspect is a basic functionality, whereas a secure logging service is a complex functionality, which is a composition of log and security aspects. A complex functionality produced by the aspect weaver must provide at least the same software quality attributes that would be provided if the aspects were the components of the ESB product. For that purpose, the AOP

specific functionality and the component model that structures the aspects were clearly separated. *Aspects-to-aspects composition* can be broadly divided into two steps.

The first step is to read the ACDL file and build aspects based on the configuration information given in the ACDL. Then, based on the point-cut definitions, an instance of the *AspectChainPair* is created. An *AspectChainPair* consists of two *AspectChain* instances namely *pre-processor* and *post-processor*. An *AspectChain* is merely a list of the instances of aspects. The *pre-processor* aspect chain is built based on the *before* advice and the *post-processor* aspect chain is built based on the *after* advice. The *around* advice populate both *pre-processor* and *post-processor* with the instances of aspects.

The second step is to structure the aspects in the *AspectChainPair* based on a given component model implementation. We encapsulate the component model into an interface – *AspectObjectModel*, which is shown in Figure 9. The implementation of the *AspectObjectModel* can be configured, or given as an object at runtime. The implementation chiefly assembles the aspects given in the *AspectChainPair* according to a particular component model. Hence, by implementing the *AspectObjectModel* interface aptly, a new component model can be easily plugged into the aspect weaver to be employed to compose aspects.

The return type of the *build* method of *AspectObjectModel* can be diverse. For instance, it can be just a sequence of aspects, or it can be an object model formulated based on a novel or an existing architectural style, or it may represent a specific structure of the components of the product that

Figure 10. A pipeline

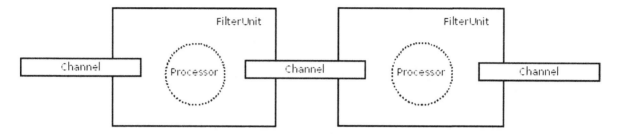

uses aspects. In the latter case, the aspects have to be transformed into the required component types using the aspect adaption technique discussed in the previous section.

We have developed a component model to be used by many different products to assemble aspects. It is based on the Pipe and Filter architectural pattern (Buschmann, Henney, & Schmidt, 2007), which is suitable for a system that is doing a staged data stream processing where each stage consists of components performing operations such as transforming data, encrypting data. Hohpe and Woolf (2003) have discussed the significance of the Pipe and Filter pattern as a fundamental architectural style for an EAI middleware such as message brokers, ESB, etc. In the aspect weaving that employs the component model based on the Pipe and Filters, the *aspects-to-aspects composition* is merely a process of creating an aspect pipeline, which consists of filter units and channels. The *FilterUnit* is the filter component of the Pipe and Filters pattern, whereas the *Channel* is the pipe. Figure 10 depicts a pipeline.

In Figure 10, A *FilterUnit* uses its in-channel to receive input data from the previous *FilterUnit*. After processing the input data, it produces and transmits output data to the subsequent *FilterUnit* via its out-channel. The main component of the filter unit is the *Processor*, which encapsulates a data processing step such as logging, caching. An aspect is a processor.

In Figure 10, a *Channel* can be a method invocation, an in-memory queue, or a sophisticated message channel. A message channel can provide

language, platform, and location independence between the filters (Hohpe & Woolf, 2003). The apt technologies for implementing the message channels are the standards used in message-oriented communication systems such as JMS (Java Message Service), proprietary MQM (Message Queuing Middleware) standards, and Web Services. Another suitable candidate for a queue based channel is in-memory queues. A queue-based channel can decompose an application into stages, which can be utilized to support event-driven, non-blocking data processing (Welsh, Culler, & Brewer, 2001). Our prototype implementation includes a method invocation based channel and an in-memory queue-based channel.

Aspects to Skeleton Component Composition

This step of the aspect weaving implements the concrete solution weaver's functionality described in chapter *Reuse across Multiple Architectures*. Different ESB products have different architectures to structure its components, and different configuration languages to define the components and their composition. Typically, based on the configuration information, the components are assembled to form a particular object model. In our approach, ideally, an object model consists only with the instances of the skeleton component and product-specific components (native components). Aspects should be weaved to the skeleton components or native components to use the functionalities offered by the aspects in the target ESB system. *Aspects-to-skeleton component*

Figure 11. The aspect composition for motivating example

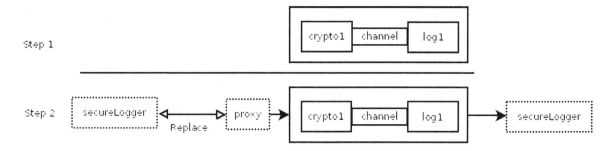

composition is responsible for that purpose and is coupled to the aspect adaption technique described in the previous section. The aspect composition technique is merely the creation of an instance of the *Proxy* and replacement of a correct instance of the skeleton component or a native component, with the created proxy instance. In order to locate the correct instance of the skeleton component, the name or type attribute of the skeleton component can be employed. For example, the identifier to locate the *secureLogger* skeleton component's instance shown in Figure 5 is *secureLogger*.

Aspect Weaving Process

In the aspect weaving process, the first step is to perform the *aspects-to-aspects composition* to formulate concrete solutions. Finally, the *aspects-to-skeleton component composition* is done. Aspect composition process for the example presented Figure 5 is shown in Figure 11. It assumes that the component model based on the Pipe and Filers pattern has been used to structure aspects.

In the first step, an aspect pipeline, which consists of log (*log1*) and crypto (*crypto1*) aspects, is created. In the second step, a proxy, which has a reference to the aspect pipeline, is created and

the created proxy replaces the *secureLogger* skeleton component. At runtime, when a request arrives at the proxy, it intercepts the request, creates a *Message* using it, and executes the aspect pipeline using the created *Message*. Finally, it delegates the control to the *secureLogger*. The *Message* was discussed in the chapter *Reuse across Multiple Architectures* as part of the *Data Access Model*. It is to encapsulate a request to an aspect, and to exchange the data among aspects in a loosely coupled manner.

To use the aspect weaver within a product, we provide a generic API for programmatically perform the aspect weaving. To make the API generic, we decoupled the aspect building process from the decoration of the component model of a particular ESB product with the built aspects. For that purpose, we introduced an interface named as – *MainObjectModelDecorator* which is shown in Figure 12.

After the aspects are built and the aspects-chains (*AspectChainPair*) are created, the aspect weaving process invokes the implementation of the *MainObjectModelDecorator* with the aspect weaver as a parameter of the *decorate* method so that within the *MainObjectModelDecorator*'s

Figure 12. MainObjectModelDecorator interface

```
public interface MainObjectModelDecorator {
    public void decorate(AspectWeaver aspectWeaver);
}
```

implementation, the aspect weaver can be accessed. In order to compose the concrete solutions to the abstract solutions, the *MainObjectModelDecorator*'s implementation should traverse the object model of the ESB product, and for each object in the object model, the aspect weaver should be invoked with the object. Upon invocation of the aspect weaver, it calculates an identifier based on the name or type of the given object, and tries to locate an *AspectChainPair* for the identifier. If there is an *AspectChainPair*, then the aspect weaver calls *AspectObjectModel*'s implementation with the *AspectChainPair*. The *AspectObjectModel*'s implementation returns a concrete solution which is a composite of the aspects in the *AspectChainPair*, made according to a particular component model. Then, an instance of the *Proxy* wrapping the resultant concrete solution is created, and the created *Proxy* instance replaces the original object in the object model of the ESB product. After the aspect weaving is completed, the object model consists of the instances of the *Proxies*, instead of the instances of the skeleton component.

The implementation of *MainObjectModelDecorator* is only the mandatory requirement to use the aspect weaver. However, if the default component model that is used to structure the aspects should be changed, then, an implementation of *AspectObjectModel* should be provided.

IMPLEMENTING ESB SOLUTIONS

The procedure for the realization of the application integration solutions is similar to the procedure which discussed in the chapter *Reuse across Multiple Architectures* under section *Implementing Solutions*. In this section elaborates on the foregoing process with a concrete ESB solution. With our approach, the first step in implementing an enterprise application integration solution with an ESB is to isolate the abstract solution from the concrete solution. Next, the abstract

solution is formulated using the instances of the skeleton component of an ESB product, and the concrete solution is implemented with the aspects. Lastly, the required ESB solution is formulated by composing the concrete solution to the abstract solution transparently using our aspect weaving mechanism.

We use the following hypothetical end-user ESB solution in the discussions of the rest of this section. The solution is simple yet effective for comprehending the ESB solution formulation process.

Hypothetical End-User ESB Solution: Allows accessing the medical records kept in a database and audits each access to them. An audit record for each access should be kept securely.

Step 1: Selecting a Suitable Product(s)

In this discussion, we use Apache Synapse ESB for implementing the above-mentioned hypothetical ESB solution.

Step 2: Building Abstract ESB Solutions

An abstract solution is the skeleton of the required solution. It involves one or more instances of the skeleton component of an ESB product. Each instance defines a particular ESB service abstractly, and the solution would be a composition of the instances according to the component model of the ESB product. The configuration language of the ESB product defines the instances of the skeleton component and their compositions. Figure 13 shows the hypothetical end-user solution modeled using Apache Synapse ESB.

In Figure 13, the *sequence* tag defines a sequence of synapse components (i.e. *Mediators*). The solution is formulated from two ESB services: secure logger and medical records access. The *component* tag is the configuration of the mediator skeleton component, and is used to

Figure 13. The abstract solution of the hypothetical ESB solution

```
<sequence name="AuditableMedicalRecordsAccess">
    <component name="SecureLogger">
    <component name="MedicalRecordsAccess"/>
</sequence>
```

define the ESB services. By only changing the name attribute, a set of different ESB services abstractly has been defined. Both *SecureLogger* and *MedicalRecordsAccess* are complex services; *SecureLogger* is a composition of security and logging, and *MedicalRecordsAccess* is a composition of cache and persistence. Mostly, to define each service, several parameters such as database driver, connection URL, etc., are required. In our approach, those details are not part of the abstraction solution. Effectively, our approach has enabled defining an ESB solution abstractly without stating the implementation details. It allows non-technical stakeholders such as business analysts, to participate in modeling ESB solutions.

Step 3: Building concrete ESB solutions

The building block of a concrete solution is the aspect (*Multi-Architecture Reusable Component*);

the instances of aspects are composed according to a given component model to form a concrete solution. The ACDL is used to define concrete solutions. Figure 14 shows the definition of the concrete solution for the hypothetical end-user solution. It only shows the essential information required to understand how to implement a concrete solution using our approach. For instance, the information such as database driver, connection URL, etc. have been omitted, but has shown the point-cut definitions, which are AOP constructs for specifying join points. Although, we do not discuss the ACDL in this paper, we believe that Figure 14 is intuitive enough to comprehend the solution defined in the ACDL.

In Figure 14, there are three aspects' instances: a log aspect' instance named as *log1*, a crypto aspect' instance named as *crypto1*, and a persistence aspect' instance named as *persistence1*. There are two concrete solution instances: the composition of the *log1* and the *crypt1*, and the

Figure 14. The concrete solution for the hypothetical ESB solution

```
define log log1
[Configuration information of the log aspect goes here as needed]
use before SecureLogger ofmain:        // a point-cut
use around crypto1:                    // a point-cut
end

define crypto crypto1
[Configuration information of the crypto aspect goes here as needed]
end

define persistence persistence1
[Configuration information of the persistence aspect goes here as needed]
use before MedicalRecordsAccess ofmain:    // a point-cut
end
```

persistence1 alone. The formation of the secure logging solution, which is the composition of the *log1* and the *crypt1*, is defined in the point-cut *"use around crypto1"* specified in the *log1*.

Step 4: Weaving Concrete and Abstract Solutions

The goal of this step is to augment the skeleton of the end-user solution created in the step 2 with the functionalities of the aspects. After the formation of the concrete solutions is completed, the aspect weaver composes the abstraction solutions and the concrete solutions to form the required end-user ESB solution. How the solutions should be composed is also defined in the ACDL as part of the definitions of the concrete solutions.

In Figure 14, the point-cut *"use before SecureLogger ofmain"* instructs the aspect weaver to compose the secure logging concrete solution (i.e. the composition of the *log1* and the *crypt1*) prior to the instance of the skeleton component with the name *SecureLogger*. The keyword *ofmain* is to identify the weaving of concrete solutions to abstract solutions. The point-cut *"use before MedicalRecordsAccess ofmain"* instructs the aspect weaver to compose the *persistence1* concrete solution prior to the instance of the skeleton component with the name *MedicalRecordsAccess*.

SecureLogger, *MedicalRecordsAccess* only the identifiers of skeleton component's instances. An identifier is a text indicating the name of the skeleton component. Hence, the above concrete solutions can be reused 'as-is' in different ESB products with our approach.

BUILDING ESB PRODUCTS

Building an ESB product reusing ESB services is similar to the process of formulating systems having different architectures reusing *Multi-Architecture Reusable Components* discussed in chapter *Reuse across Multiple Architectures*. A new ESB product is integrated only to the abstract solution space shown in Figure 1, and it requires the following artifacts.

- **Component Model and Configuration Language:** The component model to be used to assemble the components of the ESB can be constructed in several ways. If the ESB architecture is novel, then the component model has to be created from scratch. However, if the architecture is exhibited by some of the existing ESB products, and the source code of such an ESB is accessible, then extracting the component model from that ESB by refactoring the ESB would be cost-effective. Apart from the component model, its configuration must be provided (ESB configuration).

- **Proxy and Skeleton Component:** *Proxy* is not a mandatory component as Java dynamic proxies can be used as a proxy to any Java interface. The existing ESB components can be used instead of a skeleton component. A *Proxy* and skeleton component implementations can also be provided explicitly. Moreover, the skeleton component should have the methods to access either the name or type (identifier) of the component.

- **Data Access Model:** The implementation for the *Data Access Model* presented in chapter *Reuse across Multiple Architectures* must be provided. In our platform, we provide an API for the *Data Access Model*, and that API must be implemented by any ESB product. It includes a *Message*, *Interceptors*, and a *MessageFactory* that provides methods to create *Messages* and its parts, including an error entry, a message body, and headers. The *MessageAdapter*, which converts the *Message* into the parameter expected by the component of the base system and vice versa, is required.

- ***MainObjectModelDecorator*** **and** *AspectObjectModel*: The implementation of the interfaces *MainObjectModelDecorator* and *AspectObjectModel* must be provided. Those are to perform the aspect weaving programmatically.

We observed that implementing the above artifacts is only a trivial task. However, if the product should conform to a specification such as JBI, then, the development of the configuration language and component model of the product may require some efforts. Yet, as discussed in the above section, it is possible to leverage open source products to reduce efforts. For example, it is feasible to take an open source JBI engine and to refractor it.

The evolution of an ESB product can be done by modifying the artifacts in either the abstract or the concrete solution spaces. A product can change its architecture and the configuration language, or (and) it can evolve merely with the enhancements in the aspect space.

Evaluation

The evaluation of the approach for a well-planned reuse across systems having different architectures presented in chapter *Reuse across Multiple Architectures* is related to the evaluation of the research outcomes described in this chapter.

To assess aspects for its adaptability, reusability, and sustainability, we did a case study, which uses our platform in the Apache Synapse ESB for implementing application integration scenarios. The artifacts presented in section *Building ESB Products* had to develop to implement the case study. There was no refactoring in the Synapse. The case study involved twenty-two ESB scenarios, and Table 2 summarizes those.

In Table 2, all scenarios are real world EAI scenarios that typically an ESB should support. Some scenarios only needed a single aspect, whereas others needed a composite of aspects and

those composites were created only using the aspect weaving mechanism. A few Synapse components were used in some scenarios, mainly due to the unavailability of the aspects that implement the functionality of those Synapse components. Using the proxy aspect, the Synapse components were used without referring them directly. From the case study, it is evident that by developing ESB services as aspects, our approach can provide all ESB functionality Synapse needs. As a result, it is possible to remove most ESB services from Synapse and to make Synapse to use the concrete solution space. This situation should be the same with other ESB products. In other words, with our approach all ESB services from a wide range of ESB products can be extracted into the concrete solution space as aspects, which provide those ESB services, and then to make the ESB products to use the aspects to provide required ESB services. Furthermore, we used the Synapse architecture 'as is' and this situation should be same with other ESB systems. Moreover, a case study that successfully used our platform in another middleware system has been discussed in chapter *Reuse across Multiple Architectures*. Therefore, with the approach presented in this chapter, a set of ESB systems having different architectures can potentially be produced reusing the ESB services in the concrete solution space 'as-is'.

Aspects only depend on the *Data Access Model* to provide its service, and we have not done any Synapse specific modifications to the aspects. Therefore, it is evident that the aspects in our aspect space can be transparently adapted to different ESB architectures. In other words, the ESB services in the aspect library can be reused 'as is' in different ESB architectures. Furthermore, as per Table 1, most of the aspects have provided diverse features. For example, the cache aspect has provided message caching, database record caching, synchronous cache loading, and asynchronous cache loading; the load balance aspect has provided session-less and session-affinity load balancing, round-robin and dynamic round-robin,

Table 2. Results of the case study with the Apache Synapse

No	Description	Involved Aspects
1	Compose Log Aspect with Multiples ESB Components	Log
2	Log Filtering	Log
3	Passive Logging	Log
4	Secure Logging	Log and Crypto
5	Persisting Log Records	Log and Persistence
6	Sending Log Records to Remote Log Analyzers	Log and Proxy
7	Replacing and Logging Errors	Error Handling
8	Replacing Errors	Error Handling and Log
9	Retrying for Communication Errors	Error Handling and Proxy
10	Retrying for Data Access Errors	Error Handling and Persistence
11	The persistence of Data securely	Persistence and Crypto
12	The persistence of Data selectively based on a data integrity check	Persistence and Crypto
13	Caching Message Responses	Cache and Proxy
14	Caching Database Records	Cache and Persistence
15	Reactive Cache Loading	Cache and Proxy
16	Proactive Cache Loading	Cache and Persistence
17	Round-Robin Load Balancing	Load Balance and Proxy
18	Dynamic Round-Robin Balancing based on the Response time	Load Balance, Proxy and Monitoring
19	Dynamic Round-Robin Balancing based on the Remaining Capacity of Queue	Load Balance, Proxy and Monitoring
20	Session-Affinity Load Balancing based on the Client IP	Load Balance and Proxy
21	Session-Affinity Load Balancing based on the Basic Authentication Header	Load Balance and Proxy
22	Session-Affinity Load Balancing based on the Cookie	Load Balance and Proxy

etc. All these features were implemented without modifying the foundation design of aspects. This emphasizes the sustainability of the aspect formulated based on our aspect development methodology.

CONCLUSION

An Enterprise Service Bus (ESB) is the next generation EAI middleware. ESB products represent a wide range of architectural approaches such as service component architecture, java business integration, etc. An individualized ESB, which is an ESB tailored to provide sustainable integration solutions for a particular customer, is the optimal solution for a customer. Moreover, the capability to produce ESB systems on demand significantly improves the agility of an ESB vendor. In order to develop any ESB variation or individualized ESB products, a systematic reuse across ESB systems is crucial.

This chapter proposed an approach for achieving a systematic reuse across ESB systems. Our work employed the reuse approach discussed in chapter *Reuse across Multiple Architectures*. The ESB architecture was selected as the variability, and ESB services were selected as the *Multi*

Architecture Reusable Components in order to gain a vast reuse. Different ESB systems use different source codes to offer the same ESB service. Because this is a kind of code scattering, we adopted the concepts of AOP to devise a programming model for expressing reuse solutions. ESB services were identified as aspects. Our aspect weaver structures the aspects based on different architectural styles to make it suitable for component-based systems. The evaluation of our approach was performed by conducting a case study with an open source ESB. The case study concluded that the ESB services can be reused 'as is' in different ESB architectures, and most ESB variations (aspects) can potentially be produced reusing the concrete solution space, which consists of the aspect weaver, aspects, and a language for defining aspects and aspect compositions.

FUTURE RESEARCH DIRECTIONS

A potential research opportunity is to develop multiple ESB (Enterprise Service Bus) product lines based on the reuse approach and the platform presented in this chapter. Software product line (SPL) is a family of products, derived from a common platform (Clements & Northrop, 2001). Traditional SPL approaches usually develop products with the same architecture and provide a systematic reuse only within a single product family. Therefore, for an organization, the suitable approach to develop different software systems would be multiple product lines. A platform for multiple product lines should provide a systematic reuse within multiple product families and be capable of formulating products with different architectures. This chapter presented such a platform. Hence, our work can potentially form a foundation for ESB product lines.

Extending our approach to a wide range of middleware systems is another future research opportunity. We followed a component-based approach. Aspects can be reused as-is in different architectures. The aspect weaver structures the aspects based on a given architecture style. Therefore, it should be possible to extend this work to a greater variety of middleware as most middleware systems can be implemented as the component-based systems.

Our work is a prototype, and it is necessary to improve it prior to use it in a production environment. Hence, enhancing the platform for a production environment is also a major future work. Furthermore, evaluation of the results of this research must also come to the forefront. Our case study only involved one ESB product. Therefore, evaluating our approach for a systematic reuse across ESB systems with multiple ESB products, and based on the result, consolidating our approach would be a significant contribution to the software reuse sphere.

Another promising research opportunity is in the cloud computing domain. The concept of the *integration-as-a-service* is emerging, and it primarily uses EAI (Enterprise Application Integration) middleware. The ESB is the current state of art in EAI middleware. As our approach can formulate ESB systems with diverse architectures, it is possible to offer a wide range of *integration-as-a-service* products so that the user can select the cloud service that is capable of aptly supporting his or her own unique requirements.

In conclusion, while many positive steps have been made in achieving a systematic reuse across ESB systems having diverse architectures, several research aspects remain open, and each research aspect can make significant contributions to several contemporary research areas.

REFERENCES

Bai, Q., & Fitch, P. (2009). *Delivering heterogeneous hydrologic data services with an enterprise service bus application*. 18th World IMACS / MODSIM Congress.

Buschmann, F., Henney, K., & Schmidt, D. C. (2007). Pattern-oriented software architecture: *Vol. 4. A pattern language for distributed computing*. Chichester, UK: John Wiley and Sons.

Chappell, D. (2004). *Enterprise service bus*. Sebastopol, CA: O'Reilly Media.

Chappell, D. (2007). *Introducing SCA*. Retrieved October 5, 2009, from http://www.davidchappell.com/articles/Introducing_SCA.pdf

Clarke, S., & Baniassad, E. (2005). *Aspect-oriented analysis and design: The theme approach*. Boston, MA: Addison-Wesley Professional.

Clements, P., & Northrop, L. (2001). *Software product lines: Practices and patterns*. Boston, MA: Addison-Wesley Professional.

Ehcache Homepage. (2010). *Performance at any scale*. Retrieved June 5, 2010, from http://ehcache.org/

Ermagan, V., Krüger, I. H., & Menarini, M. (2008). Aspect-oriented modeling approach to define routing in enterprise service bus architectures. *MiSE '08 Proceedings of the 2008 International Workshop on Models in Software Engineering* (pp. 15-20). New York, NY: ACM.

Gamma, E., Helm, R., Johnson, R., & Vlissides, J. (1995). *Design patterns - Elements of reusable object-oriented software*. Boston, MA: Addison-Wesley Professional.

Hohpe, G., & Woolf, B. (2003). *Enterprise integration patterns: Designing, building, and deploying messaging solutions*. Boston, MA: Addison-Wesley Professional.

Josuttis, N. M. (2007). *SOA in practice: The art of distributed system design*. Sebastopol, CA: O'Reilly Media.

Kiczales, G., Lamping, J., Mendhekar, A., Maeda, C., Videira Lopes, C., Loingtier, J.-M., et al. (1997). Aspect-oriented programming. *European Conference on Object-Oriented Programming* (pp. 220-242). Heidelberg, Germany: Springer.

Laddad, R. (2003). *AspectJ in action: Practical aspect-oriented programming*. Manning.

Majumadar, B., Dias, T., Mysore, U., & Poddar, v. (2007, June). Implementing service oriented architecture. *SeTLabs Briefings*, 3 -13.

Nock, C. (2003). *Data access patterns: Database interactions in object-oriented applications*. Boston, MA: Addison-Wesley Professional.

Pawlak, R., Seinturier, L., Duchien, L., Florin, G., Legond-Aubry, F., & Martelli, L. (2004). JAC: An aspect-based distributed dynamic framework. *Software, Practice & Experience, 34*(12), 1119–1148. doi:10.1002/spe.605

Pawlak, R., Seinturier, L., & Retaillé, J.-P. (2005). *Foundations of AOP for J2EE development*. Berkeley, CA: Apress.

Petals, E. S. B. Homepage. (2010). *Petals ESB, the Open Source ESB for large SOA infrastructures*. Retrieved March 5, 2010, from http://petals.ow2.org/

Rosen, M., Lublinsky, B., Smith, K. T., & Balcer, M. J. (2008). *Applied SOA: Service-oriented architecture and design strategies*. Indianapolis, IN: Wiley.

Schmidt, M., Hutchison, B., Lambros, P., & Phippen, R. (2005). The enterprise service bus: Making service-oriented architecture real. *IBM Systems Journal, 44*(4), 781–797. doi:10.1147/sj.444.0781

Seinturier, L., Merle, P., Fournier, D., Dolet, N., Schiavoni, V., & Stefani, J.-B. (2009). Reconfigurable SCA applications with the FraSCAti platform. *SCC '09 Proceedings of the 2009 IEEE International Conference on Services Computing* (pp. 268-275). Washington, DC: IEEE Computer Society.

Seinturier, L., Pessemier, N., Duchien, L., & Coupaye, T. (2006). *A component model engineered with components and aspects. Component-Based Software Engineering* (pp. 139–153). Stockholm, Sweden: Springer.

Sun Microsystems. (2005). *Java business integration* (JBI) 1.0. Retrieved July 20, 2009, from http://jcp.org/en/jsr/detail?id=208

Suvée, D., Vanderperren, W., & Jonckers, V. (2003). JAsCo: An aspect-oriented approach tailored for component based software development. *AOSD '03 Proceedings of the 2nd International Conference on Aspect-Oriented Software Development* (pp. 21 - 29). New York, NY: ACM.

Synapse, E. S. B. Homepage. (2008). *Apache Synapse - The lightweight ESB*. Retrieved October 8, 2009, from http://synapse.apache.org/

Walls, C., & Breidenbach, R. (2007). *Spring in action*. Greenwich, CT: Manning.

Welsh, M., Culler, D., & Brewer, E. (2001). SEDA: An architecture for well-conditioned, scalable internet services. *SOSP '01 Proceedings of the Eighteenth ACM Symposium on Operating Systems Principles* (pp. 230 - 243). New York, NY: ACM.

ADDITIONAL READING

Chappell, D. (2004). *Enterprise service bus.* Sebastopol, CA: O'Reilly Media.

Hohpe, G., & Woolf, B. (2003). *Enterprise integration patterns: Designing, building, and deploying messaging solutions.* Boston, MA: Addison-Wesley Professional.

Kiczales, G., Lamping, J., Mendhekar, A., Maeda, C., Videira Lopes, C., Loingtier, J.-M., et al. (1997). Aspect-oriented programming. *European Conference on Object Oriented Programming* (pp. 220-242). Heidelberg, Germany: Springer.

Pawlak, R., Seinturier, L., & Retaillé, J.-P. (2005). *Foundations of AOP for J2EE development.* Berkeley, CA: Apress.

Rosen, M., Lublinsky, B., Smith, K. T., & Balcer, M. J. (2008). *Applied SOA: Service-oriented architecture and design strategies.* Indianapolis, IN: Wiley.

Chapter 8
Information Feedback Based Architecture for Handling the Scalability Issues in the Reusable Cloud Components

Manjunath Ramachandra
Philips Innovation Campus, India

Pandit Pattabhirama
Philips Innovation Campus, India

ABSTRACT

With the evolution of the paradigm of cloud computing in every field of application, the demand on the reusable resources while providing the service has increased substantially. Although it is transparent to the user through virtualization, that is also a strength of cloud computing, the runtime scalability of resources to cater for a variety of services is to be addressed to meet the critical factor of the agreed quality of service. In this work, an architecture based on information feedback is presented to address this issue. The findings have been supported by the simulation results. The scalable architecture makes use of a hierarchy of resources, each level capable of providing a different degree of services. The demand for resources at each level, which is also equivalent to contention for resources or service drops, is computed using Random Early Detection (RED) or similar algorithms and used as feedback signal. The effectiveness of this signal may be enhanced by predicting the same several steps ahead of time. The prediction ensures the availability of a breathing time for the allocation of the resources.

DOI: 10.4018/978-1-4666-0897-9.ch008

INTRODUCTION

In order to meet the requirements of reuse and re-configurability, software architecture with scalable & extensible components will be very useful. However, it involves increased message handling and inter-process communication. The addition of new components to the scalable and extensible software architecture poses the issue of increased memory requirements, delay/ latencies, blockheads in the queue etc. It is predominant in the distributed software architecture. In this work, a novel mechanism based on information feedback is suggested to control these parameters while the architecture is scaled up. Accurate models are required to catch up the performance with the scaling of the software components. Although a good amount of literature exists on the effect of scaling on the performance, they do not provide an insight for improving or retaining the performance. In this work, the scaling is linked to the time shifts of the feedback signal provided to the source component through active control mechanism such as Random early detection (RED). Simulation results indicate that, by controlling the shifts given to the predicted version of the feedback signal, the performance of the scaled architecture may be improved. In order to link the quality of service with the organization of the content, a hierarchical organization of the same spanning multiple levels of abstractions is proposed. Inter component communication over the internet makes them vulnerable for hacking and poses security issues that requires serious attention. The suggested mechanism of the organization of the component is addresses this problem.

The paradigm of Component based software engineering (G. T. Heineman and W. T. Councill, ed, 2001) has significantly reduced the software development cycle time and the cost. It comes with the attractive features such as parallel development, software reuse, pluggable maintenance etc.

In the distributed software architecture, the inter-component communication has increased burden over the available resources such as bandwidth, buffer space etc. The supporting network provides limited infrastructure. With the addition of every component in to the network, the contention for the resources increases.

Through advance prediction of the status of the network as proposed in this work, it should be possible to overcome the issue of the network load. The delay as well as the loss rate gets reduced which otherwise would be substantial.

The goal of this chapter is to provide a model for effective deployment of the resources in the cloud. The underlying resources for the SaaS, PaaS and IaaS (W. Kim, 2009) are organized in to hierarchical model based on the priority of the invoking application as detected by the SLA. The hierarchies are mapped on to these service parameters as well as to the availability of the results at each level.

BACKGROUND

Components in a cloud cluster the reusable portions of the code together and provide the appropriate interfaces to the external world. The programmer can use them with the right configuration minimizing the code. As a result, the efforts towards the software development have been greatly reduced.

The Cloud Model for QoS

Cloud computing supports services over the network, providing scalability and quality of service (qos) guaranteed on demand. The on demand service ensures the users can customize and personalize their settings. The hardware, software and the data of the cloud (B. Rochwerger, D. Breitgand, E. Levy, A. Galis, K. Nagin, I. Llorente, et al 2009) can get reconfigured automatically. As a result, cloud computing has shortened the software development cycle.

Cloud computing has evolved from resource virtualization and resource sharing in to an array of scalable, on demand services It provides the ability to virtualized the resources, reliving the organizations from the burden of heavy investments over the software, hardware, platform and resource infrastructures. It is an ideal solution where a large infrastructure is idle most of the time or work load is spiky. The availability of parallel infrastructure speeds up the time to market and lowers the cost. It is ideally suitable for running batch jobs (such as system testing) in parallel. It is required to ensure that the resources are not overloaded up on deploying the same dynamically. QoS is the critical part of the cloud deployment to ensure that the committed services are indeed offered with dynamic deployment of resources

Distributed Component Architecture

The component based software model has been extended to support distributed software architecture (K. Wallnau, S. Hissam, and R. Seacord, 2001) spanning multiple machines. As a result, the components or pieces of software residing on the other machines can be used conveniently. It led to the practice of distributed component based software development being widely practiced today. It calls for the transfer of the components in to the runtime environment and configuration of the same. Each instance of the component can bear separate configurations accordingly. The containers embedding the components take the responsibility of communication with reliability, scalability etc.

The Model Based Approach

Simulation model is used for a variety of applications. It provides a better understanding of the issues, based on which the design parameters are fine tuned. To make it happen, the model and the actual network over which the components communicate, are to be compared apple-to-apple.

Figure 1. The inter-component communication network

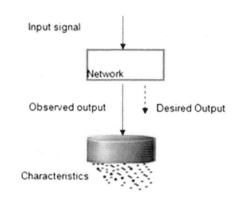

The actual network and simulation model are shown in Figure 1 and 2. The details of implementation of the model are provided in the next sections. It is expected that the model is to catch the behavior of the inter-component communication.

Relevance of the QoS in the Distributed Component Architecture

A component provides a variety of services to the users. It includes locating other components, instantiating, servicing, computation, communication etc. In applications that involve Graphical user interface (GUI) the real time response is mandated to provide a reasonably good user experience.

Components often communicate the 'services' that are require to adhere to an agreed QoS. In applications such as air ticket booking, the data gets invalid if the stringent timing constraints are not honored. Low latency high throughput systems require controllers to ensure the QoS.

The increased contention among the components takes a toll on the performance of the applications that use these components. Meeting the agreed QoS such as packet delay and loss would be difficult. The QoS defined at the network level translate on to the QoS of the inter component communication in the distributed network. It calls

Figure 2. The simulation model

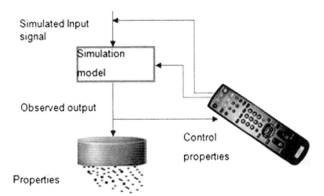

for the usage of an efficient traffic shaper at the component. The traffic shaper fairly distributes the available resources for the different components in the network considering their real time performance requirements.

The contention for resources can also happen when several applications share and try to access the same component. The paths leading to this component would get congested, leading to the dearth of resources. Prediction of the access patterns and the priority of the applications would be helpful to stagger the access.

The problem gets compounded when the number of components increases over the network. The traffic shaper or controller has to adapt to the dynamic scaling of the components that get and move out of the network over a period of time. Applications generally invoke variable number of components during the run.

Mechanisms for the Implementation of the QoS

Support for QoS at the network level involves IntServ, DiffServ (J. Harju, P. Kivimaki, 2000) etc. The QoS mechanisms are also supported in the component architectures such as CORBA for message publishing and subscriptions (OMG, 2002). However, the mechanisms are static in nature. For the runtime transport of the components, an effec-

tive adaptable QoS mechanism is required. The same is addressed in this work. Throughout this paper, the components and the nodes containing the same are used interchangeably as appropriate. The rest of this paper is organized as follows: in section 2 the model supporting information feedback is introduced. Section 3 provides an insight on the effect of scaling as seen through the model. Here the mechanism of the model handling the scaling issues is explained. The section 4 provides the summary of the work.

REALIZATION OF THE CONTROLLER ARCHITECTURE

In this section, a controller is introduced to handle the scalability issues and has been realized using a differentially fed artificial neural network. The simulation results to claim the improved performance are provided

The components exchange the data over more reliable network connection to minimize the data loss. The equations of the packet flow used for the traffic shaping are (Floyd, S., and Jacobson, V., 1993)

$$\dot{w}(t) = \frac{1}{R(t)} - \frac{w(t)w(t - R(t))}{2R(t - R(t))} p(t - R(t))$$

(1)

Figure 3. Differentially fed artificial neural network

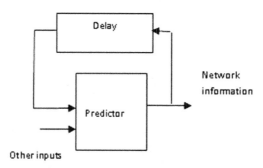

and

$$\dot{q}(t) = \frac{w(t)}{R(t)} N(t) - C \qquad (2)$$

Where $\dot{w}$ is the Data window size, q is the queue length, R is the round trip time, C is the Link capacity, N is the Load and p is the packet drop probability. The drawback with this equation is that the status of the network will be known only after the duration of the round trip time (RTT). By then, the characteristics of the network would have changed. So, a time shift is proposed for the feedback signal (Manjunath.R, K.S.Gurumurthy, 2004) to be used in the controller. In addition, if the status of the network is made known several steps ahead of time, there would be ample time for the components pumping the data to take the appropriate steps. Bigger the network more would be the traffic and the time required to control the same. The scalability of the components is linked to its performance. In this section, a traffic shaper blended with the predictor is introduced. The effect of scaling the components with such a traffic shaper in place has been analyzed in the next section and demonstrated through simulation results.

In the proposed method, instead of present value of the marking probability, its predicted value is used. This predicted value is generated with the help of a differentially fed artificial neural net-

work (DANN) (Manjunath.R, Gurumurthy.K.S., 2002) that makes use of several previous values to generate the output. The architecture of a DANN is shown in figure 3.

It consists of a predictor such as a conventional artificial neural network with the differentials of the output as the additional inputs for prediction. The other inputs are derived from parameters such as instantaneous load on the network. The immediate advantage of a DANN is that it provides the packet drop probability several time steps in advance.

Apart from the prediction of the packet drop probability, the DANN provides several interesting features suitable for shaping the inter-component communication traffic (Hwangnam Kim, Jennifer C. Hou, 2004) . The important of them are highlighted below:

- Make use of long history of inputs. This is because of the inherent autoregressive nature of the model.
- For a given number of iterations, the square error is found to decrease with the order of differential feedback.
- The model can work on a reduced set of training data
- For infinite order of differential feedback, the square error is zero
- The output with different orders of the feedback forms a manifold of hyper planes each of which is self similar (Erramilli,

A. Roughan, M. Veitch, D. Willinger, W, 2002) to the other.

- The origin of self similarity is due to the associated Long- range dependency or usage of the previous input and output samples.
- The self similar outputs have varying degrees of abstraction, each of which may be generated through the other by convolving with a Gaussian pulse.

Features of the Proposed Model

The proposed information feedback model goes well with the characteristics of the network that support the distributed components. The traffic over the network, be it LAN or the WAN, turns out to be self-similar. I.e., the shape of the autocorrelation function of the traffic observed over different time scales remain the same. The status signal such as the probability of packet loss sampled from the network, spans several time scales. I.e. It happens to be the resultant of the events happening at different timescales. The controller model precisely has all these characteristics (Manjunath.R, Vikas Jain, 2009) making it look like the network. If it sits in the feedback path, it should be easy to control the network as shown in Figure 4.

QoS is related to buffer dynamics. Though large buffers reduce the cell loss, the packet delays increases. On the other hand, small buffers could result in reduced delay at the risk of increased cell loss. It calls for different enforcements i.e. packet discard rules to ensure the QoS adaptively depending up on buffer size, growth, rate of the growth etc. These parameters are considered as the inputs of the DANN that predicts the traffic at different time scales.

As a result of the differential feedback being used in the controller, the control signal spans multiple time scales (Manjunath Ramachandra, Shyam vasudeva Rao, 2009). This important feature provides additional advantage of 'mul-

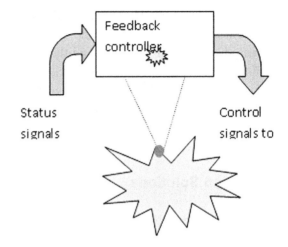

Figure 4. Feedback based controller in the network

tiple time scale control" for the inter component communication as explained in the next sections.

The usage of these previous values is equivalent to sieving the traffic through multiple time scales. Hence, when a DANN is used, it is equivalent to scale the time by a factor that is a function of the order of the feedback. DANN produces same results of scaling. Replace p(t-R(t)) with p(t). The equation may be thought of as the backward prediction starting from p(t) and up to p(t-RTT). Artificial neural network works the same way for the backward prediction. The time shift provided for the predicted samples amounts to generating the samples with future and past values. Derivative action generally reduces the oscillations .So proportional derivative with prediction may be used to reduce q variance. The idea here is to use the shifted versions of the 'near future' prediction of loss probability as the control signal that is fed back to the input. Shift provided to the feedback signal is equivalent to scaling the network with increased number of components.

Relevance of the Congestion Detection Interval

The congestion detection interval is a critical point in the design of the proposed congestion avoidance algorithm. If the interval is too long, the controller cannot adapt swiftly for the changes in the traffic input rate, making the difference between the predicted input rate and the actual input rate very large. As a result, packets get dropped in the network. On the other hand, if the interval is too short, the prediction error would be too large and the network would be left with near congestion state.

Issues and Solutions

The controller handling short timescales are to account for the bursty traffic from a single dominant or a limited number of data sources that tend to flood the buffers along the path. Such a source can be contained the earliest after RTT and adequate buffer space has to be reserved to handle the same. It leads to scaling issues with the number of components and the dynamics of RTT, Queue and window size.

Scaling of the Components

As N, the number of components interacting at a given time increases, the time slot allocated for each of them to share the common bandwidth decreases. This leads to the traffic control at different timescales. Let the communicating N components share a path with fixed link of capacity C. Let T be the propagation delay of the path.

Let q(t) and p(t) denote, respectively, the queue length and the packet dropping probability of the link at time t.

Let Wi(t) and Ri(t) denote, respectively, the window size and the round trip time of flow i at time t. Then (1) and (2) reduce to

$$\frac{dq}{dt} = \sum_{i=1}^{N} \frac{W_i(t)}{R_i(\tau_i)} - C \qquad (3)$$

$$\frac{dW_i(t)}{dt} = \frac{1}{R_i(t)} - \beta.W_i(t).\frac{W_i(\tau_i)}{R_i(t)}.p(\tau_i) \qquad (4)$$

Where

$$R_i(t) = T + \frac{q(t)}{C} \qquad (5)$$

and ß is the multiplicative parameter, p is the packet dropping probability, and $\tau_i = t_i - R_i(t)$.

The rescaling or the equivalent shift given to the feedback signal increases the link bandwidth and reduces the link delay by the scaling parameter, α. This is because each packet is served at α times larger bandwidth (which reduces its transmission time by 1/ α) and experiences 1/ α times larger delay. The time instants at which an event over the packet occur is also advanced by 1/ α. The delay reaches the stable value faster. I.e. a packet event that occurs at time t in the original network before scaling the components is advances to (1/ α)t in the scaled network as a result of scaling the components.

As seen in section 2.1, shift in the feedback signal amounts to scaling of the components or the supporting network. One of the effects of scaling is that the number of events the packets encounter gets reduced. The bandwidth delay product remains the same and is governed by the capacity of the network. Physically, it represents the capacity of the flow in terms of the amount of data packets that can be transmitted without waiting for the acknowledgment.

Let B and D represent the available bandwidth and the delay along a path in the original network and PBDP be the bandwidth-delay product along the path. Let B', D', and P'BDP be the equivalent parameters in the scaled network. Since the bandwidth-delay product remains invariant, the constraint for scaling becomes

PBDP = B . D = B'. D' = P'BDP   (6)

From the equation 6, the scaling parameter α is determined as follows:

B' = α .B;   (7)

D' =D/ α   (8)

where α >1.

The Shift changes the self similarity because shift implies a different order (Marco Ajmone Marsan et.al, 2005). In central interpolation, $\frac{d^n y}{dt^n}$ is replaced by $\frac{d^{n+1} y}{dt^{n+1}}$, i.e. the time scale would be different. This is as though the number of sources increases. Increase in the number of sources is equal to changing t to t. This is equivalent to multiplying differential by α. It takes $\frac{d^n y}{dt^n}$ to $\frac{d^{n+1} y}{dt^{n+1}}$ This is because the differentials and shifts are related by the central interpolation.

I.e. y= $A\frac{dy}{dt}$ becomes

$$y = B\frac{d^2 y}{dt^2} \qquad (9)$$

$$= C\frac{d^3 y}{dt^3} \qquad (10)$$

So on. Here A, B and C are arbitrary proportionality constants.

The outputs of the controller are central differences which are generated by providing shifts for the predicted probability of the packet drop signal. These derivatives are realized with the help of a DANN. Here the near future prediction of loss probability is being used as the control signal that is fed back to the input. The mechanism works because of the round trip time; the controller will not react immediately on the packet drop decision.

Scaling of the components resulting in increased RTT, increased load, reduced capacity, reduced buffer size, that happen dynamically in the network adversely affecting the performance of the network in terms of increased packet losses, increased delays etc. In this work, it is empha-

sized that, the shifts amount to scaling and by appropriately shifting the feedback signal and it is possible to achieve the same or better performance even when the number of components scale up. The packet sources or components can shift this feedback signal appropriately depending upon the instantaneously measured network parameters and achieve better end-to-end performance.

Scaling of the Queue Dynamics

The delay gets scaled as the available bandwidth reduces and it increases with increase in N. Last section explains that, with scaling, all the events get advanced by the factor $1/\alpha$. The queue length in the buffers of the original network is more than the same in the downscaled network. This is because, the downscaled network responds in line with the original network.

It is assumed that the channel capacity C remains the same. With this, dq'/dt reduces to

$$\frac{dq'}{dt} = \sum_{i=1}^{N} \frac{P'_{i,BDP}(t)}{D'_i(t)} - C' \qquad (11)$$

$$= \sum_{i=1}^{N} \frac{P'_{i,BDP}(t)}{\dfrac{D_i(t)}{\alpha}} - C' \qquad (12)$$

$$= \alpha \sum_{i=1}^{N} \frac{P'_{i,BDP}(t)}{D_i(t)} - C \qquad (13)$$

$$= \alpha \frac{dq}{dt} - (1-\alpha)C \qquad (14)$$

This equation shows that $\frac{dq'}{dt} \geq \frac{dq}{dt}$ indicating the effect of scaling. It may be noted that, in equation (11), the change in the queue size is computed as the difference between the arrival rate of the different flows and the link capacity. The

Table 1. Performance with RED and the proposed method for different number of components in the network with prediction step=1

No.	No. of sources	Variance with RED	Standard deviation with proposed method
1	20	125.2279	111.5828
2	30	134.0159	126.0763
3	40	140.5793	129.6867
4	60	142.8687	111.8134
5	80	177.0254	126.0417
6	100	194.5093	138.2350
7	120	219.2376	151.1265

Table 2. Performance with RED and the proposed method for different number of components in the network with prediction step=3

No.	No. of sources	Variance with RED	Standard deviation with proposed method
1	20	125.2279	106.8508
2	30	134.0159	120.8611
3	40	140.5793	128.3137
4	60	142.8687	111.8134
5	80	177.0254	126.0417
6	100	194.5093	138.2350
7	120	219.2376	151.1265

arrival rate of a flow i is computed using equation 6, by dividing the bandwidth-delay product by the delay.

The tables 1 to 4 show the variance of the packet queue for different number of components in the network. The change in the queue size variance for different degrees of the shift in the predicted feedback signal is provided. The simulation has been carried out in SIMULINK. The simulation setup for all the experiments in the paper is shown in figure 9. The block-sets that generate the desired traffic pattern available in SIMULINK have been used. The buffer size of the gateway is 8000 packets and the target queue length is 3200 packets.

Figures 5 and 6 show the instantaneous queue with the above simulation. It can be seen that, when the number of sources is 40, the ripples in

the queue settle down fast. The same is true with the average queue shown in the figures 7 and 8.

As seen in the tables, the variance will be reduced with increase in the prediction step. It continues for some time. Again the variance shows the upward trend. This is because the autocorrelation function of a long range dependent series exhibits oscillations and the data traffic over the network is self similar and long range dependent.

As the load increases, variance increases. When the transmission rate reaches the capacity of the network, the controller will be able to keep the aggregate throughput steady. As a result, the variance falls. At this stage, if the load on the network increases with the scaling of components, the feedback signal dominates and reduces the trans-

Table 3. Performance with RED and the proposed method for different number of components in the network with prediction step=4

No.	No. of sources	Variance with RED	Standard deviation with proposed method
1	20	125.2279	106.5868
2	30	134.0159	118.4315
3	40	140.5793	128.5254
4	60	142.8687	111.8134
5	80	177.0254	126.0417
6	100	194.5093	138.2350
7	120	219.2376	151.1265

Table 4. Performance with RED and the proposed method for different number of components in the network with prediction step=6

No.	No.of sources	Variance with RED	Standard deviation with proposed method
1	20	125.2279	106.6906
2	30	134.0159	119.2891
3	40	140.5793	127.5494
4	60	142.8687	111.8134
5	80	177.0254	126.0417
6	100	194.5093	138.2350
7	120	219.2376	151.1265

Figure 5. Instantaneous value of the queue for 20 sources without shift – with shift 1 --with shift 2

Figure 6. Instantaneous value of the queue for 40 sources without shift – with shift 1 --with shift 2

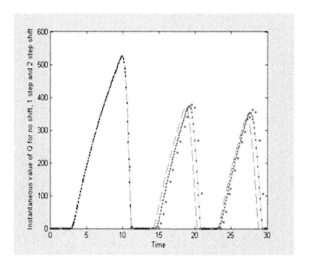

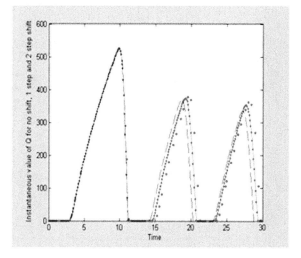

Figure 7. Time response for 20 sources without shift – with shift 1 --with shift 2

Figure 8. Time response for 40 sources . without shift – with shift 1 --with shift 2

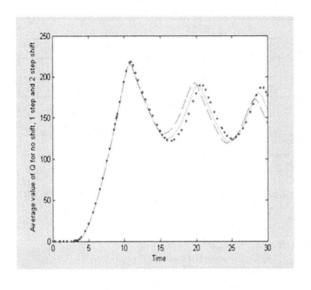

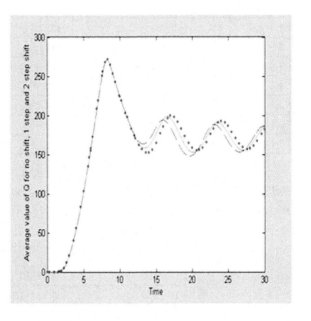

Figure 9. Simulation model

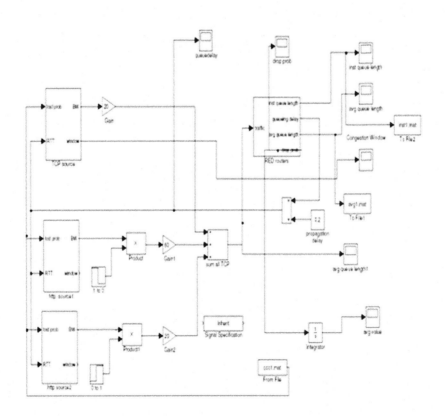

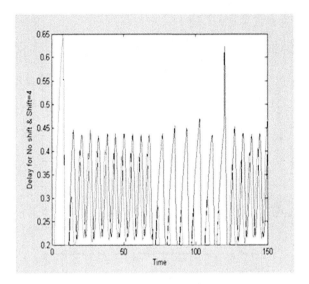

Figure 10. Packet delay for 40 sources with a shift of 4 -- without shift, - with a shift

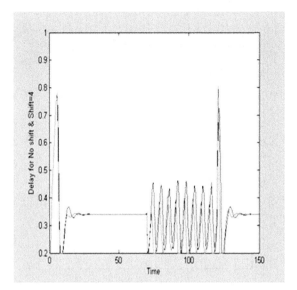

Figure 11. Packet delay for 80 sources with a shift of 4 – without shift, - with a shift

mission rate. Again the variance starts increasing. The same is evident in the tables.

RED detects the network congestion by computing the probability of packet loss at each packet arrival. As a result, the congestion detection and the packet drop are computed at a small time scale. On the contrary, in the proposed scheme, the congestion detection and the packet drop are performed at a different time scales, overcoming the issues stated above.

Because the proposed scheme detects and predicts the congestion at a large time scale, the components can react for the network conditions more rapidly. They receive the congestion status signal and reduce the data rates before the network actually gets into congestion. The reduced chances of congestion minimize the required packet buffer size and therefore reduce the end-to-end delay and the jitter evident from the Figures 10 to 13.

The queue and delay are shown in the simulation for different loads. The total number of data sources activated in each of the 120 second simulation time range from 40 to 120.

To see the effect of the shift, the number of sources has been changed to 40 & 120 respectively. The results are taken for the shifts of 4. As the load increases, the advantage due to shifts gets reduced. However, the delay with shifts is always less than the one without shifts.

The packet loss rates have been found to be 5.2% and 4.6% respectively. It makes the throughput 'with shift' 1.2 times larger compared to the one 'without shift'. The factor is 1.06 for a shift of 1. The high gain of 5.32 in the throughput factor has been observed when the load is low i.e. 20, with a shift of 1.

Scaling of the Window Dynamics

Equation 11 implies that each connection in the down-scaled scenario (reduction in the number of components) exhibits the same window dynamics but the response is $1/\alpha$ times faster than that in the original case (since the connection as a result of downscaling adjusts its rate per round trip time $R'i(t)$). The equation governing the window dynamics in the scaled network may be written as

197

Figure 12. Packet delay for 120 sources with a shift of 4 -- without shift, - with a shift

Figure 13. Queue size for 40 sources with a shift of 8 --without shift, - with a shift

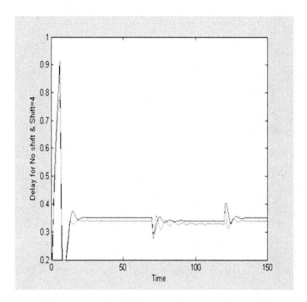

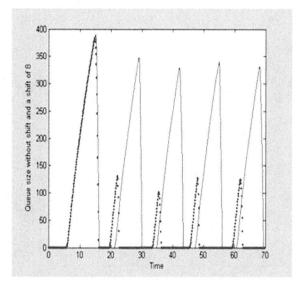

$$\frac{dW_i'}{dt'} = \frac{1}{R_i'(t')} - \beta.W_i'(t').\frac{W_i'(\tau_i')}{R_i'(t')}.p(\tau_i') \qquad (15)$$

where $\tau_i' = t' - R_i'(t')$.

By rearranging the terms, the effect of scaling becomes

$$\frac{dW_i'}{dt'} = \frac{1}{\frac{1}{\alpha}.R_i(t)} - \beta.W_i(t).\frac{W_i(\tau_i)}{\frac{1}{\alpha}.R_i(t)}p(\tau_i)$$

$$\qquad (16a)$$

$$= \alpha.\frac{dW_i}{dt} \qquad (16b)$$

where $\tau_i' = t - R_i(t)$.

It may be noted that, the current bandwidth-delay product of a data path in the network as explained in equation 6 is used as the current window size, and hence

W'ii (X'ii) = Wii (Xii) (17)

for all x'=(1/ α)x. In addition,

$$\tau_i' = \frac{1}{\alpha}\tau_i \qquad (18)$$

Because, over a short time $R_i'(t') = \frac{1}{\alpha}R_i(t)$ (Eq. (11)) and $p = p'$. Due to the advancement of the time events as a result of scaling, the window size can be reduced to achieve the same or better performance relative to the original network.

Scaling of the RTT Dynamics

The round trip time in the scaled time domain, t' is using predicted versions of the feedback signal. Here, RTT gets reduced by the same amount of the prediction or forecast.

When RTT is small, the components sensing the network respond too fast. If the network is out of congestion, all the components start increasing the transmission rate resulting in the

Figure 14. Organisation of the data/signal that get exchanged between components

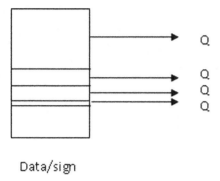

Data/sign

Figure 15. Organisation of the data/signal that get exchanged between components

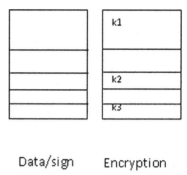

Data/sign   Encryption

network to stay in the congestion state. Hence, the phase transition of a network can happen at a lower load, much before any of the components tend to grab the network with higher data rates. The, traffic exhibits self-similarity at lower loads when the RTT is small and therefore better predictable. The same is true when the number of components gets scaled up. The contribution of individual components towards the network load is still small. Addition or deletion of a component in to the network influences the phase transition. Although contention for the resources increases with increase in the number of components, the traffic is better 'controlled' as evident from the graphs.

Organization of the Components to Meet the QoS in the Communication

The simulation results shown in the figures indicate that the quality of service of the applications driven by the components may be enhanced with the usage of the prediction feedback signal. Depending up on the availability of the network bandwidth and with the input from the prediction feedback signal, the appropriate abstract version of the data may be transferred over the network. For the end application that is calling this service, there will be a reduced service option instead of total denial of the service. The dynamic mapping

of the different abstractions of the content and the quality of service is shown in Figure 14.If the network bandwidth available is small, abstract version of the content may be transferred instead of denying the same.

Organization of the Components to Meet the Security Constraints in the Communication

The component communication has opened up security concerns with increased transactions over the Internet. Powerful encryption algorithms are required to support the same. However, providing the same degree of security among the communication of all the components, especially when the numbers are getting scaled is nearly impossible. A solution is provided to get around this problem.

The data or commands to be exchanged among the components are to be broken down in to a set of logically disjoint fragments so that they are transferred independently. Figure 15 shows the hierarchical organization of the data (or command) in to different degrees of abstraction.

Each of the abstractions is encodes with different encryption key catering for the security needs. For example, components handling financial applications are required to be encrypted with higher security.

CONCLUSION

The web based services are becoming increasingly popular handling a diverse class of applications. Each of these services often makes use of a large number of components that are hosted on a variety of machines over the cloud. The overall performance of these real time services depend up on the agreed quality of service rendered by the cluster of individual applications. With the addition of every component in distributed software architecture, the performance of rest of the components in the enabling distributed network gets affected.

Today the simulation provides encouraging results with improved quality of service. Simulation has shown improved utilization of the services as a result of prediction. For a short duration, the improvement increases with increase in the prediction step. Ultimately, the proposed architecture provides mechanisms for the service organizations to effectively manage and share the resources & 'services' in the cloud, leading to the paradigm of 'project' as a service. As an extension of the simulation, the components are to be loaded in to the actual build of a project.

FUTURE RESEARCH DIRECTIONS

Inter component communication is very important and challenging when the cloud has to support interactive services (such as web based services) where the end user application expects the data in a stipulated time. Moving forward, the web based applications such as air ticket reservation to real time medical image processing during tele-surgery involve hundreds of components communicating in real time providing the data and service with agreed QoS that in turn get reflected in the calling applications.

For test automation, the paradigm of cloud computing comes as a boon. The whole of test scripts need not be hosted by every business units. It may be rendered as a service catering for multiple vendors, versions and variants etc, all from one set of resources. The maintenance becomes easy as it absorbs the cost and supports interoperability

REFERENCES

Erramilli, A., Roughan, M., Veitch, D., & Willinger, W. (2002). Self-similar traffic and network dynamics. *Proceedings of the IEEE, 90*(5). doi:10.1109/JPROC.2002.1015008

Floyd, S., & Jacobson, V. (1993). Random early detection gateways for congestion avoidance. *IEEE/ACM Transactions on Networking, 1*(4), 397–413. doi:10.1109/90.251892

Harju, J., & Kivimaki, P. (2000). Co-operation and comparison of DiffServ and IntServ: Performance measurements. *Proceedings of the 25th Annual IEEE Conference on Local Computer Networks,* (p. 177). November 08-10, 2000.

Heineman, G. T., & Councill, W. T. (Eds.). (2001). *Component based software engineering: Putting the pieces together*. Addison Wesley.

Kim, H., & Hou, J. C. (2004). *Enabling theoretical model based techniques for simulating large scale networks*. Champaign, IL: University of Illinois at Urbana-Champaign.

Kim, W. (2009). Cloud computing: Today and tomorrow. *Journal of Object Technology, 8*(1), 65–72. doi:10.5381/jot.2009.8.1.c4

Manjunath, R., & Gurumurthy, K. S. (2002). Information geometry of differentially fed artificial neural networks. *TENCON, 3*, 1521–1525.

Manjunath, R., & Gurumurthy, K. S. (2004). *Maintaining long-range dependency of traffic in a network*. CODEC'04.

Manjunath, R., & Jain, V. (2009). Traffic controller for handling service quality in multimedia network. In Bhattarakosol, P. (Ed.), *Intelligent quality of service technologies and network management: Models for enhancing communication*. Hershey, PA: Idea Group Publishers.

Marsan, A. M. (2005). Using partial differential equations to model TCP mice and elephants in large IP networks. *IEEE/ACM Transactions on Networking*, *13*(6), 1289–1301. doi:10.1109/TNET.2005.860102

OMG. (2002). *Notification service specification*. Object Management Group, Aug. 2002.

Ramachandra, M., & Rao, S. V. (2009). *Data network performance modeling and control through prediction feedback*. ISSRE 2009.

Rochwerger, B., Breitgand, D., Levy, E., Galis, A., Nagin, K., & Llorente, I. (2009). The reservoir model and architecture for open federated cloud computing. *IBM Journal of Research and Development*, 53.

Wallnau, K., Hissam, S., & Seacord, R. (2001). *Building systems from commercial components*. Addison Wesley.

ADDITIONAL READING

Allman, M., Paxson, V., & Stevens, W. (1999). *TCP congestion control*. Internet RFC 2581, April 1999.

Christin, N. (2003). *Quantifiable service differentiation for packet networks*. University of Virginia.

Christin, N., Liebeherr, J., & Abdelzaher, T. (2002). A quantitative assured forwarding service. *Proceedings of IEEE INFOCOM 2002*, Vol. 2, (pp. 864-873). New York, NY, June 2002.

Clark, D., & Fang, W. (1998). Explicit allocation of best effort packet delivery service. *IEEE/ACM Transactions on Networking*, *6*(4). doi:10.1109/90.720870

Dovrolis, C., & Ramanathan, P. (2000). Proportional differentiated services, part II: Loss rate differentiation and packet dropping. In *Proceedings of IWQoS, 2000*, 52–61.

Evans, J., & Filsfils, C. (2007). *Deploying IP and MPLS QoS for multiservice networks: Theory and practice*.

Hoffa, C., Mehta, G., Freeman, T., Deelman, E., Keahey, K., Berriman, B., & Good, J. (2008). On the use of cloud computing for scientific workflows. In *4th IEEE International Conference on e Science*, (pp. 640-645).

Jacobson, V., Nichols, K., & Poduri, K. (1999). *An expedited forwarding PHB*. RFC 2598.

Lee, D. (1999). *Enhanced IP services*. Indianapolis, IN: Cisco Press.

Moretti, C., Bulosan, J., Thain, D., & Flynn, P. J. (2008). All-pairs: An abstraction for data-intensive cloud computing. In *IEEE International Parallel & Distributed Processing Symposium, IPDPS'08*, (pp. 1-11).

Padhye, J., Kurose, J., Towsley, D., & Koodli, R. (1999). A model based TCP-friendly rate control protocol. *Proceedings of International Workshop on Network and Operating System Support for Digital Audio and Video (NOSSDAV)*, Basking Ridge, NJ.

Vegesna, S. (2000). *IP quality of service for the internet and the intranets*. Indianapolis, IN: Cisco Press.

Wang, L., Tao, J., Kunze, M., Castellanos, A. C., Kramer, D., & Karl, W. (2008). Scientific cloud computing: Early definition and experience. In *10th IEEE International Conference on High Performance Computing and Communications, HPCC'08,* (pp. 825-830).

Xiao, X. (2008). *Technical, commercial and regulatory challenges of QoS: An internet service model perspective.*

Section 3
Reuse in Cloud Applications

Chapter 9
Understanding Cloud Computing

Qusay F. Hassan
Mansoura University, Egypt

Alaa M. Riad
Mansoura University, Egypt

Ahmed E. Hassan
Mansoura University, Egypt

ABSTRACT

Cloud computing is simply considered the realization of the long-held dream of using computing resources in the same way as accessing public utilities. Although the term "cloud computing" has been added to the IT jargon for about four years, many people are still in doubt as to what its actual meaning is. Some people even argue that cloud computing might just be an old technology under a new name. Many questions are raised when it comes to this subject. Why cloud computing? Is it the same thing as web hosting on third party servers? What is the difference between it and other popular terms such as grid computing? Why should organizations consider it? And, is it risk-free? IT, business, and academia folks are continuously asking about cloud computing with the intention of better understanding and realizing it. This chapter tries to demystify cloud computing by means of introducing and simplifying its terms to readers with different IT interests.

INTRODUCTION

Since early 2007, many of the IT professionals, business managers, and researchers have started to talk about a hot phenomenon called cloud computing. Each of these groups defined cloud computing differently according to their under-standing of its offerings (Armbrust et al. 2009). Recently, a better description for cloud computing has emerged: to outsource IT activities to one or more third parties that have rich pools of resources to meet organizations ever-changing needs in an agile and cost-efficient manner (Motahari-Nezhad et al. 2009). These needs usually include hardware components, networking, storage, software systems and applications. In addition, logistics such

DOI: 10.4018/978-1-4666-0897-9.ch009

as physical space; cooling equipment; electricity and firefighting systems; and of course, the human resources required to maintain all those items are implicitly settled.

Unquestionably, we all remember the global recession that hit the world wide economy in early 2008. During that time, many organizations were unable to keep up with the pace of change. It was really hard for many organizations to balance their IT resources with the actual demand. That is, businesses sunk, whereas IT resources and investments remained as they were.

With cloud computing, users are billed for their usage of remote IT infrastructures rather than owning them. This structure gives users the flexibility to scale up and down in response to market fluctuations. It is known that businesses usually start small with low start-up capitals and eventually flourish and start making profits. During the initial phases of new businesses, organizations usually cannot afford building mass IT infrastructures, which is why they can depend on cloud computing to access small amounts of resources. When they become popular with higher rates of hits, they can easily increase their usage of computing resources by renting more instances. Such resources can easily be disposed of to save overall expenses when not used during downturns or non-peak times.

Typically, cloud computing adopts the concept of utility computing to give users on-demand access to computing resources in a very similar way to that of accessing traditional public utilities such as electricity, water, and natural gas (Buyyaa, R. et al. 2009). In this framework, clients follow a pay-as-you-go model which provides global access as much or as little to computing resources as needed, whenever and wherever needed. Hence, IT executives are relieved from the risks of over/under-provisioning, enabling organizations to accomplish their business goals without highly investing in computing resources.

In the rest of this chapter, we review the present aspects of cloud computing with the aim of helping readers to better understand its concepts.

CLOUD COMPUTING, THE BEGINNING

Accessing computing resources in an easy manner as that of accessing water and electricity is a few-decades-old dream, which is still waiting to be achieved. Professor John McCarthy, a well-known computer scientist who launched time-sharing in late 1957, laid the groundwork for cloud computing by anticipating that corporations would sell resources by means of the utility business model (McCarthy, 1983). Soon after that, various firms started paying for their own use of computing resources, such as storage, processing, bulk printing, and software packages available at service bureaus.

A desire to allow customers to outsource processing and storage for their information has triggered some cloud-like implementations. Some of these implementations were initiated during the last two decades by providing the public with enormous IT infrastructure for their use. Such modules include:

- **Web Hosting:** A public service that provides organizations and individuals with spaces to host their websites and web applications. Web hosting providers usually offer a wide range of hosting options to clients. These Options vary from shared web hosting where tens or even hundreds of websites are being hosted on the same server, to whole servers being solely used and fully controlled by each client. Moreover, some hosting providers offer some of their solutions for free to both personal and commercial users. Rackspace, Yahoo Small Business, GoDaddy are a few examples of web hosting companies available in this field.

- **Application Service Provider (ASP):** A business model where organizations can have access to software applications offered by and remotely hosted on vendors' servers (Smith & Kumar, 2004). The advantage of the ASP model over the traditional software model is that clients are relieved from buying, installing, and maintaining prepackaged software solutions or the underlying hardware and network resources. That is to say, all these details are shifted to the providers, and clients in return pay monthly/yearly fees for their use of the offered applications. A number of ASPs are available in the market for popular ERP systems such as Oracle and JD Edwards. Although this model had a promising start, it was not able to stay in the market as a real competitor to conventional software models.

- **Volunteer Computing:** It is well-known that many of the research experiments require high volume computing powers in order to solve complex scientific problems. Many of the research experiments were able to meet this need by making use of idle computing resources available through volunteers (Sarmenta, 2001). Researchers gain access to supercomputer-like performance through this paradigm almost free of charge. Examples of volunteer computing include SETI@Home, POEM@Home, Docking@Home, Rosetta@home, FightAIDS@Home, Malaria Control, and many, many other projects.

- **Online File Sharing:** This model is based on allowing the Internet users to share files online by providing public spaces that can be easily accessed anywhere, anytime. Flicker is a famous example for this model where users are able to share and manage photos over the internet for free. Internet users also use free email services such as Hotmail, Gmail and Yahoo to host and backup their photos and office documents as well as other file types online.

- **Social Networks:** Facebook, MySpace, Blogger, YouTube, Wikipedia are all examples for websites aiming to connect and build virtual communities of users who are interested in particular issues and topics. All of the mentioned networks grant their users the opportunity to share ideas and resources such as videos, games, and even small computer applications in a friendly and effortless way. This is done by means of uploading them to central servers that are open to all community members.

WHAT IS CLOUD COMPUTING?

A cloud is an on-demand computing model composed of autonomous, networked IT (hardware and/or software) resources. Service providers offer clouds with predefined quality of service (QoS) terms through the Internet as a set of managed, easy-to-use, scalable, and inexpensive services to interested clients on a subscription basis.

The subsequent characteristics describe cloud computing:

- **Public On-Demand Computing Model:** Organizations are no longer obliged to possess their own datacenters to meet their IT needs; i.e., they have access to enormous pools of resources offered by providers in a way very much like that of accessing public utilities. "Public" word here denotes that, unlike what is being used by some articles and companies, cloud resources are neither owned nor managed by the clients themselves. To be specific, the public term cancels out the term of private (or internal) cloud (Haff, 2009). The main idea behind cloud computing is that instead of buying, installing, and maintaining computing resources, clients can rent, use and release them as needed through cloud computing. That's to say, it would be entirely against the benefits of outsourcing datacenters to third parties to build clouds within organizations for sole private uses only. In this context, readers are reminded that the "public" term should by no means contradict with the "hybrid cloud" and "community cloud" terms. Hybrid cloud, in simple terms, means the ability to amalgamate resources offered by public providers with those possessed and managed by organizations. Organizations often use Hybrid clouds during transition periods from non-cloud to cloud models, or to cover the temporary needs for extra computing resources, as those during seasonal spikes. Sharing the costs and efforts of building and maintaining datacenters within a group of organizations is something that Community cloud permits. Community clouds are generally built by huge enterprises then offered globally to their subsidiaries and business partners.

- **Autonomous:** In cloud computing, technical complexities of the offered services are hidden from the clients. This includes technologies, physical location(s), networks, cooling structures, and human resources who manage the services. Some cloud solutions are also considered as a step closer towards autonomic computing. These solutions allow systems to automatically scale up and down with the least amount of human intervention, if any at all.
- **Networked IT Resources:** Complex and powerful networks are what links both hardware devices and applications offered by providers in a way that gives access to their capabilities and allows sharing them too.

- **Predefined QoS:** Cloud providers define and state the conditions and quality of service (Qos) terms in the service level agreements (SLAs) so that clients would be informed about the expected level of service. From QoS terms, clients can compare the offerings of different providers, so they can choose from the available providers who can fulfill their technical needs.
- **Internet-based:** The name "cloud" originally emerged from the cloud shape that is being widely used in the IT field to graphically represent the Internet. This refers to the fact that actual cloud services are hosted beyond clients' boundaries and delivered over the Internet. Clients' data is also saved somewhere that may or may not be known to the client, and the way to access it is via an internet connection.
- **Management:** Providers take care of all aspects of management of fundamental resources such as installation, maintenance, and support. This feature frees clients so they could focus on their core business in lieu of caring about technical complexities.
- **Easy-to-Use:** Cloud providers deliver easy-to-use interfaces, and thus clients are able to make use of the offered services with the least effort and IT skills. Some of these interfaces include both graphical user interface (GUI) forms for IT administrators and non-technical users in addition to web services and application programmable interfaces (APIs) for developers.
- **Scalable:** Clients are not mandated to deal with fixed amounts of resources. Rather, they can scale their usage up or down according to the ever-changing business needs. This scalability gives adopters two main advantages over the on-premises models. First, it saves organizations from having to pay high up-front costs on IT resources that may never be fully utilized in the future. Second, it allows them to rap-

Figure 1. Cloud computing architecture

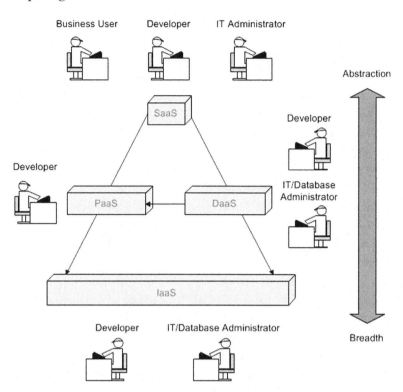

idly and flexibly add more resources whenever access traffic spikes.

- **Inexpensive:** It is known that small and medium enterprises (SMEs) cannot sustain their own datacenters. Thus, cloud computing offers them a considerably lower-cost option. The fact that resources owned by cloud providers are shared among different clients rather than being owned by or solely dedicated to a specific client (e.g., economies of scale), is what causes the service to be a money saver.

- **Subscription-based:** Clients are allowed to subscribe to services they are interested in using a utility-based pricing schema provided by cloud computing. The billing process usually takes place at the end of each month and it is based on the clients' usage of the offered resources rather than on a flat rate basis. Resources are usually metered in this form: CPU instances/day;

RAM MB/day; storage GB/month; number of I/O requests; amount of data transfer in and out; IP addresses; load balancers; number of licenses to software instances; and of course the level of offered administration and support.

ARCHITECTURE

As illustrated in Figure 1, the architecture of cloud computing is like a pyramid composed of four main abstraction layers. The base of the cloud pyramid contains extremely large sets of physical resources like those in datacenters, whereas the head represents a smaller number of software solutions and end-to-end services. Cloud computing deploys the concepts of SOA, enabling easy access to its layers by exposing them as a set of coherent services (APIs and/or GUI screens) that wrap underlying complexities. While users of top layers indirectly use bottom layers, loose-coupling between these layers is still available, giving clients the chance to use one or more of them as required. These layers are listed from bottom to top as follows (Wang et al. 2010):

- **Infrastructure-as-a-Service (IaaS):** Represents the base of the cloud computing pyramid without which the whole architecture cannot exist. IaaS provides commodity servers and hardware resources such as CPUs, memory, storage, networks, and load-balancers. Because IaaS is responsible for providing the cloud fabrics, it is sometimes called hardware as a service (HaaS). Although the HaaS term is being used in some books and papers, it is more accurate to call it IaaS instead, because this layer is not purely composed of hardware. A layer of virtualization that uses technologies such as Xen and VMware resides on top of the available resources to abstract core complexities. This virtualization enables clients to create virtual instances (very similar to physical servers) of hardware as needed. This layer is open to IT administrators and software developers who deploy/dispose virtual images. Examples of IaaS providers include: Amazon, Rackspace, GoGrid, IBM, and FlexiScale.

- **Platform-as-a-Service (PaaS):** Supplies users with operating systems and application platforms (both administration and development frameworks) that enable on-demand access to available hardware resources in a simple manner. Due to technical terms, access to this layer is only restricted to developers who write code to add scalability to their systems. Many PaaS platforms are available to enable access to IaaS resources. Some of these platforms are open source such as Nimbus, OpenNebula, and Ecyulabtus while some

other platforms are developed and provided by cloud providers such as Amazon Web Services, Google App Engine, Windows Azure, and Force.com.

- **Data-as-a-Service (DaaS):** Frees organizations from buying high-cost database engines and mass storage media. This layer abstracts underlying processing and storage infrastructures by adding database management capabilities to store client information. Database/IT administrators access this layer to configure and manage the database, while software developers write the code that retrieves data and saves its changes. One important thing about DaaS that is worth pointing out: DaaS is sometimes referred to as a part of PaaS or SaaS layers. Examples of DaaS include: Amazon Simple DB (for non-relational databases), Amazon Relational Database Service (aka Amazon RDS), Google BigTable, and Microsoft SQL Azure Database.

- **Software-as-a-Service (SaaS):** The ultimate and most abstract form of cloud resources that delivers software applications to clients in terms of accessible services. With SaaS, clients subscribe to applications offered by providers rather than building or buying them. Developers can also enrich already existing applications by integrating SaaS services into them. These SaaS services may be designed to access cloud databases through DaaS layer, or they may be designed to access hardware resources only through the PaaS layer. There are almost no restrictions on the access to this layer. . Examples of SaaS solutions and providers include: Google Apps, Microsoft Online Services, Oracle On Demand, Salesforce, NetSuite, Zoho, and IBM.

Figure 2. Convergence of cloud computing enabling technologies

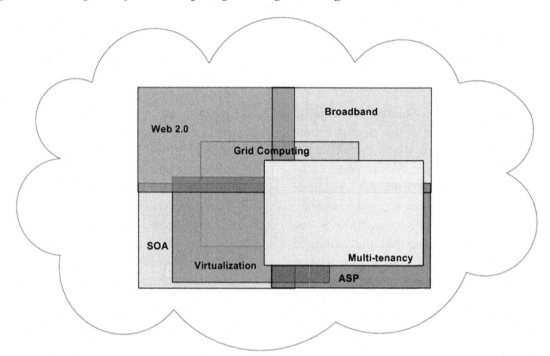

ENABLING TECHNOLOGIES

As illustrated in Figure 2, different technologies and methodologies converged and worked together to enable the emergence of cloud computing, including:

- **Broadband:** High-speed internet access enabled systems and data to reside in one continent while users access them from different continents. Furthermore, it increases accessibility to large data files such as images, videos, audios, complex datasets from different databases and other binary and large objects (BLOB). The ability to do so has given organizations the dynamicity required to overcome economic constraints in order to accomplish their goals. For example, many enterprises have chosen to host their information systems in less expensive datacenters in developing countries in Asia, Africa, and Eastern Europe to reduce their IT costs.
- **Application Service Provider (ASP):** In the mid-1990s, ASP came to the surface as a business model that enabled organizations to access tailored applications hosted by software vendors/third parties, freeing them to focus on their business rather than being distracted by IT complexities. In fact, this model was not broadly adopted due to two reasons. First, it was unacceptable to organizations which have already invested in complex and expensive systems to reinvest in other new systems. Second, SMEs with no experience of outsourcing did not like to take chances until best practice scenarios were presented by bigger adopters. In this context, it is worth mentioning that although this model could not survive, it opened the door to organizations outsourcing their applications to third parties (Seltsikas & Currie 2002).

- **Grid Computing:** Distributed computing, in general, refers to the ability to combine different computers to solve complex computational problems more rapidly. Grid computing is a distributed computing model that tends to gather computing resources (both underutilized and dedicated) from multiple administration domains to process computing-intensive tasks in a superfast manner (Foster & Kesselman, 1998). This model has given large organizations that own giant data centers, like Amazon, the idea to lease unused resources (both processing units and storage) to clients who need them. Initially, leasing unused computing resources was like a side business to these organizations before creating separate cloud computing business units. Due to such implementations, some computer scientists and technicians consider grid computing as the backbone of cloud computing (Foster et al., 2008).

- **Service-Oriented Architecture (SOA):** The idea of SOA is to turn the functionalities of both existing and new stovepipe systems and complex applications into a set of granular and reusable components (Hassan, 2009). SOA has encouraged software vendors to offer their products as a set of loosely-coupled services that clients can use, reuse and orchestrate (compose together) to fulfill business requirements in a neat style. This agility also applies to cloud computing as well as making it easier and more efficient to access available hardware and software resources.

- **Web 2.0:** This decade has brought many advances in web technologies. Innovations included different data formats and forms of accessibility to information available on the Internet such as RSS, REST, Blogs, Portals, Wikis, XML, HTML 5, AJAX, XML Web Services, and other mashups. These techniques helped organizations to offer their information as sets of services that allow others to easily access them to mix and match underlying functionalities in their own websites (Murugesan, 2007). With Web 2.0 data may be hosted on datacenters of one or more organizations whereas applications that use these data belong to totally different organizations. These data can be easily and responsively transmitted between nodes so that end users do not notice any latency or inefficiency in the accessibility or application performance.

- **Multi-tenancy:** A software architecture that allows vendors to offer a single instance of one or more of their systems to different tenants (clients). Multi-tenancy represents an evolution of the ASP model that offers similar services at lower costs. The savings mainly come from sharing the same software instance and underlying infrastructures by clients rather than dedicating resources to each single one. Technically, this model depends on a single database that stores tenants' information with virtual separation between them. The separation is usually made by partitioning data into different sets of records, each of which is marked with an account ID of a corresponding client. Multi-tenancy is commonly used by SaaS providers as a way to manage global fixes, updates, and releases of offered applications from a central point. Customization features are usually enabled to help each client configure and adapt his instance along with his distinct needs.

- **Virtualization:** Hardware virtualization is a technology that organizations are usually adopting to enable better utilization of the available computing resources. Virtualization is accomplished by installing a monitor software known as hypervisor that allows multiple operating systems to be installed concurrently on the same machine (each with the needed sets of applications) with total isolation from each other (VMware, 2007). Additionally, many hardware capabilities were added to processors to allow better support for full virtualization. With virtualization, physical hardware resources are sandboxed and assigned to each running instance as required, enabling different clients to access them in a cost-effective manner. Virtualization is usually used as a substitute for multi-tenancy due to its easy implementation and lower costs. The preference to virtualization over traditional multi-tenancy mainly results from offering a multi-tenancy-like model without the need to redesign every application to be used simultaneously by different clients. In practice, virtualization is considered as a core enabler technology to cloud computing, without which, it might not appear in the current model and usage rate.

- **Metering Mechanisms:** The ability to meter clients' usage of computing resources has enabled providers to charge them for specific usage rather than the traditional subscription model. This, with no question, has encouraged new businesses to emerge, new providers to fairly rent services, and new customers to make cost-effective use of the offered services.

BIG PLAYERS

Different companies offer commercial cloud services to both individuals and organizations (private, government, and non-profit) including (but not limited to):

- **Amazon:** It is considered as one of the first and biggest cloud computing providers in the marketplace with multiple and redun-

dant datacenters across the globe –Virginia and California in the US, Ireland in Europe, and Singapore in Asia. These datacenters are configured to host different operating systems including Windows, Linux, and OpenSolaris. What is more, they are empowered with different software systems from all categories to give support to different environments. For example, IBM DB2, Oracle Database 11g, MY SQL, MS SQL Standard 2005, Apache HTTP, IIS, IBM Web Sphere Portal, and many others. Amazon started to offer its cloud computing solutions in July 2002 by launching its project of Amazon Web Services (AWS) to enable clients to make use of its cloud offerings (http://aws.amazon.com/). AWS is a collection of public web services that grant developers access to Amazon's cloud capabilities using programming platforms such as .NET, Java, PHP and Ruby. The service includes storage services, database services, queuing services, computing instances, and hosted applications and websites. With programmatic access to cloud services, applications can scale dynamically up and down its share of resources on-the-fly. Some of Amazon solutions include, but are not limited to:

  ○ **Elastic Compute Cloud (EC2):** A simple service that allows developers to enrich applications with the ability to automatically scale their computing capacity to fit loads.

  ○ **Simple Storage System (S3):** Announced in March 2006 as a service that allows clients to store their information on Amazon redundant and replicated storage networks.

  ○ **Relational Database Service (RDS):** A solution that delivers relational databases to cloud AWS clients.

  ○ **Simple Queue Service (SQS):** Offers queues for storing messages moving between distributed components and applications.

- Amazon CloudFront: A content delivery solution that gives organizations a way to distribute content close to end users to have high transfer speeds when downloading or streaming objects.
- Elastic Load Balancing: Presented to achieve a greater fault tolerance by enabling automatic distribution for incoming traffic across multiple EC2 instances.
- Virtual Private Cloud (VPC): A solution that enables organizations to securely link their existing IT infrastructure with AWS cloud.
- Amazon Machine Image (AMI): Besides programmatic access to cloud solutions, Amazon offers a special type of virtual appliances that enables clients to rapidly run their cloud environments. Namely, AMI enables clients to easily create and configure their computing instances either by selecting from existing image templates or by defining their own sets.

- Rackspace: One of the leading web hosting companies that has been offering enterprise-level hosting solutions for businesses of all sizes since 1998 (http://www.rackspace.com/). Rackspace is based in San Antonio, TX with offices, datacenters, and clients spread around the world. In March 2006, Rackspace introduced its utility computing solutions under the name of "Mosso LLC" before renaming it "The Rackspace Cloud" in June 2009 (http://www.rackspacecloud.com/). Rackspace offers a wide range of cloud solutions to its clients, including (but not limited to):
  - Cloud Servers: Gives clients a chance to have their computing in-

stances to host and run their applications/websites in the cloud.
  - Cloud Files: Delivers high performance, unlimited, and redundant online storage for files and media.
  - Cloud Sites: A cheaper alternative (with less management options) for dedicated servers to host websites built with numerous technologies.
  - Email Hosting: Offers Microsoft Exchange Hosting, Rackspace Email, or Hybrid Exchange (both of Microsoft Exchange and Rackspace emails). All email hosting solutions are offered with up to 10GB of storage per user and connectivity support to BlackBerry and other mobile devices.
  - File Sharing: Easy ways to store, synchronize, share, access and manage files securely online either through Microsoft SharePoint or Rackspace Cloud Drive options.
  - Online Backup: Offers secured file servers known as Rackspace Server Backup to backup data online with the ability to restore all files or specific versions of needed files.

- GoGrid: An important cloud provider that has been offering dedicated servers to online clients for about nine years (http://www.gogrid.com/). GoGrid now offers hardware infrastructure to clients, with great support for Microsoft and Linux platforms, at competitive prices, available with both pre-paid and pay-as-you-go models. GoGrid competes with others by offering special pricing options such as free inbound data transfer, volume discounts, dedicated support teams at no extra cost, and free f5 hardware load balancing. It also offers unique technical features such as hybrid hosting solutions (i.e. the ability to deploy dedicated servers in the cloud), and role-based access control. Access to GoGrid infrastructure is enabled through an API that employs a REST-like query interface to send calls over HTTP. This API supports access using different languages such as Java, PHP, Python, and Ruby.

- **Microsoft:** As a legendary player in the software industry, Microsoft decided to offer some of its well-known products that are being widely deployed by organizations on-premises as SaaS solutions (http://www.microsoft.com/cloud/IT-solutions/default.aspx). Microsoft highly invests to sustain its cloud offerings both by building new datacenters in new areas around the world, and by enriching its existing ones with gigantic server containers. However, Microsoft cloud services are not yet available to all courtiers making it hard to be used by all organizations that are highly influenced by Microsoft platforms. Here is a list of cloud services offered by Microsoft, including (but not limited to):
  - **Microsoft Exchange Online:** Delivers a messaging solution similar to the traditional Exchange Server environment with an anywhere, anytime access to emails. This is delivered with up to 25GB of storage per license, and a number of optional features such as BlackBerry connectivity support, data migration services, and archiving services.
  - **Microsoft SharePoint Online:** Offers an online platform for building and managing intranet sites and contents used to share information between coworkers.
  - **Microsoft Dynamics CRM Online:** Gives organizations a centralized place to store customers information needed to automate sales and marketing functionalities.
  - **Microsoft Office Web Apps:** A set of tools that act as online counterparts to traditional Microsoft Office applications enabling clients to access, edit, and share Office documents from anywhere.
  - **Microsoft Office Communications Online:** Provides organizations with IM capabilities with the ability to use voice and video communications between coworkers.
  - **Microsoft Office Live Meeting:** Brings the tools needed to conduct virtual meetings, events, and training sessions to clients.
  - **Microsoft SQL Azure Database:** Delivers a reliable, scalable, and multi-tenant relational database service built on SQL Server technologies.
  - **Windows Azure:** In addition to readymade SaaS services offered by Microsoft, it offers a programming platform that allows Microsoft developers to easily create their own cloud applications and services based on Windows platform (Chappell, 2009). Windows Azure allows developers to write scalable applications that are hosted on Microsoft's datacenters rather than being hosted on-premises. Hosting applications on Microsoft's datacenters enables these applications to scale out whenever swamped with requests by running multiple instances of the same code across different virtual and/or physical servers.
  - **Software-plus-Services:** Another feature made available to Microsoft clients giving them the ability to combine and integrate applications hosted locally with those hosted online by Microsoft or its partners.
  - **Office 365:** A brand new cloud-based office suite that is composed of com-

munication and collaboration products for businesses of all sizes (http://office365.microsoft.com/en-US/online-services.aspx). This service was launched on October 10, 2010 and it is currently available in 13 countries as a next-generation cloud service offered by Microsoft to its clients (http://www.microsoft.com/Presspass/press/2010/oct10/10-19Office365.mspx). Applications included in this suite are: Office Professional Plus (a web version of the traditional Office program suite); Microsoft Exchange Online; Microsoft SharePoint Online; and Microsoft Lync Online (the next generation of Microsoft Office Communications Online and Microsoft Office Live Meeting together). Microsoft expects expanding to include Microsoft Dynamics CRM Online and some other features tailored for education next year.

- **Google:** Google entered the cloud computing field as a SaaS provider with a number of tools known as Google Apps that utilize Google's infrastructure and management experience (http://www.google.com/apps/intl/en/business/index.html). These tools make it possible for businesses to collaborate online in a reliable, secure, and effective manner while saving total IT costs and management burdens. These tools include, but are not limited to:
  - **Business Gmail:** Email accounts with 25 GB of storage per user, instant search tools, group calendaring system, mobile access, BlackBerry integration, IM plus voice and video chat, spam and virus filtering.
  - **Google Docs:** Office tools that let users create and edit their documents, spreadsheets, drawings, and presentations using web-based interfaces.
  - **Google Videos:** Helps organizations host videos that contain confidential information in a central and secure place with the ability to share them with coworkers.
  - **Google Sites:** Provides a portal-like way to easily create and manage intranet sites.
  - **Google Wave:** Allows organization teams to easily share ideas and discussions.
  - **Google Groups:** Enables organization employees to share docs, sites, calendars, folders, and videos with groups instead of individuals.
- **Salesforce:** A key SaaS provider in the marketplace that is specialized in delivering CRM applications over the Internet (http://www.salesforce.com/). These applications make it possible for organizations to host their customers and sales information online. Some of Salesforce's applications include, but are not limited to:
  - **Sales Cloud 2:** A sales force automation toolkit that supplies organizations with a complete set of tools needed to manage all phases of sales.
  - **Service Cloud 2:** A customer service platform composed of a number of helpful tools that enables organizations to satisfy their customers while reducing service costs.
  - **Chatter:** A collaboration platform that enables organization employees to share important information and documents in an easy manner.
  - **Force.com:** A cloud computing platform that allows developers to build, deploy, and run custom cloud applications using Salesorce's infrastructure.

Table 1 summarizes cloud offerings of the key providers available in the market.

BENEFITS

As mentioned earlier, cloud computing as a business and technical model derives many of its benefits from other terminologies such as economies of scale, distributed computing, SOA, and obviously the client/server model. These benefits are on hand to both providers and clients.

Provider benefits:

- **Better Hardware Utilization:** Underutilization is a popular characteristic of hardware resources owned by almost all organizations. In these organizations, hardware resources rarely operate at full capacity; consequently, the value of these resources becomes extremely minimized as opposed to the costs paid to obtain them. Cloud computing can help organizations with large investments in hardware resources to lease unused parts to others for some fees. This task is usually achieved by utilizing virtualization technologies to partition physical servers on hand to a set of virtual instances for public use. These virtual instances could be used by clients in line with their needs, with the ability to combine them together to form server farms.
- **Higher Revenues:** It gives the specialties that never existed before in the market the chance to run new businesses that bring high income. Furthermore, the ability to lease unused hardware resources gives organizations the ability to make extra profits that could be exploited to run and enhance their IT infrastructure.
- **Bigger Software Markets:** Software vendors can deliver their applications in the form of services to their clients at lower costs on a subscription basis. This feature could encourage clients to increase their use of these applications, which in turn, would minimize the rate of software pi-

racy, allowing providers to gain higher revenues.
- **Activities Monitoring:** With cloud computing, providers are able to monitor actions and activities performed by their clients. In doing so, providers can promote other services and products to clients with the opportunity to make more money.
- **Better Releases Management:** SaaS providers are freed from sending different patches, service releases, and upgrades to each single client separately. Given that all software applications are being hosted on provider servers, updates can be instantly and automatically applied without client intervention.

Consumer benefits:

- **Reduced Costs:** Cloud computing aims to help organizations drive a low total cost of ownership (TCO) by minimizing capital expenses (CapEx) required for IT systems. SMEs can have low cost startups resulting from renting resources offered by cloud providers instead of having their own sets. Also, large enterprises can take advantage of cloud computing as a tactical solution to face seasonal peaks without spending large sums to acquire resources that might be idle for most of the time. Operational expenses (OpEx) including salaries and energy costs are equally reduced for both small-to-medium and medium-to-large corporations.
- **Reduced Setup Time:** With cloud computing, organizations can acquire and operate necessary resources in almost no time versus the long time needed to plan, buy and install their own ones.
- **No Installation Hassles:** With on-premises, organizations spend much time and effort to setup and run IT resources. Conversely, cloud computing put all of

Table 1. Offerings of key cloud providers

Company	Products	Service Type	Pricing Model
Amazon	EC2, S3, SimpleDB, Elastic MapReduce, RDS, SQS, CloudFront, VPC, Load Balancing, many other products	IaaS and PaaS	Pay-as-you-go
Rackspace	Cloud Servers, Cloud Files, Cloud Sites, Load Balancers, Email Hosting, File Sharing, and Online Backup	IaaS, PaaS and SaaS	Subscription* and Pay-as-you-go
GoGrid	Windows and Linux-compliant Hardware Infrastructure	IaaS	Pre-paid and Pay-as-you-go
Microsoft	SharePoint Online, Dynamics CRM Online, Office Web Apps, Office Communication Online, Office Live Meeting, SQL Azure, Windows Azure, Software-plus-Services, Office 365	IaaS **, PaaS, DaaS and SaaS	Subscription* and Pay-as-you-go
Google	Business Gmail, Google Docs, Google Videos, Google Sites, Google Wave, Google Groups	IaaS **, PaaS and SaaS	Free***/Pay-as-you-go
Salesforce	Sales Cloud 2, Service Cloud 2, Chatter, Force.com	PaaS and SaaS	Free***, Subscription* and Pay-as-you-go
FlexiGrid			
IBM	CloudBurst, Smart Cloud Enterprise, Information Protection Services, Smart Business Storage Cloud, WebSphere, DB2, Informix, LotusLive, BlueworksLive, SAP Application Managed Services, Smart Analytics Cloud, Systems Director and many other products	IaaS, PaaS DaaS, and SaaS	Subscription* and Pay-as-you-go
Oracle On Demand	Oracle E-Business Suite On Demand, PeopleSoft Enterprise On Demand, JD Edwards EnterpriseOne On Demand, JD Edwards World On Demand, Oracle On Demand for Siebel CRM, On Demand for Business Intelligence	SaaS and PaaS	Subscription* and Pay-as-you-go
NetSuite	NetSuite Financials, NetSuite CRM+, NetSuite Ecommerce, NetSuite OneWorld, NetSuite OpenAir, SuiteAnalytics, SuiteFlow, SuiteCliud Platform, SuiteApp.com	SaaS and PaaS	Subscription*
Zoho	Collaboration Applications(Chat, Messaging, Docs, Projects, Discussions, Share, Mail, and Wiki); Business Applications (Assist, Marketplace, Books, People, Challenge, Recruit, Creator, Reports, CRM, Site24X7, Invoice, Support); Productivity Applications(Calendar, Sheet, Notebook, Show, Writer, Planner, Writer)	SaaS	Subscription*

* per user or license/month

** indirectly by hosting applications and data on the underlying infrastructures

*** free up to a limited use for small businesses

these complexities on the provider side enabling clients to focus on their core business. Additionally, fixes and upgrades are all made by providers giving their clients the chance to focus on the business.

- **Higher Scalability:** Organizations can effortlessly install any number of hardware/software instances wanted by business. This goal is accomplished through methods that allow clients to create, upload and install their virtual machine images either by code or GUI screens. In addition, clients can freely delete unused instances to save costs.

In addition to the aforementioned benefits for providers and consumers, cloud computing is beneficial to our environment as it is considered greener. As known, computers manufacturing and operational running are energy intensive by nature (Wiliams, 2004; DOE & EPA, 2008). With cloud computing, computation power is better utilized (as there are no idle computers), fewer computers would be manufactured (as the same server would be used simultaneously by different clients), and less energy would be consumed (as less computers would be operating). This, with no doubt, can reduce the negative impact of technology on our environment.

CHALLENGES AND RISKS

As anything new in our life, moving to cloud computing is not an easy mission. Cloud computing is still in its early phases, and this makes it suffer from a number of downsides and risks that should be taken into consideration by adopters in order to achieve successful implementations. Some of the challenges that face cloud computing adoption include:

- **Misunderstanding:** Cloud computing is yet a confusing or even an obscure term

to most organizations. Clients should first properly understand cloud computing terms in order to benefit from its advantages.

- **Immaturity:** Cloud computing is still in its formative years. Organizations usually prefer to adopt proven methodologies that come with success stories and best practices from previous adopters.
- **Lack of Standards:** Cloud computing lacks the standards needed for loose-coupling between providers and clients, and the interoperability between different systems. This lack of standards usually leads to two risks. First, *vendor lock-in* that results from using proprietary APIs created by each provider to enable access to available services. Second, *data lock-in* as every single provider uses its own structures and methods to store client's information. That is to say, *cloud lock-in*, or the inability to move from one provider to another, and the difficulty to integrate cloud systems with other solutions, either cloud or on-premises, is the inevitable result of missing cloud standards.
- **Dependability:** The questions that every client usually asks when about to adopt cloud computing is: *"Is their cloud provider going to be around in the future?", "Can they get their mission-critical information, and is there a way to use it somewhere else?"* Organizations do not want to invest in IT solutions that may depart with vital information incase cloud providers decided to leave the market.
- **Long-term Costs:** As mentioned above, cost saving is one of the benefits associated with cloud computing; however, this cost saving is not always achievable. For example, long term use of cloud services that do not require continues upgrades may cost clients more expenses than acquiring and running them on-premises. Additionally, providers usually start their

businesses with affordable offerings, and then they ask for more fees later on.

- **Lack of Security and Privacy Terms:** Organizations cannot imagine hosting mission-critical information beyond their borders. They believe that losing physical access and control over the servers that host such information means losing the information itself. Such issue makes sensitive information vulnerable to security breaches, and surveillance activities of intelligence agencies and/or business competitors. Gartner advises adopters to ask their cloud suppliers the following questions (Heiser & Nicolett, 2008): Who is going to manage hosted data/systems? Do the providers have any security certificates from reputable external auditors and certification authorities? Where are the data/systems hosted, and/or under which jurisdictions will they be processed? If mission data is to be hosted alongside data from other customers (as is the case with multi-tenancy), how will the provider segregate different customers from each other? If encryption is used to prevent confidential information, how effective are the used encryption schemas, and are they well tested? How will data be recovered in case of disasters? Can the provider support some forms of investigation if required by customers (if so, how)? How would customers get their information back (and in which format) in case the provider is no longer available in the market?

- **Unreliability and Need for Redundant Internet Connections:** Since cloud computing relies on the Internet to host information, having a reliable, redundant, and high speed internet connection is critical to successful implementations. Although broadband became available to many parts of the world, some courtiers still cannot have dependable access to the Internet.

Another concern related to this point is that although small/micro organizations can have Internet access, they cannot afford having multiple Internet service providers (ISPs) for service availability and reliability. Money saved from leasing resources rather than buying them can be lost on redundant Internet connections and high bandwidth. These limitations undoubtedly make it impossible for some organizations to move to the cloud.

- **Slow Performance:** Providers certainly offer their cloud solutions to make profits; this causes clients to fear from depending on cloud services that might be over utilized by their providers resulting in poor performance. Furthermore, latency caused by solely depending on the Internet to process clients' requests can negatively affect the performance of the used systems.

- **Availability is not 100% Guaranteed:** A crucial requirement for business stability and success. Main cloud providers invest several hundred million dollars on their hardware resources to guarantee that a high level of service is provided to their clients. Redundancy of datacenters owned by providers is an essential strategy followed to assure the reliability of the offered solutions. However, the availability and reliability of cloud services are not 100% guaranteed due to some unmanaged conditions. For instance, Internet connection may be lost for some reason; server(s) crashes may happen on the providers' side; human error may cause servers to go down, etc. Lack of availability will force organizations to locally backup their information for emergency use during cloud outages. Of course, a local backup is not an affordable solution to smaller organizations as it will add rather than save overall costs.

- **Lack of Legislations:** Laws related to cloud computing such as reliability of the presented solutions, availability of providers, and secrecy of information, as well as the providers' financial rights are still missing. Moving to cloud computing depends a great deal on the trust between providers and clients. With strong and effective legislations, trust between cloud implementers can be built and sustained.

SUCCESS STORIES

New adopters can now find hundreds of success stories on providers' websites for organizations that embrace cloud computing. Our short list of success stories is categorized according to business/organization type as follows:

Large-Scale Enterprise

- **Coca-Cola Enterprises (CCE):** As one of the largest producers of nonalcoholic beverages, its main need was to have powerful communication and collaboration platforms that span geographies and time zone. Coca-Cola met its need by implementing Microsoft Online Services (http://www. microsoft.com/casestudies/Case_Study_ Detail.aspx?casestudyid=4000004584). Coca-Cola says that it has migrated 30,000 users from its legacy email platform in five months without interrupting their business operations. This solution helped Coca-Cola to get rid of the overhead of managing 50 servers and underlying different environments. Furthermore, the organization is now able to conduct internal meetings while saving much of the travelling time and expenses. Coca-Cola is planning to move an additional 42,000 users to online services, and 15,000 users will have mobile devices that are managed by Microsoft.
- **Washington Post:** With particular emphasis on national politics, Washington

Post released documents about Hillary Clinton's activities as a First Lady during President Bill Clinton's two terms in office, from 1993-2001. The documents were composed of 17,481 pages of data as a non-searchable, images-formatted, PDF. Washington Post thought to convert this report in a searchable PDF format by using Optical Character Recognition (OCR) tools. The estimate for converting and preparing the pages was about 30 minutes per page. Washington Post decided to move to the cloud by launching 200 server instances on Amazon EC2 to speed up the whole process (http://aws.amazon.com/solutions/ case-studies/washington-post/). The company was able to cut the process time down to 1 minute per page by using 1,407 hours of virtual machine time for final expense of $144.62.

Small-to-Medium Enterprises

- **Scribd:** The largest social publishing and reading site on the Internet, with 60+ million monthly readers, 20+ million embeds, and tens of millions of documents published. Scribd was launched in 2007, using Amazon S3 to host original and converted documents, and Amazon EC2 to convert the documents from original format to Web-readable HTML (http://aws.amazon.com/ solutions/case-studies/scribd/). One of recent needs of Scribd is to switch the site from Adobe Flash to HTML5. Realizing this means having to reprocess millions of files that were already published on the website, which would be impossible with only 40 employees and without supercomputing powers. Due to these limitations, Scribd decided to make extensive use of Amazon EC2 Spot Instances for its batch conversion. Amazon EC2 Spot Instances are a way that allows clients to bid on unused EC2 instances and run them as long as their bid exceeds the current Spot Price. Scribd ran its batch job on up to 2,000 EC2 instances which led to saving about 63% (or $10,500) compared with what it would have spent on on-demand instances for the same job.

- **Author Solution:** One of world leaders in the publishing field with more than 120,000 book titles. The company wanted to develop a system that would help it to automate the publishing workflow for authors and other publishers. Author Solution required the new system to integrate with a number of disparate back- and front-office to increase the visibility into business metrics. The company created a customized application on Force.com in less than 6 months for its iUniverse self-publishing brand that enables automation for the entire workflow from editorial and cover design to marketing and distribution (http://www.salesforce.com/platform/success_stories/stories/author_solutions.jsp). Author Solution migrated more than 40,000 International Standard Book Numbers (ISBNs) and approximately 2,000 in-flight projects to the new cloud environment. The new cloud environment enabled Author Solution to develop the needed system 1.5 times faster and to save about 67% of the costs of on-premise development.

Government/Non-Profit Organization

- **American Red Cross:** Chapters of American Red Cross had a need for a CRM system that can track thousands of volunteers and donors. This system had to be powerful enough to handle heavy loads related to natural disasters such as Hurricane Katrina and the earthquake in Haiti. American Red Cross was able to create the needed CRM system using SalesForce (http://www.salesforce.com/customers/

education-non-profit/american_redcross.jsp). The implementers deployed this system in 35 chapters around the U.S. to manage issues related to volunteers, donors, trainings, events, and back-office functions. The implemented solution enabled American Red Cross to handle as many as 10,000 cases per day by two persons only. The flexibility of the implemented solution allowed emergency expansion to 50 users. The cloud environment also enabled centralized access to information and more effective communication with 700 chapters around the U.S.

- **City of Carlsbad:** A small city that is located on the southern California cost with more than 100,000 local citizens. The city government faced a situation of upgrading its ageing email service and enabling some kind of collaboration and web conferencing technologies while being constrained by low IT budgets. The IT team of the city decided to migrate to Microsoft Online Messaging Services to accomplish its goals while saving overall costs (http://www.microsoft.com/casestudies/Case_Study_Detail.aspx?casestudyid=4000004251). By moving to Microsoft Online Messaging Services, the city expects to save ~40% annually while standardizing communication technologies. Cost reduction mainly originates from saving new hardware, licensing, and training costs. The cloud solution also enabled access to emails for diskless workers using Office Outlook Web Access.

ALTERNATIVE MODELS

Without a doubt, cloud computing is not the only available model in the market that allows organizations from all sizes to have access to remote IT resources offered to host and run their systems. Thus, organizations can overcome the cloud computing downsides by choosing from the available alternative models. Some of these alternatives

Table 2. Alternative models

	Cloud Computing	**Dedicated Servers**	**Virtual Private Servers**	**Colocation Centers**
Technical Offerings	Virtual computing instances with one or more of the followings: • Physical Computing Resources • Database Engines • Storage • Software Applications and Licenses	Whole, actual servers with predefined hardware specifications	Virtual computing instances with Predefined hardware specifications and OS	Hosting infrastructures such as: • Physical spaces • Electricity • Communication links • Cooling • Firing prevention systems • Security appliances
Management	Physical servers are managed by providers. Virtual instances are fully managed by clients with the ability to create and dispose instances as needed	Could be offered with or without management	Could be offered with or without management	Could be offered with or without management
Payment Model	Clients pay only for what they have used	Clients pay for the length of time they rented the resources whether they have used them or not	Clients pay for the length of time they rented the resources whether they have used them or not	Clients pay for the length of time they rented the resources whether they have used them or not

are listed in Table 2 and briefly described in the subsequent sections below:

• **Dedicated Servers:** As its name indicates, different clients can lease servers dedicated for their use by hosting companies for a defined length of time. Clients can either define the specifications of the needed servers or they can choose from hardware packages with the ability to customize according to their needs: upgrade, downgrade, install applications (as long as they hold valid licenses), etc. Usually, companies offer dedicated servers with different options; for example, they may entirely/partially manage these servers by their own staff or not. Due to the high similarity to the cloud computing model, clients often contrast them with each other. Besides, some hosting companies and clients use the terms "dedicated servers" and "cloud computing" interchangeably. Technically, the main difference between these two

models is as follows: with dedicated servers, clients are billed for the period they leased the servers and not for the actual use, whereas, cloud computing adopts a utility model that allows clients to pay only for the resources they used during a certain period.

• **Virtual Private Servers (VPSs):** This solution leverages the capabilities of hypervisors to provide clients with a less expensive form of dedicated servers. In this model, hosting companies split each physical server into a number of virtual instances to be used by different clients concurrently. Each of these instances can run any application that is supported by the hosting operating system. Clients can also link different VPSs (aka Virtual Dedicated Servers) together to act as a farm/cluster to obtain a higher performance needed by heavy traffic websites/applications. Although this model has many similarities with IaaS layer, they are not identical. In

VPS model, physical servers are usually sold to many clients with no real isolation between them. Those clients are offered with instances composed of limited hardware resources if compared to IaaS offerings. Thus, these oversold servers can easily lead to poor performance or even system crashes. VPS model is also similar to the dedicated server model in which clients are monthly billed whether they used the resources or not.

- **Colocation Centers:** This type of datacenter hosts clients' servers without the burden of actually having their own datacenters. Colocation centers (aka Colos) are being widely used by SMEs that cannot afford building huge and complicated datacenters. This option enables business owners to easily locate their servers at datacenters powered with spaces, electricity, cooling systems, fire protection systems, communication links, and security strategies. In addition, some of these centers offer the technical expertise needed to manage servers of clients who cannot hire required human resources. Although colocation centers do not provide servers as cloud computing do, they still offer the desirable hosting and management for client servers. Clients should consider it as an alternative to cloud computing.

CLOUD COMPUTING VS. GRID COMPUTING

Because cloud computing has many similarities with grid computing, people usually compare them to each other (Foster et al. 2008). Theoretically, the idea behind both models is to group various computing resources together and share their capabilities in a scalable form in order to accomplish one or more complex tasks that are hard or even impossible to get done with one single resource.

Grid computing is a distributed computing model that combines a range of computing resources to act as a single powerful unit. These resources may include processing cycles, memory, disk spaces, networks, printers, scanners, software licenses, remote devices, etc. Grid computing is widely used for academic and scientific purposes to process computationally intensive tasks faster and cheaper. Examples of fields that utilize grid computing include drugs discovery; urban planning; economic forecasting; weather forecasting; disasters forecasting; massive data analysis and storage; graphics and videos rendering; and complex mathematical problems.

From our understanding to cloud computing and grid computing, we can briefly describe the differences between the two paradigms as follows:

- **Business Model:** As mentioned, grid computing is being widely used to solve problems that require substantial computing capabilities that are hard to be owned or controlled by one single institution. In this model, each client negotiates with the provider for its use of grid resources by providing a detailed proposal for the scope of his research study and anticipated amount of necessary resources. Grids in general are offered for free, so clients do not pay money in return of their use for computing resources; rather, they must agree to make their own computing resources available for use by others at any time needed. Conversely, cloud computing is commercially offered by large companies for public use as an affordable option for organizations that cannot (or do not like to) build or manage their computing solutions.
- **Technical Model:** Both clouds and grids are distributed computing paradigms that use special software systems to link different servers together and enable access to resources as if they are coming from a single gigantic unit. However, the way cli-

ents access available resources is different in the two models. In grid computing, the amount and specs of the resources available to clients are defined and controlled by the provider according to his understanding of the actual needs of each particular client. Cloud computing, by contrast, hinges on virtualization to enable clients to freely and quickly create as many computing instances as needed.

- **Communities and Technical Scenarios:** Grid computing is mainly used for high performance computing (HPC) to process extremely complex experiments as those performed by scientists in laboratories. This objective is usually realized by designing and coding programs that can divide each intricate computation task into large numbers of simple subtasks (aka jobs) that could be processed in parallel using available computing resources. These jobs are queued by the resources managers while clients must wait until the required resources become available. Contrarily, clouds aim to bring computing solutions that can support high throughput computing (HTC) to organizations in an extraordinarily dynamic and scalable form. This dynamicity and scalability enable organizations to meet business ever-changing requirements flexibly and efficiently.

- **Security Model:** Grid computing is very strict about security, where in most implementations each new client is obligated to have a person-to-person communication with the provider in order to be able to create a new account. Certainly, this process is difficult and time consuming. In cloud computing, security model is fairly simpler, as providers offer web forms that deploy digital certificates to allow clients to securely and instantly subscribe to services, pay fees, and create/dispose instances as needed.

REUSE IN CLOUD ERA

Cloud computing is architected to enable high rates of reuse and flexibility. Many clients can share available servers; IT resources can be better utilized; client are able to reprocess the same functionalities in various systems and applications; and of course higher layers of cloud computing stack can reuse the offerings of preceding layers in various manners.

As mentioned before, cloud computing was built on a number of prominent technologies that impressively affected the IT field. On top of this list of technologies is SOA. Cloud computing leveraged SOA to wrap the functionalities offered by its layers to users in a form of highly reusable services. This reusability is not only critical for cloud providers, but for clients as well. Providers are able to share and reuse the same hardware/software functionality in a variety of solutions and by multiple, disparate users. That is, providers are able to offer their cloud resources in terms of abstract, granular services to different clients without having to tailor these services according to the needs of each single client. Clients are able to mix and match services to meet the needs of different applications without caring about the underlying complexities.

SaaS provides the maximum level of reusability in cloud computing. With SaaS, common applications such as word processing applications and email hosting can be used over and over by all interested clients without having to reinvent the wheel. Business functionalities can also be reused by different applications leading to shorter production cycles and more efficient management of available resources. For example, there is no need to re-create a general ledger several times when it is a standard functionality in all accounting applications. This reusability leaves the chances for customization only to highly specialized requirements and applications such as unique business workflow processes.

In spite of reusing the resources offered by the cloud, using non-cloud applications in it represents a big challenge to software developers, designers, and architects. In order to run existing software applications in the cloud, organizations are forced to migrate and convert them into cloud style. This migration may take place either by rewriting the whole code from scratch using frameworks/APIs offered by chosen cloud provider(s), or by leaving the code to run on-premises and extending it with cloud-based add-ins/services (hybrid cloud). Approaches and strategies to perform this migration process are not yet well defined. Early adopters and big players may take more time to introduce the best practices to leverage cloud computing in the context of using existing software applications.

Lack of standards is again a huge obstacle that hinders the reuse of data and applications in the cloud. Moving data from one cloud provider to another is almost impossible due to the proprietary structure in which data is stored. In addition, applications built to work on one provider's resources will need to be rewritten when moving to another cloud provider resulting in more outlays.

To enable mass acceptance of cloud computing, both technical and academic communities should work together to address these challenges alongside all other risks and challenges listed earlier.

CONCLUSION

This work has presented the essential terms related to cloud computing with the aim to answer common questions frequently asked by people who are in touch with the computer field. From the presented terms, we learned that the idea of on-demand access to computing resources is not really new as it goes back to the late 1950s. We also understood how different internet-based implementations including web hosting, ASP, volunteer computing, online file sharing and social networks have given cloud computing-like behavior to the Internet users.

A more concise definition of cloud computing and its characteristics are now available, giving readers, with different interests, a better understanding of its nature and offerings. We have presented the architecture of the cloud computing model in order to give the readers an insight into its underlying layers and technical details.

This chapter also discussed how different technologies stand behind the emergence of cloud computing. These technologies include, but are not limited to, broadband, ASP, grid computing, SOA, web 2.0, multi-tenancy, virtualization and metering mechanisms.

Furthermore, the chapter talked over the cloud services and capabilities offered by the key cloud computing providers in the market. This section is meant to enable organizations to easily and efficiently acquire the best-of-breed cloud computing offerings and products.

Another important point that has been presented in this chapter is the list of benefits that cloud computing offer for both providers and clients. The benefits promised by cloud computing caused IDC to expect cloud services spending to be about $42 billion by 2012. IDC also predicts that cloud computing will form 25% of the annual IT expenditure growth by 2012 and about third of the growth by 2013 (Gens, 2008). However, cloud computing is not risk-free. The readers should note that the implementation of cloud computing is not an easy mission as it is still in its early stages with many challenges yet to be overcome. Cloud providers, clients and researchers should work together in order to address the risks linked with cloud computing. This would alleviate these challenges before diving deep into the migration phases, leading to successful and long-lasting implementations.

A small number of case-studies were lightly discussed so that new adopters could take a look at scenarios where cloud computing best fits them. These cloud computing success stories were presented to show how cloud computing is being leveraged in different sectors and at all scales.

An important thing that adopters should keep in mind is that while cloud computing represents a giant leap in information technology, other competing models should be considered as strong competitors. Dedicated servers, virtual private servers and colocation servers represent the key alternatives to the cloud computing model.

One of the main contributions of this chapter is providing a brief comparison between the cloud computing and the grid computing models. This included the similarities and differences between the two models in terms of business, technical, and security details as well as communities and technical scenarios.

Finally, the chapter pointed out how cloud computing enables the sharing and reusing of available computing assets. SOA plays a great role in making both hardware and software functionalities, offered by the cloud computing layers, highly reusable. However, this reusability is not yet in its ultimate form due to the use of proprietary APIs and frameworks. Working on creating and leveraging open-standards that allows clients to freely move from one provider to another is the real enabler to the success and continuity of cloud computing. This will not happen overnight due to the large number of cloud computing providers currently available in the market. These providers are not willing to lose their clients by enabling such facility, but certainly, a form of standardization and common API will arise in the not-too-distant future.

ACKNOWLEDGMENT

Authors would like to thank Rana S. Shaker for her great assistance in revising and editing this work.

REFERENCES

Armbrust, M., Fox, A., Griffith, R., Joseph, A. D., Katz, R., & Konwinski, A. … Zaharia, M. (2009). *Above the clouds: A Berkeley view of cloud computing*. Technical report, EECS Department, University of California, Berkeley.

Buyyaa, R., Yeoa, C. S., Venugopala, S., Broberg, J., & Brandic, I. (2009). Cloud computing and emerging IT platforms: Vision, hype, and reality for delivering computing as the 5th utility. *Journal of Future Generation Computer Systems*, *25*(6), 599–616. doi:10.1016/j.future.2008.12.001

Chappell, D. (2009). *Introducing Windows Azure*. Retrieved from http://www.davidchappell.com/writing/white_papers/Introducing_Windows_Azure_v1-Chappell.pdf

DOE (U.S. Department of Energy) & EPA. (U.S. Environmental Protection Agency). (2008). *Fact sheet on national data center energy efficiency information program*. Retrieved from http://www1.eere.energy.gov/industry/saveenergynow/pdfs/national_data_center_fact_sheet.pdf.

Foster, I., & Kesselman, C. (1998). *The Grid: Blueprint for a new computing infrastructure*. Morgan Kaufmann.

Foster, I., Zhao, Y., Raicu, I., & Lu, S. (2008). Cloud computing and grid computing 360-degree compared. *Proceedings of the IEEE Grid Computing Environments (GCE08), co-located with IEEE/ACM Supercomputing*.

Gens, F. (2008). *IT cloud services forecast – 2008, 2012: A key driver of new growth*. Retrieved from http://blogs.idc.com/ie/?p=224

Haff, G. (2009). Just don't call them private clouds. *News.cnet.com*. Retrieved from http://news.cnet.com/8301-13556_3-10150841-61.html

Hassan, Q. F. (2009). Aspects of SOA: An entry point for starters. *Annals Computer Science Series*, 7(2), 125–142. Retrieved from http://anale-informatica.tibiscus.ro/download/lucrari/7-2-12-Hassan.pdf

Heiser, J., & Nicolett, M. (2008). *Assessing the security risks of cloud computing*. Gartner. Retrieved from http://www.gartner.com/DisplayDocument?id=685308

McCarthy, J. (1983). *Reminiscences on the history of time sharing*. Stanford University. Retrieved from http://www-formal.stanford.edu/jmc/history/timesharing/timesharing.html

Motahari-Nezhad, H. R., Stephenson, B., Singhal, S. (2009). *Outsourcing business to cloud computing services: Opportunities and challenges*. Technical report, HP laboratories.

Murugesan, S. (2007). Understanding Web 2.0. *IT Professional*, 9(4), 34–41. doi:10.1109/MITP.2007.78

Sarmenta, L. F. G. (2001). *Volunteer computing*. Ph.D. thesis, Massachusetts Institute of Technology. Retrieved from http://www.cag.lcs.mit.edu/bayanihan/

Seltsikas, P., & Currie, W. L. (2002). Evaluating the application service provider (ASP) business model: The challenge of integration. *Proceedings of the 35th Hawaii International Conference on System Sciences.*

Smith, M. A., & Kumar, R. L. (2004). A theory of application service provider (ASP) use from a client perspective. *Journal of International Management*, 41(8), 977–1002.

VMware. (2007). *Understanding full virtualization, paravirtualization, and hardware assist*. VMware White paper. Retrieved from http://www.vmware.com/files/pdf/VMware_paravirtualization.pdf

Wang, L., Laszewski, G. V., Kunze, M., & Tao, J. (2010). Cloud computing: A perspective study. *Journal of New Generation Computing*, 28(2).

Wiliams, E. (2004). Energy intensity of computer manufacturing: Hybrid assessment combining process and economic input-output methods. *Environmental Science & Technology*, 38(22), 6166–6174. doi:10.1021/es035152j

Chapter 10
Social CRM:
Platforms, Applications, and Tools

Anteneh Ayanso
Brock University, Canada

ABSTRACT

This chapter provides an overview of social customer relationship management (CRM) and explores the Web-based platforms that provide social CRM solution in software as a service (SaaS) model as well as the applications and tools that complement traditional CRM systems. Based on a review of current practices, the chapter also outlines the potential benefits social CRM provides to organizations in their sales, service, and marketing efforts. Furthermore, while the Web and its new breed of technologies and applications open new opportunities for businesses, these technologies also pose several new challenges for organizations in implementation, integration, data security, and consumer privacy, among others. In addition, these technologies can be exploited in a negative way to propagate misinformation against businesses and their reputations. In view of this, this chapter also examines ethical and legal challenges businesses could face in embracing social media technologies at the core of their customer management processes and systems.

INTRODUCTION

Social media technologies have transformed the way companies build and manage customer relationships as well as how customers learn about products and services. According to a recent study

by DEI Worldwide, 70% of consumers have used social media to research a product, brand or company (DEI Worldwide, 2008; Accenture, 2009). Businesses in different industries are trying to harness the empowering forces of these technologies and apply them to their sales, service, and marketing efforts. CRM applications rely on strong relationships in order to effectively retain exist-

DOI: 10.4018/978-1-4666-0897-9.ch010

ing customers and attract new ones. Building and maintaining strong customer relationships requires accurate and timely data to leverage collaboration that extends beyond traditional boundaries. Yet, traditional CRM applications did not have the capability to capture and manage such complex interaction, and they were not usually designed to be intuitive for the people who are handling the customer-facing applications. In addition, existing CRM solutions are not very effective in leveraging collaboration with customers as well as relationships within a company. As a result, new CRM platforms and applications enabled by social media technologies have surfaced to allow organizations plan, organize and manage their CRM strategies on a much larger scale than ever before. Social media technologies redefine the Web as a platform and empower individual users with light weight computing tools to manifest their creativity, engage in social interaction and share content in ways they never could before (Parameswaran and Whinston, 2007a; 2007b). Social media technologies empower sales people to be more effective and productive by leveraging the collective knowledge and experience of the broader sales community on the social Web.

Enterprise 2.0 is the term used to refer to the use of Web 2.0 platforms by organizations on their intranets and extranets in order to make visible the practices and outputs of their knowledge workers (McAfee, 2006; 2009). "Social CRM" represents Enterprise 2.0 in a sales, service, and marketing context by enabling individual sales users to easily interact with customer information and uncover business insights that were not readily available before (Oracle, 2008). Social CRM platforms help to ground and embody this vision by delivering software as a service (SaaS) and facilitating a community based on sharing information and making content available in real time via a new wave of social tools such as blogs, mashups, podcasts, RSS, social networking, widgets and wikis. Such platforms take advantage of the Web 2.0 interactive technology and its key features which include

readily shared data and access to Web-based applications from anywhere. Therefore, social CRM applications have great potential for businesses to communicate and interact within social networks and improve the quality and quantity of interactions with customers, suppliers and partners and boost reputation and overall brand loyalty.

A study conducted by Avanade, a global IT consultancy company, with top executives examines fundamental factors shaping the impact of social media on company performance and customer relationships, including user adoption, customer engagement, barriers to deployment and employee retention (Avande, 2008). The study covers three major areas of social media technologies in a business setting which include social media technology use by employees for business communications; social media technology use by customers with companies; and company use of social media in customer relationship management. The study indicated that businesses are aware of the trend toward social media, but most have no plan in place to manage the formal adoption of these technologies. According to the survey, over half of the companies have yet to put social media on the corporate agenda. Apathy, fear and concerns over productivity were cited as the main reasons for organizations to slow down the adoption of social media in the enterprise. On the other hand, the early adopters of social media report improved customer relationships, better corporate reputation and increased sales. On social media technology use by customers, the main benefits mentioned include improved feedback, creating a perception of the company as forward looking, the reduction in time to resolution for support issues, and even an increase in sales. Furthermore, on the benefits of social media to CRM, the majority of the companies surveyed feel that social media technologies provide an excellent means of uplifting customer relationships and allow them to add new value to their customer interaction, thus playing a major role in customer relationship management.

Avanade's survey clearly shows that "social media technologies have an important and positive role to play in the enterprise, and they provide businesses the opportunity to change the way they relate to customers, shifting the focus from managing transactions to building deeper relationships." It also reminds businesses that managing the introduction of these technologies is critical given the risks and concerns involved. The main objective of this chapter is to provide an overview of social CRM and the potential benefits social media provides to businesses in their sales, service, and marketing efforts. The chapter explores the current developments in Web-based platforms that provide social CRM solution in software as a service (SaaS) model as well as the applications and tools that complement traditional CRM systems. Then, the chapter examines the ethical and legal challenges businesses could face in embracing social media technologies at the core of their customer management processes and systems.

BACKGROUND

Despite the increased attention social CRM received in recent years, there is no consensus on its meaning or definition. However, several sources echo on the basic features of social CRM and its main differences from conventional CRM. One most frequently cited and carefully constructed definition is credited to Paul Greenberg, who is widely regarded as a leader in social CRM. Greenberg (2009) defines social CRM as follows:

"Social CRM is a philosophy and a business strategy, supported by a technology platform, business rules, workflow, processes and social characteristics, designed to engage the customer in a collaborative conversation in order to provide mutually beneficial value in a trusted and transparent business environment. It's the company's response to the customer's ownership of the conversation."

Greenberg (2009) highlights that social CRM is not a replacement for CRM; it is a change primarily on how communications take place.

Another comprehensive definition/description of social CRM is provided by Gartner, an information technology research and advisory firm, in its first report on Magic Quadrant for Social CRM (Gartner, 2010):

"Social CRM applications encourage many-to-many participation among internal users, as well as customers, partners, affiliates, fans, constituents, donors, members and other external parties, to support sales, customer service and marketing processes. Social CRM works within each of these domains, for example, to provide a social enterprise feedback mechanism in the service domain, or social monitoring or product development in the marketing domain..."

Researchers at Chess Media Group also make a distinction between traditional CRM and social CRM by examining how the evolution of social CRM takes place in different areas (see Figure 1). They describe that "traditional CRM has always been a set of linear, internally focused processes based around three key areas: marketing, sales, and service and support."

As the diagram shows, collaborative relationship has not been the focus in traditional CRM when dealing with the customer. Although CRM has been commonly described as involving the management of all aspects of relationships with a customer, it has been more of a transactional approach which is primarily driven by data and information, as opposed to relationship. Thus, building upon a strong foundation of CRM, social CRM augments public relations and recognizes the social customer and the social web (Chess Media Group, 2010).

The above definitions and descriptions emphasize that social CRM adds several advantages to traditional CRM and its activities. With social CRM, service teams can broaden their understand-

Figure 1. Evolution of social CRM (Source: Chess Media Group, 2010)

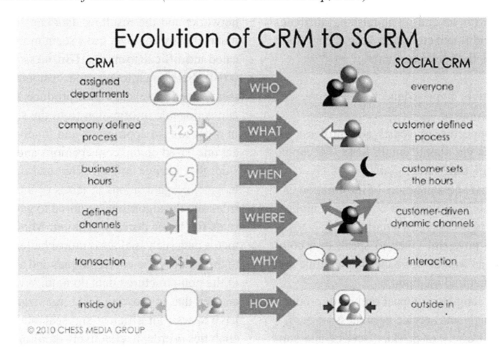

ing of the customer and her/his service expectations through conversations on social platforms. It allows service teams to redefine their roles and proactively indentify issues before they become problems (Accenture, 2009). Similarly, sales and marketing teams can take advantage of the wealth of social media technologies and information to generate more effective deals and marketing campaigns. By allowing marketers to engage in a dialogue with prospects much earlier and at many touch points, social media channels have resulted in a collapse of the marketing funnel (Accenture, 2009). While conventional CRM strategies focus on one-on-one customer interactions by leveraging integrated data and business processes across multiple touch points, social media channels, by contrast, make information freely available in order to shift influence to the community and power to the consumer (Tobey, 2010).

The Social Customer

The social Web brings new opportunities as well as challenges on the management of customers. Growing the customer base is easier but at the same time more competitive and risky. Unlike the traditional CRM environment, customers have relatively more control and power in social CRM. According to Forrester's recent survey, nearly 50% of users rank information from other consumers as more important than information from marketers (Greene et al., 2009; Accenture, 2009). Thus, social CRM represents a fundamental shift from a predominantly company-to-consumer dialogue to consumer-to-consumer dialogue (Accenture, 2009). Greenberg (2010a) describes that social customers "trust their peers, are connected via the web and mobile devices to those peers as much of a day as they would like. They expect information to be available to them on demand and at the same time have the tools and the desire to share and socialize that information with those same trusted peers." Attensity and Chess Media Group, in their social CRM series (2010), also describe the social customer with several distinguishing attributes from the traditional customer. According to their description, the social customer:

- is active, hyper-connected, creative, and collaborative
- is connected to social and professional circles via phone, email, SMS, Facebook, Twitter, blogs and forums
- is vocal and a producer of information
- is mobile and expects convenient applications to access from smart devices
- has a powerful voice to speak to a company as well as peers through a public and unstructured medium
- has a long-term impact on brand, product, company and service awareness
- has a variety of product, service and support options and expects to customize own products - "make it mine"
- expects good value that embodies either price, product quality, or service and support
- is critical of claims made by brands, influenced more by friends, family, and peers
- demands prompt dispute resolution and expects trust, transparency, and accountability
- expects consistent presence and two-way communication

Thus, along the customer dimension, the challenge for businesses pursuing social CRM strategies is to understand this cultural shift, adapt the social customer's changing expectations, and adjust the game plan in treating and servicing customers (Attensity and Chess Media Group, 2010).

Social CRM Data

One of the unique features of the social media channel is the nature and type of data that organizations have to deal with. Social CRM programs rely on conversations taking place at the various social media sites. Managing activity on social networks and the resulting data can sometimes make already complex tasks seem more complicated and difficult to manage (Business-Software, 2010). Sales, marketing, and customer service teams need to manage and produce structured and actionable information from the social Web in order to take appropriate and timely business actions based on the conversations and relationships they engage in. This brings additional challenges to organizations in terms of the business rules and the algorithms required to generate the rules for faster decision making. Mining social media data such as blogs is more challenging due to the lack of efficient techniques and algorithms in the non-structured data domain. While this is an area that is growing fast, organizations may have to wait for efficient and scalable tools and analytics in order to effectively monitor and filter online conversations and manage new forms of data related to campaigning and relationships. A related challenge on the data domain is the possible inconsistency of results from different monitoring or analysis tools, due to possible variations in data sources or data formats (Went, 2010). Thus, standards are expected to evolve in the future to facilitate these activities.

Adopting Social CRM Strategy

In order to respond to customers promptly, organizations need an organized approach to social CRM using enterprise software that connects business units to the social web (Wang and Owyang, 2010). Effective social CRM strategies require an organization to leverage existing CRM strategy and processes in a way that is both efficient and scalable to take advantage of social media resources. This means that activities and processes related to sales, marketing, and service should strategically utilize the extended collaboration and relationship opportunities provided by social media technologies. Social CRM is more than just the tools and the people hired to deal with social media channels. Simply using social media technologies does not automatically bring organizational benefits. Organizations should adopt a social CRM strategy in order to touch customers at multiple points and early in the buying process (Accenture, 2009). Nevertheless, adopting social CRM does not eliminate existing customer strategy, but requires organizations to augment or redefine their overall CRM program to support new customer interaction models as well as the culture of internal and external collaborations (Greenberg, 2009; Wang and Owyang, 2010; Attensity and Chess Media Group, 2010). Krigsman (2010) states that "social CRM represents a broader lifestyle change for many organizations and its success depends on determining goals, stepping forward on the path, and maintaining the persistence needed to achieve consistent results." He also points out three primary reasons that social CRM projects fail:

- *Poor strategy*: social CRM initiative requires specific plans, goals, and objectives to avoid a hit or miss proposition.
- *Over-focus on technology*: social CRM is more than just the technology or the collaboration forums. It should be accompanied by significant effort to engage and communicate with customers.
- *Minimizing culture*: social CRM represents a long-term process of change leading to greater commitment and engagement with customers, which in turn involves a long-term cultural shift and organizational leadership to actively support customer-oriented goals inside the company.

Wang and Owyang (2010) of Altimeter Group, based on interviews and consultations with several organizations, leading market influencers, and solution vendors, report that most organizations start their social CRM initiatives by laying out foundational (baseline) processes and deploying a customer insight program. After these initiatives, Wang and Owyang (2010) emphasize that

organizations should focus on real business values across seven categories of 18 social CRM use cases. Figure 2 shows these categories and the use cases identified under each category. The seven categories include: Customer Insight; Marketing; Sales; Service & Support; Innovation; Collaboration; and Customer Experience. In this framework, social customer insights form the foundation for all social CRM use cases. Thus social CRM projects must begin with social customer insights to engage well with a customer. Furthermore, this framework indicates that not all use cases are equally important. Organizations must prioritize based on market demand and technology maturity. Market demand reflects the urgency by organization to deploy a use case, whereas technology maturity reflects the market readiness and maturity of a solution. The detailed description of the use cases, the categorization, as well as the ranking illustrated based on the priority dimensions, can be found in Altimeter's report by Wang and Owyang (2010).

CRM Deployment Options

CRM applications can be typically delivered via *on-demand* model or *on-premise* model. In order to assess the potential benefits of social CRM applications, this section discusses the CRM deployment options that are currently available for organizations and examines some of the challenges in integrating new applications with existing offerings via on-premise versus on-demand delivery model.

On-Premise CRM: involves installing and running applications on computers on the premises of a client organization where data and software applications are held in-house by the organization. The servers, connections, access, and data are all controlled by the organization and housed internally. Major CRM vendors are providing social media management capabilities that integrate with existing CRM products installed on the premises of client organizations (Business-Software, 2010). These offerings come in the form of modules that

Figure 2. The 18 use cases of social CRM (Source: Wang and Owyang, 2010)

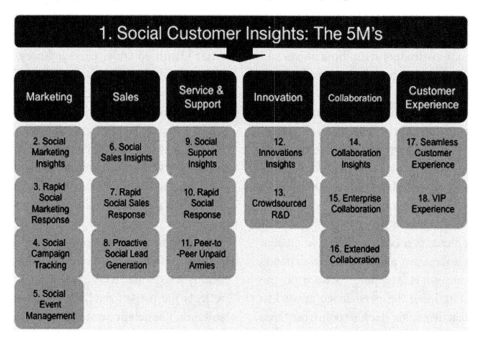

range from simple front-level integration to more complex process-level integration.

On-Demand CRM: is commonly known as software-as-a-service (SaaS) model. Under this model, data, servers, and CRM applications are available via the web, housed by the application vendor. SaaS or On-demand software application delivery models have come along in many forms such as Application Service Providing (ASP) or Business Service Providing (BSP) (Benlian et al., 2009). However, the early applications of ASPs were unable to offer greater economic benefits over locally installed applications and had limited ability for customization, data sharing and integration with other applications (Hai and Sakoda, 2007). With advances in internet technologies and software developing tools, a new breed of Web-based applications are now prevalent and SaaS is becoming a popular model for enterprise applications, particularly for social CRM. This increasing demand for SaaS applications has further led to the proliferation of SaaS platforms, third-party add-ons and integration tools. As op-

posed to buying a software license, the SaaS model bundles the cost of the infrastructure, the right to use the software, and all hosting, maintenance and support services into a single monthly or per-use charging (Sun et al., 2007). Mature SaaS offerings provide flexible software architecture and loosely coupled configurable application components. These features allow SaaS customers to quickly change presentation and logic without code modification and seamlessly access the latest version of customized services from the SaaS provider (Hai and Sakoda, 2007). The shift from traditional waterfall-like methodology to iterative methodologies in the SaaS implementation stages also promotes user adoption by incorporating user feedback early in the discovery, design, and development stages of the implementation (Hai and Sakoda, 2007).

Traditional drivers to on-demand based sourcing models include a focus on core competencies, cost-effectiveness, flexibility in technology choices, and the lack of necessary IT application skills in many firms (Kern et al., 2002). As the range of demand-driven applications grows, organizations need to evaluate several risk factors as well. One key consideration is integration with existing applications. It is important that business data and logics are properly integrated with other applications deployed by the SaaS subscriber (Sun et al., 2007). According to market surveys on the integration requirement of SaaS customers, most companies expect that the SaaS solution can be integrated with their on-premises legacy applications or other SaaS solutions (Kern et al., 2002). Some SaaS solution vendors provide integration as part of their service offerings by maintaining an integration server with prebuilt connectors to on-premise applications (Hai and Sakoda, 2007). SaaS providers also maintain a set of standard Web service application programming interfaces (APIs) to enable data integration and continuously provide seamless upgrades to functionality. There is also an emerging integration-on-demand market that calls for an integration service through menu-driven wizards and platforms for easily incorporating connectors as well as data cleansing and validation add-ons in an affordable and flexible pricing model (Hai and Sakoda, 2007).

Benlian et al. (2009) examine the main drivers and inhibiting factors of SaaS-adoption for different application types. Their analysis shows that social influence, pre-existing attitude toward SaaS-adoption, adoption uncertainty, and strategic value are the most consistent drivers. However, their study reveals that company size is not a determining factor in SaaS-adoption. Based on an empirical analysis, they find that the patterns of decisions on SaaS-adoption vary between application types, indicating that vendors should address application-specific drivers to increase SaaS adoption. Accordingly, applications with a high level of standardization, less strategic relevance, and lower technical and economic risks, have a higher degree of adoption in a SaaS delivery model. These findings have several implications for organizations when evaluating on-demand versus on-premise options for enterprise appli-

cations such as ERP and CRM. The relatively more complex design of these applications and the wide range of business processes they support require careful considerations in order to drive a successful SaaS CRM deployment. In the case of CRM, for example, organizations need to understand the customer service, sales, and marketing processes, and the associated benefits and risks involved when migrating the data and applications supporting these processes.

Among the key CRM trends outlined by Forrester Research recently is that SaaS CRM solutions become the default choice (Band et al., 2010). As SaaS deployments, on-demand CRM solutions are relatively more affordable, particularly for small and medium size businesses with limited infrastructure and the resources needed to effectively run on-premise applications. Notable examples of on-demand CRM vendors include *Salesforce.com, NetSuite*, and *RightNow Technologies* (SearchCRM.Com). These vendors also support social CRM applications. Targeting primarily small and medium businesses since its inception, Salesforce.com is the pioneer in the SaaS market that forced traditional CRM vendors to redefine their approach, including recent developments in social CRM applications. The company has been successful in establishing a sustainable business model and offering a pay-as-you-go CRM solution that includes sales force automation (SFA), marketing automation, and customer service and support automation. Salesforce.com provides an online application directory, AppExchange, and a Web-based programming tool for third party developers to facilitate integration of add-on services with other core on-demand CRM services. AppExchange's applications use the company's proprietary programming language, Apex, as their on-demand platform. Similarly, NetSuite's programming tool, SuiteFlex, enabled the company to offer customization capabilities to its customers while also allowing them to host new applications within the system (SearchCRM.Com). RightNow Technologies also offers CRM on-demand via the

SaaS model. In particular, the company gained strength in its SFA software offering after buying Salesnet Inc. in 2006. Later in 2006, the release of version 8 of its CRM application used the company's core strength in customer service to extend customer focus throughout an organization and let users design business processes around the customer via a "modular workflow engine" and a drag-and-drop design tool (SearchCRM.Com).

While SaaS CRM may seem a natural fit to smaller businesses, larger organizations are also considering SaaS CRM as most traditional CRM vendors (e.g., Microsoft and Oracle) are now moving into the SaaS territory. For example, Microsoft's first multi-tenant version of CRM came in 2007, which allows users to benefit from economies of scale, with multiple customers running on the same instance of the CRM product. Later in the same year, Microsoft also announced pricing for on-demand Dynamics Live CRM, offering pricing in multiple tiers, the most expensive of which beats Salesforce.com's cheapest rate of $65 per user per month (SearchCRM.Com). Similarly, Oracle released the latest version of Siebel CRM On Demand in 2007, which features customization capabilities to allow users to tailor the application to their processes, embed best practices, and streamline data-related activities (SearchCRM.Com).

The actual costs and benefits of a SaaS CRM deployment depend on several internal and external factors, including the unique needs of an organization, the required level of integration with on-premise applications as well as changes that may be required through future upgrades or extensions. Lashar (2009a) discusses the challenges, particularly for large organizations in deploying SaaS CRM and the tradeoffs these organizations should address in their strategy and planning. The major tradeoffs, according to Lashar (2009a), lie in idealism versus realism, adoption versus functionalism, and dynamism versus discipline. In other words, large organizations should first recognize that SaaS CRM will not be a panacea

to the challenges that have plagued their CRM initiatives in the past. Thus, organizations should expect the challenges of transformation and change realistically. Second, large organizations should expect gaps in the functionality of SaaS CRM for business requirements where SaaS solutions are less mature. While these gaps can be closed in the long-term, understanding the depth and breadth of functionality in SaaS CRM applications is important to maintain the right balance between on-premise and on-demand applications in the implementation process. Third, large organizations should be wary of the speed and frequency of changes to their SaaS CRM applications after initial deployment. For large organizations, even small changes may result in unintended impacts, thus requiring a disciplined approach to avoid costly mistakes.

In addition, Lashar (2009b) emphasizes the challenges for large organizations in integrating their SaaS CRM platforms into the rest of the technology landscape. For large organizations, technical activities such as moving data from legacy applications and integrating the new software with existing applications may involve significant risks and costs due to limitations in the capabilities of native tools as well as limitations in the SaaS CRM data structures and maintenance. SaaS CRM platforms may also pose challenges for the IT staff in large organizations in operational support, which involves technical constraints in managing availability, controlling security, optimizing performance, and migrating configuration changes (Lashar, 2009b).

Forrester outlines five best practice strategies to succeed with CRM SaaS solutions based on an interview with early adopters of SaaS CRM, leading CRM SaaS vendors and professional services organizations (Band et al., 2008). These best practice strategies include: building a solid business case; negotiating a sound contract; using a proven implementation approach; establishing strong data security procedures; and creating robust governance and support structures (Band et al., 2008). In building a solid business case, Forrester's study identified the importance of deeply understanding the total costs of SaaS CRM, and focusing on business models and economic drivers, differences in business benefits, flexibility, and risk. In the contractual agreement, the study identified the need for a formal service-level agreement (SLA) and that companies need to protect themselves from hidden cost drivers, unexpected service outages, declines in customer support, and obscure disaster recovery procedures. Concerning the implementation approach, the best practice includes defining business objectives; establishing a team (that involves an executive sponsor, a steering committee with a user group representative, a CRM SaaS solution administrator, and a CRM SaaS vendor developer or consultant); defining a timeline that outlines major tasks, milestones, and accountabilities upfront; defining a scope and prioritizing initiatives; and configuring a SaaS CRM solution that meets the specific needs of the users. In the area of data security, the study identified the need for data protection guarantees; compliance with industry standards; clearly defining roles and access rights for different users in an organization; and defining vendor data integration, conversion and exit blueprints. The final area of best practice identified in Forrester's study relates to the governance structure of the SaaS solution. Governance structure involves managing the SaaS solution; identifying the support resources and designating the support staff; establishing data backup procedures; and outlining upgrade schedules and procedures.

Social CRM Vendors and Platforms

Regardless of the delivery model, social CRM applications should leverage traditional CRM capabilities with the innovative Web 2.0 technologies to maximize relationships with customers and business partners. Recognizing the benefits of the social Web, traditional CRM vendors are incorporating social CRM features and function-

alities in their existing CRM design. New players have also emerged possessing several strengths and functionalities. This section summarizes how existing vendors are supporting social CRM applications and describe the features and functionalities provided by new platforms in the social CRM market based on different industry reports.

A comprehensive analysis of social CRM vendors is provided in Gartner's Magic Quadrant report (Gartner, 2010). Gartner's Magic Quadrant for social CRM evaluates the market and ranks the leading social CRM vendors according to two major dimensions: *ability to execute* and *completeness of vision*. The evaluation categories under the ability to execute dimension include: product/service; overall viability in terms of business unit, financial, strategy, and organization; sales execution/pricing; market responsiveness and track record; marketing execution; and customer experience. The evaluation categories under the completeness of vision dimension include: market understanding; marketing strategy; sales strategy; offering (product) strategy; business model; vertical/industry strategy; innovation; and geographic strategy. Beginning with a large list of vendors that offer some elements of social CRM, Gartner short-listed few vendors by emphasizing on processes and how vendors meet minimum inclusion requirements. Vendor categories include social-media monitoring; hosted communities; product reviews; sales contacts; and enterprise feedback management.

Gartner's four quadrants of the market based on its evaluation criteria are "Leaders", "Challengers", "Visionaries", and "Niche Players". Table 1 describes Gartner's characteristics of vendors that fall in each quadrant. For example, vendors falling in the Leaders' quadrant have software that benefits both the company and the community. Jive Software and Lithium are the only vendors identified in this quadrant. Visionaries demonstrate strong understanding of current and future market trends and directions. Vendors identified in this quadrant include Mzinga, Salesforce.com, and KichApps.

Table 1. Gartner's magic quadrants and vendor characteristics (Gartner, June 2010)

Challengers	Leaders
• Offer solutions that are poised to move into leadership, but have not yet done so. • Have strong products, as well as the market position and resources to become leaders, but may not have either the same functional breadth, marketing strategy, or rate of innovation as those in the visionaries quadrant. • Have an established presence, credibility and viability, and once their products become "good enough", they will likely cross-sell to their customer base to leapfrog others into the Leaders quadrant at some point in the future. **Vendors:** *None*	• Leaders' software must benefit both company and community: Leaders show benefits to enterprises by demonstrating ROI, by supporting KPIs, and leaders' software convinces users that they get something valuable by participating in a conversation or community. • Leaders' offerings demonstrate support for multiple CRM processes, not just one domain, and have substantial revenue coming specifically from their social CRM offerings. **Vendors:** *Jive Software, Lithium*
• Provide useful, focused technology, understand changing market dynamics and are working toward evolving their product capabilities. • Some can be held back by narrow functions, limited product road maps or by the lack of an innovative growth strategy • Many of the smaller vendors may enjoy success relative to their size, but need to grow and establish their positions before their competitive differentiation erodes in 2011. **Vendors:** *RightNow; Demand Media; Vovici; Bazaarvoice; Nielsen BuzzMetrics; LiveWorld; Thompson Reuter-Hubbard One; Radian6; Oracle CRM On Demand; Globalpark; Leverage Software; InsideView; Visible Technologies; Overtone.*	• Demonstrate strong understanding of current and future market trends and directions. • Their products and product road map exhibit innovation especially in architecture and lightweight integration, but their marketing and R&D efforts are boosted by their alignment with the open-source "ecosystem." • The Visionaries in this market have not exhibited the scope of delivery of the Challengers, but have demonstrated vision across a range of capabilities. **Vendors:** *Mzinga; Salesforce.com; KickApps*
Niche Players	**Visionaries**

Challengers have an established presence, credibility and viability, as well as strong products, market position, and resources to become leaders, but lack functional breadth, marketing strategy, or rate of innovation. Gartner did not identify vendors exemplifying these characteristics. The Niche Players provide useful, focused technology, understand changing market dynamics and work toward evolving their product capabilities, but may have limited functions, product road maps, or an innovative growth strategy. The vast majority of vendors short-listed in Gartner's study are identified in this quadrant (See Table 1).

Business-Software (www.business-software. com, 2010) also evaluated the social CRM market and reported top 10 social CRM vendors. The list includes Microsoft Dynamics, Salesforce.com, NetSuite, SAP, Sage, eSalesTrack, Jive Software, Lithium, BatchBlue, and Helpstream. Business-Software defines social CRM as "process for monitoring, engaging in, and managing conversations and relationships with existing and prospec-

tive customers and influencers across the Internet, social networks, and digital channels." It describes two basic Social CRM models: 1) the first model relates to the social media management capabilities offered by major CRM vendors in the form of modules that integrate with their existing CRM platforms, which can range from simple (just a Twitter integration) to complex (complete community management); 2) the second model is offered by Social CRM vendors whose platforms focus almost exclusively on customer relationship management through social networks. These products focus on community engagement and online communication. Some of them are standalone platforms, but they can be integrative with major CRM platforms.

Greenberg (2010b) also provided a brief, but insightful analysis of the major vendors and how they are doing in the social CRM front in terms of the extension of their applications. His assessment of the major vendors shows that few of them approach a "genuine holistic" social CRM suite that includes the customer facing departmental functionality and the social components and extensions. Greenberg's first focus was on the Big 4 which includes Oracle, Salesforce.com, SAP, and Microsoft. Greenberg mentions Oracle and salesforce.com for their emphasis on enterprise collaboration, whereas their social CRM features are not quite designed to engage customers. SAP is also mentioned, but for its component-based approach to social CRM, such as its integration of customer service monitoring tools with Twitter. Yet, SAP is not commended for its social sales or community platform integration. While Microsoft is mentioned for its high levels of personalization and contextual behaviors for customer experience, its progress on social channel integration is considered short. Others in Greenberg's list of vendors to watch include RightNow, CDC Software/Pivotal, Jive, Lithium, NetSuite, Sage, SugarCRM, Infor, INgage Networks, Get Satisfaction, and Sword-Ciboodle. One common description of most of these vendors is that they lack traditional CRM sales, marketing or customer service functionality.

Social CRM Applications and Tools

The software modules of a social CRM suite vary from vendor to vendor. Each vendor has its own design priorities depending on the market it serves and its traditional competency in different CRM processes. Research and consultancy firms have attempted to evaluate the various offerings, features, and functionalities of vendors in order to guide clients on their choices. For example, Gartner's report on Magic Quadrant for Social CRM provides a comprehensive description of social CRM applications offered by vendors identified in its Magic Quadrant (Gartner, 2010). These applications typically have customer-centric functions such as discussion forums, message boards, comments, polls and voting, surveys, reviews, ratings, chat, blogs, wikis, bookmarking, tagging, and search. In addition, social CRM applications have administrative tools for businesses which

include moderation, reputation management, dashboards, reports, event management, privacy management, and video management. Regarding the scope of applications, Gartner's study notes that vendors tend to start in one of the following four disparate approaches:

1. Hosting and supporting a branded or private-label community, and providing the surrounding functions
2. Monitoring, listening to and surveying private-label or independent social networks
3. Facilitating the sharing of common B2B or B2C contacts through the use of an internal community
4. Community product reviews to facilitate the online process

While these are currently disparate approaches, Gartner expects these approaches to form social CRM suites soon or be integrated into traditional big CRM applications provided by vendors such as SAP, Oracle, Salesforce.com, Microsoft, Amdocs, ATG, SAS, IBM and RightNow. The key functions and tools provided by the vendors identified in Gartner's Magic quadrant are outlined below (Gartner, 2010).

Bazaarvoice: community platform for social commerce that includes product reviews; ask & answer feature for customers; and stories capability for posting product and service experience.

Demand Media: community platform focusing on B2C social applications that integrates with blogs, forums, product reviews, and social networks such as Facebook, LinkedIn, Twitter and Youtube.

Globalpark: a single platform for managing surveys, panels and communities; features such as profile sharing and searching, push/pull with social media, blogs, real-time chat, multithreaded forums, wall postings, and rating systems.

InsideView: capabilities to compile news, firmographic details, management profiles, social graph information from the Web; easy to use functions for list building, lead generation, and lead qualification; features to search and extract information from sites such as Twitter and LinkedIn.

Jive Software: integrated blogs, wikis, ratings, rankings and voting, user profiles, dashboards and user interfaces, and a broad range of social capabilities; integrated social-media monitoring that connects with content repositories and applications; capability to bridge conversations between internal and external communities.

KickApps: flexible and configurable community platform, commenting and rating, user-generated content sharing such as photos, blogs, audios and videos, contests, polls, games, widgets, and event management; configurable dashboard for community management and engagement.

Leverage Software: a variety of SaaS components for social networks, such as blogs, wikis, ratings and status updates.

Lithium: hosted community and associated applications for hosting private-label social networks for B2B and B2C companies.

LiveWorld: functions for moderation services and community participation for company, product or brand issues; capability to be used with other social CRM platforms.

Mzinga: functions for social engagement with employees, customers, and partners; discussion blogs, comments, ratings, polls, surveys, events, chat, social profiles, mobile support, video and event management.

Nielsen BuzzMetrics: functions for listening to comments about products, brands and competitors in social networks.

Oracle CRM On Demand: easy-to-use user interfaces that mimic Flickr, Evite and iTunes carrousel to encourage collaboration; func-

tions for partner relationships; social media monitoring capabilities.

Overtone: text mining analytic capability for categorizing, aggregating and routing social mentions and feedback; capability to highlight statistically significant conversations and create business rules for reporting, notification and routing of records.

Radian6: social monitoring capability for aggregating and engaging in external social activities on forums, blogs, online news, Twitter, FriendFeed, LinkedIn and Facebook and video and image-sharing sites; community data aggregation and capture, filtering and configurable dashboards showing engagement levels, vote count, and links comment count; automated sentiment analysis to identify positive and negative mentions within activity.

RightNow: peer-to-peer customer care, crowdsourcing for idea capture, brand and reputation monitoring, and community ratings and reviews; B2C community-based customer service and idea capture.

Salesforce.com: social tools for sales providing in-process sales support and necessary data services; embedded social capabilities within existing CRM applications

Thomson Reuters-Hubbard One: focuses on law firms for B2B interactions; monitors e-mail logs, IM, address books, phone logs, time and billing systems, social networks and other communications traffic; features for attorneys to find, use and grow relationships with clients by sharing contacts; relationship scoring algorithms, taxonomy, matching contacts and filtering, privacy access layer, relationship search and analytics.

Visible Technologies: social media monitoring, analysis, and engagement tools to monitor, build, and manage brands online by aggregating conversations; dashboarding, reporting and analytics, including sentiment analysis and influence metrics; online reputation management services to protect brand in search engines

Vovici: functions for engaging/listening across multiple channels and communities that support forums, voting, surveys, blogs, profiles, multimedia, search, tag clouds, groups and wikis; capability for intelligent surveying, customer analysis and segmentation.

Similarly, Business-Software (2010) describes the main components of a social CRM suite to include brand monitoring, social media platforms, community support, and social CRM analytics.

1. *Brand Monitoring*: to track conversation regarding a brand or business which can take the form of sentiment tracking on third-party sites such as blogs and reviews or internal contributions, or opinions expressed in customer service/support calls.
2. *Social Media Platforms*: to access and contribute to social media platforms such as Twitter and Facebook from within the Social CRM solution.
3. *Community Support*: to create and manage customer communities from within the platform.
4. *Social CRM Analytics*: algorithms to generate reports on popular content, search keywords, and navigation paths, sentiment and behavioral analysis, and monitor customer interactions within online communities.

The social CRM applications and the key features of Business-Software's top 10 vendors are outlined below in order of their ranking (Business-Software, 2010). Some of these vendors are also listed in Gartner's top providers list.

Microsoft Dynamics: user-friendly dashboards to view and monitor activity on different networks; tool for identifying influencers and importing their profile; tool for conversation

analysis regarding brand, strength of sales and marketing initiatives.

SalesForce.com: Salesforce for Twitter to connect with customers in real-time; Facebook Toolkit to create service community for Facebook users; Salesforce Answers for posting ideas, vote on answers from peers, and add comments; Customer Feedback and interactive features for community members; Community Analytics to identify top ideas and issues, slice and dice data for more targeted campaigns.

NetSuite: extensive social network access directly within the platform to Twitter, Facebook, LinkedIn, etc.; monitoring for sentiment and risk to assess payment risk and improve collections processes; gauge suppliers' brand reputation, customer satisfaction, and service levels; assess supply chain risk; internal collaboration tools for cross-enterprise productivity directly within the NetSuite user interface.

SAP: Twitter Integration & Monitoring for connecting with customers on Twitter and converting user information to lead status; Features for troubleshooting and addressing customer problems using Twitter; Text Analyzer for sentiment analysis of conversations in Twitter; Facebook Integration for creating optimized community pages on Facebook through the CRM platform, connecting with customers and fostering brand loyalty.

Sage: social media dashboard and Web information that supports integration with many social networks; tool for importing social media information into contact management; community support and forum for platform users to discuss social media best practices and share tips on executing campaigns.

eSalesTrack: collaborative tools such as e-mail platform, integrated audio/video conferencing; dashboards and several user-centric and friendly applications.

Jive Software: Analytics Module for reporting and analytics solution; Bridging Module for connecting the employee community to the conversations customers and partners are having in public communities; Community Discovery Module for uncovering engagement and sentiment insights derived from user-generated content. Video Module for managing video libraries and moderate, tag and publish video assets; Mobile Module for mobile workforces to easily access applications and resources; connection with Microsoft Share Point that allows unified access, search results, activity streams, and document management.

Lithium: Reputation Engine that determines rank through dynamic, customer-defined formulas that take into account behavioral metrics; Lithium Mobile community platforms that are optimized for web-enabled mobile devices; Social Web Connect that allows clients to participate in conversations with customers over various social networks; Command Center Dashboards that provide an integrated view of the status of communities, alerts from customers and ROI metrics; Lithium Content Discovery (LCD) that offers solution to classify and moderate user-generated content; Content Connect that enables content integration through simple configuration or APIs; CRM Connect that connects communities with CRM systems such as Salesforce.com and RightNow Technologies.

BatchBlue: BatchBook's Contacts tool that offers contact management and a variety of filtering options; BatchBox tool for email forwarding; SuperTags for grouping contacts and creating custom fields that are searchable in Batchbook's advanced search; Social media monitoring tools; tools for building lists & reports; Web forms; and third party integration tools.

Helpstream: automatic notification for community questions and answers from experts that can be converted to solution articles; automatic data capture regarding customer experience; tool for maintaining and managing detailed social profiles for community participants to view and track; tool for identifying influencers based on scoring;

Social CRM: Ethical and Legal Challenges

Despite the potential benefits of social CRM, there are several ethical and legal risks organizations should consider and be prepared for. For example, in Avande's 2008 survey, fear and apathy toward social media were noted as key obstacles to using social media. The survey found that senior executives and IT staff tend to resist social media due to concerns over its impact on employee productivity. In addition, organizations may tend to resist social CRM adoption in order to avoid possible liability for privacy and security, intellectual property infringement or other social and legal risks. In this section, we review some of the critical ethical and legal challenges organizations may face in embracing social media in their CRM strategy.

Data Security

One of the major challenges of social CRM platforms is the security of personal profiles residing in vendor's data repositories as well as social networking sites such as Facebook and LinkedIn. The decentralized nature of social media data makes the issue of data security more serious in today's online environment. CRM solutions that rely on Web-based data repositories need to establish data security policies concerning the profiles of customers and business partners. Security should be the foundation for effective customer engagement and part of the social CRM overall strategy. Organizations that belong to industries such as financial services and healthcare are subject to extensive government and industry data security regulations that are challenging to address with SaaS solutions (Hai and Sakoda, 2007). Another operational issue that comes with data security is the service reliability. If SaaS solutions face frequent downtime, it can easily compromise the various advantages of on-demand applications. From the end-users perspectives, both data security and service reliability are critical requirements for an effective integration of social CRM applications.

Companies providing social CRM solution should avoid putting the onus only on the user. They should do more than framing the terms of use that protect themselves from potential legal liabilities. Several issues have already been the subject of discussion concerning terms of use as well as user's rights on their data with popular social networks. Adding to these challenges are policies towards the use of customer data by third-party developers. Third-party developers play a major role in extending the value of SaaS services by providing add-on services or facilitating application integrations. However, in the absence well-defined policies on the use of core customer data by these developers, the privacy and security of customers can be easily compromised with serious legal consequences. Applications that are interwoven with third-party networks are directly or indirectly affected by these issues. Today's customers are not only more sensitive about their information, but also have more power to challenge businesses on their privacy and security policies.

Analytics and Privacy

Although the analytical capabilities of social CRM helps marketers to gain marketing intelligence, mining social data poses a threat to ethical issues concerning customer privacy and individuality. Social media prompts users to disseminate data about their personal profiles which can be easily discovered, mined and combined with other data for use in a completely different purpose. This capability also raises privacy concerns for

customers because their information and actions can be easily analyzed and used for different purposes without their consent. CRM analytics can be used to discover a wealth of information on customer categories, profiles, and personal preferences. Beyond basic customer information, analytics can target a customer's specific events and actions on the social Web. This analytical capability, which is increasingly becoming better, makes customers' age-old concerns about the Internet and their privacy even more serious. In order to use this capability for productive business insights, organizations should give equal attention to the ethical issues concerning customer privacy and individuality.

Intellectual Property Rights

Social media has resulted in an explosive growth of user-generated content which presents significant legal challenges (George and Scerri 2007). As mentioned above, social CRM strategies involve the use of Web-based data repositories that allow users to store and share various types of contents. Yet, several social media companies have already been the subject of copyright issues due to loose policies on user actions. The more difficult challenge is the variation of copyright laws from place to place, while many of the social media sites cross several cultures and operate in multiple nations and geographic regions. Yet, their approach has been predominantly reactive, rather than proactive in dealing with copyright infringements. The user-friendly nature and flexible content sharing capabilities of most social media applications put unwary employees at risk of disseminating proprietary contents or violating the terms of service of partner Web sites. Several Web-based applications and features are available free of charge in order to attract the user base and enhance future functionalities based on user feedback and usage. If users do not pay attention to their proprietary contents, they can be easily exposed to copyrights infringements.

Social Media Policy

Several organizations today are active members of the social media environment. Nevertheless, policies governing their participation as well as their employees are not usually given the attention they deserve, particularly in customer-facing applications. Incidents happen on a routine basis mostly involving employees that are unaware of many legal and business issues surrounding social media technologies and their use in customer-facing activities. Thus, the decision to participate in social media, including the use of social software or application tools should consider a broad organizational policy framework that can help educate employees on their rights and limitations, as well as understand the approach or format they should follow in the day-to-day business use of social media technologies. As primary tools for engaging with customers and business partners, social CRM applications are more exposed to potential legal risks. Employees may damage company image while genuinely trying to promote their organization if they are unaware of the information they can disclose or its accuracy. In the absence of established company policies, guidelines, and appropriate training, employees are more than likely to face such risks. Thus, organizational policy governing the use of such applications and tools should be an integral part of any social CRM strategy. Furthermore, organizations should monitor any government regulations (national or international) as well as industry regulations that provide guidance on social software applications, customer interactions, management of customer data and transactions in a SaaS delivery model.

CONCLUDING REMARKS

Social CRM presents many opportunities as well as challenges for businesses (Accenture, 2009). This chapter reviewed the basics of social CRM and discussed several capabilities of social CRM applications for businesses in their sales, marketing and service activities. A review of the CRM market by analysts and research firms presented in this chapter also shows that the market will continue to grow in the next few years with the potential of more capable and integrated offerings from many vendors and Web-based platforms. The chapter also discussed an important element of the social CRM strategy, the social customer, who has higher expectations in the current business environment and is more influential than the traditional customer.

This chapter also discussed the additional challenges social CRM brings for organizations in the areas of implementation, application integration, data management, data security, and consumer privacy. In addition, while the business benefits and cost advantages of SaaS CRM solutions look attractive for organizations, industry experts advise organizations to conduct a comprehensive analysis of the deployment options and to follow a disciplined approach to the SaaS approach. To generate timely business actions using social CRM applications, organizations need enhanced business analytics and a holistic approach to the data that is coming from both structured and unstructured sources. Future research should address these limitations in order to enhance the full capability of social CRM solutions.

The various opportunities and challenges imply that social CRM requires a well-defined business strategy that helps organizations integrate the many touch points into their sales, marketing, and service processes and other internal systems. Industry experts also emphasize that organizations should not eliminate existing customer strategy, but redefine their overall CRM program to support new customer engagement and collaboration models (Greenberg, 2010; Wang and Owyang, 2010; Attensity and Chess Media Group, 2010). Organizations need to start with entry-level use cases or foundational (baseline) processes and a customer insight program, and then progress into other priority areas to derive real business values

(Wang and Owyang, 2010). To derive real business values, the strategy should also incorporate change management, training, and appropriate measures based on business goals.

Finally, in addition to the internal challenges to adopting social CRM strategy, organizations should be wary of the related ethical and legal issues. As discussed, social CRM is directly and indirectly affected by the global issues surrounding social media technologies. Therefore, establishing proactive policies, training, and staying current with national and international regulations as well as industry requirements should be part of any social CRM initiative.

REFERENCES

Accenture. (2009). *Social CRM: The new frontier of marketing, sales and service*.

Attensity and Chess Media Group. (2010). Introducing the social customer. *Social CRM Series*, Part #1, Avande. (2008). *CRM and social media: Maximizing deeper customer relationships*.

Band, W., Hamerman, P. D., & Magarie, A. (2010). *Trends 2010: Customer relationship management: Eleven trends shape CRM technology adoption agendas*. Forrester Research.

Band, W., Marston, P., Herbert, L., Leaver, S., & Rogan, M. A. (2008). *Best practices: The smart way to implement CRM SaaS solutions*. Forrester Research.

Benlian, A., Hess, T., & Buxmann, P. (2009). Drivers of SaaS-adoption: An empirical study of different application types. *Business & Information Systems Engineering*, *1*(5), 357–369. doi:10.1007/s12599-009-0068-x

Business-Software. (2010). *Top 10 social CRM vendors revealed: Profiles of the leading social CRM software vendors*.

Chess Media Group. (2010). *Guide to understanding social CRM*. Retrieved October 15, 2010, from http://www.chessmediagroup.com/resource/guide-to-understanding-social-crm/

Gartner. (2010). *Magic quadrant for social CRM*. Gartner, Inc. and/or its Affiliates. Retrieved October 15, 2010, from http://www.lithium.com/pdfs/whitepapers/Gartner-MQ-Social-CRM-t4OR7RhY.pdf

George, C. E., & Scerri, J. (2007). Web 2.0 and user-generated content: Legal challenges in the new frontier. *Journal of Information, Law and Technology, 2*. Retrieved October 15, 2010, from http://www2.warwick.ac.uk/fac/soc/law/elj/jilt/2007_2/george_scerri

Greenberg, P. (2009). Time to put a stake in the ground on social CRM. *PGreenblog*. Retrieved October 15, 2010, from http://the56group.typepad.com/pgreenblog/2009/07/time-to-put-a-stake-in-the-ground-on-social-crm.html

Greenberg, P. (2010a). The impact of CRM 2.0 on customer insight. *Journal of Business and Industrial Marketing*, *25*(6), 410–419. doi:10.1108/08858621011066008

Greenberg, P. (2010b). *A quick look at the social CRM vendor landscape*. Focus Brief.

Greene, M., Riley, E., Card, D., Mitskaviets, I., Bowen, E., & Wise, J. (2009). *Justifying social marketing spending*. Forrester Research.

Hai, H., & Sakoda, H. (2007). SaaS and integration best practices. *FUJITSU Science Technology Journal*, *45*(3), 257–264.

Kern, T., Lacity, M. C., & Willcocks, L. P. (2002). *Netsourcing: renting business applications and services over a network*. New York, NY: Prentice-Hall.

Krigsman, M. (2010). Reaching for social CRM success (or failure), IT project failures. *ZDNet*. Retrieved November 25, 2010, from http://www.zdnet.com/blog/projectfailures/reaching-for-social-crm-success-or-failure/11415

Lashar, J. D. (2009a). To SaaS or not to SaaS? *Destination CRM.Com*. Retrieved April 30, 2011, from http://www.destinationcrm.com/Articles/Columns-Departments/The-Tipping-Point/To-SaaS-or-Not-to-SaaS-53686.aspx

Lashar, J. D. (2009b). Servicing software-as-a-service. *Destination CRM.Com*. Retrieved April 30, 2011, from http://www.destinationcrm.com/Articles/Columns-Departments/The-Tipping-Point/Servicing-Software-as-a-Service-55510.aspx

McAfee, P. A. (2006). Enterprise 2.0: The dawn of emergent collaboration. *MIT Sloan Management Review, 47*(3).

McAfee, P. A. (2009). *Enterprise 2.0: New Collaborative Tools for Your Organization's Toughest Challenges*. U.S.A.: Harvard University Press.

Oracle Social, C. R. M. (2008). *It's all about the salesperson: Taking advantage of Web 2.0*. An Oracle White Paper, Oracle Corporation.

Parameswaran, M., & Whinston, A. B. (2007a). Social computing: An overview. *Communications of the Association for Information Systems, 19*, 762–780.

Parameswaran, M., & Whinston, A. B. (2007b). Research issues in social computing. *Journal of the Association for Information Systems, 8*(6), 336–350.

Searc, C. R. M. Com. (n.d.). *SaaS and CRM on demand vendor guide*. Retrieved April 30, 2011, from http://searchcrm.techtarget.com/

Sun, W., Zhang, K., & Chen, S.-K. Zhang, X., & Liang, H. (2007). Software as a service: An integration perspective. In B. Krämer, K.-J. Lin, & P. Narasimhan (Eds.), *Service-Oriented Computing- ICSOC 2007, LNCS 4749* (pp. 558–569). Berlin, Germany: Springer-Verlag.

Tobey, B. (2010). *Expand the spectrum: Integrating the social media channel enables CRM to paint a more complete picture of the customer. Teradata Magazine, Q3/2010* (p. 6184). AR: Teradata Corporation.

Wang, R., & Owyang, J. (2010). *Social CRM: The new rules of relationship management: 18 use cases that show business how to finally put customers first*. Altimeter Group.

Went, G. (2010). *The key issues in social media monitoring today*. Red Cube Marketing.

Worldwide, D. E. I. (2008). *Engaging consumers online: The impact of social media on purchasing behaviour, Volume one: Initial findings, United States*.

KEY TERMS AND DEFINITIONS

Brand Monitoring: A practice of listening to and/or measuring what customers say and write about a company or brand using social media tools.

CRM: Customer relationship Management – A technology solution for managing customers and establishing long-term relationship for companies.

Crowdsourcing: The practice of outsourcing a task to a group of people in order to take advantage of the collective intelligence of the public.

Enterprise 2.0: A term coined by McAfee (2006) to refer to the use of Web 2.0 platforms by organizations on intranets and extranets.

Sentiment Analysis: Part of social media analytics that uses analytical or computational techniques to determine the attitude or judgment of a speaker or a writer with respect to some topic, organization, brand, or products.

Social CRM Analytics: Algorithms that support various types of social media data analysis to generate reports.

Social CRM: A technology solution based on social media which includes social networks, blogs, forums, chats, audio and video sharing, etc.

Software Suite: A collection of software modules with specific functionalities that are integrated with common interface to support different business processes/objectives.

Use Case: A software engineering term used to describe system behavior from an actor's point of view or high-level functional description of requirements.

Web-Based Platform: a software solution delivered in software as a service (SaaS) model by a provider.

Chapter 11
Reusing Transaction Models for Dependable Cloud Computing

Barbara Gallina
Mälardalen University, Sweden

Nicolas Guelfi
University of Luxembourg, Luxembourg

ABSTRACT

Cloud computing represents a technological change in computing. Despite the technological change, however, the quality of the computation, in particular its dependability, remains a fundamental requirement. To ensure dependability, and more specifically, reliability, transaction models represent an effective means. In the literature, several transaction models exist. Choosing (reusing entirely) or introducing (reusing partially) transaction models for cloud computing is not an easy task. The difficulty of this task is due to the fact that it requires a deep understanding of the properties that characterize transaction models to be able to discriminate reusable from non reusable properties with respect to cloud computing characteristics. To ease this task, the PRISMA process is introduced. PRISMA is a Process for Requirements Identification, Specification and Machine-supported Analysis that targets transaction models. PRISMA is then applied to engineer reusable requirements suitable for the achievement of the adequate transaction models for cloud computing.

DOI: 10.4018/978-1-4666-0897-9.ch011

INTRODUCTION

Cloud computing is a computing service offered over the Internet. That is, a customer plugs into the "cloud" (metaphor for Internet) and uses computing scalable capabilities owned and operated by the service provider (Bernstein & Newcomer, 2009).

Two kinds of service can be offered over the Internet: either an application-specific service that offers a specific application (e-mail, search, social networking, etc.) or a general-purpose service (raw storage, raw processing power, etc.). The provider of these kinds of service may be a large company that owns many data centers, clusters of hundreds of thousands of computers.

Cloud computing represents a paradigm shift, a technological change in computing. This technological change forces cascading changes. Despite the technological change, however, the quality of the computation, in particular its dependability, keeps on being a fundamental requirement.

To ensure dependability, more specifically reliability, transactional principles, in particular ACID (Atomicity, Consistency, Isolation and Durability) properties (Härder & Reuter, 1983), which characterize the flat transaction model (Gray, A Transaction Model, 1980), represent an effective means. ACID properties combine fault tolerance and concurrency control to preserve global data consistency.

In the context of cloud computing, however, ACID properties are too strict and need to be reviewed and carefully changed, "relaxed," to achieve adequate transaction models, characterized by the right ACIDity (the right choice in terms of Atomicity, Consistency, Isolation and Durability). The traditional Atomicity, for instance, has to be relaxed when a computation is executed over a series of Internet's partitions that belong to different and autonomous service providers. Autonomy implies the possibility to decide locally about the outcome of the computation. This possibility would be denied by the *all-or-nothing semantics* (known as Failure Atomicity) that characterizes

traditional atomicity, since it subordinates local decisions to the global decision. To preserve autonomy, the *all-or-nothing* semantics has to be changed into *all-or-compensation* semantics (known as compensation (Levy, Korth, & Silberschatz, 1991)).

Scattered throughout the literature are available several relaxed notions of the traditional ACID properties. Since, however, no effective means exist to support a systematic understanding of the differences and similarities among these notions, no selectable and composable on-the-shelf-(relaxed)-ACID properties exist yet. This lack of means hinders the beneficial exploitation (reuse) of these properties.

To reduce time to market and increase quality, reuse has to be the key-leading-principle and changes have to be introduced only where needed. Changes have to be engineered. To be able to plan the changes as well as the reuse correctly and efficiently, a methodological support has to be provided. In particular, the methodological support should help engineers to identify what has to be changed and what has to be kept unchanged. More specifically, it is fundamental to be able to identify what are the changes in terms of ACIDity, that is what are the changes required to adapt each single ACID property to meet the requirements of cloud computing and provide the right transaction model. By being able to identify what has changed and what remains unchanged, engineers are able to maximize reuse.

As initially discussed in (Gallina & Guelfi, A Product Line Perspective for Quality Reuse of Development Framework for Distributed Transactional Applications, 2008), to succeed in engineering systematically common (what remains unchanged) and variable properties (what changes), a product line perspective on transaction models has to be considered.

This chapter builds on this initial discussion and presents PRISMA (Gallina, PRISMA: a Software Product Line-oriented Process for the Requirements Engineering of Flexible Transaction Models, 2010). PRISMA integrates a product line perspective and supports the reuse of reliability-oriented and transaction-based requirements for achieving the adequate ACIDity. PRISMA is an acrostic that stands for Process for Requirements Identification, Specification and Machine-supported Analysis. PRISMA is helpful as a prism (from Greek "*prîsma*") in the identification of fundamental constituting properties of transaction models to achieve, as a result of the PRISMA process, correct and valid requirements specifications.

By integrating a product line perspective, PRISMA allows similarities and differences, which are called commonalities and variabilities in the terminological framework of product lines, to be identified, systematically organized and engineered to distinguish, as well as to derive, the single "products." Specifically, PRISMA is conceived for engineering the specification of a transaction model by placing the effort in revealing its requirements in terms of ACIDity. By following the PRISMA process, then, the adequate transaction models for cloud computing can be obtained.

PRISMA proposes two phases: the first one to engineer the commonalities and the variabilities that characterize the entire product line and the second one to derive the products by reusing the commonalities and the variabilities engineered during the first phase. The ACIDity, for instance, is seen as an abstract variability which can be customized during the application engineering phase to obtain the desired ACIDity of the transaction models (products). This customization is obtained by selecting and composing the adequate notions of ACID properties.

Each PRISMA's phase consists of three activities: identification, specification and verification & validation. To perform the activities, PRISMA proposes to use the requirements elicitation template, called DRET (Gallina & Guelfi, A Template for Requirement Elicitation of Dependable Product Lines, 2007), and the specification language, called SPLACID (Gallina & Guelfi, SPLACID:

An SPL-oriented, ACTA-based, Language for Reusing (Varying) ACID Properties, 2008; Gallina, Guelfi, & Kelsen, Towards an Alloy Formal Model for Flexible Advanced Transactional Model Development, 2009).

DRET allows requirements engineers to gather requirements in a structured way. Domain concepts as well as product behaviors may be elicited through, respectively, DOMET and UCET, which are the two templates composing DRET.

SPLACID is a domain-specific specification language targeting transaction models. SPLACID integrates the above mentioned product line perspective and provides constructs for the specification of commonalities and variabilities within the product line. SPLACID offers a powerful means to maximize reusability and flexibility.

The SPLACID language benefits from a formal tool-supported semantics, which is obtained as a translation of the SPLACID concepts into Alloy concepts (Jackson, 2006). The Alloy-Analyzer tool (Alloy Analyzer 4), therefore, can be exploited to carry out automatic analysis. Because of its tool-supported semantics SPLACID contributes to improving the verifiability and reliability of transaction models.

In addition to the introduction of the PRISMA process, this chapter illustrates its application. PRISMA is applied to show how it can be used to engineer reusable Atomicity-related assets suitable for cloud computing.

The illustration of the PRISMA process is based on the current and informal understanding concerning the feasible ACIDity in the context of cloud computing (Karlapalem, Vidyasankar, & Krishna, 2010; Hohpe, 2009; Puimedon, 2009; Vogels, 2008; Pritchett, 2008). The aim of the chapter is to present a methodological support, the PRISMA process, and provide a first analysis on how it could be applied to reuse reliability-oriented and transaction-based models in the context of cloud computing. Cloud computing is still a rather new technology and therefore the

PRISMA phases will need multiple iterations before achieving the right ACIDity.

BACKGROUND

This section is devoted to presenting the background concerning the problem and the solution space. First of all, this section introduces the main characteristics of cloud computing that make ACID properties inadequate to meet the dependability's requirements. Then a step-by-step immersion into transactional principles is given. This immersion is aimed at providing the necessary elements to understand the problem space and to prepare the reader to the solution space. In particular, first, the traditional transactional properties, namely ACID properties, which allow global data consistency to be preserved, are recalled. More specifically, the role of each single property is pointed out to deeply understand the property's contribution in preserving global data consistency. Then, intuitions are given to motivate and start conceiving the potentially numerous relaxed notions of the ACID properties as well as the potentially numerous transaction models that incorporate them. Two existing transaction models are then analyzed.

Finally, before letting the main section to introduce the solution proposal, the background section provides the fundamental ingredient of the solution space: product line engineering.

Cloud Computing Characteristics

As mentioned in the introduction, in cloud computing, the customer plugs into the cloud to use the computing service that is offered over it. The cloud is a metaphor for the Internet, a medium that consists of geographically and purposely scattered computers or supercomputers that perform different parts of the computation. Several properties characterize cloud computing (Buyya, Yeo, Venugopal, Broberg, & Brandic, 2009), the following

list focuses on those that make the traditional ACID properties inadequate to meet the dependability's requirements of cloud computations.

- **autonomy**. The scattered computers and supercomputers that compose the cloud are loosely coupled and they belong to different autonomous organizations. Since autonomy implies the possibility to take decisions locally, it is not compatible with any master-slave hierarchy in which a local decision taken by a slave is subordinated to the decision of a non-local master.
- **complexity**. The computations involved in cloud computing are often complex. Complex comes from Latin past participle "complexus" and it means "composed of two or more parts." Complex computations are constituted of several operations accessing several data (complex data) and they often present parallelism. E-scientific applications, for instance, often submit to the cloud the request of executing large computations (i.e. large-matrix multiplications).
- **intra and cross-organization cooperation**. The scattered computers or supercomputers act in concert to execute very large computations. Cooperation implies that the scattered computers exchange information.
- **performance**. The computations involved in cloud computing are often expected to be executed quickly.
- **customization**. Cloud computations are supposed to be customizable. The customization may, for instance, involve reliability.
- **scalability**. Expansion, as well as contraction, of the capabilities (i.e. storage, database, etc.) needed by cloud computations is expected. Scalability can be guaranteed by scaling either vertically or horizontally (Pritchett, 2008). Vertical scaling (or scal-

ing up) consists in moving the application that needs to be scalable to larger computers. Horizontal scaling (or scaling out) consists in adding more computers (generally low cost commodities) to the system that runs the application. Since vertical scaling is expensive and limited to the capacity of the largest computer, in cloud computing, scaling is mainly achieved horizontally. Cloud computing is in fact supposed to guarantee "infinite" scaling (a seemingly inexhaustible set of capabilities).

When an application is executed on a cluster of computers (on a scaled out system) some adjustments are required. For instance, its data have to be properly distributed (scattered and replicated to guarantee low-latency access). To do that, a functionality-based approach can be followed. Functionality-based scaling consists in creating groups of data by dividing data according to functionalities and then spreading as well as replicating the groups across databases.

Horizontal scaling, however, suffers from network partitions. Since network partitions happen, they need to be tolerated.

ACID Properties

Atomicity, Consistency, Isolation and Durability, widely known under the acronym ACID (Härder & Reuter, 1983), are four properties, which, if satisfied together, ensure high dependability and, more specifically, reliability. These properties combine fault tolerance and concurrency control. The definitions of these properties, adapted from (Gray & Reuter, Transactions Processing: Concepts and Techniques, 1993) are given in what follows. The definitions make use of some terms defined in the appendix. The terms are written in *italics*.

Atomicity: a *work-unit*'s changes to the *state* are atomic: either all happen or none happen (all-or-nothing semantics, known as failure

atomicity). Atomicity guarantees that in case of failure, intermediate/incomplete work is undone bringing the state back to its initial consistent value.

Consistency: a work-unit is a correct transformation of the state. All the a priori constraints on the input state must not be violated by the work-unit (intra-work-unit, local, consistency).

Isolation: a set of work-units either is executed sequentially (no interference) or is executed following a serializability-based criterion (controlled interference).

Durability: once a work-unit completes successfully, its changes to the state are permanent.

All of these four properties aim at preserving a consistent state (global data consistency), that is the state that satisfies all the predicates on *objects*. To become familiar with these definitions and to really achieve a deep understanding of their impact, a simple example (partially inspired by (Besancenot, Cart, Ferrié, Guerraoui, Pucheral, & Traverson, 1997)) is introduced to illustrate them. Throughout the example the following notation is used:

- to refer to a *read operation* which belongs to a work-unit labelled with the number 1 and which reads an object x (where the read value is v), the following notation is used: read1[x, v];
- similarly, to refer to a *write operation* which writes an object x (where the written value is v), the following notation is used: write1[x, v];
- the symbol "$\diamond$" denotes inequality and the symbol "*" denotes multiplication.

Example:

Two objects x and y of type integer are related by the constraint: y=2x

The initial state of the two objects is:

x=1 and y=2

Since 2 = 2 * 1, in the initial state, the constraint holds.

Case 1: ACID Properties Hold

Work-unit 1 executes permanently to completion (all semantics) and in isolation, the following operations: write1[x, 10] and write1[y, 20].
Work-unit 2 executes permanently to completion (all semantics) and in isolation, the following operations: write2[x, 30] and write2[y, 60]

A possible sequential execution:

write1[x, 10] write1[y, 20] write2[x, 30] write2[y,   60]

The final state in permanent storage is:

x=30 and y=60

Since 60= 2 * 30, the a priori constraint holds. The sequential execution of Work-unit 1 and Work-unit 2 therefore transform the state correctly and preserve the consistent state.

Case 2: AID Properties Only Hold

Work-unit 1 executes permanently to completion (all semantics) and in isolation, the following operations: write1[x, 10] and write1[y, 30]
The final state in permanent storage is: x=10 and y=30
Since 30 <> 2*10, the a priori constraint does not hold. Work-unit 1 therefore does not transform the state correctly, i.e., it does not preserve the consistent state (**broken consistency semantics within the work-unit**).

Case 3: CID Properties Only Hold

Work-unit 2 executes permanently in isolation but not atomically (something in the middle semantics) the following operations: write2[x, 10] and write2[y, 20]
The something in the middle semantics has to be intended as follows: only a subset of the operations to be executed is in reality executed. Work-unit 2, instead of executing both operations, executes only the first (write2[x, 10]).
The final state in permanent storage is:

x=10 and y=2

Since 2 <> 2 * 10, the a priori constraint does not hold. Work-unit 2 therefore does not preserve the consistent state (**broken all or nothing semantics**).

Case 4: ACI Properties Only Hold

Work-unit 2 executes to completion (all semantics) and in isolation but not permanently the following operations: write2[x, 10] and write2[y, 20]. In particular, the second write operation.
The final state in volatile storage is:

x=10 and y=20

Since 20 = 2 * 10, the final state in volatile (non permanent) storage is consistent.
The final state in permanent storage is:

x=10 and y=2

Since 2 <> 2*10, the a priori constraint does not hold. Work-unit 1 therefore does not preserve the consistent state (**broken durability semantics**).

Case 5: ACD Properties Only Hold

Work-unit 1 executes permanently to completion (all semantics) but not in isolation the following operations: write1[x, 10] and write1[y, 20]

Its execution time overlaps the execution time of work-unit 2. Work-unit 2 executes permanently to completion but not in isolation the following operations: write2[x, 30] and write2[y, 60]

In particular considering the following interleaved execution:

write1[x, 10] write2[x, 30] write2[y, 60] write1[y, 20]

The final state in permanent storage is:

x=30 and y=20

Since 20 <> 2*30, the a priori constraint does not hold. The concurrent execution of Work-unit 1 and Work-unit 2 therefore does not preserve the consistent state (**broken isolation semantics, in particular an update is lost**).

ACID properties are not easy to ensure. Some research has shown that to guarantee these properties, a work-unit has to exhibit additional properties. A non-exhaustive list of these additional properties includes:

- each work-unit presents a short execution time (Gray & Reuter, Transactions Processing: Concepts and Techniques, 1993; Besancenot, Cart, Ferrié, Guerraoui, Pucheral, & Traverson, 1997).
- each work-unit accesses, during its execution time, a small number of data (Gray & Reuter, Transactions Processing: Concepts and Techniques, 1993; Besancenot, Cart, Ferrié, Guerraoui, Pucheral, & Traverson, 1997);
- the same data must not be accessed by a large number of concurrent work-units (Gray & Reuter, Transactions Processing: Concepts and Techniques, 1993; Besancenot, Cart,

Ferrié, Guerraoui, Pucheral, & Traverson, 1997);
- each work-unit accesses only non-structured (simple) data (Gray & Reuter, Transactions Processing: Concepts and Techniques, 1993; Besancenot, Cart, Ferrié, Guerraoui, Pucheral, & Traverson, 1997);
- each work-unit executes reversible work (Gray & Reuter, Transactions Processing: Concepts and Techniques, 1993; Besancenot, Cart, Ferrié, Guerraoui, Pucheral, & Traverson, 1997);
- each work-unit is executed in a non-mobile environment (mobile work-units are assimilated into long-living work-units because of long communication delays over wireless channels, whether or not disconnection occurs, that is whether or not communication connections are broken) (Walborn & Chrysanthis, 1995);
- each work-unit accesses only data belonging to a single organization (belonging to a trust boundary) (Webber & Little).

This partial list helps in defining the limits beyond which it's hard or even counterproductive to guarantee ACID properties. This list is constantly being enriched as a consequence of the continuously challenging ACID properties in new environments. As discussed in the following sub-section, as soon as a work-unit does not exhibit these properties, the ACID properties have to be relaxed.

Relaxed ACID Properties

Relaxed ACID properties are the result of a modification of the semantics of ACID properties to achieve less restrictive properties. Further, the relaxation allows the properties to meet the new requirements imposed by the application domains, which are different from those for which the original semantics was adequate. One-by-one each one of the fundamental ACID properties has been challenged in various environments to achieve realistically applicable properties, even though less simple. As a result, for each property, a spectrum of notions is available. In the following discussion are given the reasons that may lead to relax the ACID properties.

Relaxed atomicity is introduced to deal with the higher abortion frequency of longer running work-units by providing a means for guaranteeing intermediate results and selective roll-back (degradation acceptance, i.e., something in the middle semantics instead of all or nothing). Relaxed atomicity is also introduced to deal with computations that involve autonomous work-units (Levy, Korth, & Silberschatz, 1991).

The notions of atomicity differ on the basis of the allowed intermediate results. In (Derks, Dehnert, Grefen, & Jonker, 2001) intermediate results are interpreted as partial execution of operations.

Relaxed consistency is introduced to deal with the complexity of highly distributed systems. In case of complex distributed systems, when global consistency is not achievable, a relaxed consistency, for instance, allows a state to associate to a name a value that violates its domain range (Drew & Pu, 1995; Sadeg & Saad-Bouzefrane, 2000).

The notions of consistency differ on the basis of the allowed integrity violation. The domain range for instance could be violated according to a planned delta and the delta used is a criterion to differentiate the notions.

Relaxed isolation is introduced to deal with: 1) performance requirements (Adya, Liskov, & ÓNeil, 2000; Berenson, Bernstein, Gray, Melton, O'Neil, & O'Neil, 1995); 2) the higher data unavailability of long running work-units; and 3) cooperative work-units (Ramamritham & Chrysanthis, 1996).

The notions of isolation differ on the basis of the interference allowed.

Relaxed durability is introduced to deal with time constraints. In case of time constraints, write operations on persistent storage (which represent bottlenecks) have to be delayed and, in case of failures, data are lost. Relaxed durability is also introduced when permanence is not required immediately after the completion of a work-unit (Moss, 1981).

The notions of durability differ on the basis of the allowed loss.

Transaction Models

Transaction models represent a means to structure complex computations by grouping logically related operations into sets and by imposing a series of properties on them. During the last three decades, several transaction models have been proposed.

The flat transaction model, known as ACID transactions, was the first transaction model. This model, as it will be explained in the remaining part of this subsection, exhibits ACID properties. All the others models have been obtained from it by relaxing ACID properties in some way. Since these other models stem from the same model, they must have precise similarities and differences.

To try to achieve a deeper understanding of their similarities and differences, they have been deeply surveyed (Elmagarmid, 1992; Gray & Reuter, Transactions Processing: Concepts and Techniques, 1993). In (Elmagarmid, 1992), for instance, transaction models are classified by taking into consideration two important aspects: 1) the structure that they impose on a *history*; and 2) their difference with respect to ACIDity. This classification is an important starting point in revealing the dimensions according to which the original transaction model has evolved. However, since the classification assumes the final user's point of view, the dimensions do not present a satisfying level of granularity. This subsection builds on this embryonic classification and provides a more detailed analysis. Two transaction models are discussed: the Flat Transaction Model and the Nested Transaction Model. The discussion makes use of the terms defined in the appendix. The terms are written in *italics*.

The Flat Transaction model (Gray, A Transaction Model, 1980) identifies the first *transaction model*. This model presents a very peculiar multigraph as structure: the multigraph is constituted of a single node and no edges. All the work-units compliant to this model, therefore, are typed according to a single *transaction type*:

- **flat** transaction type. Work-units of type flat exhibit the following properties: Atomicity, Consistency, Isolation and Durability. Moreover, their events are delimited by a standard boundary, that is two management events mark the initiation and termination of the work-unit and all the other events are in between.

The Nested Transaction Model (Moss, 1981) represents a *transaction model* that allows work-units to be structured in a hierarchical way, forming either a tree or an entire forest. In this model, work-units are partitioned into two distinct *transaction types*:

- top-level transaction type, usually called **root**. A top-level transaction type is equal to the Flat transaction type.
- nested transaction type, usually called **child**. Work-units of type child exhibit the following properties: Atomicity, Consistency, Isolation and Conditional Durability. Conditional Durability requires that whenever a work-unit of type child successfully terminates its work, it is not allowed to save it permanently but it has to delegate the work-unit, enclosing it, to take care of the durability of the work). Moreover, the events of the work-units of type child are delimited by a non-standard boundary. In particular, in the non-standard boundary the durability management

events follow the event that marks the termination of the work-unit.

These two types constitute the two nodes of the multigraph that identify the Nested Transaction Model. A structural dependency, more precisely a containment dependency (obtained as an initiation dependency plus a termination dependency), relates these two types. Another containment dependency relates the child type with itself (a loop).

This model differs from the Flat Transaction Model according the following dimensions: structure (multigraph) and properties (a relaxed durability is introduced).

Software Product Line Engineering

Software product line engineering is a key ingredient to maximize reuse systematically. In software product line engineering, reuse embraces the entire software life-cycle. The maximization of reuse is achieved thanks to the identification/engineering of common (always reusable) and variable (not always reusable) properties that characterize a set of products. Given its effectiveness in maximizing reuse, product line engineering can be a key-ingredient to reuse transaction models in the context of cloud computing. This subsection therefore is aimed at introducing some basic concepts related to software product line engineering and at drawing the attention to the current practices for product line requirements engineering to learn fruitful lessons to engineer the requirements of the adequate transaction model for cloud computing by maximizing reuse.

Basic Concepts

The definitions of concepts listed below are mainly taken from (Clements & Northrop, 2001, Withey, 1996; Klaus, Böckle, & van der Linden, 2005).

- An **asset** is a description of a partial solution (such as a component or design document) or knowledge (such as a requirements database) that engineers use to build or modify software products.

- A **software product line** is "a set of software intensive systems sharing a common, managed set of features that satisfy the specific needs of a particular market segment or mission and that are developed from a common set of core assets in a prescribed way."

- The common set of core assets is known as commonalities. The set of assets that distinguish one product from another is known as variability.

- A **commonality** is a property that is common to all members of a software product line.

- A **variability** represents the ability of an asset to be changed, customized, or configured for use in a particular context. To characterize variability in more detail, it is useful to answer the following questions: "what varies?" and "how does it vary?." The answers to these questions lead to the definitions of variability subject and variability object, which are given here:
  - A **variability subject** is a variable item of the real world or a variable property of such an item;
  - A **variability object** is a particular instance of a variability subject.

- A **variation point** is a representation of a variability subject within domain artifacts enriched by contextual information.

- A **variant** is a representation of a variability object.

- **Feature** is a product's property that is relevant to some stakeholder and is used to capture a commonality or discriminate among products of the product line.

- **Feature diagrams** are trees (or graphs) that are composed of nodes and directed edges. The tree root represents a feature that is progressively decomposed using manda-

tory, optional, alternative (exclusive- OR features) and OR-features. A mandatory feature represents a product line commonality. Features that have at least one direct variable sub-feature (i.e. as one of its children) represent variation points.

- **Cardinality-based feature diagrams** are feature diagrams that allow features to be annotated with cardinalities.

- A **domain** represents an area of knowledge or activity characterized by a set of concepts and terminology understood by practitioners in that area. This set of concepts and terminology corresponds to "set of core assets," which is mentioned in the definition of a software product line.

- **Domain engineering** is the first phase that has to be carried out during product line engineering. This phase is meant at defining and building the "common set of core assets" that serves as a base to develop the products. Domain engineering starts with a domain analysis phase that identifies/engineers commonalties and variabilities amongst the software product line members.

- **Application engineering**, known also as "product derivation," is the second phase that has to be carried out during product line engineering. This phase represents a complete process of constructing products from the domain assets. This phase covers the process (mentioned in the definition of a software product line) of developing a "set of software-intensive systems" from "a common set of core assets in a prescribed way."

Domain engineering and application engineering are intertwined, the former providing core assets that are "consumed" by the latter while building applications. As a result of the product derivation task, feedback regarding specific products can be acquired and used to improve the software product line core assets.

Product Line Requirements Engineering

Product line requirements engineering embraces the engineering (elicitation, specification and verification & validation) of the requirements for the entire product line as well as for the single products. The set of requirements that concerns the entire product line contains all the common and variable requirements. The set of requirements that concerns a single product is derived from the set of requirements of the product line. This derived set, contains all the common requirements plus those requirements that allow the product to be distinguished from the other products (variability objects).

In the literature as surveyed in (Kuloor & Eberlein, 2002; Gallina, PRISMA: a Software Product Line-oriented Process for the Requirements Engineering of Flexible Transaction Models, 2010), several general-purpose processes for product line engineering are available. These processes embrace the entire software life-cycle and, since they are general-purpose processes, they do not suggest specific techniques for accomplishing all the process tasks. The only techniques that are suggested are those to be used during the requirements elicitation and specification. These techniques include cardinality-based feature diagrams and textual use-case scenario-based templates.

To perform the requirements specification, a common suggestion is also to use domain-specific languages. To perform verification & validation, no suggestion is given.

Despite the interest of these general-purpose processes, sharply focused processes are lacking.

WHICH TRANSACTION MODELS FOR CLOUD COMPUTING?

From the background section, it emerges that cloud computing represents a technological change and that this change is revealed by a series of key properties. To achieve dependable cloud computations, transactional principles represent an effective means. However, as it emerges clearly from the background, since cloud computations do not exhibit the typical properties that are needed to be able to ensure ACID properties, adequate transaction models for cloud computing need to be identified, either by reusing an existing relaxed transaction models or by reusing some key properties. To achieve adequate transaction models, it is fundamental to take into account what emerges from the background. In particular, it is fundamental to take into account that:

- to deal with the complexity of cloud computations, structured transaction models are needed. This consideration suggests that the adequate transaction models should be hierarchical and therefore composed by more than one transaction type (the multigraph that characterizes the Nested transaction model could represent an interesting starting point);
- to deal with autonomous computations, an adequate relaxed atomicity is needed. This consideration suggests that the all-or-nothing semantics of the traditional Atomicity should, for instance, be replaced by all-or-compensation (Levy, Korth, & Silberschatz, 1991) or by failure-atomic-or-exceptional (Derks, Dehnert, Grefen, & Jonker, 2001);
- to deal with cooperative computations scattered across the cloud, an adequate relaxed isolation is needed. This consideration suggests that the serializability-based semantics of the traditional Isolation should, for instance, be replaced by cooperative-seri-

alizability (Ramamritham & Chrysanthis, 1996);

- to deal with computations that need to be executed at high levels of performance, an adequate relaxed durability, as well as an adequate relaxed isolation, is needed. This consideration suggests that:
  - the no-loss semantics of the traditional Durability should, for instance, be replaced by an ephemeral permanence similar to the one available in in-memory databases (Garbus, 2010);
  - the serializability-based semantics of the traditional Isolation should, for instance, be replaced by the PL1 Isolation (Adya, Liskov, & ÓNeil, 2000).

Besides these considerations, it is also relevant to point out that, since the scattered computers and supercomputers that compose the cloud are expected to share data, cloud computing is governed by the CAP theorem. This theorem, initially presented as a conjecture by Eric Brewer, during his Keynote talk at PODC (Brewer, 2000), and later proved in (Gilbert & Lynch, 2002), states that of three properties of shared-data systems (data consistency, system availability and tolerance to network partitions), only two can be achieved at any given time.

Despite the fact that all the three above-listed properties are desirable and expected, a trade-off is required. Before sketching the plausible trade-off in the framework of cloud computing, the definitions (Gilbert & Lynch, 2002) of these three properties are given.

Data consistency is defined as "any read operation that begins after a write operation completes must return that value or the result of a later write operation." This definition refers only to a property of a single operation. Since the ACID properties guarantee global data consistency to be preserved, they are commonly associated to this definition. The data consistency achieved through the ACID properties, however, is a property that refers to a set of operations. This set of operations, thanks to the Atomicity property is treated as if it was a single operation. Therefore, the association that commonly is done between these two different notions of data consistency makes sense.

System availability is defined as "every request received by a non-failing node in the system must result in a response."

Partition tolerance is defined as: "No set of failures less than total network failure is allowed to cause the system to respond incorrectly."

As seen in the background, cloud computations have to be partition-tolerant. According to the CAP theorem, then a choice has to be made between availability and consistency.

In (Pritchett, 2008), the necessity of lowering the ACIDity of the ACID transaction model is advocated. The author suggests that it is time to break the unbreakable ACID paradigm and that it is time to recognize that consistency is not paramount to the success of an application. The author, then, uses the term BASE (Basically Available, Soft state, Eventually consistent) to denote a new paradigm. This term, initially introduced in (Brewer, 2000), taken from chemical reactions domain, underlines the necessity of having a less ACID transaction model. This less ACID transaction model must provide a lower guarantee in terms of global data consistency (i.e. eventual consistency). However, if some guarantees in terms of global consistency are desired, the process of relaxing the ACID transaction model by lowering its ACIDity must not lead to a neutral transaction model. To plan this relaxation process, a methodological support is needed.

From the background it also emerges that an important set of relaxed transaction models exists. Since, however, this set is not structured, it is not possible to understand, compare and reuse these models easily. As a consequence it is not easy to understand which relaxed transaction model could be adequate for cloud computing or which properties could be reused to introduce a new transaction model to satisfy specific cloud computing requirements.

To ease the understanding, comparison and reuse, the set of transaction models has to be systematically organized. To do that, the dimensions that contribute to their differences and similarities have to be systematically engineered.

As discussed in the background, the current practices adopted within the product lines' community can represent a key-ingredient in providing a solution to maximize reuse.

To structure the set of transaction models in order to ease the understanding, comparison, reuse as well as the careful planning of the adequate ACIDity, a product line perspective is adopted.

This section presents the product line perspective on transaction models. Then, it presents a new process for engineering the requirements of the desired transaction model. This new process integrates the product-line perspective. Finally, this section illustrates the application of the approach towards the achievement of the adequate transaction model for cloud computing.

A Product Line Perspective on Transaction Models

As it was pointed out previously, existing transaction models constitute an unstructured set and as a consequence it is difficult to understand, compare and reuse existing transaction models. Product line engineering represents a concrete opportunity to engineer commonalities and variabilities and, as consequence, to maximize reuse systematically.

This subsection builds on the work proposed in (Gallina & Guelfi, A Product Line Perspective for Quality Reuse of Development Framework for Distributed Transactional Applications, 2008) and enhances it by introducing a more mature product-line perspective on the set of transaction models.

The viability and feasibility of the product line composed of transaction models is justified by the fact that since transaction models have more properties/features in common (commonalities) than properties/features that distinguish them (variabilities), there is more to be gained by analyzing them collectively rather than separately.

From what was presented in the background, two main commonalities characterize transaction models:

1.   A transaction model can be seen as a multi-graph. Transaction types identify the nodes; structural dependencies inter-relating transaction types identify the edges.

2.   Each transaction model is characterized by a specific ACIDity. The ACIDity of a transaction model can be seen as the result of the selection and composition of the ACIDities characterizing the transaction types, which compose the transaction model itself. The ACIDity consists of the coexistence and synergy of four assets aimed at guaranteeing Atomicity, Consistency, Isolation and Durability (Gray & Reuter, Transactions Processing: Concepts and Techniques, 1993). All these assets, taken individually, identify a variability subject, which may give rise to different variability objects. As seen in the background, the semantics of the ACID properties has been challenged in various ways. As a consequence, for each property a spectrum of notions is available. The notions which compose a spectrum are the variability objects which instantiate the corresponding variability subject. Failure Atomicity, for instance, represents a variability object. To obtain the appropriate Atomicity asset, the adequate variability object has to be selected. A transaction model is, therefore, characterized by an ACIDity, which results from the selection and composition of the variability objects that correspond to the (relaxed) ACID notions.

Whenever an adequate variability object is not available, if reasonable, the product line should evolve and a new variability object should be introduced to cover a specific need.

Figure 1 and Figure 2 show the cardinality-based feature diagram that partially represents the product line constituted of transaction models. In this diagram, variability subjects are represented by variation points, that is by those features that have at least one direct variable sub-feature. Leafs, instead, are selectable variants at variation points and represent variability objects.

Figure 1, in particular, focuses on the common multi-graph structure and it summarizes that a transaction model can be either a pre-defined transaction model (i.e. the Flat transaction model discussed in the background) or a user-defined one. A transaction model is commonly structured as a collection of inter-dependent transaction types. Transaction types and the structural dependencies that inter-relate them can in turn either be selected among those available (pre-defined) or obtained by selecting and composing the needed sub-features.

Figure 2 shows that each transaction type is characterized by commonalities (i.e. coexistence of a boundary, an Atomicity variant, a Consistency variant, an Isolation variant and a Durability variant) and variabilities represented by, for instance, the ACID variation points. The Atomicity Type is a variation point and at this point a choice has to be made. A predefined Atomicity (i.e. Failure Atomicity) or a user-defined Atomicity has to be selected. A user-defined Atomicity requires the introduction of new features to describe the desired intermediate result. Usually, to mark the successful or unsuccessful execution of an operation, specific management events are used. For instance, the all semantics is represented by marking all the operations with a management event (a Commit Type event) that indicates full commitment. Similarly, the nothing semantics is represented by marking all the operations with a management event (an Abort Type event) that indicates full abortion. Management events are helpful to distinguish the different intermediate semantics. In Figure

2, these events, which are used to distinguish the Atomicity variants, are represented by the feature called "A-Extra Event Type."

For space reasons, dashed features are not detailed. For more details, the interested reader can refer to (Gallina, PRISMA: a Software Product Line-oriented Process for the Requirements Engineering of Flexible Transaction Models, 2010).

The PRISMA Process

As mentioned in the background, within the product line's community, a sharply focused methodological support is lacking. As stated in (Jackson M., 1998), it's a good rule of thumb that the value of a method is inversely proportional to its generality. A good method addresses only the problems that fit into a particular problem frame. Systematic and sharply focused methods help in reaching a solution.

To reuse existing transaction models either entirely or partially a sharply focused methodological support is needed. PRISMA provides that support. PRISMA stands for Process for the Requirements Identification, Specification and Machine supported Analysis. PRISMA is a new software product line-oriented requirements engineering process, which aims at being useful as a prism in revealing clearly the properties composing the transaction models.

PRISMA is compatible with the general-purpose processes surveyed in (Kuloor & Eberlein, 2002). PRISMA inherits from them. PRISMA, for instance, similar to those processes, is composed of the two typical inter-related phases: the domain engineering phase and the application engineering phase. PRISMA, however, aims at offering a sharply focused method as opposed to one that is more general-purpose. PRISMA targets a precise class of problems and aims at offering specific guidelines and techniques to perform the tasks, which make up the process. In particular, within PRISMA the following techniques are integrated:

Figure 1. Cardinality-based feature diagram: focus on the multi-graph structure

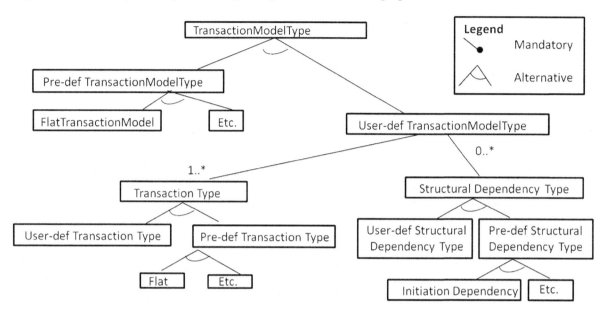

Figure 2. Cardinality-based feature diagram: focus on the transaction type's Atomicity

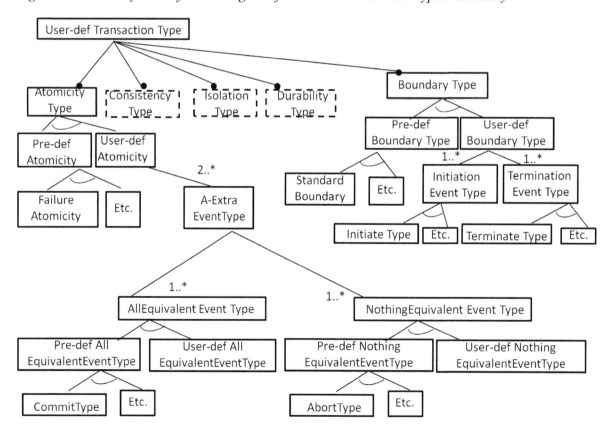

- a specific use-case-based template to carry out the elicitation, called DRET (Gallina & Guelfi, A Template for Requirement Elicitation of Dependable Product Lines, 2007);
- a domain-specific specification language to carry out the specification, called SPLACID (Gallina & Guelfi, SPLACID: An SPL-oriented, ACTA-based, Language for Reusing (Varying) ACID Properties, 2008; (Gallina, PRISMA: a Software Product Line-oriented Process for the Requirements Engineering of Flexible Transaction Models, 2010);
- a tool support (integration of the Alloy Analyzer tool) to carry out the verification and validation (Gallina, Guelfi, & Kelsen, Towards an Alloy Formal Model for Flexible Advanced Transactional Model Development, 2009; (Gallina, PRISMA: a Software Product Line-oriented Process for the Requirements Engineering of Flexible Transaction Models, 2010);

Before introducing the static as well as the dynamic structures of the PRISMA process, a brief explanation of these techniques is given.

The PRISMA's Techniques

As mentioned before, the relevance of the PRISMA process is its sharp focus. This sharp focus is achieved through the integration of sharply focused techniques, which support engineers during the different tasks that compose the process.

To ease the understanding of the following sections, these techniques (DRET, SPLACID, and the tool-supported verification and validation) are briefly introduced.

DRET is a requirements elicitation template suitable for the elicitation of dependable software product lines. This template is composed of two parts: a DOMain Elicitation Template (DOMET) and a Use Case Elicitation Template (UCET).

The DOMET allows the concepts of the domain to be elicited. The DOMET is depicted using a tabular notation. The field meaning is briefly provided in the following. **Name** labels the concept via a unique identifier. **Var Type** underlines commonalities and variabilities in the software product line and is filled with one of the following keywords: *Mand* (mandatory concept); *Alt* (alternative concept); *Opt* (optional concept). **Description** is an informal explanation of the concept purpose. **Dependencies** exposes any kind of relationship with other concept(s). **Misconception & class(es)** is an informal explanation concerning the misunderstanding of the domain (fault). **Misconception consequence & class(es)** is an informal explanation concerning the consequence (failure), observable by the stakeholders, that the misunderstanding of the domain may entail. **Priority Level** represents different levels of priority on the basis of criticality and is filled with one of the following keywords: *High*, *Medium* or *Low*.

The two fields that involve the misconception are meant to elicit the *causality chain* existing among the dependability's threats (Avizienis, Laprie, Randell, & Landwehr, 2004).

The UCET allows the software product line members' behaviour to be elicited. The UCET is an extension of the popular textual use-case scenario-based template given by Cockburn. It allows requirements to be organized in a tabular form that has a series of fields. Besides the standard fields (use case name, goal, scope, level, trigger, the actors involved, pre-conditions, end-conditions, main scenario, alternatives of the main scenario) the UCET includes fields (mis-scenarios, recovery scenarios, etc.) to elicit non-functional behaviour. The UCET may be labelled as *Collaborative* or *Single*. These labels, jointly with the labels used to characterize the resources, provide a means to distinguish concurrency's types. The explanation of the detailed structure of the UCET is outside of this scope. The names of the template's fields, however, should be understandable. Details can be found in (Gallina & Guelfi, A Template for

Figure 3. Cut of the SPLACID meta-model

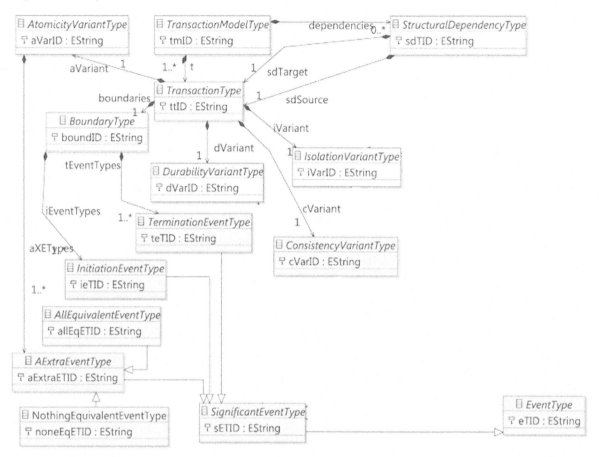

Requirement Elicitation of Dependable Product Lines, 2007).

SPLACID is a domain-specific language conceived to specify transaction models on the basis of their fundamental properties. SPLACID is based on ACTA (Chrysanthis, 1991), a unified framework that was introduced for the specification, synthesis and verification of transaction models from building blocks. The main advantages of SPLACID over ACTA are:

- a well-structured abstract syntax, given in terms of a meta-model;
- a well-structured textual concrete syntax, given in EBNF;
- a formal semantics given following a translational approach.

SPLACID integrates the product line perspective, which was discussed previously. The meta-model that defines its abstract syntax contains an abstract meta-class for each concept that was labelled as User-def in Figure 1 and in Figure 2 (i.e. TrasactionModelType, TransactionType, etc). Figure 3 illustrates a blow up the SPLACID meta-model.

Similarly, the syntactical rules, which are written in EBNF, that define the concrete syntax contain a non-terminal for each concept that was labelled as User-def.

Each concept (variant) that was a leaf of a feature labelled Pre-def in Figure 1 and in Figure 2 is represented in the SPLACID meta-model by a concrete meta-class that reifies the corresponding abstract meta-class. The concept of Failure Atomicity, for instance, is represented by a concrete meta-class that reifies the abstract meta-class corresponding to the Atomicity Type.

Similarly, these leaf-concepts have a representation in the concrete syntax and specifically they are represented as terminals.

All the concepts (abstract and concrete) are characterized by a set of constraints that define them. The constraints impose either a specific order among the events that belong to a history or require specific management events to occur in the history.

The concept of Failure Atomicity, for instance, establishes that all events, which have executed an operation on an object, have to be followed by one management event. The management event in particular has to be of type CommitType in case the "all"' semantics has to be guaranteed; it has to be of type AbortType in case the "nothing" semantics has to be guaranteed.

The tool support for verification and validation is achieved by providing a translational semantics to SPLACID. SPLACID concepts are translated into Alloy concepts. A model transformation provides rules to obtain an Alloy specification from a SPLACID specification. Once the Alloy specification is available, the tool, called Alloy Analyzer, can be used to verify and validate it. The verification consists in executing the executable Alloy specification to look for instances of it. If instances exist, it means that the specification is contradiction-free and that therefore it is consistent. A consistent specification has to be validated. To validate the specification, the instances are inspected to check that they really describe the desired requirements.

The PRISMA Process' Static Structure

The backbone of the static structure is made up of a set of activities, a set of roles, and a set of work-products. A detailed description of these elements, using the SPEM 2.0 standardized format (OMG, 2008), is given in (Gallina, PRISMA: a

Software Product Line-oriented Process for the Requirements Engineering of Flexible Transaction Models, 2010). In the following list, the set of activities is presented. For each activity, the roles, the work-products and the guidelines (if any) are given.

- **Product line requirements elicitation**. This activity is carried out by using the DRET template. This activity aims at revealing commonalities, variabilities (i.e. the Atomicity types, etc.) and dependencies (cross-cutting concerns) existing among variants at different variation points. The dependencies have to be documented to constrain the permitted combinations of variabilities.

The work-products involved are:

- input: none
- output: the filled-in DRET template.

The roles involved are:

- Concurrency control expert focuses on the Isolation spectrum.
- Fault tolerance expert (before termination) focuses on the Atomicity spectrum.
- Fault tolerance expert (after termination) focuses on the Durability spectrum.
- Application domains expert focuses on the Consistency spectrum.

The first four roles represent key-roles in engineering the requirements pertaining to the ACID spectra.

Guidelines: DRET usage in the context of the PRISMA process

- **Product line requirements specification**. This activity is carried out by using the SPLACID language. This activity aims at specifying the elicited requirements.

The work-products involved are:

- input: the filled-in DRET template
- output: the SPLACID specification.

The roles involved are:

- Analyst mastering the SPLACID

Guidelines: traceability rules to move from a filled-in DRET template to a SPLACID specification.

- **Product line requirements verification & validation**. This activity is carried out by using the Alloy Analyzer tool. This activity aims at verifying and validating the specified requirements. The work-products involved are:
  - input: the SPLACID specification
  - output: the Alloy specification

The roles involved are:

- Analyst mastering the Alloy Analyzer tool

Guidelines: transformation rules to translate SPLACID concepts into Alloy concepts.

- **Product requirements derivation**. This activity is carried out by using the DRET template. This activity aims at eliciting the requirements of a single product. The elicitation is obtained by derivation/pruning (the thick black path in Figure 4), that is by selecting from the filled-in DRET template received in input all the commonalities plus those variability objects that characterize the product.

The work-products involved are:

- input: the filled-in DRET template
- output: the pruned filled-in DRET template.

The roles involved are:

- Product requirements engineer. This role incorporates the competences of the experts in ACID spectra. In addition, this role is competent in pruning.
  - **Product requirements specification**. This activity is carried out by using the SPLACID language. This activity aims at achieving the SPLACID specification of a single product.

The work-products involved are:

- input: product line SPLACID specification (the black dashed path in Figure 4 is followed) xor pruned filled-in DRET template (the thick and horizontal black path in Figure 4 is followed).
- output: Product-SPLACID specification.

The roles involved are:

- Product requirements engineer.
- Product specifier. This role incorporates the competence of Analyst mastering the SPLACID language. In addition, this role is competent in pruning.

Guidelines: traceability rules to move from a filled-in DRET template to a SPLACID specification.

- **Product requirements verification & validation.** This activity is carried out by using the Alloy Analyzer tool. This activity aims at achieving a correct and valid Alloy specification of a single product.

The work-products involved are:

- input: product line Alloy specification (the thick grey path in Figure 4 is followed) xor product-SPLACID specification (the thick and horizontal black path in Figure 4 is followed).

- output: Product-Alloy specification.

The roles involved are:

- Product verifier and validator. This role incorporates the competence of Analyst mastering the Alloy Analyzer tool. In addition, this role is competent in pruning.
- Product user represents a key-role during validation.
- Product requirements engineer

Guidelines: transformation rules to translate SPLACID concepts into Alloy concepts.

The PRISMA Process' Dynamic Structure

Besides the static structure, to fully define a process, its dynamic structure must also be provided. A software process defines ordered sets of activities, which may be grouped into phases. The ordered sets of activities define meaningful sequences that, if followed, allow interacting roles to produce valuable work-products. Figure 3, summarizes these meaningful sequences. Globally, Figure 3 shows that the PRISMA process is made up of two inter-related phases: the domain engineering phase and the application engineering phase.

During the domain engineering phase, commonalities and variabilities characterizing the product line are engineered. Artefacts, which constitute the product line's assets, are produced. Once the domain is rich enough to allow requirements engineers to derive at least one product from the assets available, the second phase can be started. During the application engineering phase, single products are derived.

The sequence of these two phases is iterated. The iteration ends as soon as the product line loses its worthiness. Four roles are in charge of establishing worthiness of iterating the sequence: the

Product requirements engineer, Product specifier, Product verifier and validator, and Product user.

Towards Adequate Transaction Models for Cloud Computing

To achieve adequate transaction models to be used for cloud computing, the reusable assets have to be engineered. To do that the PRISMA process is applied. This subsection, first introduce a toy cloud computation to understand the characteristics that force a change in terms of ACIDity. Then on the basis of this toy computation, the PRISMA process is applied to achieve reusable Atomicity-related assets, adequate for cloud computing. In particular, the thick black path, shown in Figure 4, is followed until the achievement the SPLACID specification. The following ordered tasks are executed:

- Product line requirements elicitation;
- Product requirements derivation;
- Product line requirements specification.

The last step of the path, that is the Product requirements V&V, is not executed but simply discussed. The translation into Alloy is not presented since, to be fully understood, it requires wider background information, which for space reasons cannot be provided within this chapter.

Finally, this subsection discusses the results obtained by applying the PRISMA process.

Toy Computation

The toy computation introduced here is adapted from (Pritchett, 2008). The computation involves the modification of three different objects which are related by a consistency constraint and which are distributed on different computers. The first object x contains the purchase, relating the seller and buyer and the amount of the purchase. The second object y contains the total amount sold and

Figure 4. The PRISMA process' dynamic structure

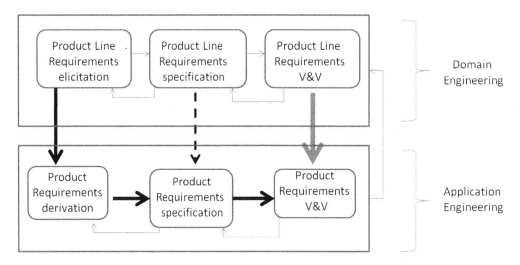

bought by a seller. The third object z contains the total amount bought by a buyer.

The modifications consist in one insert (a write operation) into the first object and in two updates (a read operation followed by a write operation) into the last two objects. The notation introduced in the background, has to be enriched to describe this computation. A read operation on an object x is denoted as read[x]. Therefore the computation consists of the following set of operations:

{write [x, 10]; read [y]; write [y, 10]; read [z]; write [z, 10]}

Due to the distribution of the objects, in (Pritchett, 2008), these modifications are not grouped altogether. Three different work-units are used to decompose the computation. These three work-units are:

Work-unit 1={write [x, 10]}
Work-unit 2={read [y]; write [y, 10]}
Work-unit 3={read [z]; write [z, 10]}

All these three work-units exhibit ACID properties. However, if at least one of them does not complete the work while the others do, the global consistency is not guaranteed. As it was explained

in the background, global consistency would be broken due to the broken atomicity.

An additional work-unit, called for example Work-unit 4, should be considered to enclose these three modifications. This work-unit is:

Work-unit 4={write [x, 10]; read [y]; write [y, 10]; read [z]; write [z, 10]}

Work-unit 4 does not exhibit ACID properties. The Atomicity property, in particular, is replaced by a weaker notion of atomicity that allows a work to be done only partially.

Product line Requirements Elicitation

To plan the adequate Atomicity-related assets, first of all a deep understanding of the characteristics of the application domain is mandatory. This understanding must be documented. According to the PRISMA process, the *Application domains expert* has to fill in the DRET template with this information. Once this information is available, the elicitation of the ACIDity-related assets may start.

The *Fault tolerance (before termination) expert*, for instance, may proceed by filling-in the sub-DOMET and the UCET concerning Atomicity.

Figure 5. Atomicity-related assets

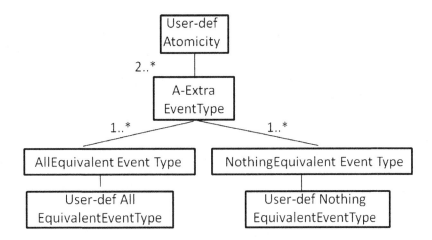

The sub-DOMET must contain all the concepts concerning the Atomicity-assets (all the Atomicity's notions and Atomicity's management events) and the UCET must contain all the behaviours.

The goal of the *Fault tolerance (before termination) expert* is to engineer the Atomicity-assets. With respect to Figure 2, the *Fault tolerance (before termination) expert* has to provide the User-def assets as summarized in Figure 5.

On the basis, of the toy computation, two notions of Atomicity seem to be necessary: the traditional notion of Atomicity (Failure Atomicity) and a new notion that allows the set of operations to complete fully or only partially. This new notion is called here "All-or-neglect Atomicity."

As mentioned in the background, the notions of Atomicity differ from each other on the basis of the completeness of the execution. To distinguish these notions (these variants), different event types can be considered. For instance, the notion of Failure Atomicity (all or nothing semantics) might be characterized by two event types: one for the "all" semantics, aimed at committing the entire work (that is each event within the work-unit has to be committed), and the other for the "nothing" semantics, aimed at aborting the entire

work (that is each event within the work-unit has to be aborted).

The sub-DOMET, presented in Figure 6, therefore, contains the two notions of Atomicity and the different notions of event types used to distinguish them.

A single UCET is used to elicit the requirements concerning the variants associated with the behaviour related to the guarantee of a property. The Single UCET filled in by the Fault tolerance (before termination) expert is:

- ID: UC2
- Single Use Case name: provide [V1] Atomicity
- Selection category: Mand
- Description: During this use-case, [V1] is guaranteed
- Primary Actor: Atomicity-Manager
- Resources: work-units (no sharing), data (competitive sharing), operations (no sharing)
- Dependency: if V1=Failure, then V3=aborts; if V1=All-or-neglect, then V3=neglects
- Preconditions: [V2] data
- Post-conditions: [V2] data

Figure 6. Sub-DOMET focuses on atomicity

Causality chain of dependability threats

Concept name	Var Type	Description	Dependencies	Misconception classe(es)	Misconception consequences class(es)	Priority Level
Failure Atomicity	Alt	Atomicity variant that classifies work-units that have to do nothing or the complete work	Exclusive w.r.t. all the other atomicity variants Requires: -Commit Event Type -Abort Event Type	Malicious/ Non-Malicious Partial results	Failure Content Consistency constraints violation	High
All-or-neglect Atomicity	Alt	Atomicity variant that classifies work-units that have to do the complete work or something in the middle	Exclusive w.r.t. all the other atomicity variants Requires: -Commit Event Type -Neglect Event Type	Malicious/ Non-Malicious Wrong Partial results	Failure Content Wrong consistency constraints violation	High
Commit Event Type	Alt	This event type variant classifies events used to commit the execution of an event on the state	None	Malicious/ Non-Malicious Wrong commitment	Failure Content Consistency constraints violation	High
Abort Event Type	Alt	This event type variant classifies events used to abort the execution of an event on the state	None	Malicious/ Non-Malicious Wrong abortion	Failure Content Consistency constraints violation	High
Neglect Event Type	Alt	This event type variant classifies events used to neglect the omission of the execution of an event on the state	None	Malicious/ Non-Malicious Wrong compensation	Failure Content Consistency constraints violation	High

- Main scenario: The Atomicity Manager guarantees [V1] Atomicity, i.e. if the work done by the work-units is complete, it commits otherwise it [V3]
- Alternatives of the main scenario: None
- Variation points description:
  ◦ V1: Type = Alt, values = {Failure, All-or-neglect}, Concerns = Behaviour
  ◦ V2: Type = Alt, values = {Consistent, Eventually consistent}, Concerns = Behaviour
  ◦ V3: Type = Alt, values = {aborts, neglects}, Concerns = Behaviour
- Non-functional: reliability
- Duration: None
- Location: None
- Mis-scenario: None
- Fault Variation descriptions: None

- Recovery scenarios: None

Product Requirements Derivation

The requirements of the single assets can be derived easily from the filled-in DRET previously obtained. Two different Atomicity assets can be derived. The derivation (pruning) of the concepts belonging to a single asset is obtained by:

- keeping all the mandatory concepts;
- choosing the desired concepts in the case of alternatives;
- choosing a concept or not in case of an option.

The resulting two pruned filled-in sub-DOMETs are:

- Pruned-filled-in-sub-DOMET related to Failure Atomicity={FailureAtomicity, CommitEventType, AbortEventType}
- Pruned-filled-in-sub-DOMET related to All-or-neglect Atomicity={All-or-neglectAtomicity, CommitEventType, NeglectEventType}

Despite the small dimension of this asset, by inspecting the two pruned sub-DOMETs, it can be seen that the set of common concepts is not empty.

Reused concepts ={CommitEventType}

The derivation (pruning) of the behaviour characterizing a single asset is obtained by:

- keeping all the mandatory UCETs;
- choosing the desired UCETs in case of alternatives, choosing a UCET or not in case of option;
- for each UCET derived for the product, selecting the desired variant at each variation point.

The two Atomicity assets differ on the basis of the choices that have to be made at the variation points.

To obtain the behavior of the FailureAtomicity asset, in UC2 the following choices must be done:

- V1=Failure
- V2=consistent
- V3=aborts

To obtain the behavior of the FailureAtomicity asset, in UC2 the following choices must be done:

- V1=All-or-neglect
- V2=Eventually consistent
- V3=neglects

The two pruned UC2 differ only on the basis of the choices made at the variation points. The remaining part is in common and can be totally reused.

Product Line Requirements Specification

The concepts and behaviours that have been previously documented must be specified using the SPLACID language. The SPLACID language offers extension mechanisms. The language is not closed but evolves in parallel with the evolution of the product line. As soon as new asset is introduced, the abstract syntax, the concrete syntax as well as the executable semantics have to evolve.

Therefore, the traceability rules detailed in (Gallina, PRISMA: a Software Product Line-oriented Process for the Requirements Engineering of Flexible Transaction Models, 2010) have to be followed to move from the work-product obtained during the elicitation (that is the filled in DRET template) to the SPLACID specification.

According to these rules, for each concept introduced in the DOMET, an abstract meta-class (if not yet available) and a concrete meta-class have to be added in the meta-model. Considering that the concepts related to Atomicity, introduced during the elicitation, represent variants of pre-existing concepts (the AtomicityVariantType, NothingEquivalentEventType, AllEquivalentEventType, etc. see Figure 5), only concrete meta-classes (namely, FailureAtomicity, All-or-neglectAtomicity, CommitType, etc.) have to be added. The concrete meta-classes represent reusable modeling concepts.

Similarly, terminals (namely, FailureAtomicity, All-or-neglectAtomicity, CommitType, etc.) have to be introduced in the concrete syntax.

The SPLACID specification for the Failure Atomicity is:

FailureAtomicity

AXE={CommitType, AbortType}

The SPLACID specification for the All-or-neglect Atomicity is:

All-or-neglect Atomicity

AXE={CommitType, NeglectType}

In the two-above SPLACID specifications, "AXE" stands for *Atomicity Extra Events* and it is the name of the set that contains all the management event types related to Atomicity.

Product Line Requirements V&V

The SPLACID concepts, newly introduced, have to be translated into the Alloy concepts. The translation rules detailed in (Gallina, PRISMA: a Software Product Line-oriented Process for the Requirements Engineering of Flexible Transaction Models, 2010) have to be followed. As a result of the translation an Alloy specification is available for both assets. As can be imagined, the two specifications differ on the basis of the concepts and behaviours that distinguish them. The remaining part is equivalent.

The resulting Alloy specification can be executed to check its consistency as well as its validity The Alloy Analyzer tool, for instance, is used to check that the All-or-neglect Atomicity allows a less constrained history.

With respect to the toy computation, more specifically with respect to Work-unit 4, the Alloy Analyzer tool, for instance, is expected to allow the instance h (given below) in the case of All-or-neglect Atomicity and forbid it in the case of Failure Atomicity.

h: write [x, 10]→read [y]→write [y, 10]

Discussion

Despite this brief and incomplete illustration of the PRISMA process, its effectiveness in easing the (partial or entire) correct and valid reuse of transaction models should be evident. The reuse embraces the entire set of the PRISMA's work-products: elicited requirements (sub-parts of the filled-in DRET template), specified requirements (SPLACID specifications), V&V requirements (results obtained by using the Alloy Analyzer tool).

FUTURE RESEARCH DIRECTIONS

The PRISMA process, which has been presented in this chapter, offers a methodological support to engineer adequate transaction models for cloud computing by customizing their ACIDity qualitatively.

Thanks to the identification of the building properties (sub-properties) which, in turn, characterize the ACID properties, it is possible to evaluate qualitatively the ACIDity of one model with respect to another one, simply by considering which sub-properties it is composed of. This evaluation capability suggests a systematic organization of transaction models into a lattice structure, which holds together many individual elements, otherwise unstructured, into one coherent and understandable order. This evaluation capability also pioneers the path to the provision of a quantitative evaluation of ACIDity.

As discussed throughout the chapter, since cloud computing is subjected to the CAP theorem, the customization of ACIDity is necessary and has to be planned carefully. To enforce the PRISMA process effectiveness in offering a valid means, it would be useful to have at disposal metrics to evaluate quantitatively the ACIDity of a transaction model. These metrics could be used to measure the ACIDity of the transaction models currently in use in the context of cloud computing so that to achieve a range of reliability.

To provide a quantitative metric for the ACIDity, the number of histories generated by the Alloy Analyzer tool, within a certain scope, could be counted. The ACIDity of two transaction models might, therefore, be compared on the basis of the number of histories allowed. For instance, with the predicate "moreACIDthan (transaction model A, transaction model B, application X)" a truth value might be assigned by verifying that the number of histories allowed by the transaction model A structuring the application X is less than the number of histories allowed by the transaction model B structuring the same application. More granularly, it would be useful to be able to establish the role of each single feature that composes a transaction model in decreasing or increasing the ACIDity of the model itself (that is, the contribution of each sub-property in increasing/decreasing the number of allowed histories).

The work presented in (Prömel, Steger, & Taraz, 2001) could represent another possibility for counting the histories.

The percentage of ACIDity characterizing a computation structured according to a transaction model could be calculated as follows:

ACIDity% = (#forbiddenHistories)/(#allpossibleHistories),

where the number of forbidden histories is obtained by subtracting to the number of all possible histories the number of allowed histories.

By decreasing the ACIDity, that is by choosing base like features, at some point a transaction model degenerates completely since its ACIDity is neutralized. A threshold that separates feasible and reasonable transaction models from non-reasonable, neutralized transaction models must exist. A metric would allow this threshold to be identified. An ACIDity metric would allow an engineer to quantify and plan the ACIDity and as a logical consequence this would allow the loss in terms of global consistency to be planned as well.

CONCLUSION

The technological change represented by cloud computing forces cascading changes and, as a consequence, several issues need to be solved to identify and adequately engineer the cascading changes. Since the quality and, in particular, reliability remains a fundamental requirement and since transaction models represent effective means to increase the quality of a computation, this chapter has been devoted to the identification of the cascading changes that involve transaction models and, more specifically, their requirements in terms of Atomicity, Consistency, Isolation and Durability. To engineer the changes, then this chapter has introduced a requirements engineering process, called PRISMA. This process integrates a product line perspective and supports engineers to reuse systematically properties of pre-existing transaction models to achieve adequate transaction models, which meet the application domain's requirements as well as the technological domain's requirements. Finally, on the basis of the current understanding, the PRISMA process has been applied to engineer Atomicity-related reusable assets. This chapter has provided a first step to achieve adequate transaction models for cloud computing.

REFERENCES

Adya, A., Liskov, B., & ÓNeil, P. (2000). Generalized isolation level definitions. *16th International Conference on Data Engineering(ICDE)* (pp. 67–80). San Diego, CA: IEEE Computer Society.

Alloy Analyzer 4. (n.d.). Retrieved from http://alloy.mit.edu/alloy4/

Avizienis, A., Laprie, J. C., Randell, B., & Landwehr, C. (2004). Basic concepts and taxonomy of dependable and secure computing. *IEEE Transactions on Dependable and Secure Computing*, *1*(1), 11–33. doi:10.1109/TDSC.2004.2

Berenson, H., Bernstein, P., Gray, J., Melton, J., O'Neil, E., & O'Neil, P. (1995). A critique of ANSI SQL isolation levels. *ACM SIGMOD International Conference (ACM Special Interest Group on Management of Data)*, (p. 24). San Jose, CA: ACM Press.

Bernstein, P. A., & Newcomer, E. (2009). *Principles of transaction processing* (2nd ed.). Burlington, MA: Morgan Kaufmann Publishers.

Besancenot, J., Cart, M., Ferrié, J., Guerraoui, R., Pucheral, P., & Traverson, B. (1997). *Les systèmes transactionnels: Concepts, normes et produits*. Paris, France: Editions Hermès.

Brewer, E. A. (2000). Towards robust distributed systems (abstract). *The 19th Annual ACM Symposium on Principles of Distributed Computing* (p. 7). July 16-19. Portland, OR: ACM.

Buyya, R., Yeo, C. S., Venugopal, S., Broberg, J., & Brandic, I. (2009). Cloud computing and emerging IT platforms: Vision, hype, and reality for delivering computing as the 5th utility. *Future Generation Computer Systems*, *25*(6), 599–616. doi:10.1016/j.future.2008.12.001

Chrysanthis, P. K. (1991). *A framework for modeling and reasoning about extended transactions*. Doctoral Dissertation, University of Massachusetts, Department of Computer and Information Science, Amherst, Massachusetts.

Clements, P., & Northrop, L. (2001). *Software product lines: Practices and patterns*. Reading, MA: Addison Wesley.

Derks, W., Dehnert, J., Grefen, P. W., & Jonker, W. (2001). Customized atomicity specification for transactional workflows. *Third International Symposium on Cooperative Database Systems for Advanced Applications (CODAS)* (pp. 140-147). Beijing, China: IEEE Computer Society.

Drew, P., & Pu, C. (1995). Asynchronous consistency restoration under epsilon serializability. *28th Hawaii International Conference on System Sciences (HICSS)* (pp. 717–726). Kihei, HI: IEEE Computer Society.

Elmagarmid, A. K. (1992). *Database transaction models for advanced applications*. The Morgan Kaufmann Series in Data Management Systems.

Gallina, B. (2010). *PRISMA: A software product line-oriented process for the requirements engineering of flexible transaction models*. Laboratory for Advanced Software Systems, University of Luxembourg, Luxembourg: Unpublished doctoral dissertation.

Gallina, B., & Guelfi, N. (2007). A template for requirement elicitation of dependable product lines. *13th International Working Conference on Requirements Engineering: Foundation for Software Quality* (pp. 63-77). Trondheim, Norway.

Gallina, B., & Guelfi, N. (2008). A product line perspective for quality reuse of development framework for distributed transactional applications. *2nd IEEE International Workshop on Quality Oriented Oriented Reuse of Software (QUORS), co-located with COMPSAC* (pp. 739-744). Turku, Finland. Los Alamitos, CA: IEEE Computer Society.

Gallina, B., & Guelfi, N. (2008). SPLACID: An SPL-oriented, ACTA-based, language for reusing (Varying) ACID properties. In *32nd Annual IEEE/NASA Goddard Software Engineering Workshop (SEW-32)* (ss. 115–124). Porto Sani Resort, Greece: IEEE Computer Society.

Gallina, B., Guelfi, N., & Kelsen, P. (2009). Towards an alloy formal model for flexible advanced transactional model development. In *33rd International IEEE Software Engineering Workshop (SEW-33)*. Skövde, Sweden: IEEE Computer Society.

Garbus, J. R. (2 February 2010). In-memory database option for sybase adaptive server enterprise. *Database Journal*].

Gilbert, S., & Lynch, N. (2002, June). Brewer's conjecture and the feasibility of consistent, available, partition-tolerant web services. *ACM SIGACT News*, *33*(2), 51–59. doi:10.1145/564585.564601

Gray, J. (1980). A transaction model. In J. W. de Bakker, & J. van Leeuwen (Eds.), *Proceedings of the 7th Colloquium on Automata, Languages and Programming*, (pp. 282-298). Noordweijkerhout, The Netherlands: Springer Verlag.

Gray, J., & Reuter, A. (1993). *Transactions processing: Concepts and techniques*. Morgan Kaufmann Publishers.

Härder, T., & Reuter, A. (1983). Principles of transaction-oriented database recovery. *ACM Computing Surveys*, *15*(4), 287–315. doi:10.1145/289.291

Hohpe, G. (2009). *Into the clouds on new acid.* Retrieved from http://www.eaipatterns.com/ramblings/68_acid.html

Jackson, D. (2006). *Software abstractions: Logic, language, and analysis.* MIT Press. Jackson, M. (1998). *Software requirements & specifications.* Addison-Wesley.

Karlapalem, K., Vidyasankar, K., & Krishna, P. R. (2010). Advanced transaction models for e-services. In *6th World Congress on Services, Tutorials, Services* (pp. xxxii-xxxiii). IEEE Computer Society.

Kiringa, I. (2001). Simulation of advanced transaction models using GOLOG. In *Revised Papers from the 8th International Workshop on Database Programming Languages LNCS 2397*, (pp. 318-341). Frascati, Italy. Springer-Verlag.

Klaus, P., Böckle, G., & van der Linden, F. J. (2005). *Software product line engineering: Foundations, principles and techniques* (1st ed.). Springer-Verlag.

Kuloor, C., & Eberlein, A. (2002). *Requirements engineering for software product lines.* 15th International Conference on Software and Systems Engineering and their Applications (ICSSEA). Paris, France.

Levy, E., Korth, H. F., & Silberschatz, A. (1991). A theory of relaxed atomicity (extended abstract). *The Tenth Annual ACM Symposium on Principles of Distributed Computing (PODC)* (pp. 95-110). Montreal, Canada. New York, NY: ACM.

Moss, J. E. (1981). *Nested transactions: An approach to reliable distributed computing.* PhD dissertation, Massachusetts Institute of Technology, USA.

OMG. (2008). *Software & systems process engineering meta-model (SPEM), v 2.0. Full specification formal/08-04-01.* Object Management Group.

Pritchett, D. (2008). BASE: An acid alternative. *ACM Queue; Tomorrow's Computing Today*, *6*(3), 48–55. doi:10.1145/1394127.1394128

Prömel, H. J., Steger, A., & Taraz, A. (2001). *Counting partial orders with a fixed number of comparable pairs. Combinatorics, Probability and Computing, 10.* Cambridge University Press.

Puimedon, A. S. (2009). *Transactions for grid computing, advanced e-business transactions for B2B-Collaboration Seminar, University of Helsinki.* Retrieved from www.cs.helsinki.fi/group/.../Transactions_grid_computing.pdf

Ramamritham, K., & Chrysanthis, P. K. (1996). A taxonomy of correctness criteria in database applications. *The International Journal on Very Large Data Bases*, *5*(1), 85–97. doi:10.1007/s007780050017

Sadeg, B., & Saad-Bouzefrane, S. (2000). Relaxing correctness criteria in real-time DBMSs. In S. Y. Shin (Ed.), *ISCA 15th International Conference Computers and Their Applications* (pp. 64–67). New Orleans, LA: ISCA.

Vogels, W. (2008). Eventually consistent. *Queue, 6*(6), 14–19. doi:10.1145/1466443.1466448

Walborn, G. D., & Chrysanthis, P. K. (1995). Supporting semantics-based transaction processing in mobile database applications. In *The 14th IEEE Symposium on Reliable Distributed Systems*, 13-15 September (p. 31). Bad Neuenahr, Germany. Los Alamitos, CA: IEEE Computer Society.

Webber, J., & Little, M. (n.d.). *Introducing WS-coordination*. Retrieved from http://www2.syscon.com/itsg/virtualcd/webservices/archives/0305/little/index.html

Withey, J. (1996). *Investment analysis of software assets for product lines*. Pittsburgh, PA: Software Engineering Institute, Carnegie Mellon University.

ADDITIONAL READING

Abadi, D. J. (2009). Data management in the cloud: Limitations and opportunities. *A Quarterly Bulletin of the Computer Society of the IEEE Technical Committee on Data Engineering, 32*(1), 3–12.

Bernstein, P. A., Hadzilacos, V., & Goodman, N. (1987). *Concurrency control and recovery in database systems*. Addison Wesley.

Burrows, M. (2006). The chubby lock service for loosely-coupled distributed systems. *7th Symposium on Operating Systems Design and Implementation (OSDI)* (pp. 335-350). Berkeley, CA: USENIX Association.

Chang, F., Dean, J., Ghemawat, S., Hsieh, W. C., Wallach, D. A., & Burrows, M. (2006). Bigtable: A distributed storage system for structured data. *The 7th USENIX Symposium on Operating Systems Design and Implementation (OSDI)* 7, (pp. 205-218). Berkley, CA: USENIX Association.

Cooper, B. F., Ramakrishnan, R., Srivastava, U., Silberstein, A., Bohannon, P., & Jacobsen, H. (2008). PNUTS: Yahoo!'s hosted data serving platform. *Proceedings of the VLDB Endowment, 1*(2), 1277–1288.

Ericson, K., & Pallickara, S. (2010). Survey of storage and fault tolerance strategies used in cloud computing. In Furht, B., & Escalante, A. (Eds.), *Handbook of cloud computing* (pp. 137–158). Springer Verlag. doi:10.1007/978-1-4419-6524-0_6

Fox, A., Gribble, S. D., Chawathe, Y., Brewer, E. A., & Gauthier, P. (1997). Cluster-based scalable network services. In W. M. Waite (Ed.), *Sixteenth ACM Symposium on Operating Systems Principles (SOSP)* (pp. 78-91). New York, NY: ACM.

Guo, H., Larson, P., & Ramakrishnan, R. (2005). Caching with "good enough" currency, consistency, and completeness. *31st International Conference on Very Large Data Bases (VLDB)* (pp. 457-468). VLDB Endowment.

Helland, P. (2007). Life beyond distributed transactions: An apostate's opinion. *Third Biennial Conference on Innovative Data Systems Research*, (pp. 132-141). Asilomar, CA, USA.

Kraska, T., Hentschel, M., Alonso, G., & Kossmann, D. (2009). Consistency rationing in the cloud: Pay only when it matters. *Proceedings of the VLDB Endowment, 2*, 253–264.

Stonebraker, M., Madden, S., Abadi, D. J., Harizopoulos, S., Hachem, N., & Helland, P. (2007). The end of an architectural era (it's time for a complete rewrite). *33rd International Conference on Very Large Data Bases (VLDB)* (pp. 1150–1160). University of Vienna, Austria. ACM.

Tanenbaum, A. S., & Van Steen, M. (2006). *Distributed systems: Principles and paradigms* (2nd ed.). Prentice Hall.

Weikum, G., & Vossen, G. (2002). *Transactional information systems*. Morgan Kaufmann.

KEY TERMS AND DEFINITIONS

Consistency Constraint: This term identifies a predicate on objects. A state satisfying all the consistency constraints defined on objects is said to be consistent.

Event: This term identifies the execution of a single operation on the state.

History: This term identifies the set of possible complete executions of a partially ordered set of events belonging to a set of work-units.

Object: (or or data-item): This term identifies a single pair <name, value>.

Operation: This term identifies the access of a single object. Two types of access are allowed. One type identifies operations that read (get the value). The other type identifies operations that write (set the value).

State: This term identifies a mapping from storage unit names to values storable in those units.

Transaction Model: This term identifies the type of structure/ordering used to organize the transaction types that are used to decompose a computation. This structure identifies a multi-graph. Nodes are identified by transaction types and edges by structural dependencies existing among the transaction types. The structure/ordering that organizes the transaction types has an impact on the ordering of events belonging to a history. A containment dependency between two transaction types, for instance, has the following impact on the history: all the events belonging to a work-unit of type "content" are enclosed within those events that represent the boundary and that belong to a work-unit of type "container."

Transaction Type: This term identifies a specific set of properties that have to be satisfied by work-units. The set of properties constrains the events belonging to a work-unit.

Work-Unit: This term identifies the set of possible executions of a partially ordered set of logically related events.

Chapter 12
Goal–Based Requirements Elicitation for Service Reuse in Cloud Computing

Lin Liu
Tsinghua University, China

ABSTRACT

Based on the existing requirements model and new service requests, the proposed service requirements elicitation framework ASREGL aims to achieve an optimal service supply and demand relationship. The current control variable is the similarity of the service requirements and capabilities. The major contents of this chapter include: (1) Service requirements elicitation questionnaires system, which uses a set of queries to narrow generic service requirements down to specific expressions of user preferences; (2) The construction process of goal-oriented service models based on the user's answers to the elicitation questions, which incorporates a Multi-strategy Task-adaptive Learning (MTL) technique with the goal-oriented requirements modelling approaches such as the i* framework; and (3) The dual feedback control mechanism, which supports the continuous interactions between service providers and requestors. The requirements elicitation process uses requirements models in the services pool matched with specific service requests, and ultimately identifies a service capability model that best fits the specific purpose of the targeted user. A virtual travel agency example is used to illustrate the proposed approach.

DOI: 10.4018/978-1-4666-0897-9.ch012

1. INTRODUCTION

The Service-Oriented Computing paradigm aims to support maximal reuse of web services according to the user's requirements. This target becomes even more viable in the cloud computing platform. At present, the user's requirements are often represented in certain existing standard interoperable service description languages such as WSDL or OWL-S. However, general service requestors may find such languages hard to use directly because service requirements are often partially understood and elicited. This chapter formulates the service-oriented requirements analysis as an automated feedback control process, in which the classical "once for all" philosophy is replaced with a continuous learning, negotiation and adaptation process. Conventional requirements analysis is a collaborative negotiate-and-decide process carried out by requirements analysts and system-to-be stakeholders. The requirements analysts usually drive requirements-related activities including elicitation, analysis and prioritization, addressing questions such as: What information shall be collected from each stakeholder? In what order should questions be asked? How to settle on a comprehensive list of functional requirements? How to settle on a comprehensive list of desired qualities of service? How to minimize the number of questions asked, while ensuring that adequate information is elicited from stakeholders? How to adjust the elicitation process according to answers obtained from earlier questions? The research discipline of Requirements Engineering (RE) has accumulated a body of knowledge that can guide an analyst in going through the requirements elicitation process. Of course, the analyst's intuitions and experiences also play a vital role.

During recent years, the Service-Oriented Architecture (SOA) paradigm (Papazoglou et al. 2007) has been recognized as a novel way to structure complex, loosely-coupled services on demand and timely. Among other advantages, SOA can adapt to changes rapidly, and provide effective inter- and intra-organization application integration. It is worth mentioning that, no matter how neatly the SOA defined the relationships between the services and the responsibility of each one, the service itself has to be built and runs somewhere. Cloud Computing embraces various techniques of networking, virtualization, software as a service (SaaS), Web 2:0, web infrastructure, distributed computing, and also Services Computing. Cloud Computing platforms provide large scalable computing resources "as a service" over the Internet to users (Peng et al. 2009). Cloud Computing has drawn more and more attention from research as well as industry community. There are some basic techniques of Cloud Computing, for example Bigtable (Chandra et al. 2006), Google File System (GFS) (Ghemawat et al, 2003), and MapReduce (Dean et al. 2008). There are some open-source Clouding Computing infrastructure such as Xen Cloud Platform (XCP), Nimbus, OpenNebula (Sotomayor et al. 2009), and Eucalyptus. Any earlier enterprise software architectures prior to cloud computing will lead to capacity problems, or chaotic situations. The estimation of capacity for business applications is challenging, estimating the capacity requirements for SOA services, especially if it is a large quantity of service, is even more challenging. Thus, cloud computing and SOA come together. Services defined within an SOA are best deployed within a cloud to gain all of the advantages of cloud-based software (Marks & Lozano, 2010). On the other hand, cloud applications are at their best when defined in terms of services. The two are inseparable.

SOA are founded on the concept of service. A service is something one actor wants and another can deliver, along with terms constraining the delivery. Service-level agreements (SLAs) and quality-of-service (QoS) requirements are two generic types of service terms. An operational framework for services actually involves three kinds of actors: requestors searching for needed services, providers who provide services and mediators who support the match-making process between requestors and providers. This framework assumes that providers know what services are needed by requestors, while requestors expect that needed service is available from some provider. When there is no acceptable match between a service request and a published service description, the elicitation process stumbles.

Compared with conventional requirements engineering, where the elicitation process usually adopts a "face-to-face" and synchronous mode, in the open environment enabled by the cloud computing infrastructure, a "back-to-back" and asynchronous mode is needed. In the former case, requirements engineers obtain requirements information directly from customers, using methods such as structured interviews (Kvale & Brinkman, 2008) and task analyses (Hackos & Redish 1998). In the latter case, the requestors and providers have to conduct a double blind search online, since they have little chance to interact face-to-face in advance of the development of services or the formation of business agreements. Back-to-back elicitation is also useful for ERP and software product families, and conventional mass-marketed software, but this chapter is focusing all usage scenarios on service-oriented systems. The extension to the proposed techniques which are also applicable for other build-once-use-many-times scenarios is left as a topic for future research. Developing a new methodology for requirements elicitation in the "back-to-back" mode is a critical task in the services era. The success of services as a business and computational paradigm depends on how well the two sides - providers and requesters - understand the requirements and constraints of each other. Ill-defined and misrepresented requirements of services may lead to unbalanced service-level agreements or, worst, complete failure to reach an agreement. Thus, requirements engineering for services plays a definitive role in service engineering. In order to achieve efficient service design, publication, discovery, binding and evolution, there is a dire

need for novel requirements concepts, techniques and tools. In addition, any such proposal needs to support adaptation of services in view of evolving requestor requirements.

Thus, the essential questions regarding requirements elicitation in this new context are: How can a provider map its current service assets or core competence into a maximum set of requested services? Where and how can one acquire and accumulate valuable service requirements knowledge? Is it from existing published service profiles, from Service-Level Agreements, or from logs of user queries? Unfortunately, the literature on requirements engineering or service engineering offers few clues on how to address these issues. Thus, we need a process to guide providers transforming system assets into easily reusable and adaptable services addressing requestor needs.

This chapter proposes an automated service requirements elicitation mechanism, ASREGL, to facilitate the process of service requirements elicitation on the cloud. First, a Service Requirements Modelling framework, SRMO, is defined (Liu et al, 2008), which extends the agent-oriented requirements modelling framework *i** with service-related concepts. Then, an automated requirements elicitation process adapts the knowledge base structure and representations such as goals, tasks and temporal constraints are introduced, in which the elicitation process is transformed into a learning process for the goal-based requirements models. To optimize the elicitation and design decision process, a process control mechanism based on a plausible justification trees is also used. In other words, the ASREGL elicitation approach uses goal-oriented graphical models as the basic representations of service requirements. A service requirements knowledge base (a goal-model base) for targeted service requirements is gradually built in this way. Through constant interaction between the two sides, the learning process matches models in the service knowledge base with the partial requirements models indicates the service requestors' preferences on the desired services, and ultimately identifies the appropriate requirements model for the targeted user.

In order to recover a service requirement model, the multi-task adaptive learning (MTL) method (Tecuci et al, 1995) is adopted. In MTL, a knowledge base with goal model fragments is first constructed, and then a group of existing goal models is used as a training set and the rules and learning strategies are defined for knowledge acquisition and improvement, with which the system can determine process and learn about new definitions of the service requirements. Model elements include the required goals, tasks, and constraints such as the temporal order of the operations. We adapt the existing MTL algorithms by changing the target of the learning process to the elicitation of a goal model (Qiao et al. 2008), which depicts how requirements goals can be achieved through a sequence of component services. The novel part of our proposal is that the method conducts bottom-up reasoning for each time interval of the satisfaction of goals and the temporal order of such intervals. A tool prototype is implemented to study the feasibility and usability of the approach. The results have shown that the method is feasible, and the correctness of the approach can be guaranteed when adequate training samples are provided.

We propose to formulate the service-oriented requirements process as a double feedback control framework. Thus, the classical "once for all" elicitation philosophy is replaced with a continuous negotiation and adaptation process. Based on the existing goal model and new service requests, the proposed service requirements elicitation system ASREGL dynamically issues elicitation questions to help form an optimal service supply and demand relationship. We control the elicitation process using the similarity between the service requirements model and the service capability model. When the service providers publish their services online, they need to specify their semantics. The questions provide a guideline on how they can rationalize this activity and specify what they actually provide. The requestors and providers are using the same model, but requestors describe what they want, while providers describe what they provide. Our web-based tool supports many requestors and many providers running in parallel.

The structure of this chapter is arranged as follows: Section 2 introduces the goal-oriented ontology for the service requirements elicitation (SRMO), the dynamic questionnaire system (DQS) and how requirements models are built from the DQS using learning techniques. Section 3 describes in detail the elicitation mechanism, including the satisfaction measurement of two models, and the feedback system. Section 4 introduces examples applying of ASREGL. Section 5 discusses related work. Section 6 concludes the chapter.

2. AN AUTOMATED SERVICE REQUIREMENTS ELICITATIONS APPROACH

Getting the requirements right is a must in the development of complex, software-intensive systems. In conventional requirements engineering, questionnaires, meetings and interviews are often used to collect original requirements data. This original requirements information is often fragmented like the pieces of jigsaw puzzle, and the requirements analyst's major contribution is to recover the complete picture from such fragments, and make design decisions based on the available information. Service engineering faces a similar situation. When a consumer issues a service request, the request expresses some intended need to be served. Our requirements elicitation mechanism is dedicated to making such service requirements explicit and to applying the mechanism to conduct automated service composition of given elementary services.

Figure 1. Service requirements modelling concepts

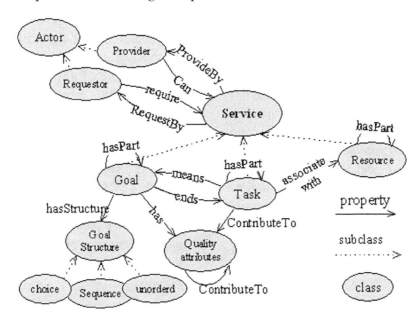

2.1 Service Requirement Ontology

Service requirements elicitation concerns three major issues: the service requirements modelling ontology, i.e., in this chapter the SRMO ontology that was first proposed in (Liu et al. 2008), the service requirements elicitation process, and the service knowledge accumulation process. *SRMO* defines the ontology for requirements modelling; it provides a conceptual guideline for the other two. The elicitation process collects requirements details and structural information with the service requestor; the service knowledge acquisition process reconciles and integrates all instance requests to build a requirements knowledge repository that contains heuristics for service publication.

The ontology-based approach is widely used to solve problems that require common knowledge and understanding. Concepts, relationships and their categorizations in ontology can be used as a source of shared knowledge in a specific application domain. By using ontology based approaches, many existing semantic processing techniques can be employed in requirements analysis without getting into rigorous NLP techniques. *SRMO* defines the ontology for service requirements modelling based on concepts of goals and actors, inherits its key modelling concepts from *i**, and extends it with the concepts of the provider actor, requestor actor and services. Providers are capable of certain services, while requestors require certain services. Every actor in the service network is motivated to get their required service provided. Figure 1 shows the concepts and their relationships in the proposed service requirements ontology. It models services at a higher level of abstraction than current service ontology such as *OWL-S* (Martin et al. 2004), which focuses more on service design details not accessible to general end-users. The level of abstraction adopted by the proposed mechanism aims to achieve more precise profiling of service requirements. Individual service requests can be easily collected and crystallized as requirements knowledge.

In the services requirements modelling ontology, services can be described as three different kinds of modelling constructs. An actor can state their desired services in terms of the goals associ-

Figure 2. Automated elicitation process in ASREGL

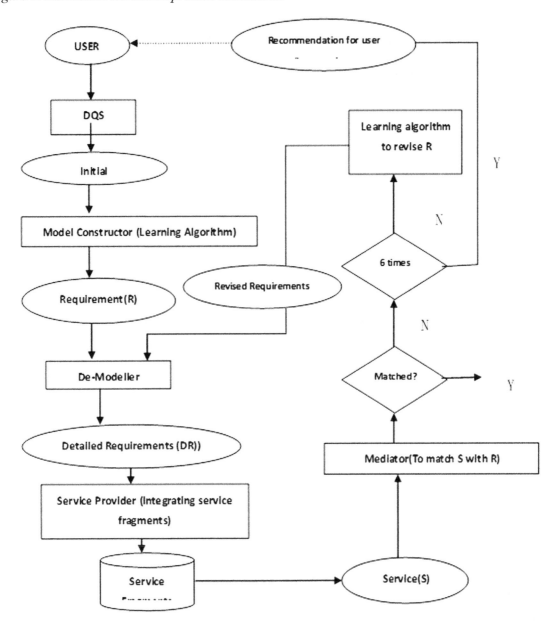

ated with the service. That is, they can express what goal the desired services should satisfy, without giving more low-level details; or, they can describe the service as a task, defining the concrete procedures and operational constraints of the desired services; or they can represent the service as a resource, pointing out the particular information entity they would access. An actor a_i is either a service requestor or a service provider. A *goal-state* g_i is a condition or state of affairs in the world that a service requestor would like to achieve. A goal can be achieved in different ways, prompting alternatives to be considered. A *task* t_i is used to represent the specific procedures to be performed by the service provider, which specify particular ways of doing something. *Tasks* are used to incrementally specify and refine solutions in the target system. *Task* is the way of achieving goals. *Resource* is a physical or informational entity, which may serve some purpose. Properties of a *resource* include whether it is available or not, the value of its quality attributes, or non-intentional properties such as amount, producer, copyright owner, colour, length, etc. A quality attribute could be any attribute that is of concern to an actor requesting or providing a service, such as cost of a service, performance, security/privacy assurance, or ease of use. In other words, anything within the scope of QoS can be described. Goal, task and resources are all subclasses of services.

Decomposition relationships between goals are represented as *part-of* (g_1, g_2), which is used to describe that goal g_2 can be achieved iff goal g_1 can be accomplished. The relationships between *goals* are represented by **Goal Structure**. *Goal Construct* is used to describe the temporal or causal relationship of *Goals*. So far, there are three structures: **Sequence, Unordered or Selection (choice).** The *goals* connected by *Sequence* must be executed one by one according to the order they appear in the goal sequence. The *Goals* connected by *Unordered* can be executed in any order or concurrently. Only one *goal* among all alternatives can be executed by *Selection*. We use *Can$_a$s* to denote that there exists an actor *a* that can provide a certain service or quality *s*. A means-ends relationship between a task *t* and a goal *g*, denoted by *me (t, g)* describes that *g* can be achieved if the task *t* is performed. Connecting a task to a goal by a means-ends link adds one possible way of achieving the goal. The **Contribution** relationship links tasks with the quality attributes it influences. The influence is evaluated from two orthogonal dimensions: *{positive, negative, unknown} × {full, partial, unknown degree}*. We use the following alias for each possible value of the contribution type: *Make = (full, positive); Help = (partial, positive); Some+ = (positive, unknown degree); Undecided = (unknown, unknown degree); Some- = (negative, unknown degree); Hurt = (partial,*

negative); Break = (full, negative). The partial order of the above types is: *Make ≥ Help ≥ Some + ≥ Undecided ≥ Some - ≥ Hurt ≥ Break.* Other qualitative or quantitative measurements can be used as scale of contributions.

The *SRMO* has inherited its key modelling concepts from *i** [35], a widely adopted requirements modelling framework. Thus, *SRMO* can be considered as a service-flavoured requirements modelling framework. The *i** framework emphasizes the actors or stakeholders distributed in different environments and the relationships among them, and is generally applicable to any distributed agent-oriented environment. In other words, the requirements model defined here is generally applicable, which means it can be applied to requirements settings other than the service-oriented paradigm.

As shown in Figure 2, *ASREGL* is an iterative process. First, rough requirements statements are extracted by a Dynamic Questionnaire System (*DQS*) residing on either the service requestors or the service providers' site. Then the requirements models, which are based on the Service Requirements Modelling Ontology (*SRMO*), are constructed using a machine learning based approach. Naturally, there are gaps between the two models constructed separately from the two sides due to their different intentions and initiation. The service providers have to meet the users' needs by adjusting their own capability and specification. On the other hand, the requestors should refine their request to remove the inconsistency, misrepresentation, incompleteness and constraints that are over or under specified. As a result, a dual adjustment is conducted to bridge the gap between the two models. A quantitative measure can help evaluate how well the two sides correspond. The feedback loop will only terminate when the similarity value reaches a preset threshold. Otherwise the feedback is provided to the *DQS*, which triggers a new set of queries and reasoning actions.

Table 1. Queries catalog

Series	Type	Purpose	Sample Queries
S1	Who	Identify actors	Who is involved in the service?
S2	What	Identify tasks	What task do you want to perform?
S3	Why	Identify goals upstream	Why is this service needed?
	How	Refine goals downstream	How can this goal be achieved or decomposed?
S4	Why	Rationalize tasks upstream	Why is this task needed?
	How	Refine tasks downstream	How can this task be decomposed?
S5	How well, When, Where	Identify and refine Quality Attributes	How well do you need this quality attribute to be met? Which task influences this quality? Does this quality influence another quality? When and where do you want the task to be performed?

2.2 Dynamic Questionnaire System

The Service Requirements Elicitation Process helps generate a requirements model based on the concepts shown in the ontology above. Thus, it is inevitable for us to raise questions such as: How does one extract the original requirements statements from a service requestor? Here, we present a series of query and answer schemas to formulate a rough sketch of the requirements model. The queries can be organized in the 5W2H style (Leite et al. 2005), that is Who, What, Why, When, Where, How and How well. According to their functions, the 5W2H questions can be categorized into five series as listed in Table 1:

Series 1: This series includes all queries regarding actors. E.g., that the query "Who is involved in the service?" is used to identify the actors. "Who can best satisfy your needs?" is used to determine the user's preferred service provider. Answers to these queries can be modelled as Actors.

Series 2: This series includes all queries to identify model elements other than actors. The answer to "What is your primary goal?" could be a goal, which states a condition to be satisfied with the help of a service; the answer to "What action do you want to perform?" could be a task, which specifies a procedure or course of actions to be performed during the service execution; the

Figure 3. Goal decomposition in SRMO

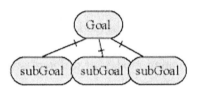

answer to "What resources do you need?" could be a resource, which is made available by the service.

Series 3: Queries in this series are used to refine goals. The WHY queries, e.g. "Why is this goal needed?" can be used to explore the goal tree upstream, finding out the fundamental intentions of the requestor. On the other hand, the HOW queries can be used to explore the goal tree downstream. Here we switch levels from questions about the needed service to questions about statements about the needed service. This is not a move from "what" to "how", it is a move between levels of abstraction. What/why/how questions can each be asked at different levels of abstraction

The query "How can the goal be broken down?" decomposes the goal into sub-goals, which is modelled in Figure 3.

The answers to "How are the states of the goal achieved?" identify the tasks required to achieve a goal. It adds a means-ends link between the goal and the task, the task is a means for achieving the

Figure 4. Means-ends refinement of a goal into a task in SRMO

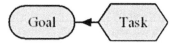

Figure 5. Decomposition of a task into sub-task in SRMO

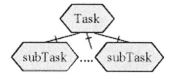

goal, while the goal is the end of performing the task.

During the elicitation process, one should obtain as much information from the requestor as possible. The how query help clarify whether the requestor have knowledge or requirements on breaking down the desired service into smaller service functionalities. Actually we consider it a merit of the propose approach to move across different levels of abstraction. We believe that requirements process is always intertwined with design, relating models of different abstraction level is necessary.

One goal may have multiple tasks, and each task stands for an alternative way of achieving this goal. The answers to the above HOW query can be modelled as in Figure 4.

Series 4: Similar to series 3, series 4 also includes WHY and HOW queries, but they are used to refine tasks. WHY queries, such as "Why is this task needed?" are used to find high-level tasks or goals, while the HOW queries, for example "How can this task be decomposed?", decompose the task into sub-tasks, which can be modelled as in Figure 5.

Series 5: HOW WELL, WHEN and WHERE queries all fall into series 5 category. They can elicit requirements on quality attributes, which

Figure 6. Quality attribute associated to a goal and a resource

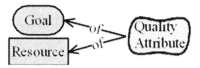

are the decision-making rules for evaluating its quality. Answers to HOW WELL queries can be modelled as in Figure 6.

This series also includes other queries to refine the quality. For example, how does a specific task influence quality of service? How does one quality attribute influence another quality attribute? Answers to these queries can be modelled as in Figure 7.

In addition, WHEN and WHERE queries also contribute to enriching the quality attributes we extract. These queries help us collect requirement fragments from requestors and providers. Figure 8 shows an example integrated view for a service requirement constructed from all query answers.

Figure 7. Contribution of a task to the quality of a goal

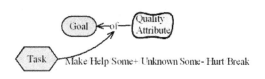

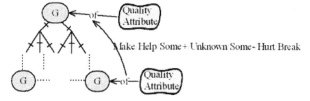

Figure 8. A hierarchical requirement model in SRMO

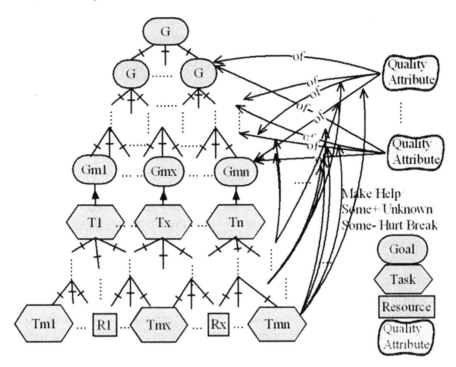

2.3 Service Requirements Reconciliation Process and Heuristics

Service requirements elicitation can help each requestor understand their requirements better and express their service demands more efficiently in the future. As mentioned, for different requestors targeting the same service goal, different requirements models can be generated, which is meant to bring benefits to not only service requestors, but also service providers. Through the integration of requirements models from different service requestors, this mechanism builds a requirements knowledge repository. Such a repository offers service providers requirements knowledge about the needs and preferences of service requestors with regards to the services offered by the provider. In the meanwhile, the provider who has the most important components in the repository will find himself in an advanced position when competing with other service providers. Having received the

corresponding position in the requirements model hierarchy, service providers could trace the goal model upstream to figure out what other influential requirements it can satisfy. This section discusses this requirements reconciliation process.

2.3.1 Matching Strategies

The key step in the reconciliation process is to combine the new incoming requirements model into the existing repository. When integrating a new requirements model into the knowledge base, the service requirements reconciliation process (SRRP) first needs to analyze all components in the new model to see if they have are similar to with any existing components of the goal model. First, we define the matching strategy. To understand them better, the components are prioritized in the following order: > *pri(Quality Attribute)* > *pri(Resource)* > *pri(Task)* > *pri(Quality Contribution)* > *pri(Goal)* to the above HOW query.

Quality attribute synergy rule: There may be overlapping quality attributes for different services. Quality attributes can be domain-specific or domain-independent. Domain-specific attributes vary from one service requirements goal to another. When matching quality attributes, we combine ranges of the domain independent attributes across services, and combine the ranges of domain-specific attributes only if their service goals also match.

Resource combination rule: A resource represents a physical or informational entity, which is the object of a certain task for the achievement of the corresponding service goal. Two resources are combined if they refer to information entities that fall into a same predefined category and have semantically equivalent properties and attributes.

Task combination rule: A task is the specific procedures to be performed by a service provider for achieving a goal. Two tasks are equivalent if they have the same capability and constraint, and if they operate on the same type of resource and provide the same function. Two equivalent tasks may have different descriptions, sub-structures or super-structures.

Quality contribution propagation rule: Each task has its contribution link to the quality attribute of the goal. Contributions from two equivalent tasks to two equivalent goals can be matched.

Goal grouping rule: Goal matching often occurs at different structure levels. A top level goal for a new incoming service requirement may be the same as a sub-goal in another goal sub-structure. The matching rule for goals is based on the task connected to it by the means-ends link. Two goals can be combined when they have matching means-ends tasks and matching quality attributes.

Other matching rules include:

R1: If two goals/tasks/resources/attributes have the same semantic meaning, they are matched. We use word net, and Wikipedia vocabulary repository to search for synonyms.

R2: If two goals/tasks/resources/attributes have the same identifier such as URI, they are matched.

R3: If two goals/tasks/resources have the same direct sub-structure, they are matched

R4: If two goals/tasks/resources have the same parent and siblings, they are matched.

R5: Match relation is transitive, i.e., for all elements, if A matches B, B matches C, then A matches C.

R6: If two goals have the same means-ends tasks, they are matched.

R7: If two tasks are matched, they have the same type of contribution link to a same quality attributes, the two contributions are matched.

These rules will help us merge the new service request model into the existing one. In this section, we have introduced the potential matching between requirement models. It is the foundation for the requirements reconciliation process to be discussed in the following section.

2.3.2 Merging Requirements Instances

The SRRP conducts a learning process based on a large number of requirements model instances to form a requirements knowledge structure. A possible scenario could be: we accept a first request, and place it in an empty requirement model. When another request comes, the SRRP reconciles the new one with the original model, constructing a hierarchy structure. The learning procedure continues when a new request comes.

We describe the process of requirements reconciliation as follows:

1. Concept learning is conducted, and the elements in the new incoming model are compared with existing ones. The models are merged by identifying various goals, tasks, resources or attributes.

2. The frequency with each element and its sub-structure link appear in the requirements

model is counted when the merge operation is performed.

3. The reinforcement of an element refers to how often it appears in the model network.

4. Redundant decomposition links are removed and the corresponding transitive links are reinforced.

5. Equivalence heuristics are applied for merging matching elements. All the matching rules mentioned above are applied.

This requirement reconciliation process helps generate an integrated requirements model. The more requests issued, the more refined the requirements are, and the richer the knowledge is.

3 GOAL MODEL CONSTRUCTIONS

We also adopt the multi-strategy task-adaptive learning (*MTL*) process (Lee et al 1997, Tecuci et. al. 1995), which is a learning strategy that combines a variety of learning strategies such as: deduction, analogy, induction and abduction. Each step of the learning process can adopt a different learning strategy, so that the learning process can automatically adapt to different tasks. Given correct premises, learning based on deduction can guarantee the correctness, while analogy, induction and abduction may lead to inconsistencies. Thus, *MTL* always tries to use deductive reasoning first; if it fails, analogy will be tried, then induction, and finally, abductive reasoning. Moreover, the results obtained using one strategy will be validated by using other strategies. Similar to human reasoning, the correctness of results are judged to be more reliable if the same results are obtained using two different approaches to the same case.

3.1 Multi-Strategy Task-Adaptive Learning (MTL)

The core structure of *MTL* is the Plausible Justification Tree (*PJT*) structure (Tecuci et al 1993). *PJT* reasons about an input case using knowledge in the knowledge base, and also records and demonstrates the correctness of the process. When using knowledge to conduct feasibility studies on the input, reasoning strategies such as deduction, analogy, induction and abduction can be used. The *MTL* is a continuous learning process of the *PJT* structure based on the input training samples. During the establishment of the *PJT* structure, inconsistencies with input may occur as a result of incorrect inference steps. In this case, a revision to the *PJT* structure is necessary, so that all input can be satisfied.

When applying *MTL* in requirements elicitation, there are several differences. The training set of requirements elicitation is a sequence of actions, and there are temporal orders between the actions. Different ordering may lead to different results. This is not the case in general conceptual learning. The actions included in the training set is not a simple predicate, trigger conditions also need to be given along with the example, the training set must also include information about whether the goal has been achieved or not.

Table 2 shows that, when the learning process starts, the requirements knowledge base will include some partial, inaccurate fractions of the model fragments, including rules for goal decomposition, a number of example models, domain definitions, event definitions, etc. In the table $<=$ represents deductive rules, $\leftarrow$ represents analogy, induction or abduction. Sources of requirements knowledge include: (1) original requirements documents or interview records from stakeholders, and (2) domain knowledge provided by domain experts or past experiences. This chapter uses the first source, in which $<=$ represents deductive rules, $\leftarrow$ represents analogy, induction or abduction. As we can see, the knowledge base is incomplete: for example, for the goal "processBidRequest", there is just one decomposition rule listed in rule 4. The example shows that the decomposition is not complete, and other rules need to be learned during the subsequent learning process.

Since the concepts in the requirements goal model have specific semantics, the *PJT* structure should consider temporal ordering, constraints and events, and give specific treatments to these concepts when establishing and updating the *PJT*. Figure 5 is an example *PLT*: its structure is fairly similar to a goal decomposition tree structure. The learning process is as follows: (1) Establish a *PJT* structure based on the first positive example, then generalize the *PJT*, i.e., use variables to substitute the constant objects in the example, then update the knowledge to include new rules identified in this process. (2) Handle the subsequent positive example e_i by instantiating the existing *PJT* with constants in e_i. If the *PJT* can justify e_i, then it is already included in the *KB*; otherwise, try to make the minimum modification to the *PJT*, so that e_i can be included. The *KB* should be updated at the same time. (3) Handle subsequent negative example n_i, by instantiating the *PJT* with the constants in n_i. If the *PTJ* cannot justify n_i. Then it is not included in the *KB*, the learning process for this example ends; otherwise, the *PJT* should be modified to exclude this example. As we can see, Figure 9 shows a plausible justification tree generated by executing step (1) based on Example1 in Table 2, and Figure 10 shows the modified justification tree integrating Example2 in Table 2. Figure 11 shows the resulting PJT after handling the negative Example3 in Table 2.

Sometimes we fail to justify a given example (positive or negative) when a simple modification is made to the PJT: i.e., we are not able to learn where the required scenario contradicts the KB. In this case, we may defer the handling of this specific case to a later time, and add the negative

Table 2. Initial knowledge base

```
Rules:
r1: ManageTask(x) <= TIME-AND(GetTask(x),
ProcessTask(x), ProcessBidRequest(x))
r2: ProcessTask(x) <= TIME-AND (AnalysisTask(x),
BidTask(x))
r3: BidTask(x) ← TIME-AND(RecordBidHistory(x),
SendBidInfo(x))
r4: ProcessBidRequest(x) ← CalculateBenifit(x)
Examples:
Example1(Positive):
  Operations & Events:
    ReceiveTaskInfo(x1)
    AnalysisTask(x1)
    RecordBidHistory(x1)
    SendBidInfo(x1)
  EVENT:
    BidSucceed(x1)
    CalculateBenifit(x1)
  Result:
    ACHIEVED: ManageTask(x1)
  Related Facts:
    [ACHIEVED] GetTask(x1)
    [ACHIEVED] BidTask(x1)
    [ACHIEVED] ProcessTask(x1)
    [ACHIEVED] ProcessBidRequest(x1)
Example2(Positive):
  Operations & Events:
    ReceiveTaskInfo(x2)
    AnalysisTask(x2)
    SendBidInfo(x2)
  EVENT:
    BidSucceed(x2)
    RecordBidHistory(x2)
    ChangeBidPolicy(x2)
  Result:
    ACHIEVED: ManageTask(x2)
  Related Facts:
    [ACHIEVED]GetTask(x2)
    [ACHIEVED]BidTask(x2)
    [ACHIEVED]ProcessTask(x2)
    [ACHIEVED]ProcessBidRequest(x2)
Example3(Negative):
  Operations & Events:
    ReceiveTaskInfo(x3)
    AnalysisTask(x3)
    RecordBidHistory(x3)
    SendBidInfo(x3)
  EVENT:
    BidSucceed(x3)
    ChangeBidPolicy(x3)
  Result:
    NOT-ACHIEVED: ManageTask(x3)
  Related Facts:
    [ACHIEVED]GetTask(x3)
    [ACHIEVED]BidTask(x3)
    [ACHIEVED]ProcessBidRequest(x3)
```

Figure 9. Goal model 1(also, plausible justification tree 1)

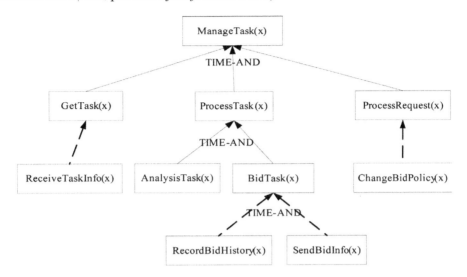

example and its derived events into the *KB* and mark it. In fact, the last *PJT* includes all the requirements information we could obtained through the model learning process.

3.2 Requirements Elicitation from Statistics

When the number of service requests grows, the integrated model becomes more refined. Based on the integrated model and the reinforcement of each goal/task/resource, both service requestor and provider can benefit from the information. Typical scenarios are:

Step 1. Elicitation results from requestor's perspective:

The integrated requirements hierarchy provides more possible alternative implementations for a service goal: for one goal/task, there can be many different ways of decomposing a goal or task; standing for different viewpoints for this goal/task. Instead of simply integrating all viewpoints from different requestors; the integrated network has an important statistic variable, reinforcement, which provides a consensus on how most people view the goal/task. For a service goal, we can find a relevant model that chooses the sub-component

link with the strongest reinforcement at every decomposition node. This model would reflect most requests' position on this goal.

Step 2. Elicitation results from provider's perspective:

Service providers will identify the goal/tasks with higher reinforcement as major revenue producers and the focus of requestors. An important issue the requirements process can help the service provider answer is how to map its core competence into a maximum set of users' requirements that can be satisfied by it. The result of the above learning process offers us a solution. Given a network, each task in the network requests a provider to execute it, and thus, the provider first locates its core service capability on a task for one goal, then it traces the network upstream to find another requirements goal it can take part in. For instance, a provider for a currency exchange service goal may find itself a role in a hospital financial service process, a result which was unknown before. Using this knowledge, the provider may map its capability to any domain, finding more potential business leads. When different service requestors have conflicting goals, the system generates more service alternatives. Each service requestor gets its own goal tree. Providers can merge hundreds

Figure 10. Goal model 2 (also a plausible justification tree 2)

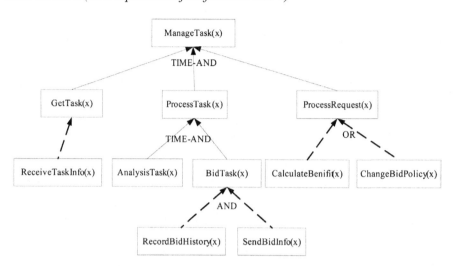

Figure 11. Goal model 3 (also plausible justification tree 3)

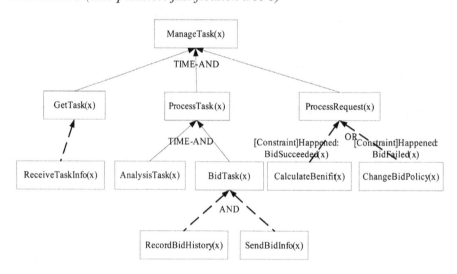

of such networks and determine which goals have high reinforcement.

3.2.1 Feedback Control of Elicitation Process

This section introduces the iterative process to allow the evolution of the requirements gathered. As a mediator, *ASREGL* supports the following functions: first, it extracts requirements fragments iteratively from several requestors. Second, it

accumulates these requirements in a knowledge repository of graphical goal-oriented models for service providers about the needs and preference of service requestors with regard to the services they are capable of providing. Third, it serves as a matchmaker for the two sides. Using knowledge provided by the repository, *ASREGL* makes it possible for requestors to find the services matching their needs as well as for providers to connect to their potential customers.

Figure 12. A provider model that needs refinement

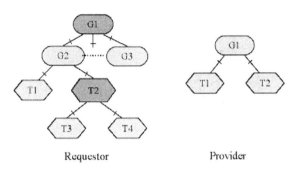

Requestor   Provider

Figure 13. A requestor model that needs refinement

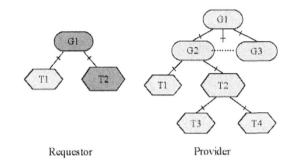

Requestor   Provider

If the satisfaction degree cannot reach the threshold, the iteration will continue. Feedback is provided to the *DQS*, which generates new elicitation queries. In general, there are eight rules including the feedback and respective actions taken by the *DQS*. The formal presentation of these rules is given by *SWRL* language in the *OWL* file.

Rule1: Provider model needs refinement.

Feedback: Certain goals or tasks of the service provider are so general that the requestor's model cannot easily match them. Suppose there are model fragments as shown in Figure 12.

It is observed that the G1 and T2 of the provider have not been decomposed enough, so we provide this information to the DQS of the providers.

Action: With this feedback, DQS should raise more HOW queries for the service provider to break down the coarse goals and tasks so that the requestor's model is matched better.

Rule2: Requestor model needs refinement.

Feedback: Contrary to the previous class, it is the requestor instead of the provider who includes high-level goals or tasks. As shown in Figure 13, the G1 and T2 of the requestor have not been decomposed completely.

Action: The DQS raises more HOW queries for the service requestor to break down the particular goals and tasks.

Rule3: Laddering the provider's model.

Feedback: In certain situations, service providers do not realize that their functional capability can achieve a higher level goal. As shown in Figure 14, the provider considers that it can only satisfy the goal G2 in the beginning. But after the requestor shows that satisfaction of G2 can lead to the satisfaction of G1, the provider knows he can raise the level of goal G2 to G1. This information can be provided to the DQS of the service providers.

Action: More WHY queries should be asked of the provider to explore the provider's goal tree upstream. By doing this, a service provider can

Figure 14. Low level of provider's goal

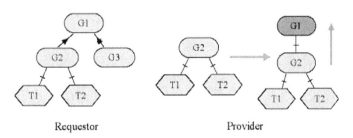

Requestor   Provider

Figure 15. Alternative selections

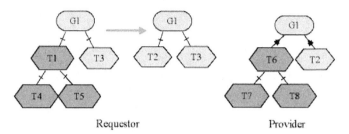

map its core competence into a maximum set of user requirements that can be satisfied by it.

Rule 4: Alternatives are sought.

Feedback: When some functional requirements, modelled as task sub-trees, are not satisfied by a provider, it is reasonable to find an alternative option (see Figure 15). If a goal of the provider is linked by some tasks through a means-end relationship, these tasks are replaceable. We can offer this information to improve the satisfaction degree.

Action: The DQS asks the requestor whether or not he wants to replace the task with another equivalent one. This action increases the opportunities of matching the two sides.

Rule 5: New Services are added or outsourced.

Feedback: If there is no alterative option to choose, and the actions introduced in rules 1-4 do not work, we should inform the DQS of the result.

Action: Suggest the provider add new services to meet the user's requirements, if necessary. We can measure the worthiness of implementing that service by utilizing the knowledge accumulated,

which indicates how often that function is requested. Within a service network, it is possible to use abundant outside services. The DQS can advise the provider to extend its competence by using outsourced services while remaining transparent to end users. This would greatly improve the matching ratio.

Rule 6: Quality conflicts are resolved.

Feedback: Quality Attributes have an extremely important impact on matching results. It is common for one task to have different types of contributions to the same quality attribute from diverse perspectives. As illustrated in Figure 16, task T1 helps the quality attribute of G1 in the requestor's view but also hurts it in the provider's view. This conflict of quality attributes will be reported to the DQS.

Action: Similar to rule 4, the DQS suggests that the requestor replace the task with an alternative that helps the quality attribute, say, T3 in this example.

Rule 7: Quality negotiation and trade-off

Figure 16. Quality attributes in conflict

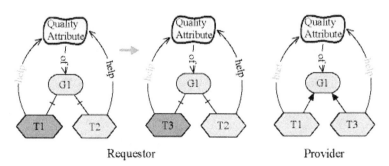

Feedback: If the quality attributes requested are too difficult to fulfill by the provided services, we should take actions to make a trade-off.

Action: The *DQS* should either suggest that the requestors to reduce the unnecessary quality requirements, or advise the providers to increase the quality degree they offer. Sometimes, quality can be traded off.

3.2.2 Satisfaction Measurement

As a matchmaker for the two sides, *ASREGL* needs a satisfaction measurement. Because the requirements models are based on ontology, the matching process is an ontology similarity calculation process in nature.

In order to get the overall similarity, it is necessary to calculate each element's MatchScore separately, including goals, tasks and resources. The MatchScore has two major considerations: functional similarity and non-functional similarity. The non-functional similarity *simSG* is captured by the following formula,

$$simSG(s,t) = \frac{1}{m}\sum_{i=1}^{m}\frac{Min[Q_i(s),Q_i(t)]}{Max[Q_i(s),Q_i(t)]} \qquad (1)$$

Where elements *s* and *t* are the elements being compared; $Q_i(s)$ means the value of the *i*-th quality attribute of element *s*; and *m* is the maximum number of quality attributes the two elements have. MatchScore is calculated as the mean of all the MatchScores:

$$MatchScore(s,t) = k^n * sim(s,t) * simSG(s,t) \qquad (2)$$

sim(s,t)=1 if the existing *t* in the service provider is the same as *s* in the service requestor; otherwise, the value is set to 0. k^n is a penalty factor that reflects the structure distance. *k* can be set to a fixed number such as 0.9, and *n* is the level distance of *s* and *t*. The combination captures the

functional similarity of the two elements. Finally, the overall satisfaction degree can be calculated as follows:

$$satisfaction(S,T) = \frac{\sum_{i=1}^{\#Nodes(S)} MatchScore(S_i,T_i)}{\# Nodes(S)} \qquad (3)$$

where *S* and *T* are the models of the requestor and provider, and *#Nodes(S)* returns the number of nodes in *S*. The calculation process will be explained in more detail with an example in section 4.

As $(S_1, ...S_m)$ is a set, there are many possible combinations between S_i and T_i. E.g., S_1 can be paired with S_2 as well as S_1. It is so-called bipartite matching. To reduce the complexity of the matching process, $(S_1,...,S_m)$ are considered tree-structured, and an algorithm to find the corresponding pairs is used here.

4. RUNNING EXAMPLES

4.1 Order Processing

We have applied the proposed approach in a simple web service of order-processing. When an order request is issued by a customer, the manufacturer, upon receiving the details of the order, checks the inventory to verify whether it has enough quantity of goods to fill the order. When there is enough stock, the manufacturer contacts its delivery partner to confirm the shipping date and address. Based on the shipment fee returned by the delivery partner and the product cost from the order detail, the accounting partner, often a bank, calculates the total price and returns the results to the customer. When there is not enough stock in the inventory, the manufacturer contacts its supplier first and then the delivery partners.

For each component service in the process, the SREP can build a requirements model. Take accounting service as an example: its service goal is "to explicitly calculate the total cost for the new order". The following figures (Figure 17-23) present the model being built. They are constructed by different requirement fragments. Different figures reveal viewpoints from different prospective providers. Due to limitation of space, labels are used for the model elements: (G for goal, T for task, R for resource and QA for quality attribute.)

G: The total cost for the new order is explicitly calculated

G1: Cost for supply service in business process is computed

G2: Cost for delivery service in business process is computed

G3: Discount for consumer is computed

G4: The tax for this order is computed

G5: The finance of the enterprise is balanced

T1: Compute the fee for supply service

T2: Compute the fee for delivery service

T3: Check the discount for customer

T4: Compute the tax cost for all costs

T5: Bank helps balance the finance of the enterprise;

T6: Perform basic computation

T7: Check the reputation of the corresponding customer

T8: Check the discount for the customer within the reputation level

R1: Supply service R2: Delivery service

R3: Customer information record

R4: Tax radio table R5: Money;

QA1: Accuracy QA2: Security

QA3: Good reputation

Figure 17 and 18 illustrate two request models which need to be merged. The integrated model from the two requests for accounting service is shown in Figure 19. The reinforcement of each goal/task/quality is labelled on the upper right side of the figure.

After building a model, when a new request comes in, the SRRP merges it into the integrated model. As we have emphasized, requirements gathered from the requestor are mostly fragmental. Suppose request 3 is as shown in Figure 20, which is a model fragment.

According to step 4 in the reconciliation process, merging this request will not change the model, but will increase the reinforcement of the corresponding goals. Through the elicitation process to merge the requirement fragments into the model, the requirement knowledge model obtained is more refined and detailed.

Among the large amount of information provided by the model, the number of reinforcement elements provides a feasible path to understand the requirement. For instance, if more requests like request 3 are received, accounting service shown i as n Figure 21 will be considered.

An important application of this model is that it can help relate requirements items, from which requestors can obtain the necessary information needed. The learning process iterates by referring to another requestor's model, and the optimal path indicated by reinforcement is a guideline for general requestors.

On the other hand, the provider expects to map its core competence into a maximum set of users' requirements. Now we discuss another scenario, in which requirement fragments come from requests for other services. Figure 22 shows the model for delivery service:

G': Goods provided by supply service delivered safely to target

G8: Cost for delivery service is confirmed

G9: The goods are received from supplier

G10: The goods are delivered at target

G11: The finances of the delivery company are balanced

T9: Delivery company discusses cost

T10: Delivery people pick up the goods

T11: Delivery people transfer the goods to the target

T12: Financial institution does the balancing for the company

Figure 17. Model of accounting service request

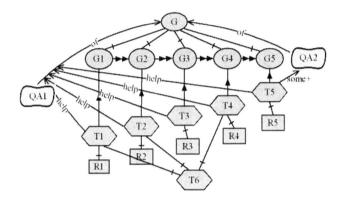

Figure 18. Model of accounting service request

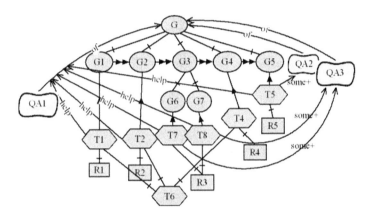

Figure 19. Merged model for accounting service

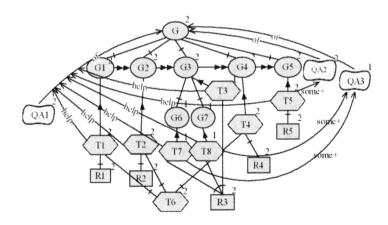

Figure 20. Model of request 3 for accounting service

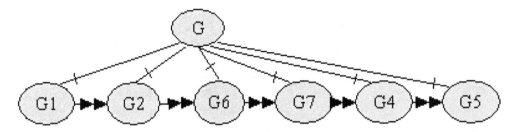

Figure 21. Reinforcement path for accounting service

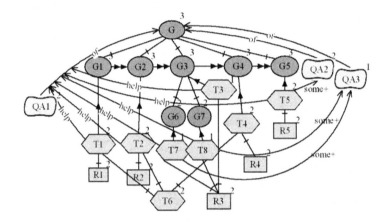

Figure 22. Model of a request for delivery service

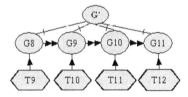

Figure 23. Integrated model with delivery service

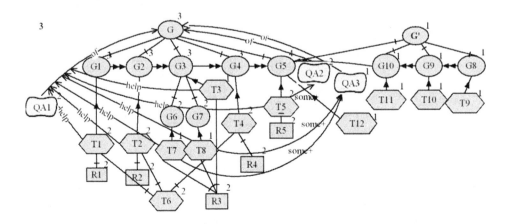

After this request is recorded, the integrated model is shown in Figure23.

G5 and G11 are providing a same service with two different implementations, namely, T5 and T12. Thus, the providers for T5 or T12 would be useful in both G and G'. Concretely, both banks and financial institutions can perform the task for accounting service and delivery service. Thus, providers capable of a task would find their other capabilities related to the task. The more requests are integrated into this model, the more providers will find users whose requirements they can meet. The model structure provides information for all service providers, to organize their legacy system to a more reasonable and comprehensive set of services.

4.2. Online Travel Agency

The proposed approach was applied to a widely referenced example in the domain of e-Tourism, which was originally built as a use case of the WSMO project. In this example, there is an online travel agency, WorldStar, which provides various e-Tourism services to customers, such as booking of flights, hotels and rental cars. Mr. Joe Liu, a customer living in Beijing, wants to enjoy his ten-day vacation in Paris. In order to save time, he decides to employ an online travel agency to make his travel arrangements for him. But Joe has not taken an international trip before, so he does not know how to express his requirements to the travel agent, or which agent will best meet his needs. In this situation, our approach, ASREGL, is applied to elicit Joe's requirements and build a model based on it (see Figure 24). In order to elicit Joe's initial requirements, a set of basic queries is generated by the DQS. Due to limitation of space, we skip the step of raising queries, and start by building an initial requirements model from the answers to these queries.

The labels represent the following services:

G1: One-stop travel services are provided.

Figure 24. Initial model of Joe Liu's request

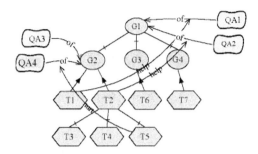

G2: Ticket to Paris is booked.
G3: Paris hotel is booked.
G4: Car is rented in Paris.
T1: Book airline ticket from Beijing to Paris.
T2: Book train ticket from Beijing to Paris.
T3: Search possible train connections.
T4: Select one train connection.
T5: Get the ticket.
T6: Book hotel room online.
T7: Book a Mercedes-Benz rental car.
QA1: Convenience. **QA2:** Cost.
QA3: Security. **QA4:** Response time.

On the other hand, models of travel agencies have been constructed using the same approach when they register. Take WorldStar as an example: the constructed model is shown in Figure 25.

In addition to the labels defined above, the following labels are added:

G5: Benefits earned by providing travel services.
G6: Travel guide is provided.
G7: Meal plan is provided.
G8: Ticket is booked.
G9: Ticket is delivered.
T8: Deliver electronic ticket.
T9: Deliver physical ticket by express.
T10: Deliver physical ticket by priority express.

ASREGL then compares Joe's initial model with all the models of currently registered travel agencies, and returns a ranking of the agency with the best matching ratio. To illustrate how to

Figure 25. Initial model of WorldStar

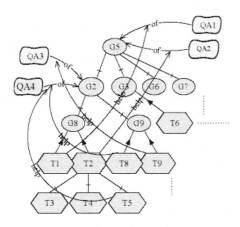

Table 3. Matching ratio calculation process

Nodes	Match Score	*simSG*	*k^n sim*
G1	0	N/A	0
G2	0.65	0.65	1
G3	1	1	1
G4	0	N/A	0
T1	0.9	1	0.9
T2	0.9	1	0.9
T3	1	1	1
T4	1	1	1
T5	1	1	1
T6	1	1	1
T7	0	N/A	0

determine the satisfaction degree, we calculate it between the models of Joe and WorldStar. Suppose all Quality Attributes can be expressed by a number, for example, the security level Joe desires can be set to 0.8 and the value WorldStar provides can be set to 1. In addition, the response time Joe desires is 15 minutes, but WorldStar can only provide service in 30 minutes. Using formula 1 we can get: $simSG(G2,G2')=1/2*(0.8/1 + 15/30)=0.65$. The functional similarity of G2 can be obtained by knsim, where $sim(G2,G2')=1$ because matched goal G2' exists in WorldStar's model. The penalty factor k is set to 0.9 and n is 0 because G2 and G2' are on the same level. The MatchScore values of all the nodes in Joe's model are calculated as shown in the following table.

According to formula 3, the overall satisfaction degree is $(0.65+1+0.9+0.9+1+1+1+1)/11=0.677$. If we set the threshold to 0.92, the iteration continues.

We can find the node with a low MatchScore in Table 3 to locate the problem. Then the heuristic rules mentioned in section 3.2.1 can be applied to adjust the two models step by step.

Iteration 1: We noticed that the MatchScores of nodes T1 and T2 in Joe's model are both 0.9 because the value of *n* is 1 in $k^n sim$. This can be easily understood: T1 and T2 are direct children of G2 in Joe's model, but they are grandchildren

of G2 in WorldStar's model. So there is one level distance between them. The level distance is caused by G8, which is not in Joe's model, meaning that G2 has not been decomposed completely. In this situation, we apply Rule 2 to refine the service requestor's goal. After receiving this feedback, the DQS raises more HOW-type queries to break down G2, such as: "In order to get the ticket, what other goals should be achieved?", "Should the ticket be delivered?" etc. By answering these queries, Joe realizes that he has overlooked the delivery step. Then our ASREGL helps append G8 and G9 in his model. Due to the limitation of space, we will skip an explanation of the process of calculating the satisfaction degree at the end of this iteration, and give the value, 0.72, directly. Although the satisfaction degree is improved, it still doesn't reach the threshold. So the next iteration begins.

Iteration 2: Because the new goal G9 has been added, it is necessary to apply Rule 2 again to elicit its means. Suppose the query "In which way do you prefer to receive your ticket?" is asked, and the answer is "By priority express". Thus T10 is attached as the means for accomplishing G9. After this adjustment, the satisfaction degree is still lower than expected, so the iteration continues.

Iteration 3: In the process of re-calculating the satisfaction degree, we find that the MatchScore of the T10 just added is zero because there is no corresponding task provided by WorldStar. Joe wants to get the ticket by priority express, but WorldStar only provides delivery services either by normal express or by sending electronic tickets by email. In order to reach an agreement, Rule 4 is applied to recommend that Joe pick another choice. The DQS asks "Your requested delivery method is not available; why not try an electronic ticket?" If Joe answers "yes", then the T10 in his requirements model is replaced by T8. Again, the process continues.

Iteration 4: Improvement of models takes place on both the customer side and the service provider side. In this step, we find the MatchScore of G4 is zero. This is also because there is no corresponding node in WorldStar's model. Joe wants to rent a car when he arrives in Paris, but WorldStar has not anticipated this customer requirement. Thus both Rules 5 and 6 can be applied. This means DQS can either recommend that WorldStar to develop a car rental support service, or outsource this service to a third-party partner. Once these actions are executed, G4 can be attached as a child node of G5 in WorldStar's model. Again, the process continues.

Iteration 5: Another node with a zero value MatchScore is G1, because no matching goal was found in WorldStar's model. Joe desires a one-stop travel services, including ticketing, hotel booking and rental car reservations. In the beginning, WorldStar did not offer the rental car reservations, so it could not be called a one-stop travel service. Thus, G1 is not contained in WorldStar's model. After G4 is added in iteration 4, WorldStar has the capability to provide one-stop travel service, so G1 is achievable. The raising of the goal level to G1 is based on the Rule 4.

Iteration 6: According to Table 2, G2 had a low MatchScore because of the mismatch of its Quality Attributes, especially QA4, the response time. Joe requests the ticket should be booked in 15

minutes, but WorldStar only promises to respond in 30 minutes. Here Rule 8 should be applied to begin negotiation. Depending on different cases, the DQS either recommends Joe lengthen the response time or suggests that WorldStar shorten it. Suppose Joe re-sets this value to 20 and WorldStar changes it to 25; then the result would be quite impressive. The overall satisfaction degree calculated here climbs to 0.973, which reaches the threshold, so the iteration can be terminated.

The above example demonstrates an execution scenario for the proposed service requirements elicitation process, including how to generate questionnaires, how to construct requirement models from the answers and how to improve these models based on rules step by step.

5. RELATED WORK

Requirements elicitation has focused primarily on developing, implementing and evaluating various techniques, methods and tools. Many of these were adopted from other research areas such as the social sciences (Berardi et. al. 2003, Zowghi et. al. 2005) and knowledge engineering (Singh et al. 2005). These approaches reduced the complexity of the elicitation process and improved the quality of the requirements. In fact, there are more than one hundred approaches used for requirements elicitation. (Gougue & Linde 1993) examined a few of the traditional techniques such as interviewing, observation and task analysis at a relatively high level. In a more recent survey on the theory and practice of requirements elicitation, more approaches were examined including those based on goals (Dardeene et al. 1993), scenarios (Anton 1996, Potts 1994), viewpoints (Sommerville et al. 1998) and domain knowledge.

There are related works on service matching using ontology-based approaches in identifying similar Web services. In Liang et al. (2008) uses categorization-based scheme to match equivalent Web services that can operate on heterogeneous domain ontology. When the upper ontology for services and domain ontology is given, the service matching scheme determines whether a given Web service is a possible replacement using a categorization utility. There is also related work in the service composition literature, which collects users' preferences in order to guide service composition. It suggests that users present a service request with an external e-Service schema of a finite state machine.

Model construction is considered a process of ontology instances elicitation in this chapter. So far, a number of methodologies for ontology development, based on the Nature Language Process (*NLP*), have been proposed. For example, the Methontology Framework [8] provides an Ontology Development Environment (*ODE*), in which the requirements engineer can use elicitation techniques, such as structured interviews, document reading and questionnaires to support the building process. It is impractical to interview each customer individually or to utilize a requirements document provided by service requestors in our services context. So a lightweight approach such as the language extended lexicon (*LEL*) (Leite et al. 1993) can be a useful complementary of this work.

6. CONCLUSION

In summary, this chapter proposes a service-oriented requirements analysis framework (ASREGL), which turns the classical "once for all" philosophy into a continuous negotiation and adaptation process. The proposed requirements analysis framework plays a similar role of recommender systems for services. Services owned by various entities in different computing levels have their capabilities. The main tasks of services computing include services classification and clustering, services migration, services recommendation, and services composition as well as services discovery and publishing in social context. Based on

existing requirements models and new service requests, ASREGL achieves an optimal service supply and demand relationship based on a dual feedback loop. The current control variable is the similarity between the service requirements model and the service capability model. Major technical contributions include: a dynamic questionnaire system for service requirements elicitation, the construction process of goal-oriented service models based on users' answers to the elicitation queries and the dual feedback control mechanism to service requestor and provider. A virtual travel agency example was used to illustrate the proposed ideas.

Our approach can be considered as a natural migration of the goal-oriented requirements elicitation approach into service-oriented computing. And this is to be deployed on the cloud computing platform. Consider the scenario in which various computing resources and basic infrastructure are powerful, cheap and easy to use where users can create or customize their services easily by utilizing various resources on the cloud computing platform. Talia & Trunfio (2010) shows that "recently Web services and Cloud computing services, became available opening the way for accessing computing services as public utilities, like water, gas and electricity". Powerful computing infrastructure allows information and services to be made available. Services may happen anytime, anywhere without space or time limitations. Service providers create their services according to their accessible resources and communication channels. Then these services are published in desired Services Computing platforms. When there are huge amounts of various services which provide certain computing functionalities, one natural problem is proposed: How service consumers can discover and access these services expediently under the condition where service consumers and service providers can register their services. From a service-oriented requirements engineering perspective, such elicitation process has to be conducted within the service life-cycle, with the assistance of web-based tools. Due to the specific requirements of the services context, a questionnaire technique is employed. Satisfaction measurement actually is the semantic similarity of ontology. Then we presented a set of adjustment rules to improve the quality of the models. Service requirements negotiation serves the same purpose.

In summary, we have present a mechanism to facilitate service requirements elicitation based on service requestors' answers to a group of queries designed based on a goal-oriented requirements language – *i**. We have elaborated on each of the elicitation strategies and the requirements reconciliation heuristics to establish a requirements hierarchical model based on *i**. The Requestor can encode its request more efficiently, and the provider can dig out the potential business leads by tracing through the requirements model. Our major contribution is threefold: first, we identified a group of service requests fragments; then we gave heuristics on how to assemble such service request fragments from the same requestor into comprehensive goal structure representing service requirements. A mechanism to reconcile service requirements knowledge about a same service from different requestors is proposed. Finally, *ASREGL* improves the requirements quality iteratively using feedbacks for matching results. For example, it can elicit relevant requirements that requestors are not aware of, or recommend that service providers adapt their function or quality to fit common user needs.

In the future, the *ASREGL* service requirements elicitation framework can be integrated with more widely applied service computing technique, so that the goal-oriented service modelling ontology *SRMO* can be used in combination with existing service ontology such as *OWL* and *WSMO*, after necessary extensions and integrations. The current matching strategy is based on a set of heuristic rules, a more rigor computational model (such as, those based on vector cosine angle distance) can be developed to improve the precision of the

matching algorithm. The reconciliation process can also be extended so that more precise suggestions can be returned to requestors and providers for effectively adjust their requirements model.

ACKNOWLEDGMENT

This chapter receives partial financial support from the National Basic Research Program of China (973) (Grant No. 2009CB320700). Contributions from Jian Xiang, Wei Qiao and Lei Lin, and inspiration from John Mylopoulos, Jianguo Lu and Hongji Yang are also gratefully acknowledged.

REFERENCES

Antón, A. I. (1996). Goal-based requirements analysis. In *2nd International Conference on Requirements Engineering* (ICRE'96) (pp. 136-144). Colorado Springs, Colorado, USA.

Berardi, D., Calvanese, D., De Giacomo, G. M., & Lenzerini, M. (2003). Automatic composition of e-services that export their behaviour. In *1st International Conference on Service Oriented Computing (ICSOC) LNCS 2910*, (pp. 43-58).

Chandra, T., Fikes, A., & Gruber, R. E. (2006). Bigtable: A distributed storage system for structured data. In *Proceedings of the 7th USENIX Symposium on Operating Systems Design and Implementation (OSDI '06)*, (p. 15).

Dardeene, A., van Lamsweerde, A., & Fickas, S. (1993). Goal-directed requirements acquisition. *Science of Computer Programming, 20*(1-2), 3–50. doi:10.1016/0167-6423(93)90021-G

Dean, J., & Ghemawat, S. (2008). MapReduce: Simplified data processing on large clusters. *Communications of the ACM, 51*(1), 107–113. doi:10.1145/1327452.1327492

Fernández, M., Gómez-Pérez, A., & Juristo, N. (1997). Methontology: From ontological art towards ontological engineering. In *Symposium on Ontological Engineering of AAAI* (pp. 33-40).

Ghemawat, S., Gobioff, H., & Leung, S.-T. (2003). The Google file system. In *Proceedings of the Nineteenth ACM Symposium on Operating Systems Principles (SOSP '03)* (pp. 29–43).

Goguen, J. A., & Linde, C. (1993). Techniques for requirements elicitation. *International Symposium on Requirements Engineering* (pp. 152-164), San Diego, CA.

Hackos, J. T., & Redish, J. C. (1998). *User and task analysis for interface design*. John Wiley & Sons, Inc.

Kvale, B. (2008). *InterViews* (2nd ed.). Thousand Oaks, CA: SAGE.

Lee, O., & Tecuci, G. (1997). MTLS: A tool for extending and refining knowledge bases. In *9th International Conference on Tools with Artificial Intelligence (ICTAI '97)* (pp. 524–531). Newport Beach, CA.

Leite, J. C. S. P., & Franco, A. P. M. v. (1993). A strategy for conceptual model acquisition. *Proceedings of the First International Symposium on Requirements Engineering*, (pp. 243-246). IEEE Computer Society Press.

Leite, J. C. S. P., Yu, Y., Liu, L., Yu, E. S. K., & Mylopoulos, J. (2005). Quality-based software reuse. *Conference of Advanced Information Systems Engineering (CAiSE 2005), Lecture Notes in Computer Science*, Vol. 3520 (January 2005), (pp. 535-550).

Liang, Q. A., & Lam, H. (2008). Web service matching by ontology instance categorization. In *Proceedings of the IEEE International Conference on Services Computing (SCC '08)*, 7-11 July 2008, Vol. 1, (pp. 202-209). Honolulu, HI.

Liu, L., Liu, Q., Chi, C., Jin, Z., & Yu, E. (2008). Towards a service requirements modelling ontology based on agent knowledge and intentions. *International Journal of Agent-Oriented Software Engineering, 2*(3), 324–349. doi:10.1504/IJAOSE.2008.019422

Marks, E. A., & Lozano, B. (2010). *Executive's guide to cloud computing*. John Wiley & Sons.

Martin, D. (Ed.). (2004). *OWL-S: Semantic markup for web services*. Retrieved from http://www.w3.org/Submission/OWL-S/

Papazoglou, M. P., & Heuvel, W. J. d. (2007). Service oriented architectures: Approaches, technologies and research issues. *The VLDB Journal, 16*, 389–415. doi:10.1007/s00778-007-0044-3

Peng, B., Cui, B., & Li, X. (2009). Implementation issues of a cloud computing platform. *A Quarterly Bulletin of the Computer Society of the IEEE Technical Committee on Data Engineering, 32*(1), 59–66.

Qiao, W., Liu, L., & Xiang, J. (2008). ASREF: An adaptive service requirements elicitation framework based on goal-oriented modelling. In *Proceedings of the 11th IberoAmerican Workshop on Requirements Engineering and Software Environments* (IDEAS'08), Recife, Brazil. Feb 13-15, 2008.

Singh, M. P., & Huhns, M. N. (2005). *Service-oriented computing: Semantics, processes, agents*. London, UK: Wiley.

Sommerville, I., Sawyer, P., & Viller, S. (1998). Viewpoints for requirements elicitation: A practical approach. International Conference on Requirements Engineering, (pp. 74-81). April 6-10, Colorado Springs, CO, 1998.

Sotomayor, B., Montero, R. S., Llorente, I. M., & Foster, I. (2009). Virtual infrastructure management in private and hybrid clouds. *IEEE Internet Computing, 13*(5), 14–22. doi:10.1109/MIC.2009.119

Sutcliffe, A., & Maiden, N. (1998). The domain theory for requirements engineering. *IEEE Transactions on Software Engineering, 24*(3), 174–196. doi:10.1109/32.667878

Talia, D., & Trunfio, P. (2010). How distributed data mining tasks can thrive as knowledge services. *Communications of the ACM, 53*(7), 132–137. doi:10.1145/1785414.1785451

Tecuci, G. (1993). Plausible justification trees: A framework for the deep and dynamic integration of learning strategies. *Machine Learning, 11,* 237–261. doi:10.1007/BF00993079

Tecuci, G. (1995). Building knowledge bases through multi-strategy learning and knowledge acquisition. In Tecuci, G., & Kodratoff, Y. (Eds.), *Machine learning and knowledge acquisition: Integrated approaches*. London, UK: Academic Press.

Vouk, M. A. (2008). Cloud computing, issues, research and implementations. In *30th International Conference on Information Technology Interfaces (ITI 2008)*, Vol. 4, (pp. 31–40).

WSMO. (2004). *Use case of "Virtual Travel Agency" (VTA)*. Retrieved from http://www.wsmo.org/2004/d3/d3.3/v0.1/

Xiang, J., Liu, L., Qiao, W., & Yang, J. (2007). SREM: A service requirements elicitation mechanism based on ontology. In *Proceedings of the 31th Annual International Computer Software & Applications Conference* (COMPSAC'07), Beijing, China, July 23-27, 2007, (pp. 196-203).

Xiang, J., Qiao, W., Xiong, Z., Jiang, T., & Liu, L. (2006). SAFARY: A Semantic Web service implementation platform. In *Proceedings of APSEC-SOPOSE'06*, Bangalore, India, December 9, 2006.

Yu, E. (1997). Towards modelling and reasoning support for early-phase requirements engineering. In *Proceedings of the 3rd IEEE International Symposium on Requirements Engineering (RE'97)* Jan. 6-8, Washington D.C., USA, (pp. 226-235).

Zowghi, D., & Coulin, C. (2005). Requirements elicitation: A survey of techniques, approaches, and tools. In Aurum, A., & Wohlin, C. (Eds.), *Engineering and managing software requirements*. Springer. doi:10.1007/3-540-28244-0_2

ADDITIONAL READING

Chung, L., Nixon, B. A., Yu, E., & Mylopoulos, J. (2000). *Non-functional requirements in software engineering*. Kluwer Academic Publishers.

Letier, E. (2001). *Reasoning about agents in goal-oriented requirements engineering*. PhD Thesis. Department of Information Engineering, Catholic University of Louvian.

Nimbus: Open Source Infrastructure-as-a-Service Cloud Computing Software. (2009).

The Eucalyptus Open-Source Cloud Computing System. (2009).

van der Raadt, B., & Gordijn, J. (2005). Exploring Web Services from a business value perspective. *Proceedings of the 13th IEE International Conference on Requirements Engineering*, (pp. 114-134).

Xen cloud platform. (n.d.). *Advanced virtualization infrastructure for the clouds*. Retrieved from http://www.xen.org/products/cloudxen.html

Compilation of References

Aalst, W. M., & Hofstede, A. H. (2005). YAWL: Yet another workflow language. *Information Systems*, *30*(4), 245–275. doi:10.1016/j.is.2004.02.002

ABCs of SOA. (2007). *CIO Magazine*. Retrieved from http://www.cio.com/article/40941

Accenture. (2009). *Social CRM: The new frontier of marketing, sales and service*.

Adya, A., Liskov, B., & ÓNeil, P. (2000). Generalized isolation level definitions. *16th International Conference on Data Engineering (ICDE)* (pp. 67–80). San Diego, CA: IEEE Computer Society.

Aebi, D., & Largo, R. (1994). Methods and tools for data value re-engineering, *International Conference on Applications of Databases, Lecture Notes in Computer Science 819*, (pp. 1-9). Berlin, Germany: Springer-Verlag.

Aebi, D. (1997). *Data engineering: A case study. Proceedings in Advances in Databases and Information Systems*. Berlin, Germany: Springer-Verlag.

Aiken, P., & Muntz, A. (1993). *A framework for reverse engineering DoD legacy information systems. WCRE*. Los Alamos, NM: IEEE Press.

Alloy Analyzer 4. (n.d.). Retrieved from http://alloy.mit.edu/alloy4/

Alluri, R. (2009). SOA adoption challenges. *BPTrends*.

Altintas, N. I., & Cetin, S. (2008). Managing large scale reuse across multiple software product lines. *ICSR '08 Proceedings of the 10th International Conference on Software Reuse: High Confidence Software Reuse in Large Systems* (pp. 166 - 177). Heidelberg, Germany: Springer-Verlag Berlin.

Amazon Elastic Beanstalk. (n.d.). Retrieved from http://aws.amazon.com/elasticbeanstalk/

Amazon Elastic Cloud. (n.d.). Retrieved from http://aws.amazon.com/ec2/

Amazon Mechanical Turk. (n.d.). Retrieved from http://aws.amazon.com/mturk

Amazon Relational Database Service. (n.d.). Retrieved from http://aws.amazon.com/rds/

Amazon SimpleDB. (n.d.). Retrieved from http://aws.amazon.com/simpledb/

Amazon Web Services. (n.d.). Retrieved from http://aws.amazon.com/

Amazon. (n.d.). Retrieved from http://www.amazon.com/

Andersson, J. (2000). Issues in dynamic software architectures. In *Proceedings of the 4th International Software Architecture Workshop*, (pp. 111–114).

Anne, T. M. (2005). *The elephant has left the building*. Retrieved from http://www.intelligententerprise.com/showArticle.jhtml?articleID=164301126&pgno=3

Antón, A. I. (1996). Goal-based requirements analysis. In *2nd International Conference on Requirements Engineering* (ICRE'96) (pp. 136-144). Colorado Springs, Colorado, USA.

Apache CouchDB. (n.d.). Retrieved from http://couchdb.apache.org

Apache Hadoop. (n.d.). Retrieved from http://hadoop.apache.org

Apel, S. (2008). An algebra for features and feature composition. In M. Johnson (Ed.), *The Twelfth International Conference on Algebraic Methodology and Software Technology* (pp. 36-50). Berlin, Germany: Springer-Verlag.

Apel, S., Kastner, C., & Lengauer, C. (2009). FEATURE-HOUSE: Language-independent, automated software composition. In S. Fickas (Ed.), *The 2009 IEEE International Conference on Software Engineering* (pp. 221-231). Washington, DC: IEEE Computer Society.

Armbrust, M., Fox, A., Griffith, R., Joseph, A. D., Katz, R., & Konwinski, A. ... Zaharia, M. (2009). *Above the clouds: A Berkeley view of cloud computing*. Technical report, EECS Department, University of California, Berkeley.

Arsanjani, A., Zhang, J.-L., & Ellis, M. (2007). A service-oriented reference architecture. *IT Professional, 9*(3), 10–17. doi:10.1109/MITP.2007.53

Atkinson, S., Bailes, P. A., Chapman, M., Chilvers, M., & Peake, I. (1994). A re-engineering evaluation of software refinery: Architecture, process and technology. *Proceedings of the Third Symposium on Assessment of Quality Software Development Tools*. Los Alamos, NM: IEEE Press.

Attensity and Chess Media Group. (2010). Introducing the social customer. *Social CRM Series*, Part #1, Avande. (2008). *CRM and social media: Maximizing deeper customer relationships*.

Aversano, L., Canfora, G., Cimitile, A., & De Lucia, A. (2001). Migrating legacy systems to the Web: An experience report. *Proceedings of European Conference on Software Maintenance and Reengineering.* Los Alamos, NM: IEEE Press.

Avizienis, A., Laprie, J. C., Randell, B., & Landwehr, C. (2004). Basic concepts and taxonomy of dependable and secure computing. *IEEE Transactions on Dependable and Secure Computing, 1*(1), 11–33. doi:10.1109/TDSC.2004.2

Axelsen, E. W., & Krogdahl, S. (2009). Groovy package templates: Supporting reuse and runtime adaption of class hierarchies. In J. Noble (Ed.), *The Fifth Symposium on Dynamic Languages* (pp. 15-26). New York, NY: ACM.

Axis2 Homepage. (2009). *Apache Axis2.* Retrieved June 8, 2010, from http://ws.apache.org/axis2/

Azure, M. (n.d.). *Service Business*. Retrieved from http://msdn.microsoft.com/en-us/library/ee732537.aspx

Bai, Q., & Fitch, P. (2009). *Delivering heterogeneous hydrologic data services with an enterprise service bus application*. 18th World IMACS / MODSIM Congress.

Band, W., Hamerman, P. D., & Magarie, A. (2010). *Trends 2010: Customer relationship management: Eleven trends shape CRM technology adoption agendas*. Forrester Research.

Band, W., Marston, P., Herbert, L., Leaver, S., & Rogan, M. A. (2008). *Best practices: The smart way to implement CRM SaaS solutions*. Forrester Research.

Bass, L., Clements, P., & Kazman, R. (2003). *Software architecture in practice*. Addison-Wesley.

Batory, D. (2004). Feature-oriented programming and the AHEAD tool suite. In A. Finkelstein (Ed.), *The Twenty-Sixth Conference on Software Engineering* (pp. 702-703). Washington, DC: IEEE Computer Society.

Bean, J. (2010). *SOA and Web services interface design: Principles, techniques and standards*. Burlington, MA: Morgan Kaufmann Publishing.

Beaty, K., Kochut, A., & Shaikh, H. (2009). *Desktop to cloud transformation planning*. IEEE International Symposium on Parallel & Distributed Processing. Los Alamos, NM: IEEE Press.

Behm, A., Geppert, A., & Diettrich, K. R. (1997). *On the migration of relational schemas and data to object-oriented database systems. Proceedings of Re-Technologies in Information Systems, Klagenfurt, Austria.* Los Alamos, NM: IEEE Press.

Benlian, A., Hess, T., & Buxmann, P. (2009). Drivers of SaaS-adoption: An empirical study of different application types. *Business & Information Systems Engineering, 1*(5), 357–369. doi:10.1007/s12599-009-0068-x

Berardi, D., Calvanese, D., De Giacomo, G. M., & Lenzerini, M. (2003). Automatic composition of e-services that export their behaviour. In *1st International Conference on Service Oriented Computing (ICSOC) LNCS 2910*, (pp. 43-58).

Berenson, H., Bernstein, P., Gray, J., Melton, J., O'Neil, E., & O'Neil, P. (1995). A critique of ANSI SQL isolation levels. *ACM SIGMOD International Conference (ACM Special Interest Group on Management of Data)*, (p. 24). San Jose, CA: ACM Press.

Bernhard, M. (2010). Stop the software architecture erosion: building better software systems. *SPLASH '10 Proceedings of the ACM International Conference Companion on Object Oriented Programming Systems Languages and Applications Companion* (pp. 129-138). New York, NY: ACM.

Bernstein, P. A., & Newcomer, E. (2009). *Principles of transaction processing* (2nd ed.). Burlington, MA: Morgan Kaufmann Publishers.

Besancenot, J., Cart, M., Ferrié, J., Guerraoui, R., Pucheral, P., & Traverson, B. (1997). *Les systèmes transactionnels: Concepts, normes et produits*. Paris, France: Editions Hermès.

Beuche, D., Papajewski, H., & Schröder-Preikschat, W. (2004). Variability management with feature models. *Science of Computer Programming - Special Issue: Software Variability management*, 333-352.

Bhati, S. N., & Malik, A. M. (2009). An XML-based framework for bidirectional transformation in model-driven architecture (MDA). *SIGSOFT Software Engineering Notes, 34*(3).

Bianchi, A., Caivano, D., & Visaggio, G. (2000). *Method and process for iterative reengineering of data in a legacy system*. WCRE. Los Alamos, NM: IEEE Press.

Bieber, G. (2001). *Introduction to service-oriented programming*. Presented at Sun's Worldwide Java Development Conference.

Bieberstein, N., Bose, S., Fiammante, M., Jones, K., & Shah, R. (2005). *Service-oriented architecture compass: Business value, planning, and enterprise roadmap*. IBM Press.

Bisbal, J., Lawless, D., Wu, B., & Grimson, J. (1999). *Legacy information systems: Issues and directions. IEEE Software*. Los Alamos, NM: IEEE Press.

Bodhium, T., Guardabascio, E., & Tortorella, M. (2002). *Migrating COBOL systems to the Web by using the MCV design pattern*. WCRE. Los Alamos, NM: IEEE Press.

Bohm, C., & Jacopini, G. (1966). *Flow diagrams, turing machines, and languages with only two formation rules. Computer Assisted Collaborative Memory, 9(5), 266*. New York, NY: ACM Press.

Booch, G. (1994). *Object-oriented analysis and design*. Boston, MA: Addison-Wesley.

Booch, G. (2007). *Object-oriented analysis and design with applications* (3rd ed.). Addison-Wesley.

Booth, D., et al. (Eds.). (2004). *W3C working group note 11: Web services architecture*. World Wide Web Consortium (W3C), February. Retrieved from www.w3.org/TR/ws-arch/#stakeholder

Borstlap, G. (2006). *Understanding the technical barriers of retargeting ISAM to RDBMS*. Retrieved June 30, 2010, from http://www.anubex.com/anugenio!technicalbarriers1.asp

Bovenzi, D., Canfora, G., & Fasolina, A. R. (2003). Enabling legacy system accessibility by Web heterogeneous clients. *Working Conference on Reverse Engineering*, (pp. 73-81). Los Alamos, NM: IEE Press.

Braude, E. (2007). Cumulative subgoal fulfillment in software development. *Proceedings of the 11th IASTED International Conference on Software Engineering and Applications*, (pp. 480-485).

Brewer, E. A. (2000). Towards robust distributed systems (abstract). *The 19th Annual ACM Symposium on Principles of Distributed Computing* (p. 7). July 16-19. Portland, OR: ACM.

Bricklin, D. (n.d.). *VisiCalc: Information from its creators, Dan Bricklin and Bob Frankston*. Retrieved from http://www.danbricklin.com/visicalc.htm

Brodie, M. L., & Stonebraker, M. (1995). *Migrating legacy systems: Gateways, interfaces, and the incremental approach*. Upper Saddle River, NJ: Morgan Kaufmann.

Buschmann, F., Henney, K., & Schmidt, D. C. (2007). *Pattern-oriented software architecture: A pattern language for distributed computing*. Boston, MA: Wiley & Sons.

Buschmann, F., Henney, K., & Schmidt, D. C. (2007). Pattern-oriented software architecture: *Vol. 4. A pattern language for distributed computing*. Chichester, UK: John Wiley and Sons.

Business-Software. (2010). *Top 10 social CRM vendors revealed: Profiles of the leading social CRM software vendors.*

Buyya, R., Yeo, C. S., Venugopal, S., Broberg, J., & Brandic, I. (2009). Cloud computing and emerging IT platforms: Vision, hype, and reality for delivering computing as the 5th utility. *Future Generation Computer Systems, 25*(6), 599–616. doi:10.1016/j.future.2008.12.001

Calder, M., & Magill, E. (2000). *Feature interactions in telecommunications and software systems V.* Amsterdam, The Netherlands: IOS Press.

Chandra, T., Fikes, A., & Gruber, R. E. (2006). Bigtable: A distributed storage system for structured data. In *Proceedings of the 7th USENIX Symposium on Operating Systems Design and Implementation (OSDI '06),* (p. 15).

Chang, J. F. (2006). *Business process management systems.* New York: NY Auerbach.

Chang, R.-S., & Chen, P. H. (2007). Complete and fragmented replica selection and retrieval in data grids. *Future Generation Computer Systems, 23,* 536–546. doi:10.1016/j.future.2006.09.006

Chang, R.-S., Wang, C.-M., & Chen, P. M. (2005). *Replica selection on co-allocation data grids, parallel and distributed processing and applications* (pp. 584–593). New York, NY: Springer-Verlag.

Chappell, D. (2007). *Introducing SCA.* Retrieved October 5, 2009, from http://www.davidchappell.com/articles/Introducing_SCA.pdf

Chappell, D. (2009). *Introducing Windows Azure.* Retrieved from http://www.davidchappell.com/writing/white_papers/Introducing_Windows_Azure_v1-Chappell.pdf

Chappell, D. (2004). *Enterprise service bus.* Sebastopol, CA: O'Reilly Media.

Chen, P.-Y., Chiang, J., et al. (2009). Memory-mapped file approach for on-demand data co-allocation on grids. *IEEE International Symposium on Cluster Computing and the Grid,* Los Alamos: IEEE Computer Society Press.

Chen, F., & Shaoyun, L. (2005). *Feature analysis for service-oriented reengineering. APSEC.* Los Alamos, NM: IEEE Press.

Chess Media Group. (2010). *Guide to understanding social CRM.* Retrieved October 15, 2010, from http://www.chessmediagroup.com/resource/guide-to-understanding-social-crm/

Chiba, S. (1998). Macro processing in object-oriented languages. In C. Mingins (Ed.), *The Twenty-Seventh International Conference of the Technology of Object-Oriented Languages and Systems* (pp. 113-126). Washington, DC: IEEE Computer Society.

Chrysanthis, P. K. (1991). *A framework for modeling and reasoning about extended transactions.* Doctoral Dissertation, University of Massachusetts, Department of Computer and Information Science, Amherst, Massachusetts.

Clarke, S., & Baniassad, E. (2005). *Aspect-oriented analysis and design: The theme approach.* Boston, MA: Addison-Wesley Professional.

Clements, P., & Northrop, L. (2001). *Software product lines: Practices and patterns.* Boston, MA: Addison-Wesley Professional.

Cleve, A., Henrard, J., & Hainaut, J.-L. (2006). *Data reverse engineering using system dependency graphs. WCRE.* Los Alamos, NM: IEEE Press.

Coffee, P. (2009, January 18). The future of cloud computing. *Cloud Computing Journal.* Retrieved November 2, 2010, from http://cloudcomputing.sys-con.com/node/771947

Colosimo, M., De Lucia, A., et al. (2007). Assessing legacy system migration technologies through controlled experiments. *International Conference on Software Maintenance,* (pp. 365-374). Los Alamos, NM: IEEE Press.

Craig's List. (n.d.). Retrieved from http://www.craigslist.com

Crnkovic, I., & Larsson, M. (2002). *Building reliable component-based software systems.* Norwood, NJ: Artech House.

Crockford, D. (2009). *Introducing JSON.* Retrieved from http://www.json.org/

Cumberlidge, M. (2007). *Business process management with JBoss jBPM: A practical guide for business analysts.* Olton, TX: Packt Publishing.

Dardeene, A., van Lamsweerde, A., & Fickas, S. (1993). Goal-directed requirements acquisition. *Science of Computer Programming*, *20*(1-2), 3–50. doi:10.1016/0167-6423(93)90021-G

De Lucia, A., Francese, R., et al. (2006). A strategy and an eclipse based environment for the migration of legacy systems to multi-tier web-based architectures. *International Conference on Software Maintenance*, (pp. 438-447). Los Alamos, NM: IEEE Press.

Dean, J., & Ghemawat, S. (2008). MapReduce: Simplified data processing on large clusters. *Communications of the ACM*, *51*(1), 107–113. doi:10.1145/1327452.1327492

Derks, W., Dehnert, J., Grefen, P. W., & Jonker, W. (2001). Customized atomicity specification for transactional workflows. *Third International Symposium on Cooperative Database Systems for Advanced Applications (CODAS)* (pp. 140-147). Beijing, China: IEEE Computer Society.

DOE (U.S. Department of Energy) & EPA. (U.S. Environmental Protection Agency). (2008). *Fact sheet on national data center energy efficiency information program.* Retrieved from http://www1.eere.energy.gov/industry/saveenergynow/pdfs/national_data_center_fact_sheet.pdf.

Drew, P., & Pu, C. (1995). Asynchronous consistency restoration under epsilon serializability. *28th Hawaii International Conference on System Sciences (HICSS)* (pp. 717–726). Kihei, HI: IEEE Computer Society.

Dugan, E. (2010). *ICST and SMEs: Theories, practices, and challenges.* Presented at IRMA Conference, Hershey, PA: IRMA International.

Eckel, B. (2002). *Thinking in Java* (3rd Edition). Boston, MA: Prentice Hall, Pearson. Retrieved from http://www.mindview.net/Books/TIJ/

Ehcache Homepage. (2010). *Performance at any scale.* Retrieved June 5, 2010, from http://ehcache.org/

Eisenbarth, T., Koschke, R., & Simon, D. (2001). *Aiding program comprehension by static and dynamic feature analysis.* International Conference on Software Maintenance. Los Alamos, NM: IEEE Press.

Elmagarmid, A. K. (1992). *Database transaction models for advanced applications.* The Morgan Kaufmann Series in Data Management Systems.

EMC VMWare. (n.d.). Retrieved from http://www.vmware.com

Endrei, M., Ang, J., Arsanjani, A., Chua, S., Comte, P., & Krogdahl, P. (2004). *Service-oriented architecture and web services* (pp. 83–102). IBM Redbooks.

Erl, T. (2005). *Service-oriented architecture: Concepts, technology, and design.* Prentice Hall.

Erl, T. (2008). *SOA design patterns.* Boston, MA: Prentice Hall, Pearson.

Erl, T. (2008). *SOA: Principles of service design.* Boston, MA: Prentice Hall, Pearson.

Ermagan, V., Krüger, I. H., & Menarini, M. (2008). Aspect-oriented modeling approach to define routing in enterprise service bus architectures. *MiSE '08 Proceedings of the 2008 International Workshop on Models in Software Engineering* (pp. 15-20). New York, NY: ACM.

Erramilli, A., Roughan, M., Veitch, D., & Willinger, W. (2002). Self-similar traffic and network dynamics. *Proceedings of the IEEE*, *90*(5). doi:10.1109/JPROC.2002.1015008

Feilkas, M., & Ratiu, D. (2008). Ensuring well-behaved usage of APIs through syntactic constraints. *The 16th IEEE International Conference on Program Comprehension* (pp. 248-253). IEEE Press.

Fergen, H., et al. (1994). Bringing objects into COBOL: Moore – a tool for migration from COBOL to object-oriented COBOL. *Proceedings of Conference of Technology of Object-Oriented Languages and Systems*, (pp. 435-556). Los Alamos, NM: IEEE Press.

Fernández, M., Gómez-Pérez, A., & Juristo, N. (1997). Methontology: From ontological art towards ontological engineering. In *Symposium on Ontological Engineering of AAAI* (pp. 33-40).

Fielding, R. T. (2000). Architectural styles and the design of network-based software architectures. In *Representational state transfer.* Retrieved from http://www.ics.uci.edu/~fielding/pubs/dissertation/rest_arch_style.htm

Flatt, M. (2002). Composable and compilable macros: You want it when? In M. Wand (Ed.), *The Seventh ACM SIGPLAN International Conference on Functional Programming* (pp. 72-83). New York, NY: ACM.

Floyd, S., & Jacobson, V. (1993). Random early detection gateways for congestion avoidance. *IEEE/ACM Transactions on Networking, 1*(4), 397–413. doi:10.1109/90.251892

Foster, I., Zhao, Y., Raicu, I., & Lu, S. (2008). Cloud computing and grid computing 360-degree compared. *Proceedings of the IEEE Grid Computing Environments (GCE08), co-located with IEEE/ACM Supercomputing.*

Foster, I., & Kesselman, C. (1998). *The Grid: Blueprint for a new computing infrastructure*. Morgan Kaufmann.

Fowler, M. (2005). *Inversion of control containers and the dependency injection pattern*. Retrieved from http://www.martinfowler.com/articles/injection.html

Fowler, M. (2005). *Inversion of control*. Retrieved from http://martinfowler.com/bliki/InversionOfControl.html

Fowler, M. (n.d.). *GUI architectures*. Retrieved from http://www.martinfowler.com/eaaDev/uiArchs.html

Gall, H. W., Eixelsberger, M., Kalan, M., Ogris, H., & Beckman, B. (1988). *Recovery of architectural structure: A case study. Development and Evolution of Software Architectures for Product Families (ARES II), LNCS 1429* (pp. 89–96). New York: Springer-Verlag.

Gallina, B. (2010). *PRISMA: A software product line-oriented process for the requirements engineering of flexible transaction models*. Laboratory for Advanced Software Systems, University of Luxembourg, Luxembourg: Unpublished doctoral dissertation.

Gallina, B., & Guelfi, N. (2007). A template for requirement elicitation of dependable product lines. *13th International Working Conference on Requirements Engineering: Foundation for Software Quality* (pp. 63-77). Trondheim, Norway.

Gallina, B., & Guelfi, N. (2008). A product line perspective for quality reuse of development framework for distributed transactional applications. *2nd IEEE International Workshop on Quality Oriented Oriented Reuse of Software (QUORS), co-located with COMPSAC* (pp. 739-744). Turku, Finland. Los Alamitos, CA: IEEE Computer Society.

Gallina, B., & Guelfi, N. (2008). SPLACID: An SPL-oriented, ACTA-based, language for reusing (Varying) ACID properties. In *32nd Annual IEEE/NASA Goddard Software Engineering Workshop (SEW-32)* (ss. 115–124). Porto Sani Resort, Greece: IEEE Computer Society.

Gallina, B., Guelfi, N., & Kelsen, P. (2009). Towards an alloy formal model for flexible advanced transactional model development. In *33rd International IEEE Software Engineering Workshop (SEW-33)*. Skövde, Sweden: IEEE Computer Society.

Gamma, E., Helm, R., Johnson, R., & Vlissides, J. (1995). *Design patterns - Elements of reusable object-oriented software*. Boston, MA: Addison-Wesley Professional.

Garbus, J. R. (2 February 2010). In-memory database option for sybase adaptive server enterprise. *Database Journal*].

Garlan, D., Allen, R., & John, O. (1995). Architectural mismatch: Why reuse is so hard. *IEEE Software, 12*(6), 17–26. doi:10.1109/52.469757

Gartner. (2010). *Magic quadrant for social CRM*. Gartner, Inc. and/or its Affiliates. Retrieved October 15, 2010, from http://www.lithium.com/pdfs/whitepapers/Gartner-MQ-Social-CRM-t4OR7RhY.pdf

Geer, D. (2005). Will binary XML speed network traffic? *Journal of Computer, 38*(4). IEEE Computer Society Press.

Gens, F. (2008). *IT cloud services forecast – 2008, 2012: A key driver of new growth*. Retrieved from http://blogs.idc.com/ie/?p=224

George, C. E., & Scerri, J. (2007). Web 2.0 and user-generated content: Legal challenges in the new frontier. *Journal of Information, Law and Technology, 2*. Retrieved October 15, 2010, from http://www2.warwick.ac.uk/fac/soc/law/elj/jilt/2007_2/george_scerri

Ghemawat, S., Gobioff, H., & Leung, S.-T. (2003). The Google file system. In *Proceedings of the Nineteenth ACM Symposium on Operating Systems Principles (SOSP '03)* (pp. 29–43).

Gilbert, S., & Lynch, N. (2002, June). Brewer's conjecture and the feasibility of consistent, available, partition-tolerant web services. *ACM SIGACT News, 33*(2), 51–59. doi:10.1145/564585.564601

Glatard, T., Emsellem, D., & Montagnat, J. (2006). *Generic web service wrapper for efficient embedding of legacy codes in service-based workflows. Technical Report, I3SC, CNRS*. France: University of Nice.

Gnu.org. (n.d.). *Free software definition*. Retrieved from http://www.gnu.org/philosophy/free-sw.html

Goguen, J. A., & Linde, C. (1993). Techniques for requirements elicitation. *International Symposium on Requirements Engineering* (pp. 152-164), San Diego, CA.

Googe PageRank. (n.d.). Retrieved from http://www.google.com/about/corporate/company/tech.html

Google AppEngine. (n.d.). Retrieved from http://code.google.com/appengine/

Google BigTable. (n.d.). Retrieved from http://labs.google.com/papers/bigtable.html

Google Docs. (n.d.). Retrieved from http://docs.google.com

Google, Large Scale Graph Computing at Google. (n.d.). Retrieved from http://googleresearch.blogspot.com/2009/06/large-scale-graph-computing-at-google.html

Google, MapReduce. (n.d.). Retrieved from http://labs.google.com/papers/mapreduce.html

Governance, I. T., & Governance, S. O. A. (n.d.). *OASIS*. Retrieved from http://wiki.oasis-open.org/soa-rm/TheArchitecture/Governance

Grameen Bank. (n.d.). Retrieved from http://www.grameen-info.org

Gray, J. (1980). A transaction model. In J. W. de Bakker, & J. van Leeuwen (Eds.), *Proceedings of the 7th Colloquium on Automata, Languages and Programming*, (pp. 282-298). Noordweijkerhout, The Netherlands: Springer Verlag.

Gray, J., & Reuter, A. (1993). *Transactions processing: Concepts and techniques*. Morgan Kaufmann Publishers.

Greenberg, P. (2009). Time to put a stake in the ground on social CRM. *PGreenblog*. Retrieved October 15, 2010, from http://the56group.typepad.com/pgreenblog/2009/07/time-to-put-a-stake-in-the-ground-on-social-crm.html

Greenberg, P. (2010a). The impact of CRM 2.0 on customer insight. *Journal of Business and Industrial Marketing*, *25*(6), 410–419. doi:10.1108/08858621011066008

Greenberg, P. (2010b). *A quick look at the social CRM vendor landscape*. Focus Brief.

Greene, M., Riley, E., Card, D., Mitskaviets, I., Bowen, E., & Wise, J. (2009). *Justifying social marketing spending*. Forrester Research.

Gregor, D., & Järvi, J. (2007). Variadic templates for C++. In Y. Cho (Ed.), *The 2007 ACM Symposium on Applied Computing* (pp. 1101-1108). New York, NY: ACM.

Griss, M. L. (1999). Architecting for large-scale systematic component reuse. *ICSE '99 Proceedings of the 21st International Conference on Software Engineering* (pp. 615 - 616). New York, NY: ACM.

Grossman, R. L. (2009). The case for cloud computing. *IT Professional*, *11*(2), 23–27. doi:10.1109/MITP.2009.40

Guo, H., Guo, C., Chen, F., & Yang, H. (2005). *Wrapping client-server application to Web services for internet computing*. PDCAT.

Gurp, J. (2002). Design erosion: Problems and causes. *Journal of Systems and Software*, *61*(2), 105–119. doi:10.1016/S0164-1212(01)00152-2

Hackos, J. T., & Redish, J. C. (1998). *User and task analysis for interface design*. John Wiley & Sons, Inc.

Haff, G. (2009). Just don't call them private clouds. *News.cnet.com*. Retrieved from http://news.cnet.com/8301-13556_3-10150841-61.html

Hai, H., & Sakoda, H. (2007). SaaS and integration best practices. *FUJITSU Science Technology Journal*, *45*(3), 257–264.

Hainaut, J.-L., Chandelon, M., Tonneau, C., & Joris, M. (1993b). Transformation-based database reverse engineering. *Proceedings of the 12th International Conference on Entity-Relationship Approach*, (pp. 1-12). London, UK: Springer-Verlag.

Hainaut, J.-L., Chandelon, M., Tonneau, C., & Joris, M. (1993a). *Contribution to a theory of database reverse engineering. WCRE*. Los Alamos, NM: IEEE Press.

Härder, T., & Reuter, A. (1983). Principles of transaction-oriented database recovery. *ACM Computing Surveys, 15*(4), 287–315. doi:10.1145/289.291

Harju, J., & Kivimaki, P. (2000). Co-operation and comparison of DiffServ and IntServ: Performance measurements. *Proceedings of the 25th Annual IEEE Conference on Local Computer Networks,* (p. 177). November 08-10, 2000.

Harrison, N. B., & Avgeriou, P. (2007). *Leveraging architecture patterns to satisfy quality attributes.* University of Groningen. Research Institute for Mathematics and Computing Science.

Hassan, Q. F. (2009). Aspects of SOA: An entry point for starters. *Annals Computer Science Series, 7*(2). Retrieved from http://anale-informatica.tibiscus.ro/download/lucrari/7-2-12-Hassan.pdf

He, H. (2004). Implementing REST Web services: Best practices and guidelines. Retrieved from http://www.xml.com/pub/a/2004/08/11/rest.html

Heineman, G. T., & Councill, W. T. (Eds.). (2001). *Component based software engineering: Putting the pieces together.* Addison Wesley.

Heiser, J., & Nicolett, M. (2008). *Assessing the security risks of cloud computing.* Gartner. Retrieved from http://www.gartner.com/DisplayDocument?id=685308

Heng, C. (1999). Free sockets and winsock libraries. Retrieved from http://www.thefreecountry.com/sourcecode/sockets.shtml

Henrard, J., Hick, J. M., Thiran, P., & Hainaut, J. L. (2002). Strategies for data reengineering. *Working Conference on Reverse Engineering,* (pp. 211-222). Los Alamos, NM: IEEE Press.

Hernan, S., Lambert, S., Ostwald, T., & Shostack, A. (2000). *Uncover security design flaws using the STRIDE approach.* MSDN Magazine.

Hohpe, G. (2009). *Into the clouds on new acid.* Retrieved from http://www.eaipatterns.com/ramblings/68_acid.html

Hohpe, G., & Woolf, B. (2003). *Enterprise integration patterns: Designing, building, and deploying messaging solutions.* Boston, MA: Addison-Wesley Professional.

Jackson, D. (2006). *Software abstractions: Logic, language, and analysis.* MIT Press. Jackson, M. (1998). *Software requirements & specifications.* Addison-Wesley.

Janke, J.-H., & Wadsack, J. P. (1999). *Varlet: Human-centered tool for database reengineering. WCRE.* Los Alamos, NM: IEEE Press.

Jarazabek, S., & Hitz, M. (1998). *Business-oriented component-based software development and evolution.* DEXXA Workshop. Los Alamos, NM: IEEE Press.

Jegadeesan, H., & Balasubramaniam, S. (2009). A method to support variability of enterprise services on the cloud. *CLOUD '09 Proceedings of the 2009 IEEE International Conference on Cloud Computing* (pp. 117-124). Washington, DC: IEEE Computer Society.

Jeusfeld, M. A., & Johnen, U. A. (1994). An executable meta model for reengineering of database schemas. *Proceedings of Conference on the Entity-Relationship Approach.* London, UK: Springer-Verlag.

Jiang, Y., & Stroulia, E. (2004). *Towards reengineering web sites to web-services providers. CSMR.* Los Alamos, NM: IEEE Press.

Joris, M. (1992). Phenix: Methods and tools for database reverse engineering. *Proceedings 5th International Conference on Software Engineering and Applications.* Los Alamos, NM: IEEE Press.

Josuttis, N. M. (2007). *SOA in practice: The art of distributed system design.* Sebastopol, CA: O'Reilly Media.

JSON-RPC. (n.d.). Retrieved from http://json-rpc.org/

Kang, K. C., Kim, S., Lee, J., Kim, K., Shin, E., & Huh, M. (1998). FORM: A feature-oriented reuse method with domain-specific reference architectures. *Annals of Software Engineering, 5.*

Karlapalem, K., Vidyasankar, K., & Krishna, P. R. (2010). Advanced transaction models for e-services. In *6th World Congress on Services, Tutorials, Services* (pp. xxxii-xxxiii). IEEE Computer Society.

Kastner, C., et al. (2009). FeatureIDE: A tool framework for feature-oriented software development. In S. Fickas (Ed.), *The 2009 IEEE International Conference on Software Engineering* (pp. 611-614). Washington, DC: IEEE Computer Society.

Kern, T., Lacity, M. C., & Willcocks, L. P. (2002). *Netsourcing: renting business applications and services over a network*. New York, NY: Prentice-Hall.

Kicinger, R., Arciszewski, T., & De Jong, K. (2005). Parameterized versus generative representations in structural design: An empirical comparison. In H.G. Beyer (Ed.), *The 2005 International Conference on Genetic and Evolutionary Computation* (pp. 2007-2014). New York, NY: ACM.

Kiczales, G., Lamping, J., Mendhekar, A., Maeda, C., Videira Lopes, C., Loingtier, J.-M., et al. (1997). Aspect-oriented programming. *European Conference on Object-Oriented Programming* (pp. 220-242). Heidelberg, Germany: Springer.

Kim, H., & Hou, J. C. (2004). *Enabling theoretical model based techniques for simulating large scale networks*. Champaign, IL: University of Illinois at Urbana-Champaign.

Kim, W. (2009). Cloud computing: Today and tomorrow. *Journal of Object Technology*, 8(1), 65–72. doi:10.5381/jot.2009.8.1.c4

Kiringa, I. (2001). Simulation of advanced transaction models using GOLOG. In *Revised Papers from the 8th International Workshop on Database Programming Languages LNCS 2397*, (pp. 318-341). Frascati, Italy. Springer-Verlag.

Klaus, P., Böckle, G., & van der Linden, F. J. (2005). *Software product line engineering: Foundations, principles and techniques* (1st ed.). Springer-Verlag.

Klein, M. (2010). *SaaS value added and risk management*. Retrieved September 15, 2010, from http://resource.onlinetech.com/

Kobielus, J. (2005). The ROI of SOA: The more you reuse, the more you save. *Network World*. Retrieved from www.networkworld.com/techinsider/2005/101005-roi-of-soa.html

Koehler, P., Anandasivam, A., & Dan, M. (2010). Cloud services from a consumer perspective. *AMCIS 2010 Proceedings*, (p. 329).

Kollhof, J. (2009). *Welcome to JSON-RPC*. Retrieved from http://json-rpc.org/

Krafzig, D., Banke, K., & Slama, D. (2004). *Enterprise SOA service-oriented architecture best practices*. Prentice Hall. Lewis, G., Morris E. J., Smith, D. B., & Wrage L. (2005). SMART: Service-oriented migration and reuse technique. *Proceedings of the 13th IEEE International Workshop on Software Technology and Engineering Practice*.

Krafzig, D. (2004). *Enterprise SOA: Service-oriented architecture best practices*. Boston, MA: Prentice Hall, Pearson.

Krigsman, M. (2010). Reaching for social CRM success (or failure), IT project failures. *ZDNet*. Retrieved November 25, 2010, from http://www.zdnet.com/blog/projectfailures/reaching-for-social-crm-success-or-failure/11415

Kuhlemann, M., Rosenmuller, M., Apel, S., & Leich, T. (2007). On the duality of aspect-oriented and feature-oriented design patterns. In Y. Coady, et al. (Eds.), *The Sixth Workshop on Aspects, Components, and Patterns for Infrastructure Software*. New York, NY: ACM.

Kuloor, C., & Eberlein, A. (2002). *Requirements engineering for software product lines*. 15th International Conference on Software and Systems Engineering and their Applications (ICSSEA). Paris, France.

Kumar, A., Neogi, A., & Pragallapati, S. (2007). *Raising programming abstraction from objects to services. ICWS*. Los Alamos, NM: IEEE Press.

Kvale, B. (2008). *InterViews* (2nd ed.). Thousand Oaks, CA: SAGE.

La, H. J., & Kim, S. D. (2009). A systematic process for developing high quality SaaS cloud services. *CloudCom '09 Proceedings of the 1st International Conference on Cloud Computing* (pp. 278 - 289). Heidelberg, Germany: Springer-Verlag.

Laddad, R. (2003). *AspectJ in action:Practical aspect-oriented programming*. Manning.

Lashar, J. D. (2009a). To SaaS or not to SaaS? *Destination CRM.Com*. Retrieved April 30, 2011, from http://www.destinationcrm.com/Articles/Columns-Departments/The-Tipping-Point/To-SaaS-or-Not-to-SaaS-53686.aspx

Lashar, J. D. (2009b). Servicing software-as-a-service. *Destination CRM.Com*. Retrieved April 30, 2011, from http://www.destinationcrm.com/Articles/Columns-Departments/The-Tipping-Point/Servicing-Software-as-a-Service-55510.aspx

Law, K., Ip, H., & Wei, F. (1998). *Web-enabling legacy applications. ICPADS*. Los Alamos, NM: IEEE Press.

Lecue, F., Salibi, S., et al. (2008). Semantic and syntactic data flow in web service composition. *Proceedings of IEEE Conference on Web Services*. Los Alamos, NM: IEEE Press.

Lee, O., & Tecuci, G. (1997). MTLS: A tool for extending and refining knowledge bases. In *9th International Conference on Tools with Artificial Intelligence (ICTAI '97)* (pp. 524–531). Newport Beach, CA.

Lee, T., Chuang, C. H., & Hou, J. S. (2009). Schema-based model composition and evolution. In H. D. Chen (Ed.), *The Twentieth Workshop on Object-Oriented Technology and Applications*. Taichung, Taiwan: Computer Society of the Republic of China.

Leich, T., Apel, S., Marnitz, L., & Saake, G. (2005). Tool support for feature-oriented software development featureIDE: An Eclipse-based approach. In M. N. Storey, M. G. Burke, L. T. Cheng, & A. ven der Hoek (Eds.), *The 2005 Object-Oriented Programming, Systems, Languages, and Applications Workshop on Eclipse Technology Exchange* (pp. 55-59). New York, NY: ACM.

Leite, J. C. S. P., & Franco, A. P. M. v. (1993). A strategy for conceptual model acquisition. *Proceedings of the First International Symposium on Requirements Engineering*, (pp. 243-246). IEEE Computer Society Press.

Leite, J. C. S. P., Yu, Y., Liu, L., Yu, E. S. K., & Mylopoulos, J. (2005). Quality-based software reuse. *Conference of Advanced Information Systems Engineering (CAiSE 2005), Lecture Notes in Computer Science*, Vol. 3520 (January 2005), (pp. 535-550).

Levy, E., Korth, H. F., & Silberschatz, A. (1991). A theory of relaxed atomicity (extended abstract). *The Tenth Annual ACM Symposium on Principles of Distributed Computing (PODC)* (pp. 95-110). Montreal, Canada. New York, NY: ACM.

Liang, Q. A., & Lam, H. (2008). Web service matching by ontology instance categorization. In *Proceedings of the IEEE International Conference on Services Computing (SCC '08)*, 7-11 July 2008, Vol. 1, (pp. 202-209). Honolulu, HI.

Li, S., & Chen, F. (2005). *Using feature-oriented analysis to recover legacy software design for software evolution. SEKE*. Los Alamos, NM: IEEE Press.

Liskov, B. (1987). Data abstraction and hierarchy. *OOPSLA 87: Conference on Object Oriented Programming Systems Languages and Applications*, Keynote Address.

Liu, H., & Orban, D. (2008). GridBatch: Cloud computing for large-scale data-intensive batch applications. *International Symposium on Cluster, Cloud, and Grid Computing*, (pp. 295-305). Los Alamos, NM: IEEE Press.

Liu, L., Liu, Q., Chi, C., Jin, Z., & Yu, E. (2008). Towards a service requirements modelling ontology based on agent knowledge and intentions. *International Journal of Agent-Oriented Software Engineering, 2*(3), 324–349. doi:10.1504/IJAOSE.2008.019422

Logan, J., & Dickens, P. M. (2007). *Using object based files for high performance parallel I/O. Intelligent Data Acquisition and Advanced Computing Systems* (pp. 149–154). Los Alamos, NM: IEEE Press.

Majkut, M. (2003). Generation of implementations for the model driven architecture with syntactic unit trees. In M. G. Burke (Ed.), *The Second Object-Oriented Programming, Systems, Languages, and Applications Workshop on Generative Techniques in the Context of Model Driven Architecture*. New York, NY: ACM.

Majumadar, B., Dias, T., Mysore, U., & Poddar, v. (2007, June). Implementing service oriented architecture. *SeTLabs Briefings*, 3 -13.

Manjunath, R., & Gurumurthy, K. S. (2004). *Maintaining long-range dependency of traffic in a network*. CODEC'04.

Manjunath, R., & Gurumurthy, K. S. (2002). Information geometry of differentially fed artificial neural networks. *TENCON, 3*, 1521–1525.

Manjunath, R., & Jain, V. (2009). Traffic controller for handling service quality in multimedia network. In Bhattarakosol, P. (Ed.), *Intelligent quality of service technologies and network management: Models for enhancing communication*. Hershey, PA: Idea Group Publishers.

Marks, E. A., & Lozano, B. (2010). *Executive's guide to cloud computing*. John Wiley & Sons.

Marsan, A. M. (2005). Using partial differential equations to model TCP mice and elephants in large IP networks. *IEEE/ACM Transactions on Networking, 13*(6), 1289–1301. doi:10.1109/TNET.2005.860102

Martin, D. (Ed.). (2004). *OWL-S: Semantic markup for web services*. Retrieved from http://www.w3.org/Submission/OWL-S/

McAfee, P. A. (2006). Enterprise 2.0: The dawn of emergent collaboration. *MIT Sloan Management Review, 47*(3).

McAfee, P. A. (2009). *Enterprise 2.0: New Collaborative Tools for Your Organization's Toughest Challenges*. U.S.A.: Harvard University Press.

McCarthy, J. (1983). *Reminiscences on the history of time sharing*. Stanford University. Retrieved from http://www-formal.stanford.edu/jmc/history/timesharing/timesharing.html

McRobb, S., Pu, J., Yang, H., & Millham, R. (2005). Visualising COBOL legacy systems with UML: An Experimental report. In Yang, H. (Ed.), *Advances in UML-based software engineering*. Hershey, PA: Idea Group. doi:10.4018/978-1-59140-621-1.ch010

Medvidovic, N., Oreizy, P., & Taylor, R. N. (1997). Reuse of off-the-shelf components in C2-style architectures. *SSR '97 Proceedings of the 1997 Symposium on Software Reusability* (pp. 190 - 198). New York, NY: ACM.

Mehoudj, K., & Ou-Halima, M. (1995). Migrating data-oriented applications to a relational database management system. *Proceedings of the Third International Workshop on Advances in Databases and Object-Oriented Databases*, (pp. 102-108). Los Alamos, NM: IEEE Press.

Mei, L., Chan, W. K., & Tse, T. H. (2008). *A tale of clouds: Paradigm comparisons and some thoughts on research issues. APSCC*. Los Alamos, NM: IEEE Press.

Mell, P., & Grance, T. (2009). *The NIST definition of cloud computing*. National Institute of Standards and Technology.

Memcached.org. (n.d.). Retrieved from http://memcached.org

Menasce, D. A., Sousa, J. P., Malek, S., & Gomaa, H. (2010). Qos architectural patterns for self-architecting software systems. *ICAC '10 Proceeding of the 7th International Conference on Autonomic Computing* (pp. 195-204). New York, NY: ACM.

Merlo, E., & Gagn, P. Y. (1995). Reengineering user interfaces. *IEEE Software, 12*, 64–73. doi:10.1109/52.363164

Mezini, M., & Ostermann, K. (2004). Variability management with feature-oriented programming and aspects. In R.N. Taylor (Ed.) *The Twelfth ACM SIGSOFT Internationl Symposium on Foundations of Software Engineering* (pp. 127-136). New York, NY: ACM.

Microsoft AppFabric Access Control Service. (n.d.). Retrieved from http://msdn.microsoft.com/en-us/library/ee732536.aspx

Microsoft Codeplex. (n.d.). Retrieved from http://www.codeplex.com

Microsoft Dryad. (n.d.). Retrieved from http://research.microsoft.com/jump/50745

Microsoft Model-View-Controller. (n.d.). Retrieved from http://www.asp.net/mvc

Microsoft SkyDrive. (n.d.). Retrieved from http://explore.live.com/windows-live-skydrive

Microsoft Skype. (n.d.). Retrieved from http://www.skype.com

Microsoft SQLAzure. (n.d.). Retrieved from http://www.microsoft.com/windowsazure/sqlazure/

Microsoft Visual Studio. (n.d.). Retrieved from http://www.microsoft.com/VisualStudio

Microsoft Windows Azure. (n.d.). Retrieved from http://www.microsoft.com/windowsazure/

Microsoft Windows Communications Framework (WCF). (n.d.). Retrieved from http://msdn.microsoft.com/en-us/netframework/aa663324

Microsoft Windows, Windows 8. (n.d.). Retrieved from http://msdn.microsoft.com/en-us/library/windows/apps/br211386.aspx

Microsoft, Entity Framework. (n.d.). Retrieved from http://msdn.microsoft.com/en-us/library/aa697427(v=vs.80).aspx

Microsoft, Model-View-ViewModel. (n.d.). Retrieved from http://msdn.microsoft.com/en-us/magazine/dd419663.aspx

Microsoft, Reactive Extensions. (n.d.). Retrieved from http://msdn.microsoft.com/en-us/data/gg577609

Microsoft, Velocity. (n.d.). Retrieved from http://msdn.microsoft.com/en-us/magazine/dd861287.aspx

Mietzner, R. (2008). *Using variability descriptors to describe customizable SaaS application templates*. Fakultät Informatik: Universität Stuttgart.

Mikkilineni, R., & Sarathy, V. (2009). *Cloud computing and lessons from the past. WETICE*. Los Alamos, NM: IEEE Press.

Miller, J., & Mukerji, J. (Eds.). (2003). *MDA guide version 1.0.1*. OMG. Retrieved May 5, 2011, from http://www.omg.org/cgi-bin/doc?omg/03-06-01.pdf.

Miller, M. (2009). *Cloud computing: Web-based applications that change the way you work and collaborate online*. Indianapolis, IN: Que Publishing.

Millham, R. (2005). *Evolution of batch-oriented COBOL systems into object-oriented systems through unified modelling language*. Unpublished doctoral dissertation, De Montfort University, Leicester, UK.

Millham, R. (2002). *An investigation: Reengineering sequential procedure-driven software into object-oriented event-driven software through UML diagrams. COMPSAC*. Los Alamos, NM: IEEE Press.

Millham, R. (2009a). *Domain analysis in the reengineering process of a COBOL system. COMPSAC*. Los Alamos, NM: IEEE Press.

Millham, R. (2010). *Migration of a legacy procedural system to service-oriented computing using feature analysis. ECDS-CISIS*. Los Alamos, NM: IEEE Press.

Millham, R., & Yang, H. (2009b). *Industrial report: Data reengineering of COBOL sequential legacy systems. COMPSAC*. Los Alamos, NM: IEEE Press.

Millham, R., Yang, H., & Ward, M. (2003). *Determining granularity of independent tasks for reengineering a legacy system into an OO system. COMPSAC*. Los Alamos, NM: IEEE Press.

Mirzaei, N. (200, January 9). *Cloud computing independent study report.*

MongoDB.org. (n.d.). Retrieved from http://www.mongodb.org

Moore, M., & Moshkina, L. (2000). Migrating legacy user interfaces to the internet: Shifting dialogue initiative. *Working Conference on Reverse Engineering*, (pp. 52-58). Los Alamos, NM: IEEE Computer Press.

Moss, J. E. (1981). *Nested transactions: An approach to reliable distributed computing*. PhD dissertation, Massachusetts Institute of Technology, USA.

Motahari-Nezhad, H. R., Stephenson, B., Singhal, S. (2009). *Outsourcing business to cloud computing services: Opportunities and challenges*. Technical report, HP laboratories.

Murugesan, S. (2007). Understanding Web 2.0. *IT Professional*, *9*(4), 34–41. doi:10.1109/MITP.2007.78

Newcomb, P., & Kotik, G. (1995). Reengineering procedural into object-oriented systems. *Second Working Conference on Reverse Engineering*, (pp. 237-249). Los Alamos, NM: IEEE Press.

Newcomb, P. (1999). *Reengineering procedural into object-oriented systems. WCRE*. Los Alamos, NM: IEEE Press.

Newton, K. (2007). *The definitive guide to the Microsoft enterprise library*. Berkeley, CA: Apress. doi:10.1007/978-1-4302-0315-5

Nock, C. (2003). *Data access patterns: Database interactions in object-oriented applications*. Boston, MA: Addison-Wesley Professional.

No-SQL Movement. (n.d.). Retrieved from http://nosql-database.org/

OMG. (2002). *Notification service specification*. Object Management Group, Aug. 2002.

OMG. (2008). *Software & systems process engineering meta-model (SPEM), v 2.0. Full specification formal/08-04-01*. Object Management Group.

Oracle Social, C. R. M. (2008). *It's all about the salesperson: Taking advantage of Web 2.0.* An Oracle White Paper, Oracle Corporation.

Papazoglou, M. P. (2003). Service-oriented computing: Concepts, characteristics and directions. *Proceeding of the Fourth International Conference on Web Information Systems Engineering.*

Papazoglou, M., & Traverso, P. (2007). Service-oriented computing: State of the art and research challenges. *Computer, 40*(11). Los Alamos, NM: IEEE Press.

Papazoglou, M. P., & Heuvel, W. J. d. (2007). Service oriented architectures: Approaches, technologies and research issues. *The VLDB Journal, 16*, 389–415. doi:10.1007/s00778-007-0044-3

Parameswaran, M., & Whinston, A. B. (2007a). Social computing: An overview. *Communications of the Association for Information Systems, 19*, 762–780.

Parameswaran, M., & Whinston, A. B. (2007b). Research issues in social computing. *Journal of the Association for Information Systems, 8*(6), 336–350.

Pawlak, R., Seinturier, L., Duchien, L., Florin, G., Legond-Aubry, F., & Martelli, L. (2004). JAC: An aspect-based distributed dynamic framework. *Software, Practice & Experience, 34*(12), 1119–1148. doi:10.1002/spe.605

Pawlak, R., Seinturier, L., & Retaillé, J.-P. (2005). *Foundations of AOP for J2EE development*. Berkeley, CA: Apress.

PayPal.com. (n.d.). Retrieved from http://www.paypal.com

Peng, B., Cui, B., & Li, X. (2009). Implementation issues of a cloud computing platform. *A Quarterly Bulletin of the Computer Society of the IEEE Technical Committee on Data Engineering, 32*(1), 59–66.

Perovich, P., Bastarrica, M. C., & Rojas, C. (2009). Model-driven approach to software architecture design. In P. Lago, P. Avgeriou, & P. Kruchten (Eds.), *The 2009 ICSE Workshop on Sharing and Reusing Architectural Knowledge* (pp. 1-8). Washington, DC: IEEE Computer Society.

Petals, E. S. B. Homepage. (2010). *Petals ESB, the Open Source ESB for large SOA infrastructures*. Retrieved March 5, 2010, from http://petals.ow2.org/

Peterson, G., & Lipson, H. (2006). *Security concepts, challenges, and design considerations for Web services integration security.*

Pizette, L., Semy, S., Raines, G., & Foote, S. (2009). A perspective on emerging industry SOA best practices. *The Journal of Defense Software Engineering, 22.*

Pomerlani, W. J., & Blaha, M. R. (1993). *An approach for reverse engineering of relational databases. WCRE.* Los Alamos, NM: IEEE Press.

Pritchett, D. (2008). BASE: An acid alternative. *ACM Queue; Tomorrow's Computing Today, 6*(3), 48–55. doi:10.1145/1394127.1394128

Prömel, H. J., Steger, A., & Taraz, A. (2001). *Counting partial orders with a fixed number of comparable pairs. Combinatorics, Probability and Computing, 10.* Cambridge University Press.

Puimedon, A. S. (2009). *Transactions for grid computing, advanced e-business transactions for B2B-Collaboration Seminar, University of Helsinki.* Retrieved from www.cs.helsinki.fi/group/.../Transactions_grid_computing.pdf

Qiao, W., Liu, L., & Xiang, J. (2008). ASREF: An adaptive service requirements elicitation framework based on goal-oriented modelling. In *Proceedings of the 11th IberoAmerican Workshop on Requirements Engineering and Software Environments* (IDEAS'08), Recife, Brazil. Feb 13-15, 2008.

Qun, Y., Xian-Chun, Y., & Man-Wu, X. (2005). A framework for dynamic software architecture-based self-healing. *ACM SIGSOFT Software Engineering Notes, 30*(4), 1–4. doi:10.1145/1082983.1083007

Rackspace.com. (n.d.). Retrieved from http://www.rackspace.com

Raines, G. (2009). Leveraging federal IT investment with service-oriented architecture. *The Journal of Defense Software Engineering: CrossTalk, March.*

Ramachandra, M., & Rao, S. V. (2009). *Data network performance modeling and control through prediction feedback.* ISSRE 2009.

Ramamritham, K., & Chrysanthis, P. K. (1996). A taxonomy of correctness criteria in database applications. *The International Journal on Very Large Data Bases, 5*(1), 85–97. doi:10.1007/s007780050017

Redhat Hibernate. (n.d.). Retrieved from http://www.hibernate.org

Riad, A. M., Hassan, A. E., & Hassan, Q. F. (2009). Investigating performance of XML Web services in real-time business systems. *Journal of Computer Science and System Biology, 2*(5). Retrieved from http://www.omicsonline.com/ArchiveJCSB/2009/October/01/JCSB2.266.pdf

Rob, P., & Coronel, C. (2002). *Database systems: Design, implementation, and management* (pp. 1–800). Boston, MA: Thomas Learning.

Rochwerger, B., Breitgand, D., Levy, E., Galis, A., Nagin, K., & Llorente, I. (2009). The reservoir model and architecture for open federated cloud computing. *IBM Journal of Research and Development, 53.*

Rodriguez, A. (2008). *RESTful Web services: The basics.* Retrieved from http://www.ibm.com/developerworks/webservices/library/ws-restful/

Rosen, M. (2008). *Applied SOA: Service-oriented architecture and design strategies.* Indianapolis, IN: Wiley.

Rosen, M., Lublinsky, B., Smith, K. T., & Balcer, M. J. (2008). *Applied SOA: Service-oriented architecture and design strategies.* Indianapolis, IN: Wiley.

Roshen, W. (2009). *SOA-based enterprise integration: A step-by-step guide to services-based application integration.* McGraw-Hill.

Ruby on Rails. (n.d.). Retrieved from http://www.rubyonrails.org/

Sabanis, N., & Stevenson, N. (1992). Tools and techniques for data remodeling COBOL applications. *Proceedings 5th International Conference on Software Engineering and Applications.* Los Alamos, NM: IEEE Press.

Sadeg, B., & Saad-Bouzefrane, S. (2000). Relaxing correctness criteria in real-time DBMSs. In S. Y. Shin (Ed.), *ISCA 15th International Conference Computers and Their Applications* (pp. 64–67). New Orleans, LA: ISCA.

Salesforce.com. (n.d.). Retrieved from http://www.salesforce.com

Saradhi, V., & Akula, N. (2002, August). Understanding requirements of large data-intensive applications. *Information Management Direct.*

Sarmenta, L. F. G. (2001). *Volunteer computing.* Ph.D. thesis, Massachusetts Institute of Technology. Retrieved from http://www.cag.lcs.mit.edu/bayanihan/

Schluting, C. (2010). *Sorting out the many faces of cloud computing.* Retrieved September 9, 2010, from http://www.internet.com/IT/NetworkingAndCommunications/VirtualInfrastructure/Article/42644

Schmelzer, R. (2005). Right-sizing services. *ZapThink.* Retrieved from www.zapthink.com/report.html?id=ZAPFLASH-20051115

Schmidt, M., Hutchison, B., Lambros, P., & Phippen, R. (2005). The enterprise service bus: Making service-oriented architecture real. *IBM Systems Journal, 44*(4), 781–797. doi:10.1147/sj.444.0781

Searc, C. R. M. Com. (n.d.). *SaaS and CRM on demand vendor guide.* Retrieved April 30, 2011, from http://searchcrm.techtarget.com/

Seinturier, L., Merle, P., Fournier, D., Dolet, N., Schiavoni, V., & Stefani, J.-B. (2009). Reconfigurable SCA applications with the FraSCAti platform. *SCC '09 Proceedings of the 2009 IEEE International Conference on Services Computing* (pp. 268-275). Washington, DC: IEEE Computer Society.

Seinturier, L., Pessemier, N., Duchien, L., & Coupaye, T. (2006). *A component model engineered with components and aspects. Component-Based Software Engineering* (pp. 139–153). Stockholm, Sweden: Springer.

Seltsikas, P., & Currie, W. L. (2002). Evaluating the application service provider (ASP) business model: The challenge of integration. *Proceedings of the 35th Hawaii International Conference on System Sciences.*

Shaw, M. (1995). Architectural issues in software reuse: it's not just the functionality, it's the packaging. *SSR '95 Proceedings of the 1995 Symposium on Software Reusability* (pp. 3-6). New York, NY: ACM.

Singh, M. P., & Huhns, M. N. (2005). *Service-oriented computing: Semantics, processes, agents.* London, UK: Wiley.

Singh, V. (2010). Service-oriented architecture (SOA) as a technical framework for web-based support systems (WSS). In Yao, J. T. (Ed.), *Web-based support systems.* London, UK: Springer. doi:10.1007/978-1-84882-628-1_19

Smith, D., O'Brien, L., & Kontogiannis, K. (2006). *Program comprehension and migration strategies for web service and service-oriented architectures. Working Session: ICPC.* Los Alamos, NM: IEEE Press.

Smith, M. A., & Kumar, R. L. (2004). A theory of application service provider (ASP) use from a client perspective. *Journal of International Management, 41*(8), 977–1002.

Sneed, H. M. (1996). *Encapsulating legacy software for use in client/server systems,* (pp. 104-109). WCRE. Los Alamos, NM: IEEE Press.

Sneed, H. M. (2008). *COB2WEB: A toolset for migrating to Web services. WSE.* Los Alamos, NM: IEEE Press.

Sommerville, I., Sawyer, P., & Viller, S. (1998). Viewpoints for requirements elicitation: A practical approach. International Conference on Requirements Engineering, (pp. 74-81). April 6-10, Colorado Springs, CO, 1998.

Sotomayor, B., Montero, R. S., Llorente, I. M., & Foster, I. (2009). Virtual infrastructure management in private and hybrid clouds. *IEEE Internet Computing, 13*(5), 14–22. doi:10.1109/MIC.2009.119

Spiegel, D. S., Frye, L. M., & Day, L. L. (2008). Issues in the instantiation of template classes. *ACM SIGCSE Bulletin, 40*(2), 48–51. doi:10.1145/1383602.1383633

Spruth, W. (2007). *The future of the mainframe. EuroCMG.* Philadephia, PA: CMG Group.

Strobl, S., Bernhardt, M., & Grechenig, T. (2009). *Digging deep: Software reengineering supported by database reverse engineering of a system with 30+ years of legacy. ICSM.* Los Alamos, NM: IEEE Press.

Sun Microsystems. (2005). *Java business integration* (JBI) 1.0. Retrieved July 20, 2009, from http://jcp.org/en/jsr/detail?id=208

Sun, W., Zhang, K., & Chen, S.-K. Zhang, X., & Liang, H. (2007). Software as a service: An integration perspective. In B. Krämer, K.-J. Lin, & P. Narasimhan (Eds.), *Service-Oriented Computing- ICSOC 2007, LNCS 4749* (pp. 558–569). Berlin, Germany: Springer-Verlag.

Sun, W., Zhang, X., Guo, C. J., Sun, P., & Su, H. (2008). Software as a service: Configuration and customization perspectives. *SERVICES-2 '08 Proceedings of the 2008 IEEE Congress on Services Part II* (pp. 18-25). Washington, DC: IEEE Computer Society.

Sutcliffe, A., & Maiden, N. (1998). The domain theory for requirements engineering. *IEEE Transactions on Software Engineering, 24*(3), 174–196. doi:10.1109/32.667878

Suvée, D., Vanderperren, W., & Jonckers, V. (2003). JAsCo: An aspect-oriented approach tailored for component based software development. *AOSD '03 Proceedings of the 2nd International Conference on Aspect-Oriented Software Development* (pp. 21-29). New York, NY: ACM.

Synapse, E. S. B. Homepage. (2008). *Apache Synapse - The lightweight ESB.* Retrieved October 8, 2009, from http://synapse.apache.org/

Szyperski, C. (1997). *Component software: Beyond object-oriented programming.* Addison-Wesley.

Talia, D., & Trunfio, P. (2010). How distributed data mining tasks can thrive as knowledge services. *Communications of the ACM, 53*(7), 132–137. doi:10.1145/1785414.1785451

Tan, K., Ip, H. H. S., & Wei, F. (1998). *Web-enabling legacy applications. ICPADS.* Los Alamos, NM: IEEE Press.

Tecuci, G. (1993). Plausible justification trees: A framework for the deep and dynamic integration of learning strategies. *Machine Learning, 11,* 237–261. doi:10.1007/BF00993079

Tecuci, G. (1995). Building knowledge bases through multi-strategy learning and knowledge acquisition. In Tecuci, G., & Kodratoff, Y. (Eds.), *Machine learning and knowledge acquisition: Integrated approaches*. London, UK: Academic Press.

Teng, T., Huang, G., & Hong, M. (2006). *Interference problem between web services caused by data dependencies. CEC/EEE.* Los Alamos, NM: IEEE Press.

Thakar, A., & Szalay, A. (2010). *Migrating a (large) science database to the cloud.* Center for Astrophysical Sciences and Institute for Data Intensive Engineering and Science (IDIES), The Johns Hopkins University. Retrieved from http://dsl.cs.uchicago.edu/ScienceCloud2010/s08.pdf

Tilley, S. R., & Smith, D. B. (1995). *Perspectives on legacy system reengineering. Technical Report.* Pittsburgh, USA: Software Engineering Institute, Carnegie Mellon University.

Tobey, B. (2010). *Expand the spectrum: Integrating the social media channel enables CRM to paint a more complete picture of the customer. Teradata Magazine, Q3/2010* (p. 6184). AR: Teradata Corporation.

Top, O. W. A. S. P. 10 – 2010. (2010). *The ten most critical Web application security risks.* Retrieved from http://owasptop10.googlecode.com/files/OWASP%20Top%2010%20-%202010.pdf

Trujillo, S., Batory, D., & Diaz, O. (2007). Feature oriented model driven development: A case study for portlets. In J. Knight (Ed.), *The Twenty-Ninth International Conference on Software Engineering* (pp. 44-53). Washington, DC: IEEE Computer Society.

Tsai, W. T., Chen, Y., & Paul, R. A. (n.d.). *Service-oriented computing and system engineering.* Unpublished book.

Tsai, W. T., Malek, M., Chen, Y., & Bastani, F. (2006). Perspectives on service-oriented computing and service-oriented system engineering. *Proceedings of the Second IEEE International Symposium on Service-Oriented System Engineering.*

Tulach, J. (2008). *Practical API design: Confessions of a Java framework architect.* Apress.

Ubayashi, N., & Nakajima, S. (2007). Context-aware feature-oriented modeling with an aspect extension of VDM. In Y. Cho (Ed.), *The 2007 ACM Symposium on Applied Computing* (pp. 1269-1274). New York, NY: ACM.

Universal Description. (2004). *Discovery and integration specification,* version 3.0.2. OASIS UDDI Technical Committee. Retrieved from http://uddi.org/pubs/uddi_v3.htm

van Deursen, A., & Kuipers, T. (1999). Identifying objects using cluster and concepts analysis. *Proceedings 21st International Conference on Software Engineering.* Los Alamos, NM: IEEE Press.

Velte, T., Velte, A., & Elsenpeter, R. (2010). *Cloud computing: A practical approach.* New York, NY: McGraw-Hill.

Vemuri, P. (2008). *Modernizing a legacy system to SOA – Feature analysis approach. IEEE TENCON.* Los Alamos, NM: IEEE Press.

VMware. (2007). *Understanding full virtualization, paravirtualization, and hardware assist.* VMware White paper. Retrieved from http://www.vmware.com/files/pdf/VMware_paravirtualization.pdf

Vogels, W. (2008). Eventually consistent. *Queue, 6*(6), 14–19. doi:10.1145/1466443.1466448

Vouk, M. A. (2008). Cloud computing, issues, research and implementations. In *30th International Conference on Information Technology Interfaces (ITI 2008)*, Vol. 4, (pp. 31–40).

W3 Schools, HTML5. (n.d.). Retrieved from http://www.w3schools.com/html5/default.asp

W3 Schools, REST Protocol. (n.d.). Retrieved from http://www.xfront.com/REST-Web-Services.html

W3 Schools, Simple Object Access Protocol. (n.d.). Retrieved from http://www.w3schools.com/soap/default.asp

W3Schools, Ajax. (n.d.). Retrieved from http://www.w3schools.com/ajax/default.asp

Walborn, G. D., & Chrysanthis, P. K. (1995). Supporting semantics-based transaction processing in mobile database applications. In *The 14th IEEE Symposium on Reliable Distributed Systems*, 13-15 September (p. 31). Bad Neuenahr, Germany. Los Alamitos, CA: IEEE Computer Society.

Wallnau, K., Hissam, S., & Seacord, R. (2001). *Building systems from commercial components.* Addison Wesley.

Walls, C., & Breidenbach, R. (2007). *Spring in action.* Greenwich, CT: Manning.

Wang, L., Laszewski, G. V., Kunze, M., & Tao, J. (2010). Cloud computing: A perspective study. *Journal of New Generation Computing, 28*(2).

Wang, R., & Owyang, J. (2010). *Social CRM: The new rules of relationship management: 18 use cases that show business how to finally put customers first.* Altimeter Group.

Ward, W. A. Jr. (2000). Algorithm 803: a simpler macro processor. *ACM Transactions on Mathematical Software, 26*(2), 310–319. doi:10.1145/353474.353484

Web Services Architecture. (2004). *World Wide Web consortium* (W3C). Retrieved from http://www.w3.org/TR/ws-arch

Webber, J., & Little, M. (n.d.). *Introducing WS-coordination.* Retrieved from http://www2.syscon. com/itsg/virtualcd/webservices/archives/0305/little/index.html

Weber, C. (2006). *Assessing security risk in legacy systems.* Cigital, Inc. Retrieved August 26, 2010, from https://buildsecurityin.us-cert.gov/bsi/articles/best-practices/legacy/624-BSI.html

Weiderhold, G. (1995). Modelling and system maintenance. *Proceedings of the International Conference on Object-Orientation and Entity-Relationship Modeling.* London, UK: Springer-Verlag.

Welsh, M., Culler, D., & Brewer, E. (2001). SEDA: An architecture for well-conditioned, scalable internet services. *SOSP '01 Proceedings of the Eighteenth ACM Symposium on Operating Systems Principles* (pp. 230 - 243). New York, NY: ACM.

Went, G. (2010). *The key issues in social media monitoring today.* Red Cube Marketing.

Wilde, N., & Scully, M. C. (1995). *Software reconnaissance: Mapping features to code. Software Maintenance: Research and Practice, 7.* Hoboken, NJ: John Wiley.

Wiliams, E. (2004). Energy intensity of computer manufacturing: Hybrid assessment combining process and economic input-output methods. *Environmental Science & Technology, 38*(22), 6166–6174. doi:10.1021/es035152j

Withey, J. (1996). *Investment analysis of software assets for product lines.* Pittsburgh, PA: Software Engineering Institute, Carnegie Mellon University.

Wong, K., & Sun, D. (2006). On evaluating the layout of UML diagrams for program comprehension. *Software Quality Journal, 14*(3), 233–259. doi:10.1007/s11219-006-9218-2

Worldwide, D. E. I. (2008). *Engaging consumers online: The impact of social media on purchasing behaviour, Volume one: Initial findings, United States.*

WSMO. (2004). *Use case of "Virtual Travel Agency" (VTA).* Retrieved from http://www.wsmo.org/2004/d3/d3.3/v0.1/

Xiang, J., Liu, L., Qiao, W., & Yang, J. (2007). SREM: A service requirements elicitation mechanism based on ontology. In *Proceedings of the 31th Annual International Computer Software & Applications Conference* (COMPSAC'07), Beijing, China, July 23-27, 2007, (pp. 196-203).

Xiang, J., Qiao, W., Xiong, Z., Jiang, T., & Liu, L. (2006). SAFARY: A Semantic Web service implementation platform. In *Proceedings of APSEC-SOPOSE'06,* Bangalore, India, December 9, 2006.

Yee, G. (2010). Cloud computing bandwidth requirements - Trends and future. Retrieved September 7, 2010, from http://EzineArticles.com/?expert=George_Yee

Yu, E. (1997). Towards modelling and reasoning support for early-phase requirements engineering. In *Proceedings of the 3rd IEEE International Symposium on Requirements Engineering (RE'97)* Jan. 6-8, Washington D.C., USA, (pp. 226-235).

Zhang, J. (2004). *Better, faster XML processing with VTD-XML.* Retrieved from http://www.devx.com/xml/Article/22219/0/page/1

Zhang, J. (2008). *VTD-XML: XML processing for the future* (Part I). Retrieved from http://www.codeproject.com/KB/cs/vtd-xml_examples.aspx

Zhang, Z., & Yang, H. (2004). *Incubating services in legacy systems for architectural migration. APSEC*. Los Alamos, NM: IEEE Press.

Zhou, M., Gao, M., & Hou, X. (2008). Design method for parameterized IP generator using structural and creational design patterns. In D. Guo (Ed.), *The Second International Conference on Anti-counterfeiting, Security and Identification* (pp. 378-381). Chengdu, China: IEEE Chengdu Section.

Zhou, Y., & Kontogiannis, K. (2003). *Incremental transformation of procedural systems to object-oriented platform. COMPSAC*. Los Alamos, NM: IEEE Press.

Zimmermann, O., Krogdahl, P., & Gee, C. (2004). *Elements of service-oriented analysis and design: An interdisciplinary modeling approach for SOA projects.* Retrieved from http://www-128.ibm.com/developerworks/webservices/library/ws-soad1/

Zou, Y. (2001). Towards a Web-centric legacy system migration framework. *Proceedings of the 3rd International Workshop on Net-Centric Computing: Migrating to the Web, ICSE*. Los Alamos, NM: IEEE Press.

Zoufaly, F. (2002). *Issues and challenges facing legacy systems.* Retrieved May 23, 2010, from http://www.developer.com/mgmt/article.php/1492531/Issues-and-Challenges-Facing-Legacy-Systems.htm

Zowghi, D., & Coulin, C. (2005). Requirements elicitation: A survey of techniques, approaches, and tools. In Aurum, A., & Wohlin, C. (Eds.), *Engineering and managing software requirements*. Springer. doi:10.1007/3-540-28244-0_2

324

About the Contributors

Hongji Yang is Leader of SERG at the Software Technology Research Laboratory at De Montfort University, UK. He serves in the Department of Computer Technology. His research interests include software engineering and distributed computing. He teaches Software Architecture and Software Evolution. He served as a programme co-chair at IEEE International Conference on Software Maintenance 1999 and as programme chair at IEEE Computer Software and Application Conference 2002.

Xiaodong Liu is a Reader in the School of Computing at Edinburgh Napier University. He is active in a number of research activities, and his roles include the PI of externally funded research projects, chair and PC member of international conferences, editorial board member of three international journals, workshop organisor, and he is also supervisor and examiner of PhD and MPhil students. In addition to computer science, he is interested in tennis and playing cards.

* * *

Anteneh Ayanso is an Associate Professor of Information Systems at Brock University at St. Catharine's, Canada. He received his Ph.D. in Information Systems from the University of Connecticut, USA, and an MBA from Syracuse University, USA. His research interests are in data management, business analytics, electronic commerce, quantitative modeling, and simulation in information systems and supply chains. He has published in journals such as *Communications of the AIS, Decision Support Systems, European Journal of Operational Research, Journal of Computer Information Systems, Journal of Database Management, International Journal of Electronic Commerce, Journal of Information Technology for Development, International Journal of Healthcare Delivery Reform Initiatives, Government Information Quarterly, Industrial Management*, as well as in proceedings of major international conferences in information systems and related fields. He has also contributed several book chapters on various topics in information systems. His research in data management has been funded by the Natural Sciences and Engineering Research Council of Canada (NSERC).

Eric Braude has a PhD from Columbia University in Mathematics. He taught at Penn State and the City University of New York before a 12-year period working in government and industry as a Software Engineer, Scientist, and R&D Manager. He has been an Associate Professor of Computer Science at Boston University for a number of years. His papers cover simulation and mathematics. He has edited or written five books, including "Software Engineering" (2001; second edition with M. Bernstein, 2010).

Chandana Gamage is a senior lecturer at the University of Moratuwa in Sri Lanka. He is a graduate of the University of Moratuwa and studied at AIT in Thailand for his Masters in Computer Engineering and obtained a PhD in Computer Science from Monash University in Australia specializing in computer network security and cryptography. He has worked in Industry, in Academia and in the Military. A Commissioned Officer in the Sri Lanka Army, Chandana has lived and worked in several countries. Most notably, he has been a computer security specialist at the Free University in Amsterdam in The Netherlands working with the world-renowned computer scientist Prof Andy Tanenbaum. His research interests are in the fields of software engineering, cryptography, and computer and network security.

Barbara Gallina is a Post-Doc Researcher at MRTC, Mälardalen University. Currently, she is involved in the European Project ARTEMIS-JU100022 CHESS. Her research interests include dependability, transaction models, reuse-based methods for software engineering, and failure behavior analysis of component-based systems. Her main research area focuses on the requirements engineering of flexible transaction models. Her PhD thesis has contributed to foster the reuse of transactional properties thanks to the adoption of a product line perspective on transaction models, which has made possible the systematization of knowledge and reuse.

Nicolas Guelfi is Professor at the University of Luxembourg. Currently, he is the head of the Laboratory for Advanced Software Systems (http://lassy.uni.lu). His topics include the engineering and the evolution of dependable systems based on semi-formal or formal methods. Focus is made on model driven engineering and reuse based on product line engineering methods. He is the author of around 80 publications in books, journals, conferences, and workshops. He is co-chairman of the ERCIM working groups on Software EngineeRing for rEsilieNt systEms (SERENE - http://serene.uni.lu).

Ahmed E. Hassan is an Associate Professor of Computer Engineering at Mansoura University, Egypt. He has received a PhD in Computer Engineering from West Virginia University, USA, and an M.S in Computer Engineering from Stevens Institute of Technology NJ, USA; he also got an M.S of Artificial Intelligence from Mansoura University, Egypt. Ahmed E. Hassan is IEEE Member since 1998, IEEE Computer Society since 1999, IEEE Education Society since 2002, IEEE Computational Intelligence Society since 2002, ACM Member since 2002, and ACM Education Society since 2002.

Qusay F. Hassan is a PhD Researcher in Information Sciences at Faculty of Computers and Information Systems, Mansoura University, Egypt, where he received a BS and a MS in Information Sciences. His research interests include software engineering, Web Services, SOA, distributed systems, grid computing, and cloud computing. He has authored and co-authored a number of papers and articles that have been published in international journals, magazines, and conferences. Mr. Hassan also works as a Senior Software Engineer for the United States Agency for International Development (USAID) in Cairo.

Jhih-Syan Hou received his B.S. degree in Information Engineering from Ming Chuan University and M.S. degree in Electrical Engineering from National Sun Yat-Sen University. His research interests include software engineering and design reuse.

Dino Konstantopoulos is a Lead Information Systems Engineer with MITRE's Center for Air Force Command and Control Systems, where he specializes in Geographical Information Systems and Mission Planning for the Air Force. Prior to MITRE, Dino helped develop point-of-sale clinical information systems for Blue Cross/Blue Shield, multi-function copier operating systems for Xerox Corporation, and fluid dynamics numerical simulations for the department of Nuclear Engineering at MIT. Dino received his Bachelor's of Science in Mechanical Engineering from Universite de Grenoble (Joseph Fourier) in Grenoble, France, and his Master's of Science and Doctorate in Aerospace Engineering from Boston University.

Indika Kumara is a Software Engineer at WSO2 Inc. He received his BSc in 2006 and an MSc in Computer Science in 2010 from the University of Moratuwa. Indika's experience at WSO2 covers a broad range of technical areas, including service oriented architecture, enterprise application integration, business rules management, business process management, and complex event processing. He has contributed to the Apache open source projects including Apache Synapse ESB and Axis2 Web Service Engine. His research interests are in the fields of software engineering, service oriented computing, distributed computing, and cloud computing.

Tsung Lee received his B.S. degree in Electrical Engineering from National Taiwan University, and his M.S. and Ph.D. degrees in Computer Science from University of California, Los Angeles. In 1992, he joined National Sun Yat-Sen University where he is currently an Associate Professor in the Department of Electrical Engineering. His research interests include computer architecture and software engineering.

Lin Liu is Associate Professor at the School of Software, Tsinghua University, Beijing, China. She received her Ph.D. in Computer Science from the Institute of Mathematics, Chinese Academy of Sciences. Her interests are in the areas of requirements engineering, information systems engineering, and services computing. Her research emphasizes concepts and techniques for modelling and systematically analyzing software systems that can reason and learning to satisfy human needs.

Richard Millham received his PhD in Software Engineering in 2006 from De Montfort University in Leicester, England. He has complemented his academic experience with over fifteen years of experience in industry working in diverse fields such as telecommunications, oil/gas, and finance. He is currently both a faculty member at the University of Bahamas and a postgraduate supervisor/external examiner at Durban University of Technology in Durban, South Africa. His research interests are in software and data evolution, service oriented computing, software systems management, and software security.

Pattabhirama Pandit is a Technical Manager for Global Test Automation Group in Magnetic Resonance Imaging Group in Philips Healthcare. He has 11 years of experience in the field of software testing and Test Automation. He has experience in building test frameworks (both White Box & Black Box) and has experience of working in various technological domains. He has published several papers in international journals and conferences.

Mike Pinkerton was born in 1958 in Montana. He has dual Bachelors from California State University, San Bernardino in 1981 in Pure Mathematics/Computer Science, Master's in Applied Mathematics from University of California, Santa Barbara in 1983, and he entered Aerospace in 1983 with Logicon, an IV&V and software development company. Logicon was purchased by Northrop Grumman in 1995, and Mike is now a Senior Systems Engineer at Northrop Grumman. Mike is an early practitioner of the Booch Object Oriented approach with Ada. He refined and evolved multiple approaches to improved software productivity and quality through OO, formal Fagan inspections, processes for development, developmental test, reuse identification, reuse management, and design for reuse. Mike has championed the use of UML, DoDAF/MoDAF, SysML, model driven engineering, model driven design, and model driven development by implementing practical approaches and processes. Mike has provided training and developer support resources including tools, collaboration and contact support, and reuse repositories on multiple programs and for multiple vendor teams. Programs supported primarily include flight and mission planning and management, guidance systems, ground stations for satellite systems and unmanned vehicles, and large scale system infrastructure (hardware and software). Mike surfs daily in small and XXL waves in southern California.

Manjunath Ramachandra is currently working at Philips, Bangalore. He has about 17 years of work experience in the overlapping verticals of signal processing including image processing, wireless/mobile, and networking. Research in the same field led to his PhD, about 100 international publications, patent disclosures, and a book. He represented Philips in international standardization bodies such as Digital Living Network Alliance (DLNA), and heserves as the industrial liaison for CE-Linux Forum. He has chaired about 14 international conferences. His areas of interests include networking, signal processing, multimedia, database architecture, et cetera.

Alaa M. Riad is a Professor and a Head of the Department of Information Systems in Faculty of Computers and Information Systems, Mansoura University, Egypt. He has received a PhD. in Electrical Engineering in 1992 from Mansoura University, Egypt, and an MS in Electrical Engineering in 1988 from Mansoura University, Egypt. Dr. Riad has authored and coauthored many research papers in a number of published journals. He also has supervised many IT-related Master and Doctorate studies.

Vishav Vir Singh works in the Computer Aided Design/Engineering group at Intersil Corporation where he leads enterprise software development efforts. He earned his Master's in Software Engineering from San Jose State University, California, USA and his Bachelor's in Technology (BTech) in Computer Science and Engineering from Punjabi University, Patiala, India. Prior to joining Intersil, he was with the acclaimed PureXML DB2 Database team at IBM Silicon Valley Laboratory in San Jose, California, USA. He has extensive and substantial experience in the field of service oriented software architectures and cloud computing applications. At IBM, he was also the Chief Engineer for the World Wide Web Consortium (W3C) XQuery Test Suite Study and Analysis team that did the analysis of the XML Query Test Suite (XQTS), which assesses the native XML capabilities of IBM's flagship DB2 database. He was awarded the prestigious IBM Thanks award for technical excellence for this project. Vishav has also co-authored a book titled "Web-based Support Systems" with a chapter on "Service-Oriented Architecture (SOA) as a Technical Framework for Web-Based Support Systems (WSS)." He is a regular speaker at universities and other educational institutions on diverse topics related to service orientation of technology, cloud based architectures, and applications. His highlight lectures include a talk at Massachusetts Institute of Technology (MIT) on a service-oriented XML based support system and a presentation at Stanford University on service-orientation and persuasiveness of technology. He is also a regular participant at various IEEE conferences related to the field of technology architectures and support systems.

Index

A

abstract components 127, 172
abstract solution space 126
accountability 61
ACID properties 249, 252, 254
Amazon 212
American Red Cross 221
API handshake principle 149
    service syndication 136, 150-152
Application Programming Interface (API) 136-138, 145
Application Service Provider (ASP) 206, 210, 227
architectural erosion 108, 115
architectural mismatch 115
aspect adaptation 116, 172
aspect composition 175
aspect library (aspect space) 167
Aspect-Oriented Programming (AOP) 29-30, 114, 159-160, 163
    on Component-Based Systems 165
    on Enterprise Service Bus (ESB) 164
    on Middleware 164
aspects-to-aspects composition 175
aspect weaver 171
aspect weaving process 177
Author Solution 221

B

brand monitoring 241
Business Process Management System (BPMS) 110

C

cache aspect 169
call analysis
    of legacy systems 6
City of Carlsbad 221

cloud computing 2, 55, 144, 188, 204-206, 249
    alternative models 221
    architecture 208
    challenges 218, 225
    characteristics 206, 251
    consumer benefits 216
    five model characteristics 144
    provider benefits 216
    reasons to move 2
    ten best practices 61
    vs. grid computing 223
cloud computing infrastructures 111
cloud model 144
    for QoS 187
Coca-Cola Enterprises (CCE) 220
colocation centers 223
community support 241
component-based development (CBD) 74, 107
component-based source code 53
component libraries 52
component-oriented architectures 52
components 52
computation independent model (CIM) 30
configurable 65
congestion detection interval 191

D

data access model 180
Data-as-a-Service (DaaS) 209
data consistency 259
data-intensive applications 10
data reengineering 9
dedicated servers 222
Denial of Service (DoS) 81
dependency injection 54
design erosion - See architectural erosion.
differentially fed artificial neural network (DANN) 190